1996

CANADIAN FAMILY POLICIES:
CROSS-NATIONAL COMPARISONS

With poverty, unemployment, and one-parent families on the rise in most Western democracies, government assistance presents an increasingly urgent and complex problem. This is the first study to explore Canada's family policies in an international context. Maureen Baker looks at the successes and failures of social programs in other countries in search of solutions that might work in Canada.

Baker has chosen seven industrialized countries for her comparative study: Australia, France, Germany, The Netherlands, Sweden, the United Kingdom, and the United States. These countries experience social and economic strains similar to those felt in Canada, and though they share certain policy solutions, major differences in policy remain. Baker considers which of the policies in these countries are most effective in reducing poverty, enhancing family life, and improving the status of women, then applies her findings to the Canadian situation.

Bringing together research and statistics from the fields of demography, political science, economics, sociology, women's studies, and social policy, this rich multidisciplinary study provides a unique resource for anyone interested in Canadian family policy.

MAUREEN BAKER is a professor in the School of Social Work at McGill University.

Canadian Family Policies

Cross-National Comparisons

MAUREEN BAKER

UNIVERSITY OF TORONTO PRESS
Toronto Buffalo London

© University of Toronto Press Incorporated 1995
Toronto Buffalo London
Printed in Canada

ISBN 0-8020-2963-9 (cloth)
ISBN 0-8020-7786-2 (paper)

Printed on acid-free paper

Canadian Cataloguing in Publication Data

Baker, Maureen.
 Canadian family policies

 Includes bibliographical references and index.
 ISBN 0-8020-2963-9 (bound). ISBN 0-8020-7786-2 (pbk.)

 1. Family policy – Canada.   2. Family policy –
 Cross-cultural studies.   I. Title.

 HV700.C3B3 1995   362.82'56'0971   C95-931546-2

The research for this book was generously funded by National Welfare Grants,
Human Resources Development Canada.

University of Toronto Press acknowledges the financial assistance to its
publishing program of the Canada Council and the Ontario Arts Council.

Contents

7 Child protection, family violence, and substitute care

x   Contents

List of tables

Preface

When I worked in Ottawa as a senior researcher for the Research Branch of the Library of Parliament from 1984 to 1990, numerous members of Parliament asked me for comparative data on family policies, especially relating to child care, child support, and maternity/parental benefits. Although I had been studying Canadian family trends and policies for some years, at that time my knowledge of comparative family policies was sketchy. The logistical problems of finding information quickly from so many different sources, and the ever-present question of what generated such discrepant policy solutions, solidified my desire to carry out a major research project when I returned to university teaching and research.

When I came to McGill University, I applied for a research grant from National Welfare Grants within their Child and Family Poverty program. Terrance Hunsley, from Queen's University School of Policy Studies, had also applied for funding for a similar project and we were encouraged to combine our applications. Consequently, National Welfare Grants generously funded our joint project, which was called 'Inputs and Outcomes: A Comparison of Policies to Reduce Child and Family Poverty.' Our labour was divided so that Terry focused on poverty and lone parents while I prepared this scholarly book on comparative family policies. Throughout the project, we shared ideas, articles, data bases, and the work of our research assistants, and profited considerably from our collaboration.

In addition to thanking Terrance Hunsley for his collaboration and support, I would like to thank Fran McIninch of National Welfare Grants for organizing the collaboration and for overseeing the project with such enthusiasm and interest. Évariste Thériault, from National

Welfare Grants, also read the draft manuscript and provided useful suggestions. The three anonymous reviewers and the final evaluator from the University of Toronto Press provided constructive criticisms of the manuscript which were invaluable in preparing the final version. For the time they spent carefully reading this manuscript and for their ideas and references, I am very grateful.

In the early stages of this project, Virgil Duff from the University of Toronto Press expressed a great deal of interest in the research. I am very grateful for his faith in my ideas, for his continued support, and for the efficient way in which he expedited the publication of this book.

Most of all, however, I would like to thank my three research assistants, Anna Michetti, Barbara Mitchell, and Erica Penner, who were all students at McGill University. These research assistants spent months in the library, at the photocopy machines, and at their own computers. They gathered information and statistics, summarized research, and discussed the material with me over a period of two years. Without their assistance, this project would have taken ten years instead of two!

And finally, I would like to thank my husband, David Tippin, for discussing the ideas with me and for reading various drafts. Without his continued support and enthusiasm for the project, it would not have been so stimulating and enjoyable!

CANADIAN FAMILY POLICIES: CROSS-NATIONAL COMPARISONS

1

State intervention in family life

INTRODUCTION

During the 1980s, poverty and inequality increased in most Western democracies, placing considerable strain on social welfare programs. Global trade and production have led to major changes in labour markets, resulting in unemployment, underemployment, and economic insecurity (McFate 1991, 1). As social programs, most of which were developed from the 1950s to the 1970s, become more costly, governments are questioning their ability to improve them or even to maintain them. Yet many people have come to perceive these benefits as entitlements or rights. Furthermore, an increasingly 'globalized' economy has created more opportunities for the harmonization of social programs among countries sharing an economic partnership. Consequently, governments and policy advisers not only are questioning the fundamental premises of the welfare state but also are becoming more interested in new policy options. Within this context, understanding the social policy solutions of other countries becomes a necessity.

In most industrialized countries, birth rates have fallen below the 'replacement level' of 2.1 births per woman, or the level of fertility necessary to replace the parents plus 0.1 to compensate for the small number of deaths that occur before the next generation reaches reproductive age (Beaujot 1991, 75). Birth rates have fallen as raising children becomes more costly and complicated, as an increasing percentage of women enter the labour force, and as birth control becomes more effective and acceptable. The percentages of one-parent and two-income families have risen, and in many industrialized countries parents are experiencing serious problems in coordinating their work and family life. Yet as more comparative research is completed, it becomes apparent that some countries have created social programs which protect families and children from poverty and work-family conflicts better than others.

This book is the result of a two-year research project originally designed to compare policies to reduce child and family poverty in eight industrialized countries (Australia, Canada, France, Germany, the Netherlands, Sweden, the United Kingdom, and the United States).[1] These countries were chosen because of their cultural/legal similarity or proximity to Canadian conditions, because their family policies and income support programs were considered unique by Canadian standards, or because their policies have proven unusually effective in reducing work-family conflicts and child poverty.

As the result of studying policies to reduce family poverty, I decided to broaden the scope of the book to include recent family trends and family-related policies specifically affecting family income. These include programs for low-income families with dependent children, family allowances, tax benefits for families with dependent children, child care funding and services, maternity and parental leave and benefits, child protection and adoption policies, and custody and the enforcement of court-awarded child support after divorce. A book on 'family' policy could include numerous other policies, especially those relating to birth control, same-sex couples, and violence against women. Because I was comparing the policies of eight countries, however, it was necessary to restrict the scope of the research. Consequently, I focused on policies designed to reduce poverty or allow parents to remain in the labour force, although I have made brief reference to other policies. Canadian trends and policies are compared with those from the other countries, and policy changes are discussed within their historical, cultural, social, economic, and political contexts. I also analyse the ideological assumptions inherent in these policies, drawing on the perspectives of both political economy and feminism.

The effectiveness of family policies in both maintaining living standards and assisting parents to combine work and family are assessed throughout this book. The book attempts to answer five central questions:
1. What sorts of family policies have been enacted in the eight countries?
2. How can we explain the fact that some countries have developed expensive and comprehensive programs for families, women, and children, while others have expected family members to assist each other, with little government support?

3. What is the relationship between the comprehensiveness of family policies and other social welfare programs within each country?
4. Which policies most effectively reduce family poverty, enhance family life, and improve the status of women?
5. Which of these 'successful' policies might work in Canada?

WHAT IS FAMILY POLICY?

Family policies can be divided into three categories. The first includes laws relating to family issues, such as marriage, adoption, reproduction, divorce, custody, and child support. The second category includes policies to help support family income, including tax concessions, family and child allowances, maternity and parental leave and benefits, and the enforcement of court-ordered child support. The third category involves the provision of direct services, such as child care, child protection services, visiting homemakers, home care health services, and subsidized housing (McDaniel 1990). In this book, aspects of all three types of family policies will be discussed for the eight countries, because all of them influence the economic well-being of families with children in some way. However, because the scope of this project was already very broad, I have glossed over huge policy areas, such as reproductive health and contraception, family violence (especially violence against women and elder abuse), and deinstitutionalization and home care.

Family policy could be defined as a coherent set of principles about the state's role in family life which is implemented through legislation or a plan of action. When I refer to 'the state,' I am talking about government departments and officials, agencies funded by government, and organizations implementing laws or government policy. There are many reasons why the state would pay close attention to family structure and interactions, as families provide invaluable services.

Although adults bear children for their own personal or family reasons, the state needs its citizens to reproduce and sustain the taxpayers, consumers, and labour force of the nation (D. Smith 1977; Ursel 1992). In raising their children, parents usually encourage them to be law-abiding citizens and to perpetuate the nation's culture and social institutions. For example, school administrators, teachers, social workers, and the police all expect parents to teach their children to fit into our educational systems, to meet labour force requirements, and to behave in such a way that social order is preserved.

Laws and social practices also assume that families, supplemented by organized religion and education, are responsible for the regulation of sexual activity and reproduction. Families help define and enforce at what age a person is allowed to engage in a sexual relationship and with whom, and what degree of closeness is considered too close for a sexual liaison, for marriage, and for reproduction. Parents are also expected to encourage their children to establish permanent relationships and reproduce as they grow older.

In order to plan and provide public services and facilities, governments need to collect information on marriages, births, and deaths. Governments and their agencies regulate marriages and births to minimize social conflict and birth defects, and to help the transmission of culture and property from one generation to the next. Child-rearing practices and interpersonal relations among families are monitored to protect more vulnerable members and to maintain social order. All this suggests that there are many reasons for governments to be interested in personal and family life, and to want to maintain at least some control over these areas of life.

Some governments have developed an *explicit* written family policy, in which the role of the state in family life is made very clear. Occasionally, a special government department is created which is responsible for 'the family' or for children, and this department is granted the power to ensure that all laws and regulations impact consistently on family life. During the 1930s and again in the 1950s, France created a family policy designed specifically to increase the birth rate and assist parents to raise their children. Generous family allowances were developed which were financed through social insurance, as well as a state-run system of preschools in which 94 per cent of three- to five-year-olds are now enrolled (Kamerman and Kahn 1991a). In the late 1980s, Quebec articulated a unified family policy which included a series of programs to assist child-rearing and the integration of family and work. A government department was established which is responsible for family policy development and enforcement, with the authority to ensure that government decisions in all other departments conform to this policy. In addition, financial incentives for childbirth have been provided since 1988, with higher amounts ($8,000 in 1994) for third or subsequent children (Le Bourdais and Marcil-Gratton 1994).

On the other hand, most governments create *implicit* family policies or establish general legislation and social programs which imply a particular view of the role of the state in family life. Rather than being collated into one document, implicit family policies can be found within laws, social policies, and regulations, and are especially suggested within labour market and social welfare programs. In order to uncover notions about how a family is defined, what are the responsibilities of family members according to the government, and under what circumstances the state will assist or intervene in family life, it may be necessary to review a variety of laws or to 'read between the lines' of these laws.

In Canada, the family policies of the federal government are largely implicit. They have been developed over the years in an ad hoc way by different political parties, and were influenced by the ideology of the party in power, the concerns of the day, and the pressure of powerful advocacy groups. Because of this ad hoc development and the involvement of two levels of government (federal and provincial), Canadian family policies are not always consistent between the levels of government or even within the same level.

Family policies may also passively assist adults to bear and raise children or may actively encourage or coerce adults to marry and procreate. Most governments devise enabling policies and programs in order to assist parents to raise their children and to combine paid work and child-rearing. Enabling policies and programs could include income support programs which provide a fixed amount of money for each child, the provision of child care services for parents who need them, or legislated leave for parenting.

In contrast, some governments have developed family policies which are pronatalist, or actively encourage couples to reproduce or to have more children than they might otherwise have. Pronatalist policies, which originate from concerns about the social and economic consequences of declining birth rates, may provide larger benefits for each subsequent child or penalties for couples who fail to marry or reproduce. These penalties could include higher income tax for childless married couples or housing policies which give preference to families with children. While both France and Quebec have actively tried to raise the birth rate through positive means such as financial bonuses, some Eastern European countries, such as Romania, have created relatively punitive anti-abortion laws, have taxed childless couples at a higher rate, and have provided subsidized housing only for families with young children. In the last chapter of this book, I attempt to assess the effectiveness of pronatalist policies.

Family programs and benefits may also be universal or selective. If they are universal, all families with dependent children, regardless of

family income, are eligible for a benefit. This may be government acknowledgment of the high cost to parents of raising children, as well as
of the importance to the nation of child-bearing and child-rearing. Universal benefits are often associated with preventive programs designed
to ensure that all children are properly cared for. The philosophy behind
universality is that the nation has a social responsibility to put programs
in place to support child-rearing, sustain family income, and prevent
family crises.

On the other hand, selective programs are targeted to certain categories
of people, usually those with lower family incomes, one-parent households, or families experiencing abuse, neglect, or some other crisis. Selective benefits are usually justified as cost-saving measures and are
often based on a residual notion of social welfare – the ideology that the
family is private and government should intervene only when parents
are experiencing financial or other difficulties. Anti-poverty groups such
as Canada's Campaign 2000 have argued that targeting social programs
to the poor is economically wasteful because supporting only those in
dire need provides help that is often too little and too late to be effective.
They also argue that targeting is divisive, playing off modest-income
families struggling for a decent life (those who pay taxes but receive
few benefits) against poor families living in deprivation (Campaign 2000,
1994). Yet increasingly, Canadian family benefits are being targeted to
families with middle and lower incomes (Baker, Hunsley, and Michetti
1993).

Family policies are essentially principles about the state's role in family
life which are implemented through social programs. There are a number of different ways to deliver social programs. For example, governments can assist parents with dependent children by providing cash
benefits, such as child or family allowances, which are usually paid
bimonthly or monthly to mothers or guardians. Benefits can also be
delivered as income tax concessions, such as Canada's Child Tax Benefit
or the Equivalent to Married Credit. In addition, benefits can be delivered
as social insurance, paid for by contributions from all employers and
employees, and provided to eligible contributors in time of need. An
example of this would be maternity and parental benefits under Canada's
Unemployment Insurance Program. Governments or agencies also deliver services directly to families, such as child care, family counselling,
school lunch programs, or medical attention. Finally, programs can be
delivered through government vouchers to purchase certain services,
such as child care or housing, on the private market. As we will see in
the following chapters, variations in delivery mechanism depend on

the political ideology of the government in power, the purpose of the program, the target group, the level of social concern about the extent of the problem, notions of collective responsibility, and the cultural/political tradition within the jurisdiction.

DEFINING FAMILIES

Before continuing this discussion of family policies, it may be useful to define more carefully what is meant by 'family.' Many different definitions have been used in the formulation of social policy, the delivery of social benefits, census taking, and academic research. Government policies need to be based on explicit definitions of family, since the way in which the institution is defined establishes who will be eligible for government benefits such as family allowance, social assistance, or child tax credits. For the purposes of gathering census data and producing statistics on family life, the term 'family' needs to be defined consistently in order to enable long-term comparisons.

Several different definitions of family have been used in Canadian policy formulation. The two-parent one-earner family consisting of a married heterosexual couple and their biological offspring still haunts our images of family. Yet most new definitions now include lone parents, unmarried couples living in permanent unions with or without children, married couples with or without dependent children at home, two-earner couples, couples living apart for employment reasons, and extended families involving grandparents, aunts, uncles, and cousins. Few definitions, however, include same-sex couples or people who live in a caring relationship.

The most prevalent definition used in Canadian policies is Statistics Canada's 'census family,' which includes a husband and wife (with or without never-married children regardless of age) or a lone parent of any marital status, with one or more children (regardless of age but who have never married) living in the same dwelling. Yet for many social scientists and cultural groups in Canada, this definition is both too narrow and too broad. Some argue that a family comprises two or more people considered to be related by blood, adoption, or marriage or involved in a 'caring relationship,' who cooperate and share resources and sometimes housing. The definition used by the Canadian government approximates the 'nuclear family' of mother, father, and children, whereas many cultural groups living in Canada consider their family to be a larger, more encompassing group, closer to an 'extended family.'

Statistics Canada also refers to the 'economic family,' which is a group of two or more persons who live in the same dwelling and are related to each other by blood, marriage, or adoption (M. Baker, ed. 1990, 4). Heterosexual persons cohabiting or living 'common law' for a year or longer are now regarded as married by the Canadian government, whatever their actual legal status. Homosexual or gay couples would, however, be considered as unrelated 'room-mates' for most government benefits, although this matter is currently under discussion.

Recently, academic researchers have been arguing that the Canadian government's definition of family does not reflect the realities of how people now live. While governments often deliberately narrow their definitions to restrict entitlement to benefits, some researchers have expanded their definitions to encompass a wider variety of living arrangements. In order to consider all the variations in family structure, it is necessary to specify the type of family being considered, whether it be a blended family, a lone-parent family, a dual-earner family, a commuter family, or a same-sex couple (M. Baker, ed. 1990, 5). However, for the purposes of this cross-national study, standard definitions accepted by the governments of each country will be adopted, so that government statistics may be used and cross-national data compared.

PROBLEMS WITH CROSS-NATIONAL RESEARCH

One problem with cross-national research is that the definitions are not always consistent among all the countries involved. The best example in this study is the term 'single parent.' Some countries consider cohabiting couples to be 'married,' while others consider them to be 'single parents' unless they have lived together for a specified length of time or produced a child together. This definitional discrepancy could lead to serious problems in cross-national comparisons.

Several studies have attempted to circumvent these problems by encouraging governments to standardize definitions and to participate in international data bases. One such data base is the Luxembourg Income Study, which includes income, labour force, taxation, and population statistics from most industrialized countries. The other way of circumventing the problem of non-standardized data is to note the inconsistencies, and refer to them before offering explanations of unusual differences among national statistics. In this book, whenever possible, I rely on international statistics which have been standardized. When they are not standardized, I note inconsistent definitions.

Some critics argue that it is difficult to make sense of the findings of cross-national studies because cultural and political circumstances are so different that social policies acceptable in one country might not be transferable to another. Although there is some truth to this observation, understanding why social welfare systems and family policies developed in varying ways is an important intellectual exercise in itself. However, there are more practical reasons for comparing policy solutions.

Canada has always been influenced by the development of social programs in other countries, especially Britain and the United States. When Britain developed its unemployment insurance program in 1911, for example, there was considerable discussion in Canada's Parliament about the need for such a program, even though the Canadian unemployment insurance program was delayed by ideological and jurisdictional disputes until 1940 (Cuneo 1979). Similarly, social policy debates in the Canadian House of Commons were influenced by the British Beveridge Report in 1942 and the subsequent introduction of health insurance (Guest 1985). More recently, Canadian policy discussions concerning the enforcement of child support were based on an examination of policies in Wisconsin, Delaware, Australia, and Sweden. In other words, there has always been some interchange in policy solutions among countries with similar cultural backgrounds, especially among Canada, the United States, Britain, and Australia.

Now, there is an added incentive to understand the social policies of other countries with the development of economic agreements such as the European Union and the North American Free Trade Agreement (NAFTA). Canadians might learn from observing the European experience of protecting social programs within their economic partnership (Malcolm Hill 1992). In the European Union, for example, a *Social Charter* was signed which agrees on certain employment-related benefits, as well as the protection of children and elderly people. There has been considerable discussion in Europe – and opposition to the proposed from the British government – about 'harmonizing' social programs, especially those relating to maternity benefits. However, the varying cultural, ideological, and political systems have so far prevented convergence (Hantrais 1994).

Some Canadians have been concerned that the U.S.–Canada Free Trade Agreement (FTA) and the inclusion of Mexico in NAFTA will eventually erode certain Canadian social programs. However, we should keep in mind that policy influence is not entirely one-sided. The United States has referred to Canadian programs as models when discussing reform.

For example, the Clinton administration studied (and then rejected) the details of Canada's medicare program when attempting to develop a national health insurance program in 1993. Whether or not convergence will actually occur between Canada and the United States or among European countries, cross-national comparisons of economic and social policy may become much more relevant in the future with increasing travel, communication, trade, and economic/political agreements.

Finally, a more thorough understanding of social policies in industrialized countries, including the ways in which they are shaped by cultural and political differences, can contribute to our knowledge and repertoire of alternatives. Without an understanding of policy alternatives, it is difficult to recognize government- or employer-initiated ideologies about the range of possible solutions to social problems. When governments tell us that they cannot afford to maintain the present level of social programs, we might believe them if we did not know that some European countries have successfully maintained more generous levels of family benefits despite rising unemployment and debt and the international recession.

IDEOLOGIES BEHIND FAMILY POLICIES

Social programs always include implicit values about equality and justice. Many researchers have argued that the welfare state is not just a set of services but rather a system of ideas about society, the family, and women (Wilson 1977; F. Williams 1989; Lewis 1993). Family-related policies include both explicit or implicit ideas about who constitutes a family, what obligations family members have towards each other and to government, and what rights individual family members can expect to have protected by the state.

Despite the official and articulated goals of social programs, they do not always accomplish what they officially say they intend to accomplish. Numerous researchers from several countries have demonstrated that, contrary to explicit objectives, taxation policies, pension regulations, welfare regulations, federal unemployment insurance benefits, and family benefits provide little or no redistribution of wealth and actually contribute to the gap between the rich and the poor (Banting 1987a; Dominelli 1991; McQuaig 1987; D.B. Perry 1987). Kitchen (1986) detailed the male bias in Canadian income tax policies, despite claims of equity. Mossman and MacLean (1986) have shown how inconsistency among the principles underlying Canadian family law and social assistance legislation contributes to the 'feminization of poverty' despite the fact that these laws are supposed to lead to equality.

Historically, Canadian social policy has favoured the traditional model of family life, in which women and children are seen as men's dependants, while men are viewed as individuals (M. Baker 1990b, 171). Until law reform in the 1970s and 1980s, marital roles were seen as complementary, but both roles were considered to be necessary and of equal value to family and society. Men were expected to provide financial support for their wives and children, and women were expected to maintain the household and care for the children. As more women entered the labour force from the 1960s to the 1990s, this traditional division of labour became less feasible and less appropriate, providing new challenges for policy makers. Furthermore, feminist researchers have demonstrated that so-called complementary roles were not treated as equal before the law by judges, especially after marriage breakdown (M.E. Morton 1988). For example, as I will discuss in chapter 8, the financial settlement of the Murdoch case in Alberta in 1971 indicated that women's unpaid contribution to marriage was not considered equivalent to men's paid contribution (Dranoff 1977, 52).

Although the law no longer requires this division of labour, it remains implicit in some social policies. One example of the tendency to perceive all men as potential breadwinners and all women as dependants of men is the welfare regulation (now repealed in some Canadian provinces) called 'the man in the house rule.' If a man even temporarily lives with a woman who is on social assistance, it is assumed by welfare agencies that he should be supporting the woman and her children, regardless of his legal relationship to her or the children. Consequently, her social assistance cheque is reduced to compensate for his assumed paycheque.

Although state involvement in family life has changed over the years, it has not kept pace with family trends and is no longer, and perhaps never was, based on accurate information about how people live. Instead, social policies specific to families are based on preconceived notions about the importance of family in society, the role of women in families, and the responsibilities of parents towards their children. Although these ideas permeate our culture, they are not static but change with economic and social trends. Misconceptions about family life which insinuate their way into legislation originate in a combination of the unrepresentative social characteristics of policy makers and their advisers, pressure from vested interests, the complex and incremental nature of legislative change, and attempts to limit government expenditures (M. Baker 1990b).

Although legislators are expected to represent 'the people' in modern democracies, their ideas are influenced by their background and personal characteristics, especially their gender, social class, cultural background, and political world-view. Most legislators are middle-class or upper-middle-class men with occupational backgrounds in business, agriculture, or law. Both legislators and their advisers have often received their training in specialized areas such as law, business administration, or economics, and do not always reflect the thinking of everyday people or even the wide range of social science disciplines (ibid.). In addition, legislators implicitly or explicitly tend to defend their own interests and protect their own world-view when selecting their advisers, amending existing legislation, or creating new policies. Publicly recognizing that the traditional one-earner, two-parent family is no longer the most prevalent would require an admission that major reforms are needed to programs which are based on the assumption that husbands are breadwinners and wives are homemakers. Yet most legislation is developed through incremental changes or amendments to existing legislation. Altering the basic premise behind social policy would require unusual political will and would be very controversial. Those lobby groups which would stand to lose benefits through the change would oppose reform.

Lastly, recognizing women's permanent presence in the labour force would require costly changes. These might include the provision of public child care, which the (Cooke) Task Force on Child Care estimated would cost the Canadian federal and provincial governments $11.3 billion in 1986 (Krashinsky 1987). Expanded leave for family responsibilities would also be necessary, as well as equity for women in hiring, pay, and promotion. In the present economic climate of restraint, costly changes are likely to be rejected as unrealistic or postponed until the economy improves or an election is imminent.

We cannot blame only politicians for misrepresenting family life, as social scientists have also misconstrued families in their research and theories. The homogeneity or uniform nature of families has been overemphasized, especially by social scientists using the structural functional perspective, implying that most people live in nuclear family units of breadwinner/father and homemaker/mother, legally married and living with their two or three children (Eichler 1988a). Recently, however, there has been greater acknowledgment by both researchers and policy makers of the rise of one-parent households, two-income families, and same-sex couples. Even so, some social scientists and many policy makers still talk about 'the family' as though there were few variations in structure. In addition, variations from the nuclear family model are still seen as unusual or 'deviant.'

'The family' has been discussed as though it were one institution which means the same thing to all people (Eichler 1988a). The academic portrayal of family life in North America has been conservative and sexist, and has focused on the experiences of middle-class white families with two married parents living together. Many U.S. studies from the 1950s to the 1970s have been based on the perceptions and opinions of one family member, generalized to all others. The concerns of male family members, however, were traditionally given precedence over those of women or children. Yet as a consequence of the new research and priorities of feminist social scientists, the multidimensional nature of family life is now being emphasized, and in some cases overemphasized. Present-day family research has focused on the gendered nature of family experience, the variety of family structures, family conflict, and the impact of the economy on family life.

Family policies form part of a larger set of income security programs and social benefits often called 'the welfare state.' In discussing the development of the welfare state in various countries, some authors have assumed greater unity among the different categories of programs than may actually exist (Esping-Andersen 1990). Even though a country may have relatively generous work-related programs, such as workers' compensation, unemployment insurance, or employment pensions, this does not necessarily mean that the same nation will provide universal family allowances, subsidized child care services, or state enforcement of court-awarded child support. Yet there may be a relationship between the generosity of social programs for workers and those for parents, and this relationship will be explored throughout the book.

Recent feminist scholarship has highlighted the gendered, two-tiered, or dual nature of the welfare state (Fraser 1989; Forestall 1993; Little 1993; Sainsbury 1993). In Canada, as in several other industrialized countries, one category of social benefits, such as unemployment insurance and workers' compensation, is financed through social insurance. Entitlement is seen as a right because it is based on previous work-related contributions, benefit levels are based on income-replacement, and claims are made mainly by men because they are more likely than women to be employed in the standardized[2] labour force. The second category of benefits, such as social assistance or mothers' allowances, is financed through public taxation. Benefits are not work related, but entitlement is based on need, tied to household income, and geared to mothers/homemakers. Judgments are made about whether the client is 'deserving,' benefit levels are minimal, and beneficiaries are mainly women. In addition, women recipients are often treated as men's 'dependants,' and eligibility rules usually force them to exhaust their savings, thereby reinforcing their dependence on both men and government. This dual nature of the welfare state is based on the premise of the separation of home and work and 'separate spheres' for men and women. Actually, however, the duality illustrates that these spheres have been separate but unequal (Fraser 1989). The dual welfare state reinforces gender inequality, women's dependence, and patriarchy (Sainsbury 1993).

Although family benefits and programs could fall into either or both categories of the welfare state, most fit into the social assistance model in Canada and the English-speaking countries. In addition, most are written to be gender neutral, despite the fact that most recipients are pregnant women or mothers with dependent children. The over representation of women recipients of family programs reflects the fact that women get pregnant and men do not, that women are more often poor, and that one-parent households are usually led by mothers. Yet some policies contain an ideological component which suggests that women *should* be the primary caretakers of children, that their 'place' is in the home, and that they should not expect much government support for their 'motherwork' because it is not 'real' or paid work. Does the fact that most recipients of family policies are women and children influence the generosity of the benefits? When benefits become gender neutral, do they rise in value? These issues will also be further explored throughout the coming chapters.

The 'private versus public' distinction

Regardless of their world-view, most researchers now agree that families are not always – and indeed have never been – 'havens in a heartless world' (Lasch 1977) of politics, the economy, and work. The distinction that used to be made between the 'private' world of family and the 'public' world of work is now criticized as not only inaccurate but very consequential to women and children (I.M. Young 1987; McDaniel 1990; Ursel 1992).

Viewing family life as 'private' and outside the realm of government regulation has inhibited the development of some kinds of social policy and encouraged others. For example, this view has allowed governments to assume that domestic services will be provided by wives at home for no pay, and that workers leave family responsibilities at home when they enter the workplace. Therefore, employees do not need child care services, flexible hours, or special leave for family responsibilities. In addition, this false dichotomy has enabled the state and the community to turn a blind eye to violence against women and children if it takes place within the home.

Because of public pressure, largely from women's groups, to find policy solutions to problems of integrating work and family and of violence against women and children, there has been a new emphasis placed on strengthening families through social policy. Yet many feminists, gays, and those on the political left are suspicious of the new calls for 'a family policy.' Creating policies which deal adequately with the multidimensional aspects of family life without being biased against different family structures has proven to be very challenging.

Ideology and 'child poverty'

In the late 1980s, Canadian parliamentary committees and politicians began using the term 'child poverty' when discussing poverty and inequality. They concluded that using the imagery of impoverished children allowed greater political consensus about the need to reduce income inequality, because the dichotomy between the 'deserving' and the 'undeserving' poor still looms large in the public's thinking. If children are living in households with low incomes, they cannot be blamed for their poverty. People cannot argue that children are poor because they are lazy, do not want to work, cheat on their unemployment insurance forms, or defraud the welfare system. Children must always be perceived as innocent victims. For this reason, the term 'child poverty' has been an effective way to draw the public's attention to poverty and at the same time elicit empathy rather than blame.

At the same time, there is a danger that using the concept of 'child poverty' could redirect attention from the real causes of poverty, focusing instead on symptoms. The symptoms of child poverty could be reduced by providing school lunch programs, school social workers, child-oriented preschools, enriched after-school programs, medical and dental services for children, or child allowances based on the needs of children. If we talk about child poverty, we could almost forget that children are poor because of their parents' employment circumstances. It would not be constructive to direct policy solutions away from discussions about achieving full employment, creating jobs, re-education and skills training, public child care programs, raising the minimum wage, reforming unemployment insurance and welfare benefits, or reforming the tax system. If using the concept of child poverty generates more public concern about poverty, then it should be retained. But the results of the present study show that solutions to child and family poverty lie in a combination of child-centred programs, labour market strategies (job sharing, job creation, education and training), taxation changes, and changes in our national priorities rather than in a focus mainly on the condition of low-income children.

The Luxembourg Income Study has gathered comparable data from many industrialized countries, and analyses have shown how child and family poverty differs cross-nationally, depending on government transfers and tax benefits. These data indicate that 17.7 per cent of Canadian families with children were poor in 1987, compared with 18.6 per cent of Australian families and 25.4 per cent of U.S. families. In Germany and Sweden, however, comparable rates are only 8.9 and 4.7 per cent. A family is defined as 'poor' using a relative poverty line based on median gross income and family size.[3] Using this data base, researchers have argued that variations in income support programs are essential to understanding differences in outcomes for families with children (McFate 1991; Phipps 1993a, 1993b, 4). But because the research does not take into account the development of the programs, these statistics cannot tell us why there are such dramatic differences among countries in the generosity of their income security programs.

Not only do the United States and Canada have higher rates of poverty among families with dependent children than do most European countries, but a higher percentage of poor families in North America experience longer spells of poverty. For example, in the Netherlands, almost 45 per cent of poor families overcame poverty after only one year. In Sweden, this figure was one-third, while one-quarter of the poor escaped poverty after only one year in France and West Germany. In Canada and the United States, the figure was closer to one in eight. Furthermore, one in seven U.S. families remain in poverty for at least three years (McFate 1991, 11). These studies indicate that it is possible to develop social programs to reduce the extent of child and family poverty, and to help impoverished families quickly move out of poverty. But the solutions are either not widely known, not politically acceptable in all countries, or difficult to implement because of government structure or existing social programs.

Although researchers and policy analysts have devised new solutions to income inequality and family poverty, there are numerous reasons why reforms are not implemented. Motivations for policy reform and constraints impeding change include economic, political, structural, and demographic factors, which will be discussed in the next section.

SOCIAL POLICY REFORM: IMPETUS AND CONSTRAINTS[4]

For many years, social scientists have debated the various explanations for the uneven development of the welfare state in different parts of the world. For heuristic purposes, we have placed these arguments into three broad categories: demographic, economic, and political; however, many authors use components from more than one category to explain why some countries are able and willing to provide generous social programs while others are not. In the last chapter, after reviewing the data on family policies from the eight countries, I attempt to assess the applicability of these theories.

Demographic factors

One category of explanation for the uneven development of family policy relates to demographic change which alters people's circumstances, influences ideas about the need for reform, and serves as an impetus for political lobbying for new legislation. Demographic variables such as fertility rates, population aging, and women's rate of participation in the labour force (as well as political variables) are often used in quantitative studies to try to explain family policy differences among nations (Pampel and Adams 1992; Wennemo 1992, 1994).

The early development of more generous family benefits in France and Sweden relative to countries such as Canada has been explained by differences in demographic and social trends (as well as political ideologies and the structure of government). For example, these countries industrialized much earlier than Canada, and urbanization and indus-trialization are usually related to increasing labour force participation by women, declining birth rates, and an aging population.

In France, concern about declining fertility dates from the 1930s when Nazi Germany was rapidly increasing its population. The threat of a rapidly expanding population across the border encouraged pronatalist policies to develop in France, but these policies were expanded considerably after the deaths of so many young people during the Second World War (Smolowe 1992). In the 1970s and 1980s, as women's labour force participation and divorce rates increased and birth rates fell, France continued its pronatalist policies through child allowances, taxation policies, and child-rearing leaves.

Since the 1930s, the participation rate of women in the labour force and divorce rates have been considerably higher in Sweden than in North America. Women's entrance into the labour force, which encouraged lower birth rates and population aging, soon led people to worry about whether the future of social insurance programs could be assured if the percentage of the population of working age was shrinking. In Sweden, policies to enable people to combine work and family more effectively were initiated from the 1930s to the 1950s. During the prosperity of the 1960s and 1970s, coverage was expanded and the programs were improved. Population aging, caused mainly by the decline in fertility rates, appears to be a powerful motivating factor influencing the development of lobby groups pressuring for changes in family policy in much of Europe in the 1980s and 1990s.

Using this demographic theory, we could predict that family policy will become more developed and more explicit in Canada after several decades of below-replacement fertility rates, population aging, and increased rates of labour force participation by mothers. This has already occurred in Quebec, where family policy was made more explicit and was expanded in 1988 after two decades of dramatic decline in fertility rates and increased labour force participation by women. Policy makers were concerned about the implications of declining fertility for future economic productivity, but Quebec nationalists were also worried about the future of Quebec's French culture within English North America. Clearly, demographic trends alone cannot explain the development of family policy in Quebec, as I discuss in chapter 9. In other words, demographic changes are not sufficient in themselves to explain the creation and development of family policies. These trends may, however, serve as a major impetus or focal point for generating ideas about possible policy initiatives and for political lobbying.

Economic factors

Most social programs were not developed until industrialization and wage labour created economic prosperity for both governments and citizens, allowing for the expansion of the public sector. Because social programs are very costly to the state, they require massive public support (Cameron 1978). Between the 1950s and the 1970s, a period of economic prosperity and expansion, social security programs were developed and expanded in many industrialized countries. Since the mid-1970s, however, when the world economy took a downturn, however, most industrialized countries have not expanded their social programs but rather have cut back or at best maintained them (Mishra 1990). Since many governments, including Canada's, are preoccupied with deficit reduction and spending cuts, the expansion and even the maintenance of social programs are sometimes considered to be economically impossible.

While a degree of sustained economic prosperity may be necessary for the expansion of social programs, prosperity does not always lead to expansion. For example, economic prosperity did not translate into more generous social programs in all countries during the expansionist period of the 1960s and early 1970s. The chief example is the United States, which, despite prosperity, failed to develop national social insurance programs such as unemployment insurance and maternity benefits, a public health care system, or a universal family allowance, as was done in most European countries, Australia, and Canada. The U.S. government clearly had the funds to invest in defence, space exploration, and transportation infrastructure, but chose not to expand income security for ideological reasons.

Despite a downturn in economies around the world, not all governments have felt it necessary to reduce income security programs or family benefits during economic hard times. Sweden, for example, increased the basic child benefit from 1990 to 1992 by 34 per cent, while Canada increased its benefit by only 4.5 per cent (Campaign 2000, 1994). Throughout this book I will show that, despite the recent recession, most of the European countries studied have maintained or improved the level of benefits for families with children and have worked harder to combat poverty and unemployment. The European countries studied (excluding the United Kingdom) tend to view universal child benefits and services for families as important measures to prevent future social problems, and are prepared to put more money rather than less into dealing with unemployment, training, and income security during a recession.

Another prevalent but misleading economic argument is that federal government policies in nations such as Canada increasingly are constrained by 'economic globalization.' The expansion of world markets, foreign investment, and the plans and preoccupations of multinational corporations and foreign investors are alleged to limit government options and action. Most Canadian political parties now share the same concern about the rising debt and the interest rates owed on the deficit. If interest rates rise for governments who need to borrow, because bond rating organizations lose confidence in that government's ability to reduce the deficit, the problem worsens (Courchene 1987; Gray 1990).

Yet there are varying ideas about what has caused the public debt to rise, what should be done to curb it, and how much control a government really has over its economy. While some conservatives and 'think-tanks' such as the Fraser Institute have argued that overly generous social programs are the major cause of government debt, Mimoto and Cross (1991) demonstrated that the Canadian debt has increased not because of social programs but for several other reasons. First, high unemployment has reduced government revenue from income tax and sales tax. Unemployed people pay lower or no taxes and spend less money, which results in reduced sales tax revenue for governments. In addition, interest rates have risen since the 1960s, forcing the federal government to pay more to finance the deficit, from 1.8 per cent of GDP in 1967 to 6.1 per cent in 1991 (ibid.). Furthermore, the tax system was gradually altered in the late 1970s by the Liberals and throughout the 1980s by the Conservatives so that corporations pay lower taxes than they used to and than corporations in other Group of Seven (G7) countries pay (Campaign 2000, 1994; Canada, Department of Finance 1994). For example, government revenue from personal income tax increased in Canada from 4.7 per cent of GDP in 1966–7 to 8.9 per cent in 1990–1, while revenue from corporate income tax declined from 2.7 per cent to 1.8 per cent during the same period (Mimoto and Cross 1991).

Although curbing spending is one alternative to reducing the deficit, government revenue could also be increased through reforms to the income tax system to require higher earners and corporations to pay more and to end some tax concessions used mainly by higher-income individuals (Laxer 1993). In addition, interest-free loans to corporations could be reduced (Ternowetsky 1987; McQuaig 1993). Making such economic reforms would require a strong Canadian government willing to develop economic policies which are less rather than more like those of the United States. At present, the opposite is occurring, policies are becoming increasingly 'harmonized' with U.S. policies, especially since the advent of the Free Trade Agreement. While many Canadians now agree that the deficit is a problem, not everyone thinks that it should be reduced through cuts to income security programs, as these programs are even more necessary in times of high unemployment. Instead, full employment and taxation reform need to be government priorities, along with spending cuts.

In Canada, economic globalization has been used as a rationale by employers for cutting payroll costs by laying off permanent employees and replacing them with temporary workers in order to 'become more competitive.' Governments have been pressured by employers' groups to cut social spending in order to lower taxes. Yet cross-national comparisons indicate that governments have responded to economic globalization in different ways. Although globalization has de-industrialized the Swedish economy and growth has been slow, the nation has not experienced the same high unemployment rates as Canada or the proliferation of 'non-standardized' (part-time, temporary) jobs which has typified the North American labour market since the 1970s. Reasons for this include the fact that the nation has a stronger commitment to full employment, especially for women (who are employed mainly in the public sector), and that the government intervenes more in the economy and has created new positions in health, social services, and education, as well as more comprehensive labour legislation. In addition, Swedish labour unions are more involved in decision making, and there are fewer levels of government required for decisions (Esping-Andersen 1990; Boreham and Compston 1992; Laxer 1993; Clement and Mahon 1994).

Laxer (1993) argues that the Conservative Canadian government (since Brian Mulroney became prime minister in 1984) and the conservative governments in the United Kingdom and the United States have made too many sacrifices or concessions to the false god of 'globalization,' driven by pressure from business interests. The Canadian government used 'globalization' and the inevitability of a growing world economy as reasons to enter the Free Trade Agreement with the United States. Laxer argues that Canadians have lost sovereignty to the United States by entering into an agreement with a much more powerful trading partner. Before signing the agreement, Canadians did not openly and adequately discuss the implications and ramifications for sovereignty because decision-making structures exclude interest groups. Laxer also argues that Canada needs both to revoke the agreement and to initiate a more consultative process which would converge not only business, labour, and government interests, but also regional, environmental, and social interests. Germany and Austria have turned to corporatism as a method of decision making, which Laxer sees as more effective because it grants everyone a stake in economic restructuring. Laxer also maintains that both government economic planning and a fair and progressive tax system are vital. This discussion indicates that economics alone are insufficient to explain variations in the development of economic policy or social programs. Policy varies with the structure of decision making, prevalent ideologies, and political coalitions of a particular nation.

Political factors

Although demographic and economic trends have led to major structural changes in family life and in labour markets, these trends themselves are not sufficient to lead to policy change. Advocacy groups need to organize and form coalitions with others in order to make an impact on the decisions of policy makers. Despite similar demographic and economic trends among industrialized societies, interest groups and their conflicts differ with each nation. Therefore, policy solutions vary considerably.

Political theorists have classified industrialized nations according to their approach to 'social welfare,' aggregating many types of programs together but generally focusing on work-related programs such as unemployment benefits, workers' compensation, and employment pensions. For example, Esping-Andersen (1990) divided the major industrialized nations into social democratic (supporting full employment and basing universal benefits on citizenship), 'liberal' welfare regimes (characterized by means-tested benefits and a residual role for the state), and conservative regimes (also called corporatist or Catholic, in which benefits are based on social insurance programs). Although Esping-Andersen's categories are widely used, they have been viewed as male-oriented in their emphasis on class to the neglect of gender (Simm 1993). Feminists have noted that social insurance programs, which have benefited working-class men, have tended to perpetuate a strict division between men as breadwinners and women as wives and mothers, and consequently disadvantage women (Langan and Ostner 1991; Lewis, ed. 1993). For the purpose of analysing family policies, Esping-Andersen's categories are somewhat confusing to a Canadian audience, partly because the words 'liberal' and 'conservative' also represent political parties here, and also because social insurance is not associated with conservatism. The categorization is also less appropriate for family policies than for employment policies. For example, the family policies under the 'liberal' regimes seem more conservative than those under the 'conservative' regimes. Clearly, his categorization was designed for employment-related benefits, and countries may fall into a different category for labour market policies than for family-related benefits.

Ware and Goodwin (1990) presented a simpler model, arguing that states follow either a rights-based model, in which benefits are determined by citizenship; a social insurance model, in which benefits are determined by contributions; or a residual model, in which benefits are determined by 'need.' However, this typology still does not allow for the fact that categorization could vary by the type of social program. For example, in Canada, medical benefits are based on a rights model, unemployment benefits are based on a social insurance model, and child and family benefits are now based on a residual model. It would therefore be inaccurate to argue that Canada falls into any one category, although more social benefits may be residual than universal. We can conclude, therefore, that broad theories of 'the welfare state' are too general for a specific discussion of family policies, even though there may be many lessons to learn from attempts to classify the different approaches to social welfare.

In explaining the development of social policies, most political theories focus on the effectiveness of political alliances, the ideology of the party in power, or the structure of decision making within the country.

a) The effectiveness of political alliances

Countries with strong social welfare programs tend to be those in which the prime beneficiaries of the programs have united to form effective coalitions to pressure the government. Because there are so many groups lobbying governments for change, politicians tend to listen to those who appear to represent greater numbers, who are apt to make their lives most difficult, or who are willing and able to create alliances with a powerful political party (Esping-Andersen 1985; Kangas and Palme 1992–3). The existence of demographic change and the perception of a problem are not enough to lead governments to reform policy. Politicians need to be persuaded that something must be done and then pushed into action.

One example of the importance of coalitions was the development of old-age pensions in Canada. With the advent of assembly-line production in the early 1900s, many older workers were displaced by new workplace technologies emphasizing speed and efficiency while downplaying experience and skill. Employers often preferred to replace older workers, who they felt were not adapting well to the changes,

with younger unskilled workers in order to reduce payroll costs, acquire a more flexible labour force, and increase productivity. In order to avoid the disagreeable task of laying off older workers and contributing to their poverty, employers' groups lobbied the government to create mandatory retirement laws as well as a government pension plan. They were successful because they were able to unite with other groups who were concerned about rising poverty among the elderly, including the labour party, trade unions, and religious groups (Myles 1989). As a result of increasing political pressure and deepening poverty among the elderly, the federal government was convinced that government intervention was needed and created a means-tested program to share the cost of old-age pensions with the provinces. After the Depression of the 1930s, when it became increasingly apparent to everyone that thrift and hard work were no guarantee of financial security in old age, and that a national program would better guarantee uniformity of payment across the country, the Canadian government made the program federal and made eligibility universal for those aged seventy and above (M. Baker 1988, 79).

A modern example of alliances working against social reform is in the debate over maternity and parental benefits in the United States in the 1990s. Small business and the Chamber of Commerce united against the introduction of paid and statutory benefits, which were advocated by feminist groups. Appealing to American values of individualism and non-intervention into employment practices by government and stressing the assumed high cost of parental leave and its effect on economic productivity, the business lobby persuaded the conservative U.S. government to require only medium and large employers to provide unpaid leave for maternity. Despite the pressing need for paid leave and the fact that the United States remains the only country of the eight in this study without statutory maternity benefits, the business lobby was successful in limiting the scope of the 1993 legislation.

Canadian governments, like all others, have historically been responsive to some groups more than others. Employer or business groups have successfully influenced government fiscal policy and policies on the minimum wage and unemployment insurance, especially during economic hard times. The medical profession, especially in concert with hospital administrators, has had a stronger influence than other health professionals (such as nurses or chiropractors) on the development of medicare. Labour unions have been relatively uninfluential in Canada except during labour shortages (in the 1960s) or when they threatened social unrest (for example, during the 1930s Depression). In recent years, unionization rates, which have always been lower in North America than in Europe, have declined, and many trade unions have withdrawn their support for specific political parties. Until recently, women's groups and Native people have not been very effective in influencing government policy, although their influence has increased considerably in the past decade.

Governments will not seek policy solutions or develop new social programs just because citizens or employees experience problems which they think need to be resolved. The problems must be perceived to be within the mandate and capability of the government to resolve. Effective political alliances must be developed among like-minded groups, and these groups must attract the attention of politicians with power. Although groups with opposing views may try to influence politicians, the successful lobby must gather support from many different constituencies, or be well funded and well organized, in order to influence the government in power. Years may pass before any legislation is created or reformed, because different members of the government may be influenced by different groups and consensus may be difficult. When the Canadian *Divorce Act* was under review in 1984–5, for example, feminist and fathers' rights groups fought hard for politicians' attention. In the 1990s, these groups continue to present the government with opposing solutions in child support and custody discussions.

When groups are able to create coalitions, they are more likely to gain strength and influence politicians. The ideology of the party in power is also important, however, in determining whom governments listen to and which policy alternatives and outcomes they finally choose.

b) The importance of political ideology

Many theorists argue that political ideology remains the decisive factor in explaining the development or maintenance of social programs (Castles 1978; Boreham and Compston 1992; Väisänen 1992). Over the years, political parties were created precisely because different philosophical assumptions exist about such issues as: (1) the role of government in personal life, (2) how best to keep a nation and its citizens prosperous, and (3) whether and how wealth should be redistributed from the rich to the poor, or from individuals without dependent children to families caring for dependent children. Traditionally, various political parties have supported different kinds of policies, emphasizing either social policy or economic policy. Some parties have favoured more generous benefits to families with children, while others have been more supportive of policies benefiting individuals, corporations, or foreign investors. For example, left-wing parties have been more involved in the development of social welfare programs than conservative or right-wing parties.

In the 1990s, there has been considerable ideological convergence among Canadian political parties on some economic and labour issues. For example, provincial New Democratic parties (especially in Ontario) have become more concerned with reducing the deficit, down-sizing government, and lowering labour costs. Traditionally, these concerns have been associated with Conservative party ideology. Furthermore, the federal Conservatives abolished universal family allowances before they were soundly voted out of office in 1993 and, despite earlier traditional commitments to universality, the Liberals have made no move to reinstate the family allowance.

The 1993 election was dramatic for both the Conservative party and the New Democratic party (NDP).[5] While the Conservatives were replaced by the right-wing Reform party, the left was demolished. With the demise of the federal NDP, Canadian political parties are now concentrated in the political centre and the right, with no social democratic or socialist party having much support. Furthermore, there appears to be little difference between the platforms of the present Liberal and the former Conservative government, a fact which may reflect the level of structural constraints preventing innovative policy implementation in Canada.

Many social scientists have suggested that political ideology has become less important in influencing government decisions than economic realities and entrenched political structures. As we discussed above, economic constraints such as a 'globalized economy' with foreign control inhibit decision making by national governments because so many decisions are relegated to international bodies. In addition, as the size and complexity of government bureaucracy increase, reforms become more difficult to negotiate. Established political structures, such as federalism, make policy reform time-consuming and cumbersome, because federalism requires consensus among so many governments. And entrenched social and economic programs make it difficult for political parties to change policy or even maintain different ideological positions. Furthermore, parties need to win elections, and if for whatever reason certain ideologies are not popular, parties must modify their policies in order to stay in power or win the next election. These economic and political constraints have led some to argue that the importance of ideology in political decision making is decreasing. For this reason, the argument has been called 'the decline of ideology' thesis' (Banting 1987a; Smardon 1991).

c) The importance of political structure

Aside from coalitions and the ideology of the party in power, the structure of decision making is important in policy reform. Countries with centralized governments, such as Sweden, have been able to expedite social reform more effectively than these with decentralized governments, such as Canada and the United States.

In Canada, the federal system and the division of powers between federal and provincial governments have served as barriers to the development of several social programs (Banting 1987b; McGilly 1990). For example, the introduction of unemployment insurance required an amendment to the Constitution in the 1940s because initiating an employment-related program was outside federal jurisdiction.

Many family policies in Canada fall under provincial jurisdiction, and changes require agreement among provincial premiers and the federal prime minister. Since the early 1980s, Canadian politics has been preoccupied with constitutional reform and national unity, and agreements among provincial and federal governments have been few. Within this political climate, reforming family policies or any social policies has become difficult. In the spring of 1994, the federal government promised a review of social programs (excluding old age pensions and medicare), but concrete policy reforms were delayed partly because the provinces would not accept federal proposals. In contrast, income security and the enforcement of child support have remained under federal jurisdiction in Australia, and nation-wide reforms were made in the 1980s.

Who is involved in decision making and the legal requirements of consultation also influence which policies are deemed acceptable. In Sweden, many social policy decisions are made by boards with representatives from labour, employers, and government, and governments cannot make decisions without the representation and participation of these groups. In Canada, there is no formal procedure for governments to negotiate with interest groups apart from non-binding consultations in parliamentary committees. Members of Parliament sometimes go through the motions of asking interest groups who have appeared before parliamentary committees to make time-consuming recommendations to amend legislation, even when they have been told by 'the whip' not to accept any. In other words, submissions to parliamentary committees are merely advisory to Parliament.[6] In addition, there is no strong, visible, and continuing alliance between labour unions and any federal party in power. In contrast, there has been a historical alliance between labour unions and the Social Democratic party in Sweden. Therefore, the structure of decision making, as well as coalitions and political alliances, influences the development of social policies.

d) The theoretical emphasis in this book

Although these three categories of theories (demographic, economic, and political) have been discussed individually, most researchers combine them in searching for explanations of the uneven development of the welfare state. For example, researchers argue that Sweden has been successful since the 1930s in developing social insurance programs, a guaranteed minimum income, and full employment policies partly because it has had a strong central government, a history of social democratic governments, an age-old alliance between the labour movement and the Social Democratic party, and established procedures for negotiations among employers, government, and employees, referred to as corporatism (Traves 1991; Smardon 1991). In addition, Sweden has experienced declining birth rates since the 1930s and public concern about financing future social programs. As a result of the expansion of the public sector and labour shortages, the participation rate of mothers in the workforce has been higher than in other countries for many decades, a circumstance which has altered family structure and the need for child care and parental benefits. Furthermore, Sweden has always had a relatively homogeneous population, sharing common social values, and until recently has enjoyed a strong economy.

In this book, all the political explanations outlined above (the strength of coalitions, political ideology, and the structure of decision making) receive more emphasis than demographic or economic theories in explanations of the uneven development of family policy. Although demographic, social, and economic changes made existing family policies obsolete and created the need for policy reform, subsequent action depended on the political factors identified above. The study of the eight countries in this project has indicated that the thrust for improved family policies came largely from social democrats, labour organizations, and feminist groups. Demands for family policy reform were most likely to be incorporated into the government agenda in countries with social democratic governments, a history of left-wing parties, strong labour unions, homogeneous values, structures requiring negotiation among various interest groups, and a centralized government.

Although political explanations are given primacy throughout the book, considerable space is devoted to economic and demographic considerations which serve as a context or impetus for reform. For example, falling birth rates alone have not led to the development of family policy in Quebec. Some connection had to be made between population decline and nationalist concern about the demise of Quebec's power and culture within the Canadian federation, and these nationalist voices had to be heard by the Quebec government. Therefore, arguments based solely on demographic change (or economic determinism) are not considered to be valid. Yet structural constraints make certain decisions or their implementation difficult, which suggests that any explanation for the uneven development of family policy must be multidimensional. In chapter 9, these theoretical complexities will be discussed in more detail.

Before specific family trends and policies can be considered and the question of why policies developed unevenly in the different countries can be examined, additional information is needed about each country in the study.

COUNTRY PROFILES[7]

In this book, Canadian social policies relating to families with dependent children will be compared with those of seven other industrialized countries – Australia, France, Germany, the Netherlands, Sweden, the United Kingdom, and the United States. As I mentioned at the beginning of this chapter, these countries have been selected for several reasons. Australia is similar to English Canada in its legal, cultural, and linguistic tradition and its development as a society based on immigration. France is important because it was the source of Canada's French tradition in Quebec. France, Germany, the Netherlands, and Sweden have been selected as European societies with a longer history and/or a more comprehensive system of family policy, social insurance, and transfer programs than Canada. The United Kingdom was selected because English Canada was once its colony and many cultural traditions and most of the legal system (with the exception of Quebec's) originate in the United Kingdom. The United States was chosen because of its

TABLE 1.1
Overview of eight countries, 1992

	Population in Jan. 1993 (millions)	Real GDP growth (%)	Consumer price inflation (%)	Unemployment rate 1992	Percentage of MPs who are women (1987)	Major religion (%)
Australia	17.6	-1.9 (1991)	3.2 (1991)	10.1	6.1	Prot. 50%
Canada	28.6	1.6	1.5	10.2	9.6	RC 46%/Prot. 44%
France	57.5	1.2 (1991)	3.2 (1991)	10.1	6.4	RC 90%
Germany	80.6	0.8	4.0	5.0	15.4 (West) 32.2 (East)	RC 45%/Prot. 44% (West)
Netherlands	15.2	1.1	3.7	6.4	20.0	RC 36%
Sweden	8.7	-1.3	2.3	4.1	28.5	Evang. Lutheran 94%
United Kingdom	58.0	-0.8	3.8	9.9	6.3	Prot. 53%
United States	256.9	-1.2 (1991)	4.2 (1991)	6.7	5.3	Prot. 61%

Abbreviations: Evang. – Evangelical; Prot. – Protestant; RC – Roman Catholic
SOURCES: OECD 1993; Economic Intelligence Units: no. 3, 1992 (*Country Report – Australia*), no. 4, 1992 (*Country Report – France*), no. 1, 1993 (*Country Reports – Canada, Germany, Netherlands, Sweden, United Kingdom, United States*); D. Anderson, 1991.

proximity and cultural similarity to Canada, and its strong influence on the Canadian economy and culture, as well as for the policy contrast it provides to the European countries.

In order to understand the policies and programs of these countries, it is necessary to acquire some knowledge of their political culture and economic, social, and demographic trends. We would be naïve to think that social programs could be identified as 'effective' and then simply transferred to a different cultural environment. Sweden, for example, has a long history of social insurance and guaranteed minimum income programs which arise from social democratic governments, population homogeneity, a corporatist model of government, acceptance of high tax rates, early industrialization, and low marriage and birth rates. A few aspects of Swedish family policies would never be politically acceptable in Canada, although some ideas may be transferable. Nevertheless, it is important to understand how the countries are similar and how they differ.

Australia

The population of Australia is 17.6 million, with 100 females for every 100 males. Sixty-two per cent of women aged twenty-five and over are currently married, and 6 per cent of women aged twenty-five to forty-four are currently divorced. The total fertility rate in 1992 was 1.9 births per woman, and the infant mortality rate was 7 per 1,000 births. According to United Nations statistics, 23 per cent of households are headed by women with children and no spouse. Women made up 38 per cent of the workforce in 1990, and the unemployment rate in 1992 was 10.1 per cent for both men and women (OECD 1992a, 43). Real GDP growth in 1992 was minus 1.9 per cent (OECD 1993).

Australia is a federal parliamentary state with six states and two territories. In 1987, 6.1 per cent of parliamentary seats were occupied by women. The population is 95 per cent Caucasian, 4 per cent Asian, and 1 per cent Aboriginal and other, and English is the official language. The reported religious affilations of the population are 50 per cent Protestant (of which 26 per cent are Anglican) and 26 per cent Roman Catholic.

Because Australia is a federal state, some of the issues related to family policy fall under state jurisdiction. The federal (Commonwealth) government has control over income security programs and the enforcement of child support after divorce.

Canada

In 1990, Canada had a population of 28.6 million, with 102 females for every 100 males. As in Australia, 62 per cent of women aged twenty-five and over are currently married; 5.4 per cent of women aged twenty-five to forty-four are currently divorced,[8] a rate slightly lower than Australia's. The total fertility rate was 1.7 births per woman, and the infant mortality rate was 6.4 per 1,000 births during 1992. According to United Nations statistics, 25 per cent of households are headed by women with children and no spouse. Women constitute 44 per cent of the workforce, and about 20 per cent of them work part time (D. Anderson 1991, 198). The unemployment rate in 1992 was 10.2 per cent (OECD 1992a, 43), which was the highest among the countries in this study. Real GDP growth was 1.6 per cent in 1992 (OECD 1993).

Canada is a confederation with a parliamentary democracy, and the country is divided into ten provinces and two territories. In 1987, 9.6 per cent of parliamentary seats were occupied by women. English and French are both official languages. In terms of religious affiliation, 46.5 per cent of the population is Roman Catholic, 44.3 per cent is Protestant, 1.2 per cent is Jewish, and 0.6 per cent is other non-Christian; and 7.3 per cent has no religious affiliation.

Many issues relating to family policy fall under provincial jurisdiction. While divorce law is federal, marriage laws, the division of matrimonial property, and the enforcement of child support are under provincial jurisdiction. Child care is under provincial jurisdiction, but is also cost-shared between the federal and provincial governments for low-income parents. The federal government provides maternity and parental leave under the Unemployment Insurance Program, but leave from employment is governed by provincial legislation for most Canadian employees.

France

France has a population of 57.5 million, with 105 females for every 100 males. Fifty-five per cent of women aged twenty-five and over are currently married, and 7.5 per cent of women aged twenty-five to forty-four are currently divorced. The total fertility rate was 1.7 births per woman in 1992, and the infant mortality rate was 7.3 per 1,000 live births. According to United Nations statistics, 17 per cent of households are headed by women with children and no spouse – far fewer than in Australia and Canada. About 42 per cent of the workforce is composed of women workers, about 23 per cent of whom work part time (D. Anderson, 1991, 108). The unemployment rate in 1992 was 10.1 (OECD 1992a, 43). Real GDP growth was 1.2 per cent in 1991 (OECD 1993).

France is a republic, divided into twenty-two administrative regions. In 1987, 6.4 per cent of parliamentary seats were occupied by women. About 90 per cent of the population gave their religious affiliation as Roman Catholic, 2 per cent as Protestant, 1 per cent as Jewish, and 1 per cent as Muslim; 6 per cent reported no religious affiliation.

France is often used as an example of a country with an explicit and pronatalist family policy. According to D. Anderson (1991, 109), France has among the best maternity leave and public child care systems in the world. Children are supported regardless of the living arrangements of their parents. At the same time, women's maternal role in the family has been emphasized in the legal system and social policies, and the Napoleonic Code historically gave men more legal rights than women (ibid, 109).

Germany

In January 1993, Germany had a population of 80.6 million. In 1990, the former West Germany had a population of 61 million, with 108 women for every 100 men. Fifty-four per cent of women aged twenty-five and over are currently married, and 10.9 per cent of women aged twenty-five to forty-four are currently divorced. East Germany had a population of 16.5 million, with 109 women for every 100 men. Fifty-seven per cent of women aged twenty-five and over are currently married, and 1.8 per cent of women aged twenty-five to forty-four are currently divorced. Although the two countries were united in October 1990, some of our statistics pertain to the former divided country because of the time lag in gathering international data.

The total fertility rate in the united Germany was 1.3 in 1992, the lowest of the countries in our study. The infant mortality rate was 6.9 deaths per 1,000 births in 1991. Of all families with children, 13.8 per cent were led by one parent, and in 86 per cent of cases this parent was the mother (Hohnerlein 1992, 126). In West Germany, women constituted about 39 per cent of the workforce, and about 30 per cent of them worked part time. Women earned about 74 per cent of what men earned (ibid.). On the other hand, 90 per cent of women in East Germany worked outside the home. The German unemployment rate in 1992 was

5.0 per cent (OECD 1992a, 43) – the second lowest rate in this study. Real GDP growth in 1992 was 0.8 per cent (OECD 1993).

Until 1990, West Germany was a federal republic with ten states. In 1987, 15.4 per cent of parliamentary seats were occupied by women. About 45 per cent of the population reported being Roman Catholic, 44 per cent Protestant, and 11 per cent 'other.' East Germany was a Communist state until October 1990, when it joined with West Germany. In 1987, 32.2 per cent of parliamentary seats in the former East Germany were occupied by women – the highest rate among all the countries in this study. Although 47 per cent of the population gave their religious affiliation as Protestant, only about 5 per cent were active church-goers; about the same percentage (46 per cent) reported 'other' or no religious affiliation.

Considering the discrepancy in the participation rates of women in the two parts of the country, and considering the different political ideologies, it is not surprising that their family policies differed substantially. The former West Germany provided fourteen weeks of maternity leave at full pay, as well as up to eighteen months' parental leave, with a child-raising allowance worth more than U.S. $400. East German women received twelve months' maternity leave: five months on full pay and seven months at 80 per cent pay (D. Anderson 1991, 88). There is a long history of both private and public kindergartens in Germany, but many of these are open only half-days. East Germany, however, always provided more subsidized child care spaces with a high level of subsidy than did West Germany (ibid.). In addition, Germany offers a child allowance which rises with each additional child in the family (up to three).

The implications of reunification are not entirely clear. The unemployment rate has reached 30 per cent of the registered workforce (including people on retirement schemes), and youths and those near retirement age are particularly vulnerable. But unemployment is especially high among the female labour force (Ostner 1994). It is expected that policies in the eastern part of the country will become less generous to women and families as they are harmonized with the policies of the western part. Already, the government is stressing the idea of 'the family' as a safety net (ibid.).

The Netherlands

In January 1993, the population of the Netherlands was 15.2 million, with 102 women for every 100 men. Fifty-seven per cent of women aged twenty-five and over are currently married, and 7.1 per cent of women aged twenty-five to forty-four are currently divorced. The total fertility rate was 1.6 births per woman in 1992, now relatively low by European standards, although it had been high before the 1970s (Jonker 1990, 279). The infant mortality rate was 6.3 per 1,000 births in 1992. The unemployment rate in 1992 was 6.4 per cent (OECD 1992a, 44). Real GDP growth in 1992 was 1.1 per cent (OECD 1993).

The government of the Netherlands is a constitutional monarchy, and the country is divided into twelve provinces. In 1987, 20 per cent of parliamentary seats were occupied by women. Thirty-six per cent of the population is reported to be Roman Catholic, 27 per cent Protestant, 4 per cent 'other' and 33 per cent unaffiliated.

Family policy in the Netherlands has been characterized by Kamerman and Kahn (eds 1978) as largely 'implicit.' In contrast to other Western European countries, the Netherlands was concerned in the postwar period about a rapid growth rate and the negative effects of overpopulation (Jonker 1990). The government therefore adopted a non-interventionist policy with families. The general philosophy has been one of equality of opportunity: equality of welfare, well-being, and health. The government does not pursue a centrally coordinated and integrated policy directed towards the position of the family in society. Instead, there is a strong emphasis on autonomy, personal responsibility, and public education (ibid.).

The government's emphasis on controlling public expenditure and reducing the deficit throughout the 1980s has evoked criticism from the International Labor Organization for neglecting low-income people and measures that are more specifically directed towards families (such as higher allowances, parental leave, and child care). Politically, only a small minority of people belonging to right-wing parties favour the idea of creating a more explicit family policy. The left-wing majority is not very enthusiastic because it fears that such a policy would encourage overpopulation and regressive political changes (Jonker 1990).

Sweden

In January 1993, Sweden had a population of 8.7 million, with 103 females for every 100 males. Forty-seven per cent of women aged twenty-five and over are currently married (the lowest percentage in our study), and 10.2 per cent of women aged twenty-five to forty-four are currently divorced. The total fertility rate was 2.1 births per woman in 1992, which is the highest among the countries in our study and up from

1.7 in 1990. The infant mortality rate was 5.4 per 1,000 births in 1992, the lowest among the countries in our study. About 50 per cent of the workforce consists of women, 43 per cent of whom work part time. The gap between men's and women's wages is among the lowest in the world, as women employed full time earn about 90 per cent of what men earn (D. Anderson 1991). The unemployment rate in 1992 was 4.1 per cent (OECD 1992a, 44) – the lowest in our study. Real GDP growth in 1992 was minus 1.3 per cent (OECD 1993).

Sweden is a constitutional monarchy, and the country is divided into twenty-four provinces. In 1987, 28.5 per cent of the parliamentary seats were occupied by women. Ninety-four per cent of the population is reported to be Evangelical Lutheran, 1 per cent Roman Catholic, and 5 per cent other.

It is often said that Sweden has the best social service system in the world, a high standard of living, and an established system of working out political problems through negotiations among employers, employees, and governments (referred to as corporatism). Instead of creating family focused policies, as in France, Sweden has emphasized full employment for both men and women, and a variety of labour market policies. In addition, the government provides housing subsidies and universal child allowances. At the birth of a child, parental leave is available for either parent at 80 per cent to 90 per cent of previous earnings for eighteen months. Government-run child care centres have been operating since the 1940s, with fees based on parents' income (D. Anderson 1991, 230).

The United Kingdom

In January 1993, the United Kingdom had a population of 58 million, with 105 females for every 100 males. Fifty-seven per cent of women aged twenty-five and over are currently married, and 8.8 per cent of women aged twenty-five to forty-four are currently divorced.[9] The total fertility rate was 1.8 births per woman in 1992, with one in five parents unmarried (D. Anderson 1991, 150ff). The infant mortality rate was 7 infants per 1,000 live births in 1992. According to United Nations statistics, 32 per cent of households are headed by women with children and no spouse. About 44 per cent of the workforce consists of women, 45 per cent of whom work part time. On average, women earn about 70 per cent of what men earn (ibid.). The unemployment rate in 1992 was 9.9 per cent (OECD 1992a, 44). Real GDP growth in 1992 was minus 0.8 per cent (OECD 1993).

The United Kingdom is a constitutional monarchy and is divided into forty-seven counties (as well as other administrative regions). In 1987, 6.3 per cent of parliamentary seats were occupied by women. About 53 per cent of the population is Protestant (mostly Anglican), 11 per cent Roman Catholic, 1 per cent Jewish; most of the rest report no affiliation.

Although Britain has one of the highest marriage rates in Europe, it also has one of the highest divorce rates. Child care is subsidized by government for low-income parents, but there is a serious shortage of subsidized spaces. For example, there are subsidized places for only about 2 per cent of children under three who need care (D. Anderson, 1991, 151). Forty weeks of maternity leave is available, with six weeks paid at 90 per cent of previous earnings, but eligibility requirements are strict. This is the shortest period of maternity benefits among the countries in the European Union (ibid.), a fact which has been a source of controversy.

The United States

In January 1993, the United States had a population of about 256.9 million, with 105 females for every 100 males. Fifty-seven per cent of women aged twenty-five and over are currently married, and 11.4 per cent of women aged twenty-five to forty-four are currently divorced, the highest rate in our study. The total fertility rate was comparable to Sweden's at 2.1 births per woman in 1992, up from 1.8 in 1990. The infant mortality rate was 8 per 1000 births during 1992, down from 10 in 1985–90, but still the highest among the countries in this study. Roughly 45 per cent of the workforce comprises women, about 26 per cent of whom work part time. Women earn only about 65 per cent of what men earn – one of the lowest ratios in the Western democracies (D. Anderson 1991, 171). The unemployment rate in 1992 was 6.7 per cent (OECD 1992a, 44), which was moderate compared with the other countries in our study. In 1991, the real GDP growth was minus 1.2 per cent (OECD 1993).

The United States is a federal republic, divided into fifty states and one federal district. In 1987, only 5.3 per cent of parliamentary seats were occupied by women, the lowest rate of all the countries in this study. The reported religious affilation of the population is 61 per cent Protestant, 25 per cent Roman Catholic, 2 per cent Jewish, 5 per cent other, and 7 per cent unaffiliated.

The United States has never had a comprehensive national family or child policy. Many issues relating to family policy are governed by state legislation, including divorce law and child support. Until 1993, the United States had no federal statutory maternity leave provision, and still does not provide maternity benefits at the national level. Unlike all the other countries in this study, the United States has never had a universal family allowance. Moreover, there is no national child care program in the United States.

U.S. social policy has been influenced by a tradition of individualism, the separation of church and state, puritanism, social Darwinism, a strong work ethic, a relatively open immigration policy, racial segregation and disharmony, late development of the federal bureaucracy, and *laissez-faire* economic policies (Kamerman and Kahn, forthcoming 1996). Although the New Deal and its aftermath (1933 to The Second World World) created the foundation for a minimalist welfare state that included federal social insurance programs, the Second World War did not lead to major new social policy initiatives. From the mid-1960s to the 1970s, new policies were oriented to equal opportunity and racial justice, and social welfare expenditures increased. The old voluntary sector and grass-roots social services became publicly funded, but much of this was dismantled during the Reagan years. From the 1970s to the 1990s, the feminist movement has focused its efforts on workplace discrimination, equal rights, and abortion (ibid.), but the backlash from the 'moral right' has diminished the feminists' impact on social policy.

CONCLUSION

Behind family policies and income support programs lie different philosophies concerning the role of the state in private life, the importance of child-bearing and child-rearing, and the role of parents (especially mothers) in families and in society. While some nations have focused on providing direct services or benefits for children, others have targeted income support to the family unit. Still others have emphasized individual rights, full employment and equal opportunity to combine paid work and child-rearing.

In this book, family-related programs in each country will be explored, including income support and tax benefits for families with dependent children, parental and maternity leave, child care funding or services, child welfare services, and the enforcement of child support after divorce. In discussing variations in funding and program delivery, we will explore the reasons why some countries have developed a complex system of transfer programs to protect families with dependent children from poverty and to help parents combine family life with earning a living. The political and economic circumstances under which these countries have made trade-offs for better social programs will also be examined.

Intellectually, it is important to understand which factors have influenced the development of the welfare state and family policy, and under what conditions ideas become politically acceptable. It is also worthwhile to understand that there are different delivery mechanisms for social programs, some of which are more effective than others in assisting families to live above the poverty line and to resolve conflicts between work and family life.

Most industrialized countries in this study are experiencing similar trends in the economy, labour force, and family structure. These trends include declining or stable economic growth, increasing numbers of mothers in the labour force, rising divorce rates, declining fertility, and increasing proportions of one-parent households. There has also been some convergence in policy solutions, including more liberal divorce laws, more equitable division of marital property after divorce, government support for low-income parents and one-parent families, the provision of paid parental leave, and greater government intervention in child care services. Yet there remain major differences in policy responses by country.

Policy responses to economic, social, and demographic change vary with the political and cultural traditions of the country and whether or not trends are perceived as 'problems.' Throughout this book, I compare and contrast countries' responses, searching for solutions which are applicable to the Canadian context and seeking theoretical explanations for the diversity. But first, I examine some demographic and social trends which have influenced family life over the past decades and have served as a rallying point for policy reform in most countries.

2

Changing family trends

Social policy is often developed or amended when influential groups create alliances and lobby governments to resolve what they perceive to be 'social problems' arising from rapid economic, demographic, and social change. For example, inflation, the decline of the family wage, and increasing family poverty encouraged more wives and mothers to enter the labour force, creating the need for maternity leave, child care, and family law reform. Rising divorce rates have also decreased the incomes of one-parent families. Most families who became poor in the 1980s, however, did so because of labour market changes rather than changes in family status (McFate 1991, 12). Nevertheless, these trends encouraged various groups to press for family policy reform.

In order to comprehend the development of family policies, we need to understand how family life has changed over the past few decades. Socio-economic and demographic changes influencing family life will be outlined, the reasons behind them discussed, and the implications for social policies gleaned from them.

Rising life expectancy at birth

Throughout this century, many industrialized countries have experienced a gradual rise in life expectancies. In 1931, the average life expectancy of Canadian males was 60 years, and of females 62 (Statistics Canada, Annual (c) 1974). By 1950, these figures had increased to 66.3 for males and 70.8 for females, and by 1992 had reached 74.2 for males and 80.7 for females, as Table 2.1 indicates. The trend of rising life

TABLE 2.1
Life expectancy in eight industrialized countries, 1950 and 1992

Country	1950		1992	
	M	F	M	F
Australia	67.1	72.8	74.4	80.3
Canada	66.3	70.8	74.2	80.7
France	63.6	69.3	73.1	81.3
Germany	—	—	72.1	78.7
West	64.6	68.5	—	—
East	65.1	69.1	—	—
Netherlands	70.6	72.9	74.3	80.3
Sweden	70.5	73.4	75.3	80.8
United Kingdom	66.4	71.2	73.2	78.6
United States	65.6	71.1	72.2	79.1

SOURCES: United Nations 1979, 548–61; Statistics Canada 1994, 18.

expectancies, especially for women, has been similar in the other nations in our study. Canada's life expectancies are now higher than those in Germany, the United States, and the United Kingdom, but slightly lower than those in Sweden.

There are several reasons for the rise in life expectancy within industrialized countries. Since the late 1800s, they have all developed improvements in living standards, including safer accommodation with better heating and sanitation. Knowledge has increased about the importance to health of cleanliness, exercise, and nutrition. As well, there have been major advances in medical knowledge and health services, and medical and pharmaceutical interventions have prolonged life and raised the average age of death.

In the early part of the twentieth century, infant mortality rates and maternal death rates declined in response to these improvements in sanitation, nutrition, housing, and health services. In particular, the invention of antibiotics has helped fight infections, and inoculation to eliminate certain deadly contagious diseases (such as smallpox and typhoid fever) has become standard practice. At the same time, however, pollution has increased and rates of cancer and other fatal diseases are still high, especially for the middle-aged and elderly.

Reducing deaths during childbirth increased the life expectancy of women relative to men, as men continued to take on high-risk occupations (such as construction, forestry, fishing and mining) and dangerous leisure pursuits (such as smoking, drinking, and fast driving). Although

the life expectancies of women in industrialized countries tend to sur-
pass men's, the reverse is usually true in developing nations where the
cause of premature death is often related to reproductive complications.
In addition, the widespread development of income security programs
and medical insurance in industrialized countries has enabled lower-
income individuals and families to afford healthier lifestyles and medical attention. Premature death rates have also been reduced through
improved health and safety standards in the workplace.

Rising life expectancies led to several other trends. At the beginning
of industrialization, a reduction in infant and maternal deaths led to an
initial increase in the population. Eventually, however, declining infant
mortality rates contributed to a declining birth rate, because couples
modified their expectations of family size to correspond with the greater
number of babies who lived to maturity. The reduction in maternal
deaths increased the average life expectancy for women and enabled
them to expand their horizons beyond child-bearing and child-rearing.
Now women in industrialized countries tend to outlive their husbands,
creating more widows than widowers. Unattached older women often
need financial assistance from their governments because lower labour
force attachment and greater financial dependence throughout their lives
mean that they have fewer savings and no or lower employer-sponsored
pensions.

Declining rates of premature death, especially of women in childbirth,
combined with an increasing acceptance of government social assistance,
had the potential of creating a more stable family life for children. The
need for orphanages and children's institutions was reduced after the
Second World War, as fewer mothers died in childbirth and widows,
widowers, deserted lone parents, and low-income parents were encouraged to care for their own children. They were assisted in this by the
introduction of mothers' allowances, welfare payments, and subsidized
child care, and by women's increased labour force participation. Today,
many children experience family disruption through parental divorce
rather than the premature death of a parent, and the former can be just
as detrimental as the latter in terms of its economic and emotional
consequences for children.

Rising life expectancies also suggest the potential for longer marriages
or more than one marriage per lifetime. In the last century, people
endured unhappy marriages for several reasons, including feelings of
obligation and commitment, the inability to function economically as a
lone parent, the absence of any notion of 'free will,' the lack of provisions

for legal divorce or permission from the state or church to remarry, and the knowledge that life was relatively short. Perhaps one of the reasons why we have more divorces today is that we expect to live longer and therefore need to create an artificial end to some of our relationships. Living to the age of eighty gives us enough time to experience several marriages of the same length as the one marriage people had when more of them died prematurely.

When few people reached old age, governments tended to assume that elderly people would depend on personal savings or family support. But when a substantial portion of the population began to survive into old age, especially at a time of rapid industrial expansion, governments faced growing pressure by employers' groups as well as unions, religious organizations, and anti-poverty groups to create mandatory retirement policies and public pensions to stave off increasing poverty in old age (M. Baker 1988; Myles 1989). With the rise in the cost of public pensions, however, governments are now trying to persuade employers to develop their own pension plans and individuals to invest in their own retirement future in order to supplement the costly public programs. Similarly, governments and the public are trying to reform health care systems to focus more on cost-effective interventions, prevention, and long-term care.

Declining birth rates

Since the mid-1800s, birth rates have been falling in most industrialized countries, and Canada is no exception. We can see from Table 2.2 that the crude birth rate in Canada – that is, the number of live births per year for every 1,000 population – was 45 in 1851–61. For twenty years after the Second World War, birth rates increased in Canada and the United States in what came to be called the 'postwar baby boom,' which was not experienced to the same extent in Europe (Beaujot 1991). In the mid-1960s, the crude birth rate fell again to reach 14.4 in 1987 before rising to 15.2 in 1990. Since 1990, the Canadian birth rate has continued to decline to 14.0 in 1992.

Canadian census data indicate that different ethnic and language groups have varying fertility rates. Contrary to popular myth, immigrants to Canada have traditionally experienced lower birth rates than Canadian-born women, as many immigrants come to Canada to improve their standard of living and need two incomes to accomplish this. Women's labour force participation has historically been related to lower

TABLE 2.2
Crude birth rates* in Canada, 1851–1992

Year**	Births per 1,000 population
1851–61	45
1861–71	40
1871–81	37
1881–91	34
1891–1901	30
1901–11	31
1911–21	29
1921	29.3
1931	23.2
1941	22.4
1951	27.2
1961	26.1
1971	16.8
1981	15.3
1986	14.7
1987	14.4
1990	15.2
1991	14.3
1992	14.0

* The number of live births in a given year per 1,000 population
** Rates for 1851–1921 are estimates.
SOURCE: Statistics Canada, Annual (a).

birth rates and smaller family size. In addition, immigrants tend to adjust their lifestyles to reflect the pattern of the majority (Beaujot 1991).

Religious variations used to be evident in Canadian fertility rates, although some of these differences are rapidly diminishing. Historically, Roman Catholics have produced larger families than Protestants, but there have always been substantial differences in birth rates among Protestant denominations. Like Roman Catholics, Mennonites, Hutterites, and Mormons have opposed birth control and encouraged large families. On the other hand, Jewish people (except Hassidic Jews) have generally produced smaller families than other religious groups (Kalbach and McVey 1979, 107).

In the past thirty years, Quebec birth rates have declined considerably, despite the Catholic background of most French Quebeckers. Only a generation ago, Quebec women were still having large families in comparison to all Canadians. In 1959, for example, the total fertility rate

(TFR) in Quebec was 4.0 children per woman but fell to 2.1 in 1970 and 1.3 in 1987 (Le Bourdais and Marcil-Gratton 1994). In the same years, the Canadian TFR rate was 3.93, 2.33, and 1.58, respectively (Statistics Canada, Annual (a) 1987–92).

The falling Quebec birth rates since the 1960s have been attributed to the sweeping cultural changes known as the 'Quiet Revolution,' when the Catholic church lost much of its control over Quebec society, the education system became more secularized, young people placed more emphasis on occupational success, and young women played down their traditional role as mothers (Lachapelle and Henripin 1982, 116ff). Another reason for the lower birth rates probably relates to women's high labour force participation and their personal reaction against their mothers' experience in child-bearing and child-rearing, which many young women perceived to be emotionally and physically draining.

Fertility rates declined in all countries in our study from 1970 to 1990, as Table 2.3 indicates, and all have experienced fertility rates below replacement level, although Sweden's and the United States' are now above replacement. This table also shows that Canada's fertility rate is moderate compared with rates in the other countries in this study. We should add, however, that total fertility rates in Quebec have been among the lowest in the industrialized countries in the past few years (Le Bourdais and Marcil-Gratton 1994, 103), and fertility rates among indigenous people living in the North have been well above the Canadian average.

TABLE 2.3
Total fertility rates, 1970–1992

Country	1970	1992
Australia	2.9	1.9
Canada	2.5	1.7
France	2.6	1.7
Germany	—	1.3
West	2.3	—
East	2.3	—
Netherlands	3.2	1.6
Sweden	2.1	2.1
United Kingdom	2.5	1.8
United States	2.6	2.1

SOURCES: United Nations 1991c, 26; Statistics Canada 1994, 19.

There are many reasons why fertility rates tend to decline when societies industrialize and urbanize. One relates to the consequences for the living costs of families with children. As societies industrialize, people tend to seek work in towns and cities where the cost of food and housing is higher than in the countryside. In addition, the technological changes accompanying industrialization usually require a more educated labour force, and parents are expected to keep their children in school rather than allowing them to work to help support the family. This expectation is usually reinforced by compulsory education laws, but also by the inability of young people to find work without adequate schooling. Despite personal preferences, large numbers of children per family become economic liabilities rather than assets for parents.

When the cost of living rises and one wage is no longer adequate to support a family, both husbands and wives need to work for pay. Unless grandparents or other relatives are available to care for the small children, child care becomes difficult and expensive. Having fewer children is often the only way couples can reduce conflicts between earning a living and raising a family. As the public demand for birth control increases, birth control technology is developed or imported and family planning becomes more widespread and socially acceptable. Ideologies supporting a more economic and less domestic role for women gain strength, and birth rates continue to decline.

Declining birth rates may have different consequences for women, families, and society (Eichler 1988b). From a woman's perspective, fewer children may mean more time and opportunity to become educated, acquire some leisure time, participate in the labour force, and gain a higher standard of living. For families, fewer children may mean higher quality care for each existing child, a higher standard of living, and, often, daytime care by non-relatives, because the mother is likely to be in the labour force. From the state's viewpoint, however, falling birth rates lead to an aging population and could trigger concern about higher dependency ratios,[1] a declining tax base, and greater pension and medical expenditures.

Some economists and demographers, especially those in Quebec, have suggested that lower birth rates will lead to declining economic productivity and prosperity (Mathews 1984; Henripin 1989). Rapidly declining birth rates have also been interpreted by some nationalists as decreasing Quebec's power within Canada. Yet in Sweden, for example, declining birth rates do not necessarily relate to lower productivity or lower prosperity. Some of the decline in productivity which may accompany a larger percentage of retirees in a population can be counteracted by encouraging fuller labour force participation for women and visible minorities (OECD 1987; Lasserre et al. 1988). Certainly, the Swedish model of high female labour force participation has kept productivity high despite falling birth rates. The other solution to declining birth rates is raising immigration rates and giving priority to young working-age immigrants with desirable job skills, which both Canada and Quebec have done.

Not only are birth rates declining in Canada and other industrialized countries, but more women are delaying childbirth. In Canada, the number of first births to women in their thirties more than tripled from 1971 to 1988 (Wadhera and Millar 1991, 154). Reasons for delayed childbirth include the fact that the average age of marriage has risen since the 1970s, but this is another symptom rather than a cause. Improvements in contraception have allowed couples to experience more child-free years of marriage, in which both work full time and have some opportunity for leisure, self-development activities, or travel. Many couples wait until they feel they are psychologically ready for childbearing, until they can establish a financially secure environment for a child, or until they have saved enough money to buy a house. Sometimes, one or both of the couple are still in college or university in the early stages of the marriage. In addition, a small percentage of single women are deciding to reproduce without first marrying, as they approach the end of their child-bearing years and are more financially secure.

The timing of pregnancy may also be influenced by maternity leave and benefit programs. Finding a permanent job before becoming pregnant is important in countries such as Sweden, which have relatively generous parental leave programs that replace 80 to 90 per cent of previous pay. In countries such as the United States, which have no statutory maternity benefits and little public child care, the timing of pregnancy may be related to personal factors more than to social policies. Although women in full-time jobs may obtain leave without pay, or in some cases receive maternity benefits negotiated in a union contract, others must quit their jobs in order to give birth and care for their infant, planning to return to the labour market later. Early pregnancy, however, is correlated with incomplete education, diminished job possibilities, and lower lifetime earning potential in most countries of this study (Wong, Garfinkel, and McLanahan 1992).

In Canada, wages have not kept up with inflation over the years, and two incomes have become necessary to maintain the same living standard as a generation ago (Maynard 1988). Many two-income couples feel that they cannot afford to lose a portion of the wife's income while she is on maternity leave, and consequently delay the decision to reproduce. Some delay for so long that conception becomes more difficult. At the same time, adopting a baby is increasingly difficult in Canada, and almost impossible in Europe, unless couples turn to international adoption, as I will discuss in chapter 7.

Over time, declining birth rates and increasing life expectancy contribute to population aging. As the average age of the population increases, governments and social planners need to reform social programs and services to ensure their continued relevance to the needs of older people. This may require a shift of monies to organizations catering to elderly persons from those catering to children and youth. On the other hand, as children become a scarce resource, a greater social value might be placed on childbirth and child-raising because children represent the future labour force whose contributions will finance the pensions and health care of the elderly. In several European nations, such as Sweden and Germany, population aging has precipitated both strong pension plans and generous benefits for children.

Although Canada's population has been aging noticeably since the 1960s, most European countries have experienced low birth rates and a growing percentage of elderly people since the 1930s. While 11.4 per cent of the Canadian population is now sixty-five or older, the percentages in the European countries studied are generally higher – as high as 17.7 per cent in Sweden, as Table 2.4 indicates. Although Canada's population is relatively young compared with Europe's, it is old compared with those of developing countries, in South America and Africa, for example. These countries tend to experience higher birth rates, more children per family, and fewer older people in the population.

Increase in common-law marriages

In comparison with previous decades, more Canadians are now living together without being legally married. In 1990, Statistics Canada reported that 12 per cent of all couples were in common-law relationships compared with 6 per cent in 1981 (Stout 1991, 18). Of the Canadian provinces, Quebec had the highest percentage of residents aged fifteen and over living in common-law relationships (13 per cent), while New Brunswick had the lowest (5 per cent). Belliveau, Oderkirk, and Silver (1994) note that 19 per cent of all couples (married and common law

TABLE 2.4
Percentage of the population aged 65 and over, 1985 and 1990*

| Country | Percentage 65+ | |
	1985	1990
Australia	10.1	—
Canada	10.4	11.4
France	12.4	13.8
West Germany	14.5	15.5
Netherlands	11.5**	12.7
Sweden	16.9	17.7
United Kingdom	15.1	15.1
United States	12.0	12.2

* Projected
** 1980
SOURCES: R.L. Brown 1991, 13; Sorrentino 1990, 43.

combined) in Quebec lived common law in 1991, but this rose to 61 per cent among couples in which the woman was under thirty five and there were no children. Furthermore, they found that French-speaking Quebeckers are more than twice as likely to live common law as English-speaking Quebeckers.

The vast majority of individuals living common law have never been legally married; this is not surprising because, on average, they are a young group. More than half the women and 43 per cent of the men who lived common law in 1986 were younger than age thirty. However, since 1984, the median age of common-law partners has continued to rise (Stout 1991, 19). From 1984 to 1990, the proportion of Canadians aged eighteen to sixty-four who had ever lived common law nearly doubled, but among those aged forty to forty-nine, the proportion almost tripled.

Statistics Canada's Family History Survey of 1984 found that 63 per cent of first common-law unions end in marriage, while 35 per cent end in separation (2 per cent and with the death of one of the partners). Consequently, some have referred to common-law living as a new 'courtship' pattern, or 'trial marriage.' On the other hand, a minority of people see cohabitation as an alternative to legal marriage, especially if they are separated but not divorced. Some feel, for example, that the government has no right to meddle in people's personal or sexual lives or that legal marriage involves rigid gender roles and expectations of behaviour that they would prefer to avoid.

Although common-law relationships in Canada used to be considered temporary arrangements, they are coming to be viewed more as legal marriages. Statistically, however, common-law relationships still differ from legal marriages in that they are shorter in duration and are characterized by lower fertility rates (although the latter are rising). Furthermore, some researchers have found that marriages preceded by cohabitation have slightly higher rates of dissolution (Burch and Madan 1986; Beaujot 1990). Yet the 1991 census has shown that living together is becoming more prevalent, especially in Quebec. Furthermore, 48 per cent of first-born children in Quebec are now born to parents who are not legally married, although 90 per cent of these parents live 'common law' (Le Bourdais and Marcil-Gratton 1994). In Canada as a whole, 41 per cent of common-law families had children living at home, up from 34 per cent in 1981 (Belliveau, Oderkirk, and Silver 1994).

These trends are very similar to those in many European countries, where the distinction between legal marriage and cohabitation is even more blurred, both legally and socially. In fact, several countries (including Canada) now consider couples to be married if they have cohabited in a heterosexual relationship for at least one year or produced a child from that relationship. For this reason, comparative statistics of common-law or de facto relationships are difficult to find. Sweden is an example of a country with a low rate of legal marriage. While 62 per cent of Canadian women aged twenty-five and over were legally married in 1990, only 47 per cent of Swedish women were legally married (United Nations 1991c, 26). Although low rates of legal marriage used to be related to low birth rates, total fertility rates are now higher in Sweden than in Canada, despite low Swedish marriage rates (Statistics Canada 1994, 19).

Increase in mothers working for pay

In 1941, about 4.5 per cent of married women were working in the labour force (Baker, ed. 1990, 8), but by 1992, this had risen to 61.4 per cent (Statistics Canada 1992c, B8). Women's labour force participation in the 1960s used to be influenced by marriage, the presence of children, and the employment status and income of their husband. Now younger women are more likely than older women to be in the labour force, regardless of the presence of young children, and about three-quarters of mothers with children under twelve are now working for pay (ibid.).

TABLE 2.5
Economically active* population, aged 15 and over, 1970 and 1990

Country	Women		Men		Women as % of economically active population
	1970	1990	1970	1990	1990
	%	%	%	%	%
Australia	37	46	82	77	38
Canada	37	49	79	78	40
France	39	45	75	71	40
Germany					
West	39	41	79	75	37
East	54	62	79	83	45
Netherlands	26	31	74	71	31
Sweden	41	55	76	71	45
United Kingdom	41	46	82	77	39
United States	42	50	78	77	41

* Economically active is defined as earning a wage or salary, or participating in the labour force, either part time or full time.
SOURCE: United Nations 1991c, 104.

Table 2.5 shows United Nations figures comparing the 'economic activity' or labour force participation rates of women and men aged fifteen and over in the eight countries studied. Note that the rates for men declined from 1970 to 1990 as more young men stayed in school, more adult men returned to college and university, and many male employees took early retirement. The rates for women have increased in all countries, however, despite the fact that women are also staying in school longer, returning to school in mid-life, and retiring earlier, and that many older women have never worked for pay.

Table 2.5 also indicates that the labour force participation rates of Canadian women have increased faster than those for women in the other countries studied. This trend can be explained largely by the rising cost of living and by high male unemployment during the 1970s and 1980s in Canada, which forced wives into the workforce, but also to some extent by ideologies, laws, and policies which promoted financial independence for women.

There are five major reasons for the increased participation of Canadian women and mothers in the paid labour force since the 1960s. The first was the need for two incomes per family because of the relative decline in wages compared with the rising cost of living. We should keep in mind that, prior to the Second World War, male breadwinners in a number of countries were paid a 'family wage' to enable them to support themselves and their dependants. A man's pay raises were often based on changes in family status such as marriage and the birth of additional children. As the cost of living increased during the 1960s, the family wage could no longer support men and their dependants. Furthermore, the idea of paying an employee on the basis of family status was challenged and eventually replaced by an emphasis on individual qualifications, experience, or merit. As the service sector and public bureaucracies expanded in the 1960s, jobs grew faster than the labour force, and married women were encouraged to accept these positions. Although they had always served as a temporary reserve labour force, more married women and mothers began to work full time. The rapid development of part-time jobs also encouraged mothers with young children, as well as high school and university students, to enter the paid workforce.

The second reason for women's increased labour force participation relates to changing roles for women. As women gained political rights and greater access to higher education, they raised their expectations about using their education to support themselves and their families and to make a contribution to society. Since the 1960s, liberal feminist ideas of equal opportunity have become widespread in many industrialized countries, especially agreement on the right to equal education, to paid work, and to employment equity. Some countries, such as Sweden, have actively promoted and reinforced the ideal of labour force equality between men and women by providing public child care, generous employment benefits for family responsibilities, and the right to work part time when children are young, with the option to return to full-time work later. Other countries, such as the United States, have taken the concept of 'equal opportunity' more literally, without acknowledgment that women's life chances are not always the same as men's. These policies have left women to compete with men in a system designed by men, without acknowledgment that pregnancy and family responsibilities can interfere with work life and without public support for parenting. Table 2.6 shows the rates of economic activity or labour force participation for women with children under age eighteen and under age three.

The third reason for the increased participation of mothers in the labour force is that they are not leaving their jobs to raise children as they used to do in the 1960s. Considering how unemployment rates have increased over the past thirty years in Canada and many other

TABLE 2.6
Labour force participation rates of women with children under 18 and under 3, 1986
or 1988*

Country	All women with children		Lone mothers with children	
	Under 18 years old	Under 3 years old	Under 18 years old	Under 3 years old
Canada	67.0	58.4	63.6	41.3
Germany	48.4	39.7	69.7	50.4
France	65.8	60.1	85.2	69.6
Sweden	89.4	85.8	—	—
United Kingdom	58.7	36.9	51.9	23.4
United States	65.0	52.5	65.3	45.1

* Data for Canada, Sweden, and the United States are from 1988; for all other countries, they are from 1986.
SOURCE: Sorrentino 1990, 53.

countries, it is now more difficult for women to quit their jobs when they become pregnant and to find another one when their children reach school age. Now mothers are more likely to take a temporary maternity leave from work.

Fourth, since the 1970s, laws relating to maternity and parental leaves and benefits have been reformed in Canada and most other countries in the study after pressure from labour unions, reproductive health advocates, and women's groups. These laws allow women who have worked continuously for the same employer for a certain length of time (which varies by jurisdiction) the right to retain their positions while giving birth, to receive a portion of their previous earnings while on leave, and to return to their jobs within a few months. In Canada, maternity benefits were first paid under the Unemployment Insurance Program (UI) in 1971, and parental benefits were added in 1990. Although UI replaces up to 57 per cent of previous earnings (recently reduced from 60 per cent), some union contracts top up this amount to as much as 100 per cent. As we will see in chapter 5, Canada's maternity and parental benefits are not very generous compared to those in the European countries. However, they look favourable compared to policies in the United States.

The fifth reason for the rise in labour force participation by mothers relates to improvements in birth control. Although the birth control pill was available in Canada as early as 1963, the dissemination and sale of contraceptive information and devices were illegal until the end of the decade. Hospital abortions were also illegal except when the life of the mother was in danger. These laws were reformed in 1969 by the Liberal government led by Prime Minister Pierre Trudeau. The legalization of contraception and the liberalization of abortion laws have enabled women and couples to plan pregnancies to fit in with educational plans, work requirements, and personal ideals. Now, fewer women than in previous decades have to curtail their education or quit their jobs because of unexpected pregnancies.

Many social implications arise from the increased labour force participation of married women and mothers. When married men and fathers left farms during the Industrial Revolution in order to find work, their authority as family heads was gradually undermined. The decline of patriarchy continued when wives and mothers began to gain their own source of income. Subsequently, public support for the patriarchal family has been further diminished through family law reform, which has eroded the breadwinner-homemaker model of the family, and through the development of child protection legislation, which provides abused or neglected children with advocates.

Now that men are no longer sole breadwinners and wives can no longer be assumed to be their financial dependants, many laws and social policies need to be reformed in order to make them more responsive to social reality. Changes have also been occurring in the division of labour in many homes, although recent Canadian research indicates that wives both retain responsibility for most household chores and perform most of the routine tasks even when they work full time (Marshall 1993), as I will discuss further in chapter 5.

Labour force participation rates have been higher for Canadian wives and mothers than for those in some other countries in this study (such as Germany, the Netherlands, and the United Kingdom) for several reasons. First, the cost of living rose rapidly in Canada, and unemployment among men has been higher than in the other countries. Second, divorce rates have been rising rapidly since the 1970s, and family law reform is based on the assumption that women earn their own money or can do so if they wish. Consequently, separated and divorced women are expected to contribute to child support payments and become self-supporting soon after divorce. Third, both liberal and more radical feminist ideologies have promoted the idea that financial dependence can lead to emotional dependence and that women should have their own money if they want to retain their self-respect, dignity, and personal freedom. Fourth, family benefits were insufficient to keep mothers at home and out of the labour force. The former family allowance was only $33 per month before it was abolished in December 1992, and provincial welfare policies no longer encouraged mothers with preschool children to remain on social assistance. Although lone mothers or low-income mothers used to be considered 'unemployable' if they had preschool or school-aged children, and therefore qualified for social assistance, these women increasingly were encouraged into the labour force. As we will see in chapters 5 and 6, in some other countries, such as the Netherlands, lower rates of economic activity for women can be explained by religious-based ideologies promoting maternal child care and subsequent policies which pay mothers to care for their children at home.

Rising rates of separation and divorce

Despite high personal expectations of marriage – or perhaps because of them – marital instability has been increasing in most industrialized countries, especially since the 1960s. The extent of marriage instability is usually based on legal divorce rates, which in Canada are calculated each year by Statistics Canada. They measure the annual number of divorces per 100,000 population or the number of divorces per marriages in the same year. Yet not all marriage dissolution is formalized and reported to authorities. The rate of marital separation may be as high as the divorce rate, which means that marriage dissolution in any year could be twice as high as government divorce rates imply (McVey and Robinson 1981).

Numerous factors have influenced divorce rates to rise in modern societies. With industrialization in Europe and North America, many young people were forced to leave home to find work or become educated. In moving away from their communities, young people avoided some of the restrictions of family life but also raised their expectations about personal development and fulfilment. Growing individualism discouraged the view of marriage as sacred or related primarily to family lineage, obligation, or procreation. People began to feel that they had the right to personal happiness, fair treatment, and love in marriage. The entrance of married women into the labour force enabled them to support themselves without a husband, and provided increased opportunities to meet new people and to compare their personal situations. Improved birth control made it possible to separate sex and marriage,

TABLE 2.7
Divorce rates in Canada, 1921–1990

Year	Rate per 100,000 population
1921	6.4
1931	6.8
1941	21.4
1951	37.6
1961	36.0
1971	137.6
1981	278.0
1982	285.9
1983	275.5
1984	259.5
1985	244.4
1986	308.3
1987	355.1
1988	308.1
1989	307.8
1990	294.0

SOURCES: Statistics Canada, Annual (b); Millar
1991, 83; Lindsay 1992, 11.

permitting more discreet non-marital relations for both men and women, but placing a strain on existing marriage. Furthermore, the backlog of applications for divorce and the activities of lobby groups (including civil rights advocates, lawyers, and feminist groups) pressured governments to liberalize divorce laws, and more liberal laws enabled divorce rates to rise. In chapter 8, some of these laws will be examined in detail.

As Table 2.7 indicates, the divorce rate in Canada rose almost consistently from 1921 to 1982, but especially after 1968 when the divorce laws were liberalized. After the 1983 recession, the rate declined slightly until 1986, when it sharply increased. The 1986 and 1987 increases were influenced by the legal change which redefined 'marriage breakdown' as one year of separation. A backlog of petitioners were probably waiting for the law to change before they applied for divorce. The decrease at the end of the 1980s likely reflects the end of the backlog, but also (and more importantly) a declining economy in which legal divorce is considered to be too expensive for many couples to contemplate.

Despite public concern about marriage breakdown, Canada's divorce rate used to be moderate compared to rates in other industrialized countries. As Table 2.8 illustrates, however, Canada had a rate of 2.8 divorces per 1,000 population in 1992, which is higher than that of most countries in our study except the United Kingdom and the United States. Canada's high divorce rate may partially reflect the lower average age of Canadians compared to Europeans, and the fact that most divorces occur at younger ages. The rate may also reflect the higher marriage rate in Canada than in European countries such as Sweden, as well as the liberalization of Canadian divorce laws in 1986.

Although divorce rates have been rising in Canada, many divorced people remarry and move back into two-parent families. In the mid-1980s, about three-quarters of divorced men and two-thirds of divorced women remarried, although these figures have been declining in recent years with more common-law relationships (O.B. Adams and Nagnur 1990, 144). Nevertheless, most divorced parents move into a new live-in relationship within a few years of their divorce. Women were divorced an average of five years and men an average of three years before remarriage in the mid-1980s, up from two years for women and one for men in 1971 (ibid.). Statistics Canada data from 1984 indicated that female lone parents (including those widowed, separated, divorced, or never married) spent an average of 5.5 years as lone parents (Lindsay 1992, 18). Thus, many children of divorced parents are living in one-parent households for only a few years, although these years might represent a large and influential portion of their lives.

TABLE 2.8
Marriages and divorces per 1,000 population in eight countries, 1992

Country	Marriages per 1,000 population	Divorces per 1,000 population
Australia	6.6	2.6
Canada	5.9	2.8*
France	4.7	1.9*
Germany	5.6	1.7*
Netherlands	6.2	2.0
Sweden	4.3	2.5
United Kingdom (1990)	6.5**	2.9**
United States	9.3	4.8

* 1991
** 1990
SOURCE: Statistics Canada 1994, 19.

As societal changes have led to rising rates of divorce, so certain social and psychological conditions that contribute to conflict within marriage have increased the likelihood of separation. Researchers have found, for example, that those who marry well below the average age, especially if the bride is pregnant, have above-average chances of being unhappy in their marriages and of divorcing (Ambert 1980, 75; Albrecht et al. 1983, 29ff). This suggests that emotional and social immaturity, an incomplete education, the inability to be self-supporting, and lack of opportunity to adjust to marriage before the strains of pregnancy tend to jeopardize the stability of marriage.

Studies have also found that the previously divorced and those with divorced parents are more likely to terminate unsatisfactory marriages (Beaujot 1990). This may simply suggest that people with previous family experience of marriage dissolution see divorce as a viable alternative to an unhappy marriage. With a 'role model' of a divorced person, they know from personal experience that there is 'life after marriage' or that a smooth transition from marriage to a single life is possible. They also may be aware of the legal procedures involved. On the other hand, this correlation may indicate that people learn unhealthy ways of resolving marital conflict from their parents or previous relationships. An increase in the numbers of Canadian young people with divorced parents will likely contribute to higher divorce rates in the future.

Large age discrepancies, differences in the cultural, religious, or socio-economic background of marriage partners, and the absence of religious affiliation have also been correlated with high divorce rates. This does not mean that anyone who enters a 'mixed' marriage or who does not attend religious services will get a divorce. It simply means that these people have a higher probability of divorcing, presumably because they are less bound by tradition. With increased urbanization, higher rates of Third World immigration, and more people studying in colleges and universities, more marriages now take place between peole from different social and cultural backgrounds. In addition, attendance at religious services has declined throughout North American society. All these trends may influence future divorce rates.

Rates of child-free marriage appear to be rising in Canada (M. Baker 1993b, 150), and couples without children have higher probabilities of divorce. This should not imply that child-free couples are not as satisfied as parents with their marriages, because the opposite tends to be reported, but rather that it is easier to obtain a legal divorce and survive economically afterwards if you do not have to agree on the custody and financial support of children.

There is also evidence from American research that employed married women consider divorce as an option more often than homemakers (Huber and Spitze 1980; Albrecht and Kunz 1980). Women who can support themselves financially initiate the decision to separate more often than women who are financially dependent on their husbands. In Canada, Ambert (1983) further concluded that divorced high-income women felt less social and financial pressure than low-income women to remarry.

These and other studies suggest that although all marriages experience conflict, some may experience more conflict than others. Furthermore, the ways in which conflict is resolved relate to parental role models, social circumstances, and opportunities to leave the marriage. Whether or not separation is legalized in the form of a divorce, however, also depends on laws, social values, and economic circumstances.

Increase in births outside marriage

One-parent families may also result from a growing trend for more babies to be born outside marriage (as illustrated in Table 2.9). In Canada, 24 per cent of live births in 1990 were to unmarried women, compared to 4 per cent in 1960 (Vanier Institute of the Family 1994, 58). In Quebec, where there is a higher rate of cohabitation, 38 per cent of children were born outside legal marriage in 1990 (Le Bourdais and Marcil-Gratton 1994). However, many of these children are born to couples in their twenties and thirties who are living in a relatively permanent though non-legal relationship.

There are several reasons for an increase in births outside marriage. As society has become increasingly secularized, attitudes have changed about the state's right to be involved in personal life or moral issues. Sexual attitudes and practices have become more liberal in North America since the 1950s, especially with respect to committed relationships (Hobart 1989). Legislative changes to protect women and children have made legal marriage and cohabitation, as well as the rights of children born inside and outside of marriage, very similar. In most Canadian provinces, the concept of an illegitimate child, or of one who has no legal rights to financial support or inheritance from the father, has been abolished.

Compared to the United States, relatively few children are born outside marriage to adolescent women in Canada. Of all births outside marriage, only 20 per cent are to women under twenty years old while 60 per cent are to women between twenty and thirty (Vanier Institute of

TABLE 2.9
Births outside marriage per 1,000 births, 1960–1988

Country	1960	1970	1980	1988
Canada	43	96	113	201 (1987)
France	61	68	114	263
Germany	63	55	79	101
Sweden	113	184	397	484 (1986)
United Kingdom	52	80	115	251
United States	53	107	184	234 (1986)

SOURCES: Lewis, ed. 1993, 7; Statistics Canada, Annual (a) 1992; Sorrentino 1990, 41–58.

the Family 1994, 58). Teenage birth rates have declined considerably in Canada since the 1950s with improved contraception, legalized abortion, public health insurance, and social assistance benefits, which have enabled poorer women to receive medical attention and prescription drugs.

Low adoption rates

Although there have always been pregnancies outside marriage, prior to the 1960s such events were generally considered to be socially unacceptable and detrimental to the woman's reputation. Unmarried pregnant women used to be sent away to relatives or maternity homes run by religious or charitable organizations. When they gave birth, their babies were subsequently adopted by married couples. Alternatively, many women obtained illegal abortions, while others who gave birth to their babies suffered the social disgrace, and struggled to raise their children with minimal public support. A few were fortunate enough to be given emotional support, money, a place to live, or child care by their own parents. Very occasionally, financial assistance came from the father, but it was often surreptitious. The law did not require unmarried fathers to support their child financially unless they declared paternity or there was a successful lawsuit proving paternity.

The development of birth control technology and the legalization of abortion have reduced birth rates for women of all ages and marital statuses in Canada. For those giving birth outside marriage, changing attitudes towards sexuality and illegitimacy have discouraged women from relinquishing their babies for adoption. More women are able to support themselves and their children outside marriage through paid employment. New laws and social benefits have been developed to protect all children from poverty and discrimination, regardless of the marital status of their parents. Furthermore, social workers and psychologists now consider that giving up a child for adoption can be psychologically damaging for both mother and child. They often advocate social assistance for unmarried mothers raising their children alone, or pre-adoption counselling, open adoptions, and state assistance for post-adoption reunions.

As more of the legal distinctions between marriage and cohabitation and between legitimate and illegitimate children have been removed, some mothers have made a deliberate choice to reproduce outside marriage. Nevertheless, most 'unmarried' mothers are living in relatively permanent but non-legal relationships and are not parenting alone.

Rising percentage of lone-parent families

From 1961 to 1991, lone-parent families as a percentage of all families with children increased from 11 per cent to 20 per cent in Canada (Lindsay 1992, 15). Separation and divorce are the major reasons for this increase, while the rising number of births outside marriage is a secondary reason. The Canadian government uses the term 'lone' parent rather than 'single' parent to avoid confusion over legal status, as 'single' usually means never-married. My terminology will be consistent with the federal government's.

Most one-parent families in all industrialized countries are led by mothers because they bear the children and are readily identifiable as parents, because mothers are more likely than fathers to choose custody, and because judges have tended to assume that children's interests are better served by maternal custody after divorce. In addition, laws have not encouraged unmarried fathers to accept custody. In Canada, women head 82 per cent of lone-parent families (Statistics Canada 1993b). Table 2.10 shows the composition of family households with children under eighteen during the 1980s in all the countries studied. Canada has a moderate percentage of one-parent households, while Sweden and especially the United States have high rates of one-parent households.

Despite the increased availability of social assistance and jobs for women and the growing respectability of raising a child in a one-parent family, many women find that they cannot earn enough to support their children without contributions from the child's father or from the government. Only 10 per cent of male lone parents do not participate in the labour force compared to 24 per cent of female lone parents (Statistics

TABLE 2.10
Composition of family households with children under 18 years of age

Country	Married or cohabiting	Lone parent
	%	%
Australia (1982)	88.6	11.4
Canada (1986)	85.2	14.8
France (1988)	89.1	10.9
Germany (1988)	86.5	13.5
Netherlands (1985)	87.7	12.3
Sweden (1985)	83.1	16.9
United Kingdom (1987)	87.5	12.7
United States (1988)	77.1	22.9

SOURCES: U.S. House of Representatives, Select Committee on Children, Youth and Families 1990; Sorrentino 1990, 50.

Canada 1993b). Yet even when women work for pay, they tend to earn lower wages than men and are also more likely to work part time. Consequently, 61.9 per cent of lone mothers were living below the poverty line in 1991 and 58.4 per cent in 1992, with very little support from the non-custodial father (National Council of Welfare 1994a, 14). This is a much higher percentage than in the other countries studied, apart from the United States. Consequently, Canadian policies relating to child custody after divorce, the awarding of support, and the enforcing of support agreements have recently been questioned, although little discussion has taken place about employment equity, minimum wages, or low rates of social assistance.

The period of time children spend in lone-parent households appears to be increasing as marriage rates decline. Many parents who do not remarry, however, live with a new partner. Until 1992, two lone parents with children living in Canada could receive more taxation benefits or transfer payments if they lived common law than if they legally married (Morrison and Oderkirk 1991). However, this loophole has recently been eliminated by a policy that considers a couple to be 'married' if they live together for more than one year or produce a child within the year.

The principle of equality enshrined in Canadian family law is often not reflected by reality. Mothers who were formerly full-time caregivers and homemakers often need government assistance in job training, finding work, obtaining higher wages, and enforcing court-ordered child support payments after divorce. Staying at home and caring for children reduces women's future opportunities, and many never recover from this disadvantage when they try to become self-supporting. The increase in one-parent families has raised welfare costs, as many of these women cannot support their children without government assistance. Additional social services are especially needed for young mothers who are still adolescents themselves and may have interrupted their education to give birth. In order to become self-supporting, many of these mothers will require special education and training programs, child care services, and improved social benefits.

Not all countries, however, reveal high poverty rates for lone parents, as I will discuss in chapter 3. Cross-national differences in poverty rates for lone-parent families with children are related to several factors. In some countries, lone mothers are more likely to be in the labour market and working full time. Second, countries vary in the availability and generosity of family benefits or social welfare programs, as well as in the degree of stigma attached to receiving these benefits. While some countries provide a government pension for lone mothers, or child-rearing allowances, others do not; some countries encourage married mothers but not lone mothers to stay at home to care for their children. In addition, social welfare programs may provide people with a strong disincentive to look for part-time work while they are receiving social benefits. A third reason for variations in child poverty relates to both male and female unemployment rates, which vary dramatically among the countries in our study. Other aspects of the structure of the labour market vary as well, including the availability of part-time jobs, minimum and average wages, policies on employment equity for women, and job training programs (McFate 1991, 13).

Among all categories of lone parents (separated, divorced, widowed, unmarried), women who have a child outside a couple relationship are most vulnerable to poverty. This is especially true if the mother is an adolescent or has not completed her education. Higher unemployment rates are associated with lower levels of education and less job experience in all countries in our study.

As we will see in later chapters, low poverty rates among lone-parent families are a result of a combination of factors: generous income support packages for families with children, direct services such as child care to enable mothers to enter the labour force during child-rearing years, and government-guaranteed support payments for a child of divorced parents (McFate 1991, 15).

SUMMARY OF TRENDS

Family life in all the countries of our study has been altered by trends in the structure of the economy and the labour force, family law reform, demographic patterns, and changing social attitudes. Life expectancies at birth are increasing, especially for women, and families and households are becoming smaller. Women and couples are delaying childbirth as higher levels of education are required to find permanent work and marriage is postponed. In many countries, all adults in the family are expected to work for pay, and child care is increasingly becoming a necessary public service.

As a result of the pressures of raising children and earning a living, families are becoming smaller and less permanent units. High rates of separation and divorce have led to rising percentages of one-parent households, most of which are led by mothers. In some countries, including Canada, female lone parents experience very high rates of poverty, causing concern about the implications for the development and future prospects of these women and, especially, their children. Much of the concern in North America focuses on the cost of supporting lone-parent families on social assistance.

Although the popularity of legal marriage is declining, most people eventually marry, remarry after divorce, or live in relatively permanent heterosexual relationships. Despite economic, legal, and social changes affecting the structure of family life, people still value intimacy and lifestyle stability. If we combine the percentage of people who are legally married with those living in common-law marriages, we could argue that the popularity of 'marriage,' loosely defined, is not declining (Vanier Institute of the Family 1994).

Although there are cross-national variations, it is generally the case that raising children and earning a living are difficult without public support. In all industrialized societies, people tend to produce fewer children than they actually want because of the high cost of children in terms of time, money, and emotional investment. Second, marriage to one person for life is not always feasible or desirable, given the changes required to fit into industrial or post-industrial society. It is often necessary to move away from home to attend university or to find work. The difficulties presented by job transitions, especially when there are two jobs per family, place added pressure on relationships. Although having two earners per family adds stress to some marriages, it has also encouraged more egalitarian relationships and has expanded women's horizons.

3

Poverty, labour markets, and social assistance

INDICATORS OF CHILD POVERTY

In Canada, in 1992, over 18 per cent of the population, or 1.2 million people, lived in families with an income below the poverty line (National Council of Welfare 1994a). The most widely used indicator of child poverty has been the percentage of children living in low-income families, based on various measures of low income, or 'poverty lines' (these will be discussed later). Other indicators of child poverty would be the percentage of children living on social assistance, the frequency with which families with children rely on food banks, and high rates of infant and child morbidity and mortality.

Using the percentage of children living in low-income families as an indicator of 'child poverty,' we find that Canadian rates are high, especially for mother-led families. Statistics Canada uses low-income cut-offs (LICOs) as poverty lines. To ensure that poor families were well above average in allocating income to necessities, Statistics Canada calculated that the percentage of income that the average family spends on necessities (shelter, food, and clothing) is 36.2 per cent and added 20 per cent to this figure. Therefore, LICOs measure the income level below which families must spend more than 56.2 per cent of their income on bare necessities, and these lines vary by family and community size. In 1989, 8.5 per cent of children in all families and 52.9 per cent of children in mother-led families were living on low incomes. In 1991, with the deepening recession, 10.7 per cent of children living in all families and 61.9 per cent of children living in lone-parent families headed by women lived in poverty (ibid.). These rates fell slightly in 1992, as Table 3.1 indicates.

TABLE 3.1
Percentage of Canadian families with children living in poverty,*
1980–1992, by family structure

Year	Female lone-parent families	Two-parent families
1980	57.7	9.4
1986	58.8	10.8
1987	59.0	10.1
1988	56.7	8.9
1989	52.9	8.5
1990	60.6	9.6
1991	61.9	10.7
1992	58.4	10.1

* As measured by Statistics Canada's low-income cut-offs (LICOs)
SOURCE: National Council of Welfare 1994a, 14.

Poverty in Canada varies by family structure, but it also differs con-siderably by province. For the children of lone mothers, for example, Prince Edward Island had the lowest rate of child poverty in 1992, at 47.1 per cent while Newfoundland had the highest child poverty rate, at 73.0 per cent (ibid., 17). Variations among provinces relate to differ-ences in unemployment rates, minimum wages, average wages, the availability of child care, and levels of provincial social assistance.

In November 1989, Canada's House of Commons unanimously passed a resolution affirming that members of Parliament would seek to elimi-nate child poverty by the year 2000. This resolution arose from United Nations decisions about children's rights, international studies revealing comparative child poverty rates, and the work of several Canadian par-liamentary committees.

The United Nations had declared 1979 International Year of the Child, and in 1989, tenth anniversary statements were made about accom-plishments and challenges during the decade with respect to children's rights. Two international parliamentary conferences on children's rights were also held in 1989. In addition, a U.N. Convention on the Rights of the Child, which is a binding international legal agreement, became effective in that year, thirty years after the U.N. Declaration on the Rights of the Child. As one of many countries, Canada signed this convention, which promised certain protections to children's financial, emotional, and physical well-being. These U.N. activities placed pressure on the Canadian government to promote children's rights and resolve child poverty.

Additional pressure was placed on the Canadian government when a number of international studies (especially those using the Luxembourg Income Study data base) compared income distributions in a number of industrialized countries. All these studies indicated that the United States had the highest, Australia the second-highest, and Canada the third-highest rate of poverty for families with dependent children in the mid-1980s.[1] These statistics were revealed in public hearings before several parliamentary committees and published in a book by Ross and Shillington (1989), which was used widely by Canadian anti-poverty groups (such as the National Anti-Poverty Organization and the Child Poverty Action Group).

Since 1980, various Canadian parliamentary committees had been studying 'child poverty' and federal child benefits, with the intention of restructuring them.[2] These committees made the political decision to use the term 'child poverty' rather than just 'poverty' to avoid any implication of distinguishing the 'deserving' poor from the 'undeserving' poor, and to elicit concern and willingness to act from all political parties. Both committees produced reports on child poverty, measuring it as the percentage of children living in families with incomes below the Statistics Canada LICOs.

The Senate committee, jointly chaired by one Liberal and one Conservative senator (both women), produced two reports. The interim report in 1989 drew a connection between child poverty and its consequent social problems, including behavioural and academic problems at school, higher rates of morbidity, premature school leaving, high future unemployment, and reliance on unemployment insurance and social assistance.[3] The senators argued that doing nothing about child poverty will, in the long run, be more expensive than developing new programs to deal with it. The final report in January 1991 noted some international comparisons of child poverty and contained a number of recommendations, while recognizing the jurisdictional constraints involved in solving the problem. These recommendations included giving top priority to poverty among Aboriginal children, raising the federal minimum wage, modifying income security programs to enhance employability, creating a more generous fully indexed child benefit, focusing on prenatal education and high-risk pregnancies, providing family allowance benefits during pregnancy, and giving federal assistance to low-income families for home ownership and rent.

The House of Commons committee, on the other hand, produced a different report. Its Sub-Committee on Poverty, chaired by a Conservative MP,[4] produced a report in December 1991 called *Canada's Children: Investing in Our Future.* The recommendations also focused on the future cost of child poverty but included an educational campaign about women's health, nutrition, infant care, and family studies; improved child care funding and services, especially for high-risk communities; the promotion of school lunch and snack programs; and national standards for social assistance. The report also recommended a *study* on the possibility of raising the federal minimum wage and of creating a guaranteed earned income supplement. It argued that federal family benefits should be reformed and child care deductions converted to credits. In addition, it recommended continued negotiations towards Native self-government, with the goal of reducing poverty among Aboriginal children.

In contrast to the Senate report, the House of Commons report made fewer recommendations that recognized that children are poor because their parents suffer from unemployment, underemployment, low minimum wages, or inadequate social security programs. This report led right-wing critics[5] to argue for a redefinition of the poverty line to make it lower relative to the incomes of other Canadians and less generous. It was noted in these discussions that 'poor' children living in Canada would be considered wealthy by Third World standards, and that the government should therefore be using an absolute rather than a relative measure of poverty.

After these parliamentary reports were tabled, the child poverty rate increased as a result of the deepening recession. In response to these reports, the (Conservative) Canadian government introduced an initiative in 1992 called 'Brighter Futures.' This initiative provided $500 million over five years for children who are 'at risk' because of poverty, ill-health, unhealthy living conditions, neglect, or abuse. Yet the money amounts to only $100 per year for every Canadian child 'at risk' (Hubka 1992b). At that time, no campaign was launched to fight unemployment or bolster income security programs. However, a national, non-partisan advocacy and public-education group called Campaign 2000 was organized to pressure the government to act on its 1989 promise to eradicate child poverty by the year 2000. This group, which comprises sixteen national organizations and a cross-country network of thirty community partners, has continued to produce a *Report Card* each year to indicate the government's progress, or lack of it, towards eliminating child poverty.

TABLE 3.2
Child poverty rates, 1987

Country	All families with children	One-parent families
Australia	18.59	53.19
Canada	17.67	48.83
Germany	8.82	32.09
Sweden	4.71	8.29
United Kingdom	16.63	25.00
United States	25.41	53.92

SOURCE: Phipps 1993a.

As Table 3.2 shows, the rate of child poverty for families with children in Canada was higher than that in the European countries in this study. The Luxembourg Income Study data base defines families as 'poor' if their gross family income is less than 50 per cent of the median income after taxes, adjusted for family size in that country (Phipps 1993b). The rate of poverty for all families with children was 17.67 per cent in Canada in 1987,[6] compared to 25.41 per cent in the United States. At the same time, Germany and Sweden have managed to keep their rates of child poverty at 8.82 per cent and 4.71 per cent, respectively. If we look at child poverty in one-parent families, the Canadian rate was much higher, at 48.83 per cent, while in Sweden the rate was only 8.29 per cent (Phipps 1993b).

If we use a poverty line based on 40 per cent of median income instead of 50 per cent, the poverty rates for Canada and the United States stand out among those of the seven countries. Table 3.3 shows that although one-parent families are always more likely to be poor than two-parent families, this is especially the case in North America.

Not only are child poverty rates higher in Canada than in most European countries, but the Luxembourg Income Study data also indicate that, based on data from the mid-1980s, child benefits were worth less in Canada, especially in comparison to other income sources. For example, O'Higgins, Schmaus, and Stephenson (1990) calculated that wages and salaries formed 75.7 per cent of gross income in Canada, and that child benefits (including tax benefits and government transfers) were worth only 0.9 per cent. If we add all cash benefits received from governments, this is raised to only 9.1 per cent of gross income. In Sweden, by comparison, wages and salaries represented only 64.5 per cent of

TABLE 3.3
Percentage of households in more severe poverty* in the mid-1980s, by nation and household structure

Country	All households	All families with children	All lone-parent families with children
Canada	8.9	9.3	29.4
France	6.1	5.3	10.7
West Germany	3.2	3.1	12.5
Netherlands	5.7	3.9	5.1
Sweden	5.9	2.9	3.6
United Kingdom	7.0	8.6	7.7
United States	13.6	17.5	44.9

* More severe poverty is defined as household income of less than 40 per cent of the national adjusted median income.
SOURCE: McFate 1991(Table 1), 2.

gross income, while child benefits formed 1.3 per cent, and all cash benefits formed 29.2 per cent of gross income.

In another analysis based on LIS data from the mid-1980s, the researchers examined the percentages of families with children who were raised out of poverty by government tax and transfer programs (McFate 1991; Smeeding and Rainwater 1991). Table 3.4 indicates that for couple-headed families, France and Sweden stand out as providing beneficial programs. For one-parent families, France, the Netherlands, Sweden, and the United Kingdom pull substantial percentages of lone parents out of poverty through government taxes and transfers. Among these seven countries, however, Canada and the United States perform poorly by comparison. In fact, in the United States, poor two-parent families are worse off after taxes and transfers than before, while poor one-parent families are marginally better off after government interventions. While some countries, including Canada, have changed their tax rates and family benefits since this analysis, we have no reason to believe that Canada would look much better today in comparison to the other countries.

While arguing that child poverty had to be eradicated by the year 2000, the Canadian Conservative government in 1990 placed a five-year ceiling on transfer payments to the three 'fiscally strong' provinces (Ontario, Alberta, and British Columbia) for the Canada Assistance Plan

TABLE 3.4

Percentage of all poor families with children lifted out of poverty by government interventions (mid-1980s)

Country	Couple-headed	Lone-parent
Canada	17.6	19.3
France	58.7	47.0
West Germany	13.4	33.8
Netherlands	20.0	89.5
Sweden	47.4	81.1
United Kingdom	26.5	75.0
United States	−9.1	4.6

SOURCE: Luxembourg Income Study data, McFate 1991, Figure 13.

(CAP), which is a federal-provincial cost-sharing program for social assistance (including child care subsidies for low-income families). This ceiling, known as 'the cap on CAP,' limited federal increases to 5 per cent a year, rather than leaving the contribution open-ended and dependent on provincial expenditures. Increases to federal transfers to the provinces for post-secondary education and health were also limited, in an attempt to reduce the federal deficit. Both these moves have forced provincial governments to pay for a larger share of social programs or to reduce services.

Another recent change made by the Conservative government was the 'reform' to child benefits in December 1992. This is discussed in detail in chapter 4. When Canadians were in the midst of a constitutional crisis, legislation was passed to abolish the Family Allowance and combine the money saved with the child tax credits to create the new Child Tax Benefit. This 'reform' was seen by many critics to be regressive because it added no new money for poor or middle-income families and because the benefit is not fully indexed to the rising cost of living. Furthermore, it removed the universality of the previous Family Allowance, which used to make a statement about the social value of child-rearing. Now the government assists parents with dependent children only if their income is moderate or below average.

Despite public statements in the United Nations and Canada's Parliament, it appears as though the Conservative government placed other priorities before the elimination of child poverty and lacked the political will to fight the obstacles. Yet it is difficult for the federal government unilaterally to reduce child poverty, since many factors which contribute to it, such as low minimum wages and low social assistance rates, are outside federal jurisdiction and require federal-provincial negotiations. Furthermore, poverty is largely caused by unemployment or underemployment, and reducing unemployment is difficult for Canada when its economy is so closely tied to markets in the United States and elsewhere. Poverty can be reduced through more effective transfer payments, but reforming these would cost money. Finding the money would require major changes in spending priorities, cuts to popular programs, or revamping the income tax system.

It appears as though the present (Liberal) government (which came into power in October 1993) will shy away from major reforms to social programs and instead attempt to cut costs. The Green Paper released in October 1994 discussed the possibility of making cuts to unemployment insurance and transfers to the provinces for secondary education, and of changing the funding arrangements for social assistance, while ruling out a guaranteed annual income program as impractical and costly. In 1995 the federal government announced its intention to phase out the Canada Assistance Plan and to use block funding for social assistance, post-secondary education, and health services. This will make less federal money available for provincial programs, but reduce federal regulations about how the money is spent.

POVERTY AND LABOUR MARKET CONDITIONS

In the last decade, Canada has experienced higher unemployment rates than other industrialized countries, as Table 3.5 indicates. Canadian governments and employers' groups have tried to persuade the public that unemployment is a result of natural market forces and that the country must adapt to these rates (Kerans 1990). An examination of other countries shows, however, that at the worst of the recession in 1983 to 1984, five countries had unemployment rates between 1.1 per cent and 4.2 per cent: Japan, Switzerland, Austria, Norway, and Sweden. These countries did not have similar governments, nor did they all have high inflation. Rather, their success seemed to depend upon an institutionalized government commitment to full employment as the top priority in labour market policy (ibid.).

While unemployment has resulted from technological change and international market trends, continued high unemployment reflects political decisions to use fiscal policy to curb inflation, decisions which

TABLE 3.5
Unemployment rates in eight industrialized countries, 1964–1992

Country	1964	1970	1984	1987	1992
Australia	1.6	1.6	8.9	8.1	10.1
Canada	4.3	5.6	11.2	8.8	10.2
France	1.2	2.5	9.7	10.5	10.1
Germany	0.6	0.6	8.2	7.9	5.0
Netherlands	0.5	1.0	11.9	9.8	6.4
Sweden	1.6	1.5	3.2	1.9	4.1
United Kingdom	1.4	2.2	11.1	10.3	9.9
United States	5.0	4.8	7.4	6.1	6.7

SOURCES: OECD, 1989, 30–1; OECD 1993.

have exacerbated existing unemployment rates (Gunderson and Muszynski 1990). Contrary to conservative political and business ideologies, there is no correlation between high levels of social spending and high unemployment rates. In 1981, welfare state expenditures were 15.3 per cent of the GDP in Canada and 26.8 per cent in Sweden (Kerans 1990). By 1990, Canada spent 18.8 per cent of GDP on social programs,[7] while Sweden spent 33.9 per cent (V. Smith, 1994, A6). In other words, throughout the 1980s Sweden experienced low unemployment and high social spending.

The problem of unemployment is the most serious contributor to poverty among working people (Gunderson and Muszynski 1990; National Council of Welfare 1994a). As unemployment rates remain high, food banks[8] have become an institutionalized response to poverty and hunger. Yet official unemployment rates do not tell the whole picture, as 'discouraged workers' who stop looking for work are no longer considered to be 'unemployed.' Others have found work but are underemployed in part-time or temporary positions.

The increase in jobs in recent years has occurred mainly in the service sector, but these positions are characterized by low pay, lack of job security, and lack of union or statutory protection (Ternowetsky and Riches 1990). Typically part-time or temporary, service sector positions have been referred to as 'non-standard employment.' These non-standard positions tend to be occupied mainly by women, as women have formed the majority of new entrants into the labour force in recent years and are more likely to accept part-time work because of family responsibilities and employment discrimination (Jenson 1994).

Governments can use three possible economic approaches to poverty: require the poor to adapt to the market-place, relieve their distress with social programs, or adapt the social and economic system to the needs of the poor. A review of Canadian programs indicates that federal and provincial governments have generally employed the first or second approaches. Unlike some other countries, the Canadian state has abandoned its goal of full employment and relies primarily on the private sector for economic growth (Guest 1990).

Many policy analysts have argued that full employment should be one of the principal goals of government policy (Guest 1990; Novick 1990; Windschuttle 1990). Our governments have responded to unemployment with fiscal policy to stimulate the private sector, direct public sector job creation, wage subsidies, regional policies, and employment programs for disadvantaged groups. Workfare and training have also been seen as solutions to unemployment, yet payment is often low, few jobs are available at the end of training programs, and newly created jobs are often temporary. Although job training is often organized by the federal government in Canada, local employment initiatives may be most successful in dealing with long-term unemployment (Windschuttle 1990).

Poverty among the working poor has increased relative to all poverty, and women make up nearly half of the Canadian working poor (Gunderson and Muszynski 1990). Furthermore, approximately 15 per cent of the working poor live in lone-parent households. The average poverty gap, or the difference between actual income and the official poverty line, was higher for lone-parent than for two-parent families. Between 1970 and 1985 the real total income of poor people rose, but this was primarily due to increases in transfer income, as real minimum wages fell by between 20 per cent and 30 per cent. The prosperity of the 1980s polarized rather than reduced the extremes of economic status in Canadian society (Ternowetsky and Riches 1990). Although real wages have risen throughout this century, wage growth was the lowest between 1980 and 1990, when men's real wages actually fell, while women's increased. Furthermore, women's real wages remain well below men's, although they increased from 53 per cent of men's in 1980 to 60 per cent in 1990 (Rashid 1994).

Although the majority of Canadian women now participate in the labour force, their participation is influenced by their parental roles as well as the structure of the labour market (Kitchen 1990a). Among full-time full-year employees, women tend to make about 72 per cent of men's earnings, but among all workers, women earn only 64 per cent (Statistics Canada 1993a). Not only are women's wages lower than men's, but their benefits are also fewer, they more often hold temporary positions, and they are less likely to belong to a trade union. Women's job mobility and promotional possibilities tend to be restricted by the additional responsibility for housework and child care, and consequently women are more likely than men to accept part-time work. The devaluation of women's work in both the home and the labour force places them in an economically vulnerable position, especially as more women become family heads and the sole source of family income. A key issue to be resolved is how to address the traditional undervaluation of women's work (Kitchen 1990a).

Without enforceable employment equity programs and family support programs, many women will be unable to achieve the minimum liberal feminist goals of employment and financial equality with men. Companies pay lip-service to the idea of job sharing and the consideration of employee needs, but few changes have been made in the labour force to accommodate the growing number of employees who have family responsibilities (Duxbury and Higgins 1994). New policies are clearly needed, including legislated leave for family responsibilities, flexible hours, and wages sufficient to support families. Yet a recent poll for *Report on Business* magazine (August 1994, 8) indicated that only 2.6 per cent of Canadian companies offer a four-day work week, only 7 per cent offer flextime, and only 7 per cent allow job-sharing. Furthermore, according to this poll, less than 3 per cent of business owners and senior executives were planning to initiate such flexibility in the near future.

While labour force participation for Canadian women has increased over the past twenty years, only 36 per cent of all women held full-time jobs year-round in 1987 (National Council of Welfare 1990b). The likelihood that women will leave their jobs for one year or more for family reasons has not changed much in recent generations, but this more tenuous connection than men's to the labour force has an impact on wages and future pensions. Job segregation also continues, and women tend to be clustered in lower paying jobs. Without the wife's earnings, however, 51 per cent of Canadian families now above the poverty line would become poor (ibid. 1990).

Equal pay legislation was created in 1956, with the *Female Employees Equal Pay Act*, which was later revoked and consolidated into the *Canada Labour Code* in 1966. In 1970, the *Canada Labour Code* expanded the scope of the original act by changing 'identical or substantially identical work' to 'same or similar work' limited to the same establishment. In court decisions, however, employers needed only to raise reasonable doubt about the similarity of work to be acquitted from a discrimination charge. The law placed a heavy burden on the complainant, which may account for the lack of success of complaints (Goodwin 1984).

In 1978, the *Canadian Human Rights Act* was enacted, which ensured equal pay for work of equal value, objective methods of job evaluation, and cooperation with employers' and workers' organizations in implementing the principle. This act prohibits sex discrimination and wage differentials for employees in the same establishment performing work of equal value, but relies substantially on complaints initiated by the victim. In 1984, the federal government passed the *Employment Equity Act*, targeting four groups as vulnerable to employment discrimination in hiring, promotion, and pay: women, Native persons, persons with disabilities, and visible minorities. Although this legislation requires that employers under federal jurisdiction provide employment statistics for all four groups, it has been criticized for its lack of effective enforcement procedures (Armstrong and Armstrong 1990, 124).

Despite legislation guaranteeing equal pay for equal work, equal pay for work of equal value, and employment equity, women still earn about two-thirds of men's wages. Employment equity laws have not substantially altered the position of women working under federal jurisdiction. New pro-active legislation which does not operate on a complaint basis, such as Ontario's 'equal pay for work of equal value' legislation, may eventually be more effective in raising wages (National Council of Welfare 1990b, 29). Not all provinces have created this kind of legislation, however, and when they do, the legislation sometimes covers only public sector employees.

Since 1982, wage inflation in Canada has shown a pronounced deceleration, and wage settlements have declined to their lowest levels in twenty-five years (Kumar 1987). The deceleration has been broad-based and more severe in length and depth than in any other postwar recession. Canada recorded the fastest deceleration in wage inflation of any OECD country in 1982 and 1983. Accompanying these trends have been changes in the collective bargaining process, including more wage freezes, individualized and organization-specific settlements, a trend towards multi-year contracts, and a decline in the relative importance of cost-of-living-allowance clauses.

Since the Second World War, economic slowdowns in the United States have resulted in increasingly higher peaks in unemployment (Aldous and Tuttle 1988). Unemployment rates thought to be intolerable in the early 1960s were reached in the 1980s, and the average length of unemployment increased from twelve weeks in 1972 to twenty weeks in 1984. Since the Second World War, male participation in the labour force has declined, while it has risen for women, especially white women. Black unemployment in the United States has been and is consistently higher than white unemployment, especially among men. Although the rise in two-earner families has offset some of the impact of unemployment, the number of involuntary part-time workers increased and about 19 per cent of this group is living in poverty. There are no federal standards for unemployment insurance in the United States, and states vary widely in their provision of unemployment benefits (Aldous and Tuttle 1988).

In the 1990s, North American governments have allowed economic globalization to influence employment practices and the availability of ongoing full-time jobs. More positions are now part time, temporary, or involve irregular work hours, and women are overrepresented in these types of positions. Numerous researchers have used the dichotomy 'good' jobs and 'bad' jobs, arguing that recent private and public sector job creation has created mainly 'bad' jobs, with little mobility, low income, no union protection, and little legislative protection. Not all governments have been equally influenced by globalization, however. Many European countries, including Sweden and Germany, have resisted some of the negative effects of globalization through government economic planning, labour legislation, and strong union participation in decision making (Clement and Mahon 1994).

POVERTY AND ONE-PARENT HOUSEHOLDS

Many policy makers and researchers have focused on one-parent households because of their rising numbers and high poverty rates before government transfer payments are made. The increase in lone-parent families, most of which are headed by women, has occurred in all countries since the early 1970s, ranging from 20 per cent in France to more than 50 per cent in the United States and Australia (Duskin 1990). The majority of OECD countries have experienced an increase of between 30 per cent and 50 per cent, while lone parents typically constitute between 10 per cent and 15 per cent of all families with children in OECD countries. However, the percentage in the United States is closer to 25 per cent, as we saw in chapter 2 (Table 2.11).

Lone parents are not a homogeneous group, but rather differ in economic and demographic characteristics, as well as in the circumstances that led them to lone parenthood. As we saw in chapter 2, the major reason for the rise in lone-parent families in all countries is marital dissolution, although never-married lone parents constitute 40 per cent of the lone-parent population in the United States (Ermisch 1990).

The percentage of births to unmarried teens compared to all births to teens varies considerably, from a high of 33 per cent in the United States to 10 per cent in France and 6 per cent in Sweden (Sorrentino 1990). In Europe, the rise in births to unmarried women is more an indication of the decline of legal marriage and increased numbers of cohabiting couples than of the growth in numbers of lone mothers. For example, births to women living alone accounted for only 2 per cent to 3 per cent of all births in France in 1985. This statistic is similar in other countries in Western Europe (ibid.). In the United States, on the other hand, births outside marriage are more prevalent among women who are not living as part of a couple. In most OECD countries (except Australia, Canada, and the United Kingdom), a greater proportion of lone mothers than married mothers are in the labour force (Duskin 1990).

Wong, Garfinkel, and McLanahan (1992) compared the economic status of lone-parent families relative to each other and to two-parent families in eight Western countries: Australia, Canada, France, West Germany, Norway, Sweden, the United Kingdom, and the United States. With data from 1979 to 1984, they used multivariate regression analysis to examine the factors contributing to differences in economic status. In particular, they focused on the influence of demography, labour force participation, and public policy on relative economic status. The heavy reliance on income-tested programs in the United States, in contrast to universal programs in other Western industrialized countries, is the main reason for higher poverty rates among families with children in the United States, they concluded. Differences in the demographic composition of lone mothers across countries (including age of head, age of youngest child, and number of children), however, also accounted for notable differences in the relative economic position of lone mothers. The younger the mother is when she has a child and the more children she has, the higher her risk of poverty. In the United States, lone mothers tend to be younger and to have more children than in European countries (Wong, Garfinkel, and McLanahan 1992).

There are several reasons why U.S. women have children at a younger age and outside marriage or cohabitation. One relates to lack of public birth control programs and public health insurance which would enable women to obtain birth control devices and regular check-ups without paying a fee. Another is the extremely high rate of poverty, especially among U.S. blacks, which discourages the higher education and career-planning that usually delays pregnancy and marriage for middle-class women. Furthermore, becoming pregnant and having a child may provide recognition, self-esteem, and independence that is impossible for young women to realize through other means. In addition, without statutory maternity leave programs requiring a period of continuing employment, there is less incentive for U.S. women, as compared to Swedish women, to find permanent work before becoming pregnant.

In some jurisdictions of North America, there is a great deal of concern about lone mothers and a fear that many become pregnant in order to receive state support. Although social service agencies indicate that lone parents form a significant portion of their client population and that lack of financial resources is the most common reason for referral, there is no evidence that withdrawing social benefits will reduce the birth rate among unmarried women. In fact, many agencies complain of gaps in services and argue that the present system encourages chronic dependency for lone mothers (Nova Scotia Social Services Council 1982).

Although Canada and the English-speaking countries tend to focus less on prevention than the European countries, as we will see in later chapters, numerous reports have recommended such programs to support young single mothers both before and after giving birth. Several jurisdictions have created pilot projects which focus on young pregnant women considered to be at risk of producing low-birth-weight children or of abusing or neglecting their child. Special services are provided for these women, such as prenatal care, including nutritional supplements, and postnatal health and social services, although these are not part of regular statutory services. In 1994, for example, Quebec added a $50-per-month bonus to social assistance payments for mothers who breast-feed their babies, since breast milk is considered to be more nutritious than formula, may protect the immune system from certain diseases, and is less costly. Later in 1994, the Canadian government announced an educational program for pregnant women focusing on lifestyle risks (such as smoking) and nutritional needs.

In addition to efforts to address health concerns, attempts have been made by social and health workers to reduce the number of young women becoming lone parents. Birth control programs are provided in some jurisdictions, although they remain controversial in others. In the American Midwest and the Canadian prairies, the 'pro-family' movement's opposition to contraception and sex education is based on fundamentalist Christian beliefs that sex education will encourage pre-marital sexual experimentation, that sex outside marriage is 'sinful,' and that the purpose of marriage is procreation. On the other hand, recent attempts by the social service department to introduce the long-lasting birth control device Norplant to lone mothers in a Boston (black) ghetto led to accusations of attempted genocide by community leaders. They argued that this drug was experimental and that poor black women were being used as guinea pigs.

Programs designed to promote self-sufficiency among lone mothers have also become popular in North America. These programs focus on literacy training, job skills development, and employment assistance, combined with free or subsidized child care services. Some have also attempted to encourage mothers to provide information which will help the social service agency establish paternity and locate the fathers, with the goal of enforcing paternal child support. Programs targeted to the American urban poor have often been criticized by radical feminists and black advocacy groups as racist, sexist, and class-biased, as they tend to promote the middle-class white patriarchal family as the pre-ferred model.

In Europe and Australia, governments have provided special allow-ances for one-parent families, in recognition that they are more vulner-able to poverty than other family structures. The allowance is usually above the level of basic social assistance, and allows mothers to remain at home with their children for a specified period. These programs have been criticized by liberal feminists, however, for keeping women out of the labour force, for perpetuating the gendered division of labour both inside and outside the home, and for making the future transition to work more difficult.

POVERTY AND SOCIAL ASSISTANCE IN CANADA

In the nineteenth century, individuals were expected to be protected from poverty by their own thrift and hard work, by other family mem-bers, and by benevolent associations, community groups, and religious organizations. Government social assistance programs developed in Canada during the twentieth century from the experiences of disability, widowhood, and unemployment arising out of the First World War, and poverty and desertion during the 1930s Depression. Initially based on the assumption that families can normally take care of themselves, Canadian social programs also acknowledged that parents occasionally need the assistance of the state. Programs were especially promoted by the growing voice of labour (Ursel 1992, 146–7) as well as by religious and charitable organizations.

In the conservative or 'residual' view of the state's role in family life, intervention is limited to situations in which the family cannot cope, either emotionally or financially, especially when children are in need of protection. In Canada, this residual view of social welfare used to be implicit in all social programs. With the exception of social assistance, however, this approach has been largely replaced by a more liberal or 'institutional' view in which all families are thought to benefit from planning and institutionalized social support, such as income security programs, day care, counselling services, and other social services (Guest 1990; Armitage 1993, 42).

Social assistance programs in Canada fall within provincial jurisdiction, although their cost is shared with the federal government. Consequently, welfare rates vary substantially by province and are well below established poverty lines. The National Council of Welfare annually calculates welfare incomes for each province. Including basic provincial social assistance, additional provincial benefits, the former federal Family Allowance, the former Child Tax Credit, child-related benefits, sales tax/ Goods and Services Tax (GST) credits, and provincial tax credits, the total welfare income in 1993 for a single parent with one child ranged from $10,150 in New Brunswick to $16,790 in Ontario. For a couple with two children, total welfare income ranged from $12,151 in New Brunswick to $22,334 in Ontario (National Council of Welfare 1994b).

The adequacy of benefits was also calculated, comparing the total welfare income to the poverty line as defined by Statistics Canada's low-income cut-offs. Single 'employable' persons on welfare could receive as little as 24 per cent of the poverty line income if they lived in New Brunswick, or as much as 62 per cent in Prince Edward Island. Similarly, couples with two children would receive 45 per cent of the poverty line income if they lived in New Brunswick compared to 73 per cent in Prince Edward Island and Ontario. As a percentage of the average provincial income, welfare incomes for single 'employable' people ranged from a low of 16 per cent in New Brunswick to 40 per cent in Prince Edward Island. For a couple with two children, the range was from 23 per cent in New Brunswick to 38 per cent in Prince Edward Island in 1993 (ibid.). In 1993, welfare recipients in many parts of Canada were worse off financially than in 1992, as Alberta cut its welfare rates, and benefits in most provinces failed to keep pace with inflation. The lack of generosity in some provinces relates to high unemployment rates, low economic growth, and a less prosperous provincial government, but also to a more punitive philosophy about why people need government assistance and what role the state should play in personal life. Furthermore, the definition of 'employable' varies by province.

Provincial social assistance programs contain both incentives and disincentives for recipients to enter the labour force. One disincentive is lack of affordable child care. Another is the high tax-back rate that exists in welfare programs across Canada, which is usually 75 per cent or more. This means that for every $100 earned in part-time work, a welfare recipient would lose $75. In some cases, recipients lose all social assistance money, as well as government subsidies for dental care and prescription drugs, if they take on part-time work. In addition, many low-income working people pay relatively high income tax rates (by international standards) and could benefit from a low-income tax credit (National Council of Welfare 1993, 2).

In a Quebec study, Bellware and Charest (1986) found that female-headed lone-parent families comprised 24 per cent of the clients receiving social assistance (or social aid) and that they stayed on assistance longer than other groups. The median length of time for receiving social aid for all recipients was thirteen months while for lone parents it was two years. Among the under-twenty-five age group, 90 per cent were single but only 25 per cent had never lived with the father of their child(ren). However, the unions were 'of short duration, usually one year or less. The most frequent reason for separation was related to their partner's lifestyle, including drug and alcohol use or a relationship with another woman. For the entire group, applying for social aid was most often precipitated by a change in family situation, such as separation from their partner or parents. One in four mothers said her pregnancy was planned.

According to Bellware and Charest, social assistance benefits were clearly inadequate for the lone-parent families. In terms of the sample budget developed by the Montreal Diet Dispensary, most families spent more than suggested on rent, which reduced the amount left for other items such as food. One in two recipients supplemented their income through the 'underground economy' (babysitting or housecleaning), a strategy they saw as necessary for survival. Family and friends provided help in kind, but half the group retained debts to social assistance, to schools, or to retail stores for furniture and/or appliance purchases. Although only one in ten recipients received child support, most were reluctant to pursue it because they feared violence if they contacted the father, or doubted his willingness or ability to pay. Two out of five fathers never or no longer saw their children, although some helped out with child care, insurance premiums, gifts, and the purchase of some items for the children.

Lone mothers in Canada tend to have low levels of educational attainment (Bellware and Charest 1986; Clark 1993; Statistics Canada 1993b). In Bellware and Charest's study, half the women had less than high school completion, which was lower than the Quebec average for women. Without high school diplomas they were seldom eligible for training programs. More than one in six had never held a paying job, and for those who had, the last job was usually low skilled, low paying, and in a female-dominated occupation. One in three said that they quit their last job for 'family reasons.'

The minimum wage did not provide sufficient income for the mothers in Bellware and Charest's study to relinquish social assistance. The researchers calculated that the minimum wage would provide an extra $1.19 an hour if there were no child care costs and would provide nothing if child care had to be paid. Given the educational and employment backgrounds of these mothers, there was little possibility of obtaining more than minimum wage. In a follow-up study over a year later, 12 per cent of the mothers were no longer receiving social assistance. Of the ten who were contacted, seven had obtained jobs (only one of whom had a preschool child), one had received higher child support payments, and two had remarried or found a new partner.

Schragge (1990) argued that welfare reform in Quebec, through the Parental Wage Assistance Program, has provided valuable subsidies for parents working for low wages but has also encouraged low pay and cheap labour. In addition, it reduced benefits for recipients who are childless and are low-wage workers. And while the Employment Incentive Program provides benefits for the 'deserving poor' (including custodial parents with children under six), even these benefits are far below the minimum wage and the poverty line.

Riches (1990b) analysed the welfare reform in Saskatchewan in 1984 which was intended to reduce dependency on social assistance by single employable recipients and to provide equitable benefits for families and others unable to work. Welfare payments were redistributed in favour of families, but this was largely achieved through cuts in the rates to single, employable individuals. Riches argues that rate increases have been insufficient, entitlements have been eliminated by the 'reform,' and benefits to families relative to the cost of living have actually decreased. Consequently, people have had to turn to food banks and other forms of private charity in order to survive. The federal government and some provincial governments, in 'reforming' social programs, are 'robbing the poor to pay the poor' (Riches 1990a).

Not only do social assistance rates vary, but also child care services, labour legislation, job training programs, and social housing vary by province, making for many inconsistencies across the country. It would be difficult to create a uniform system of programs across Canada because, although the federal government would be the logical entity to ensure consistency, such matters fall outside its jurisdiction. Furthermore, poorer provinces would probably argue that they could not afford to raise social assistance payments without federal help, or that raising minimum wages would drive away employment.

THE INTRODUCTION OF UNEMPLOYMENT INSURANCE IN CANADA

During the 1890s and in 1913–14, when unemployment was high in Canada, discussions concerning an unemployment insurance program took place in the House of Commons (Cuneo 1979). In 1911, Britain introduced a national unemployment insurance plan, which led Canadian labour organizations to lobby for a similar plan in Canada, especially after high unemployment in 1913 and 1914. However, labour shortages during the First World War diffused some of this political pressure. After the war, some returning veterans experienced serious unemployment problems. In places such as Winnipeg, high unemployment, combined with prejudice against growing numbers of immigrants and concern about the rise of socialism, led to considerable labour unrest in 1918. Consequently, the Conservative government (under Prime Minister Robert Borden) established a commission to investigate industrial and international relations and report on potential solutions to unrest. The commissioners reported in 1919 that labour unrest was largely caused by unemployment or fear of future unemployment which led to an atmosphere of insecurity, and recommended 'state insurance against unemployment, sickness, invalidity and old age' (Cuneo 1979). A few months later in 1919, the Liberal party included these proposals for social insurance in its platform, but did not implement them when it held power from 1921 to 1926.

The need for unemployment insurance (UI) was argued many times by labour MPs (including J.S. Woodsworth) in the House of Commons and by labour organizations. The MPs argued that federal involvement in unemployment insurance would guarantee uniformity in services, and that the general taxing powers of the federal government were best fitted to assume the costly responsibilities of modern welfare. The opposition to UI came mainly from the Canadian Manufacturers' Association and the Canadian Chamber of Commerce, both of which viewed it as a tax on business which would put Canadian business at a competitive disadvantage in international markets. Furthermore, the lack of labour unrest and high employment rates from 1922 to 1929 meant that there was no pressing motivation for the government to introduce new legislation.

In 1929, a House of Commons committee recommended an unemployment insurance program, but another House committee concluded that such a program was outside federal jurisdiction. As the 1930s Depression worsened, however, there was increased pressure for UI, which was seen by some to be 'insurance against political radicalism' (Cuneo 1979). In 1933, the official unemployment rate reached nearly 20 per cent and temporary 'relief' was provided to the provinces by the federal government. By 1935, the demand for UI became very loud from labour, and cracks were forming in the opposition. For example, the Canadian Manufacturers' Association was concerned that unemployed workers were losing their purchasing power, municipalities were in debt over relief and could not repay the banks, and the housing market was falling (Cuneo 1979, 164).

Just before the election in 1935, Prime Minister R.B. Bennett's Conservative government introduced the Employment and Social Insurance Bill, which set out a contributory plan of UI modelled on the British plan, requiring contributions from employers, employees, and the federal government. The bill quickly passed, but after the 1935 election when the Liberals under Mackenzie King returned to power, the Supreme Court declared the act *ultra vires* in June 1936 because it invaded provincial jurisdiction according to the *British North America Act* (1867) (Guest 1985, 89). The industrial unrest and financial hardship of the

1930s had, however, convinced many people, including Mackenzie King, of the need for UI (Cuneo 1979).

The Royal Commission on Dominion-Provincial Relations (the Rowell-Sirois Commission) discussed unemployment insurance from 1937 to 1940 and eventually recommended a new program. The last provincial premiers (Quebec and Alberta) finally agreed to allow the federal government to create such a program in May 1940. The Unemployment Insurance Bill was introduced into the House of Commons in July 1940 (when unemployment was low and contributions could build up in the fund for problems expected after the war). Benefits, which were designed to be less than the minimum wage and based on contributions, were not to be seen as 'relief.' Claimants had to be capable and available for work but unable to find 'suitable' employment. UI initially covered involuntary and temporary unemployment for lower-wage employees who were normally employed on a regular basis.

Although all political parties supported the bill by 1940, many groups (including the Canadian Manufacturers' Association, the Canadian Chamber of Commerce, the Canadian Bankers' Association, the Canadian Transit Association, and the Canadian Life Insurance Officers' Association) continued to voice their opposition when it went to committee (Cuneo 1979). They argued that it was a tax on business which would add to personnel costs and raise prices; employees would expect higher wages because of lost money in contributions; and the competitiveness of their industries would falter on foreign markets (even though many of their competitors, such as Britain and several European countries, already had UI programs). Most labour organizations supported the bill, but wanted more categories of workers included in the plan. The original plan included mainly skilled labour and excluded white-collar and government employees, seasonal workers, domestic workers, hospital workers, and workers in primary industries (such as loggers and fisherman).

The Unemployment Insurance Program began in July 1941, but by 1942 covered only 50 per cent of the labour force (Cuneo 1979, 167). In 1992, 95 per cent of the labour force was covered (Hess 1992a, 37). The administration of the act was entrusted to a commission but was financed by the federal government. A ceiling was established on earnings, based on the assumption that higher-income earners had a lower probability of unemployment. Few changes took place in the program between 1940 and 1970 apart from extensions of coverage to loggers, hospital workers, and non-permanent government employees.

In 1970, the Trudeau government produced a White Paper on UI which proposed universal coverage, higher rates, taxable benefits, reduced emphasis on work record as the basis for eligibility, and special maternity, retirement, and sickness benefits. Although these changes were opposed by the Canadian Manufacturers' Association and the Canadian Chamber of Commerce, the government pushed ahead and the *Unemployment Insurance Act* (1971) formalized these changes. Fifteen weeks of maternity benefits were added for eligible female employees, with a two-week waiting period before the collection of benefits. In 1977, the Unemployment Insurance Commission became known as the Canada Employment and Immigration Commission, and was relocated under the jurisdiction of Employment and Immigration Canada (part of the federal government) rather than remaining an independent commission supported by labour, employers, and government representatives.

In November 1990, ten weeks of parental benefits were added as an amendment to the *Unemployment Insurance Act*. At the same time, amendments influenced how long employees have to work before they become eligible for UI benefits (between ten and twenty weeks, depending on the regional unemployment rate). Regular benefits are now financed by employee and employer contributions, with a maximum weekly benefit of $408 and an average weekly benefit of $244 in 1991 (Hess 1992a, 36). The federal government share is now being used for retraining, job creation, and fishing benefits in excess of premiums (which serves almost as a regional development program).

The idea behind unemployment insurance was that the risk of unemployment was pooled among employees, employers, and the federal government because all three groups had a vested interest in maintaining high levels of employment. Employees need their wages to live and should not be blamed if they are laid off during a recession. Employers depend on high levels of consumer spending and low rates of labour unrest, and have a social responsibility to assist workers to make ends meet. Governments want to maintain order, assist the needy, and sustain domestic purchasing power. Cuneo (1979) argued that UI was viewed by the government not only as a way of reducing poverty and providing temporary relief to the unemployed, but also, implicitly, as a mechanism for social control (to avoid labour unrest and a repeat of the 1918 riots) and a way to deal with a certain level of permanent unemployment resulting from technological changes in a modern industrial society.

Although we have moved far away from the original idea that UI recipients must be available for work (as indicated by the provision of maternity and parental benefits and winter benefits for seasonal workers such as fishermen), the idea of pooling the risk – the key idea of social insurance – remains. Now, higher-income people are sharing the risk with those who have higher probabilities of unemployment.

Eligibility for UI depends on the unemployment rate in the region and varies from a minimum of ten to fourteen weeks of continuous employment for at least fifteen hours a week. The benefit now replaces up to 57 per cent of insurable earnings to a maximum, reduced from 60 per cent in 1993. In 1992, the maximum benefit was about $426, while the average was $261 (Torjman 1994). Eligibility for unemployment insurance is independent of family income. When benefits expire, however, unemployed persons with another wage earner in the household are expected to rely on their income. Those without another earner in the household may be forced to deplete their savings before turning to provincial social assistance.

In October 1994, the federal government released a Green Paper suggesting that the Unemployment Insurance Program has moved away from its original intention of providing temporary income replacement for regular workers who became unemployed for short periods. They proposed that UI could be divided into two programs. One would be a social insurance program for contributors who are normally employed full time but become temporarily unemployed. The second would be a new unemployment benefit which would provide training and skills development, job search services, and a (lower) benefit with eligibility based on household income for long-term unemployed people. This potential two-tiered system is presently used in Germany, but the suggestion has created concern in Canada about the intention behind the suggested 'reform.' The proposal was presented by the government as an improvement to UI which would help people move back into the workforce, but many anti-poverty groups, unions, and policy analysts are interpreting it as essentially a cost-cutting exercise.

A CROSS-NATIONAL COMPARISON OF SOCIAL ASSISTANCE PROGRAMS

Between the 1950s and the 1970s, many European countries developed social insurance programs to cover disability, illness, childbirth, and unemployment, in which eligibility was independent of income. Yet most countries retained some programs which were targeted to low-income families or those 'in need.' In addition, programs were modified over the years, and some universal programs have been converted to income-tested benefits as cost-cutting measures. Targeted programs carry with them assumptions about who deserves assistance from governments and under what social circumstances.

Sainsbury (1993) examined the beneficiaries of income maintenance programs in the United Kingdom, the United States, the Netherlands, and Sweden, noting that, with the exception of Sweden, these countries retain 'dual welfare systems.' One system is based on social insurance, and the other on means-tested social assistance. These systems differ in terms of benefit levels; political legitimacy, visibility, and support; level of administration; work incentives; and intervention in private lives. Sainsbury noted that women tend to be the recipients of social assistance while men predominate as beneficiaries of the more generous social insurance programs. While social insurance is perceived as an 'earned right' and involves income replacement from work, social assistance entails penalties, stigma, work enforcement, invasion of privacy, and a minimum benefit level. Sainsbury suggested that the realities of social welfare differ for men and women in three of the four countries she studied.

Kamerman and Kahn (1989c) outlined four models of intervention for lone-parent families in Britain, France, Germany, Norway, and Sweden: the anti-poverty strategy, the strategy of supporting single mothers at home, the universal young child strategy, and a strategy combining labour market and family policy to permit a successful combination of parenting and work. All of these strategies contain advantages as well as disadvantages. Britain was used as an example of a country that focused on the anti-poverty strategy. Kamerman and Kahn argued that although this strategy does somewhat reduce poverty rates, it tends to create a 'poverty trap' in which recipients cannot easily improve their situation without losing benefits. The strategy of supporting mothers to stay at home (as in Norway) creates a work disincentive for unskilled women and reduces their labour force participation, although this strategy provides generous benefits for children. The universal young child strategy, typified by French policy, also provides generous benefits until children reach a certain age, but requires a transition period for women to help them back into full-time work. Combining labour market and family policy, as is done in Sweden, helps maintain mothers' incomes but creates time pressures and requires non-family child care for long hours each day. Although the authors did not indicate which strategy is most effective, they argued that the United States can learn from European policies by recognizing the need for an infrastructure to support lone-parent families. This would involve state health insurance, child care services, maternity and parental benefits, and housing subsidies.

McLanahan, Casper, and Sorenson (1992) examined the relationship between women's roles and poverty status in eight industrialized countries – Australia, Canada, Germany, Italy, the Netherlands, Sweden, the United Kingdom, and the United States. Using Esping-Andersen's typology of welfare states and their income transfer systems, the authors divided the countries studied into social democratic, corporatist, and liberal welfare states. The researchers conclude that if risk factors are combined, women who are married/childless/workers have the lowest risk of poverty and women who are single/mothers/homemakers have the highest risk of poverty in most of the countries. Those who are wives/mothers/homemakers fall into the bottom half of the rankings in most countries. While marriage and work reduce the risk of poverty for women in all countries, motherhood increases the chances of being poor. Women are especially vulnerable when motherhood occurs outside marriage. However, women in the liberal welfare states (Australia, the United Kingdom, the United States, and Canada) experience higher poverty rates on average than women in other countries. Especially women in non-traditional situations fare better in countries which promote gender equality, such as social democratic Sweden.

Before I discuss the details of specific family policies, I will examine benefits for low-income families and especially lone mothers, as well as programs for unemployment, in each of the eight countries under investigation. Discussion of the philosophy behind the programs, the eligibility requirements, the benefit levels, and the criticisms of the programs should shed some light on the child poverty rates outlined at the beginning of this chapter.

Australia

Although Australia, like Canada, developed a federal constitution, income support programs are provided by the central or Commonwealth government and not by individual states (Bolderson and Mabbett 1991). All social security payments are funded from general taxation revenue and administered by the Commonwealth Department of Social Security (DSS) (International Social Security Association 1992c). Eligibility for benefits varies by category (e.g., old age, disability, unemployment, or lone parent). Once the category has been established, entitlement for most benefits is income-tested and asset-tested.[9]

Australia has provided a widow's pension since 1942 and a supporting mother's benefit since 1973, based on the assumption that a woman who is engaged in the full-time care of children should not be forced into the labour force because of the absence of a breadwinner (Stanton and Herscovitch 1992, 160). In 1944, Australia developed an unemployment assistance program for people who lose their jobs involuntarily, are registered as unemployed, and are available for work. Unemployment assistance was paid to men aged sixteen to sixty-four and women aged sixteen to fifty-nine, to coincide with the lower retirement age for women. Supplements have been available for those with children or a dependent spouse. The basic unemployment benefit in 1991 was the same as the sickness benefit: A.$145.85 a week (Can. $131.99) if single with dependants and A.$243.20 a week (Can. $220.10) if married with a dependent spouse (U.S. Dept of HHS,[10] 1992, 12). Unlike Canada's Unemployment Insurance Program, Australia's program is financed through general revenue and is means-tested.

An initiative was introduced in March 1989 called the Jobs, Education, and Training (JET) scheme. Designed to integrate income support and labour market programs, it provided counselling to sole-parent pensioners on the availability of education, training, and employment, as well as access to child care. It was voluntary and was phased in over three years. Priority was given to teenage lone parents, those whose youngest child is approaching sixteen, and those who have children over six and have been receiving the sole-parent pension for more than twelve months (Saunders and Matheson 1991).

In July 1991, the unemployment benefit was abolished and replaced by a job search allowance (JSA) for those unemployed for less than twelve months and a NEWSTART allowance for those unemployed for twelve months or more. Under these new policies, the unemployed are compelled to undertake retraining and demonstrate that they are actively searching for work in order to receive a government allowance (Lambert 1994). In addition, the government initiated a wage subsidy program (JOBSTART), which provides a six-month subsidy to employers who hire people from targeted groups, including lone parents. The subsidy for lone parents was A.$230 (Can. $209) a week in 1991 (Perry 1991).

The Australian sole-parent pension was introduced in March 1989, combining the previous supporting parent's benefit and the widow's pension. To qualify, the parent must be unmarried, live with at least one child under sixteen, have been previously married or previously living in a de facto (common-law) relationship, have been a resident of Australia for at least five years, and have a low income and few assets. If a woman becomes a single parent in Australia, the residence requirement for eligibility is minimal. The pension is not payable if a parent is presently in a de facto relationship, because that person is assumed to be married. Eligibility for the sole-parent pension ceases when the youngest child turns sixteen unless the child has disabilities (U.S. Dept of HHS 1992, 13).

The basic rate of the sole-parent's pension is equivalent to one-quarter of average weekly earnings (Stanton and Herscovitch 1992, 158) and is indexed to the consumer price index. The 1991 maximum rate was about A.$333 (Can. $300) every two weeks, plus A.$53 (Can. $48) for each child under age thirteen and about A.$77 (Can. $70) for each child aged thirteen to fifteen. A lone parent living in privately rented accommodation is also eligible for rent assistance.[11] As of April 1991, 71 per cent of lone parents received this pension (Perry 1991).

The sole-parent's pension is targeted to low-income sole parents, and the amount of income permitted before the pension is reduced varies by its source. For example, maintenance or child support payments received are subject to a separate income test from other income.[12] The standard pension is reduced by fifty cents for each dollar of non-pension income over A.$42 (Can. $38) a week, plus A.$12 (Can. $11) a week for each child. Once the basic pension entitlement is fully reduced, the supplementary payments are reduced sequentially by fifty cents for each dollar of other income. Pensioner fringe benefits are lost entirely when weekly income exceeds A.$103 (Can. $93.53), plus A.$20 (Can. $18) for each child (Saunders and Matheson 1991).

Australia also requires an assets test for the sole-parent's pension (which varies for homeowners and renters), but it is set at a relatively high level. Homeowners are allowed to accumulate A.$103,500 (Can. $93,978) of assessable assets in addition to an owner-occupied home without losing entitlement. The limit for renters is A.$177,500 (Can. $161,170). The limits are indexed each year, and the pension is reduced by A.$2 (Can. $1.82) per week for every A.$1,000 (Can. $908) by which the value of assets exceeds these limits (Stanton and Herscovitch 1992).

The Department of Social Services also provides sole-parent pensioners entering employment with an employment entry payment of A.$100 (Can. $91) and an earnings credit which allows them to receive the full rate of pension until their earnings accumulate to A.$1,000 (Can. $908). As of January 1992, sole-parent pensioners participating in education courses are eligible for an A.$200 (Can. $182) education entry payment to assist them with initial costs (International Social Security Association 1992c).

The Australian government provides rent assistance to low-income families but at a relatively low level because the basic pension (including the sole-parent pension) is expected to cover normal housing costs. However, housing costs vary markedly among the beneficiaries of different kinds of pension. For example, while old age pensioners are likely to own their houses, sole parents are more likely to be renters or to pay mortgages, and therefore to have higher expenses. Rent assistance pays half the difference between the basic rent allocation and the rent actually paid, up to a maximum. Since 1988, the maximum levels of rent assistance have increased, with the aim of achieving more effective targeting of benefits (Bolderson and Mabbett 1991). In 1991, the maximum rent assistance was A.$40 (Can. $36.32) per week, varying by the number of children in the family (U.S. Dept of HHS 1992).

A concern with such a selective approach to income support is the emergence of high effective marginal tax rates on recipients. Some people think that these high tax rates discourage beneficiaries from trying to earn more money and create a 'poverty trap' which encourages overreliance on income support. A study by Whiteford, Bradbury, and Saunders (1989) indicated that beneficiaries of the sole-parent pension could, over certain income ranges, have faced effective marginal tax rates of more than 80 per cent in 1988, well above the highest personal income tax rate in that year (Saunders and Matheson 1991). Therefore, the incentive to earn extra money is reduced.

Another concern relates to the cost of the sole-parent pension. In the financial year 1989–90, A.$2.33 billion (Can. $2.11 billion) was spent by the Commonwealth government on sole-parent pensions, only 22 per cent less than was spent on unemployment benefits (Lambert 1994). Furthermore, the pension has been blamed by conservatives for contributing to marriage breakdown and the rise of sole parents in Australia. Sole-parent families as a percentage of all families with dependent children have increased from 9.2 per cent in 1974 to 15.7 per cent in 1990. While 80 per cent of sole mothers receive the pension, only 35 per cent of sole fathers do, although the percentage of male beneficiaries has been rising (ibid.).

In addition to the pension, sole parents, along with two-parent families, are also eligible to receive family allowance payments for dependent children. Although the family allowance was originally a universal benefit, it is now income-tested on the basis of total family income in the previous financial year, as I will discuss in chapter 4. Family allowance is no longer payable when annual family income exceeds A.$62,057 (Can. $56,348), plus A.$3,104 (Can. $2,818) for the second and subsequent children. The definitions of resources and requirements in the means test for family allowances are currently pitched so that the average production worker will qualify (Bolderson and Mabbett 1991).

The Family Allowance Supplement (FAS) dates back to 1987. The objectives are to direct an increased and uniform family assistance payment to low-income families not receiving social assistance, regardless of their labour force participation. The payment is indexed, includes rent assistance, and is directed to the parent primarily responsible for child-rearing (Cass 1989, 171). The FAS varies by the child's age, and the payment is higher for adolescents than for younger children.[13] The full rate is payable if family income is lower than A.$18,000 per year (Can. $16,344), with additional income allowed for each child, and the rate is reduced by 50 per cent for income above that level (Perry 1991). While income-testing for the FAS began only in 1988, it is now subject to asset-testing as well, a change that indicates further targeting of family benefits (Bolderson and Mabbett, 1991).

Health care without fees is provided to all residents of Australia. In addition, sole parents are eligible for a concession card which entitles holders to a range of free or subsidized public services (Saunders and Matheson 1991).

Australia's social security programs for unemployment and for low-income families are income-tested and financed through general revenue rather than payroll taxes. Despite the fact that the family allowance supplement and the sole-parent's pension are seen as social assistance and are stigmatized, they provide valuable support for low-income families. Because they are federal programs, benefit levels are uniform across the country, and moving from one state to another does not disqualify recipients.

Historically, women's participation rates in the labour force were lower in Australia than in most other countries in this study, and their wages were set at a lower rate than men's until the 1970s. Most industrial and labour relations matters fall within state jurisdiction, and each state provides legislation which establishes a tribunal to handle industrial disputes and set wages (Goodwin 1984). The Commonwealth Conciliation and Arbitration Commission, the most important single authority, is a federal tribunal, and half of the Australian workforce is covered by federal awards. The tribunals set a minimum wage which must be paid for each job category regardless of gender (ibid.).

Until 1950, the basic wage of females was 54 per cent of the male wage, but after the Second World War, the federal tribunal set wages for women at 75 per cent of male wages. In 1969, the tribunal decided in favour of equal pay for equal work, and female wages were set at 100 per cent by 1972. However, predominantly female occupations were excluded from this decision. In 1972, the tribunal set the goal of equal pay for work of equal value with full implementation by 1975. Differential pay scales based on gender were eliminated, but occupational segregation remained. Yet these tribunal decisions increased the average earnings of a full-time female worker by 30 per cent (Goodwin 1984).

Between 1969 and 1979, female union membership increased from 35 per cent to 47 per cent, which raised women's pay and further decreased wage differentials between men and women (Goodwin 1984). In 1984, Australia passed legislation to create equal pay for work of comparable value, which significantly raised female wages. Furthermore, the National Wage Decision in 1988 emphasized the need for award restructuring to remove indirect discriminatory practices, such as discrimination against employees with family responsibilities (Heitlinger 1993, 209).

In 1994, the Australian government released a White Paper entitled *Working Nation*, announcing changes to unemployment benefits as of 1995. These include work incentives for unemployed people, additional training opportunities, and a Parenting Allowance paid directly to the spouses of unemployed and low-income parents caring for children under sixteen. The Parenting Allowance replaces the practice of paying unemployment benefits to a married couple at the 'married rate.' Beginning in 1995, spouses will be treated as unemployed individuals. If an unemployed husband finds a low-paying job, the wife could still receive the Parenting Allowance. On the other hand, spouses who do not care for young children will be encouraged to enter the labour force. If spouses of unemployed persons are over forty years old and have little job experience, however, they may not be expected to work for pay and may be eligible for a Partner Allowance (Australian Government 1994).

In the past few years, unemployment has been rising in Australia, as it has in most countries in this study. New Right critiques of welfare programs and social benefits have been prevalent, focusing on widening the gap between the 'deserving' and the 'undeserving' poor (Cass 1992) and reducing social security fraud (Lambert 1994). The 1993 Green Paper (*Restoring Full Employment*) and the 1994 White Paper (*Working Nation*) suggest that Australian policies are being reformed to acknowledge labour force trends such as the increasing employment of married women, high youth unemployment, the expansion of non-standard work, and growing long-term unemployment. At the same time, however, the reforms are attempting to reduce government expenditures.

France

Revenu minimum d'insertion (RMI) is both a conditional and a supplemental benefit which has something of the flavour of social assistance. It is known as the minimum income for job reintegration, and its aim is to help combat poverty by integrating or reintegrating people into the workforce (Barbier 1992). The word *'insertion'* distinguishes RMI from other statutory benefits in that a condition, or *'contrat d'insertion,'* is attached to benefit payments. Under certain conditions, the payments may be suspended.

RMI is geared to parents over the age of twenty-five who have dependent children, and the amount of the benefit depends on the size and composition of the household. The RMI was designed as a 'final safety net,' and the government attempted to prevent it from becoming a disincentive to work by setting the maximum allowance below the minimum wage. RMI includes a housing benefit, a medical benefit, and occupational integration assistance, as well as contact with social workers (Legros and Simonin 1991).

France also offers a benefit designed to provide lone parents with a basic living income. The *Allocation de parent isolé* (API), introduced in 1976, is an income-tested benefit paid and administered by the family allowance authorities to lone parents with a child under the age of three or for one year after a person becomes a lone parent. It is available to those who enter lone parenthood through the death of a spouse, divorce or separation, or a birth to an unmarried woman. Since RMI was established as a minimum social income, the API is no longer a public assistance benefit but is becoming more of a social wage (International Social Security Association 1992a). In practice, only about 10 per cent of lone parents receive API (Roll 1990–1) because they qualify for other family benefits or for RMI (social assistance). As with the family allowance, API is financed through employer payroll taxes (U.S. Dept of HHS 1992, 108).

The API, or the lone-parent allowance, is non-taxable, has an effective marginal tax rate of 100 per cent, and could last up to forty-four months, including during pregnancy. Benefits usually cease after twelve months or when the youngest child reaches the age of three and therefore can enter a state-run preschool (*école maternelle*). For a mother of two children, the ceiling is equal to minimum gross wage. In 1984, the lone parent allowance was received by more than 100,000 lone parents and 99 per cent were women (Ray 1990).

France is one of the few countries in which unemployed lone mothers are almost as well off as those in paid work (Lewis, ed. 1993, 20). The lone-parent allowance has been criticized as a disincentive to work, to marriage, and even to cohabitation. For eligible women, the probability is high that they will stay home and accept this allowance, unless they are very motivated to work, can command high wages, or can find convenient day care arrangements. A study using 1983 data found that only one in ten women receiving the lone-parent allowance actually worked for pay. Even this figure was surprisingly high given that, with the 100 per cent marginal tax rate, these women actually received less income when employed. Reasons given for working included improving chances of success for future jobs, and psychological and social reasons. For those not working for pay, the majority expressed a preference to work, but cited difficulty in finding work and the presence of young children as reasons for staying home. If marginal tax rates were reduced on earned income, fewer lone parents would leave the labour force completely (Ray 1990).

Starting in 1978, on-the-job training contracts with no age restrictions have been offered to single mothers. To become eligible, they must have at least one dependent child, receive the lone-parent's allowance (API), and return to work within a period of two to five years after birth or adoption (Brocas et al. 1990).

In addition to the family allowance, which is universal for families with at least two children, France provides an income-tested supplement to the family allowance and a family support allowance. These benefits are also financed through payroll taxes. The family support allowance is worth 22.5 per cent of the 'base wage' or Fr 1,848.40 (Can. $439) a month per orphan or lone mother (U.S. Dept of HHS 1992, 108).

Since 1905, France has provided an unemployment insurance program financed by employees, employers, and the government. This program is for insured employees who are unemployed involuntarily for a temporary period of time. The duration of the benefit varies with the length of contributions, the age of the employee, and family situation. The level of benefit is calculated as a basic allowance plus a percentage of previous earnings (U.S. Dept of HHS 1992, 107).

In France, the preamble of the French Constitution of 1946 guarantees gender equality, and explicit gender differences in basic wages established by collective agreement were eliminated at that time. In 1972, equal pay legislation was enacted which covered paid work which is the same or of equal value. New legislation against gender discrimination was passed in 1975, but employers have experienced little difficulty in persuading courts to make exceptions allowing wage differentials. In 1983, the *Law on Equality in the Employment Field between Men and Women* was enacted, which applies to both the public and private sectors and specifically outlaws gender discrimination. Extensive power has been given to labour inspectors who can themselves seek redress as well as complain. The law includes provisions for fines and imprisonment for failure to comply (Goodwin 1984).

Germany

In Germany, persons are eligible for social assistance only when they have neither income nor capital and cannot obtain assistance from relatives. Under the law, welfare recipients are required to search for work, yet working outside the home is not obligatory if it would endanger 'the normal upbringing of a child.' If a child is under the age of three, the parent is not obliged to enter the labour force, and from the time the child is three to six, only half-time work is required. Yet social assistance is a subsidiary benefit, and the lone parent must use all other possible funds before becoming eligible. The person must not have accumulated more household capital than DM 2,500 (Can. $1,995), plus DM 500 (Can. $399) savings for each child. Lone parents must expect that the income and assets of their parents will be brought into the assessment (Hohnerlein 1992).

Under German law, people living common law are considered to be married for purposes of determining eligibility for social assistance. To determine whether a quasi-marital relationship exists, the social assistance institution is empowered to carry out home investigations and the couple must allow entrance to the dwelling (ibid.).

Although family support in Germany is generally perceived as the responsibility of family members rather than the state, some protection for lone parents and their children is set forth in the Constitution. Since

1977, divorced spouses have been permitted to split old-age or disability pensions with their former spouses as part of a policy of fair compensation. Divorced or widowed parents who are prevented from working because of the need to care for children may be eligible for the child-rearing benefit (*Erziehungsrente*). This pension is paid to a divorced parent who has not remarried or to a survivor after the death of a spouse, if he or she has contributed to the insurance program for sixty months prior to divorce or if the deceased spouse was a pensioner at the time of death (ibid.).

A striking inequality in the German system is the lack of pension support for unmarried mothers. The child-rearing pension for widowed or divorced mothers is linked to the absence of a former husband, serving the double purpose of replacing both income and child support. Although it is assumed that child support by the deceased or divorced parent has lapsed, former support is not a condition. Unmarried mothers do not receive a similar benefit to replace or compensate lost income. Even in the case of the death of the father liable for child support, there is no entitlement to the survivor's pension (Hohnerlein 1992).

In 1986, a child-rearing benefit was introduced for parents caring for their children at home and unable to work full time. This benefit is available both to parents in the labour force and to homemakers. For those in the labour force, the benefit provides job protection and protection against dismissal, as well as the opportunity to work up to eighteen hours per week. Mothers or fathers of children born after 30 June 1989 may receive a child-raising benefit of DM 600 per month (Can. $479) for the first fifteen months. For children born after 30 June 1990, the period was extended to eighteen months. After the seventh month, the benefit is income-tested.[14]

Unemployment and child-rearing benefits cannot be received at the same time. If the child-rearing benefit is insufficient to cover expenses, a lone parent may also apply for public assistance under the housing allowances law or even under federal assistance law. Various state governments (Länder) assist young families by means of their own programs. For example, in Bavaria the amount is DM 500 (Can. $399) per month for six months and in Baden-Wurttemberg DM 450 (Can. $359) per month. The state benefits are not taken into account when considering eligibility for other benefits.

Aside from the state benefit, a family may claim family assistance under the 'young family' program for children born on or after 1 July 1989. This is a one-time payment for young families on the occasion of the birth or adoption of a child (Hohnerlein 1992), similar to the newborn allowance in Quebec.

In 1927, Germany developed an unemployment insurance program which covers employed persons, including agricultural workers and homeworkers, and is funded by contributions from employees, employers, and government (U.S. Dept of HHS 1992, 114). To receive unemployment benefit, a person must officially report as 'unemployed,' be available for work through the placement services, and complete the qualifying period. A person is considered 'unemployed' if for the time being he or she cannot find work or is working less than eighteen hours per week. A person is also entitled to unemployment insurance if, as a lone parent, she or he can work only part time or only at specific times because of the need to care for children. The qualifying period is met if the person contributed to the social insurance program for three years before becoming unemployed. For unemployed parents, the benefit replaces 68 per cent of previous net earnings, which is higher than for individuals. Depending on age and previous length of employment, the benefit is paid for between six and thirty-two months (Hohnerlein 1992).

In addition to unemployment insurance, there is also a means-tested benefit called unemployment assistance for those ineligible for insurance or who have exhausted their benefits. There is no limit on the duration of this assistance, but there are annual qualifying examinations (ibid.). For unemployed parents, the rate is 58 per cent of previous net earnings from work. Since January 1986, eligibility for unemployment assistance is also dependent on the income and capital of the partner, whether married or unmarried (Hohnerlein 1992).[15]

The German government also pays allowances or provides loans to encourage vocational training. One program may be relevant to divorced lone parents who previously were employed and now want to return to work after raising children. The assistance consists of cash benefits for maintenance and the payment of training costs.

The introduction of a 'partial maintenance allowance' is also of importance for lone parents. This assistance is available for part-time training of at least twelve hours per week, provided such parents have temporarily left employment in order to raise children and cannot work or study full time because they have to look after their children (Hohnerlein 1992).

As I will discuss in chapter 4, family allowances in Germany are income-tested. There are no special rules for lone parents under the general family allowances scheme, but the permissible income limit for lone parents with two children is DM 37,880 (Can. $30,164.40) net annual income. Child allowance supplements can be claimed by persons who cannot fully use the tax concessions under the child exemption law or who have low incomes. The maximum supplement is DM 48 (Can. $38.30) per month per child (Hohnerlein 1992).

A housing allowance is also available for both owners and tenants. The level of subsidy depends on family size, amount of rent payable, and family income. For lone parents, there are some special rules. Widowed parents can receive a housing allowance for twenty-four months after the death of their spouse and, in addition, lone parents can deduct an increased exemption of DM 100 (Can. $79.80) per month for each child under twelve (ibid.).

The Netherlands

Social assistance in the Netherlands has ensured that lone-mother families have a lower rate of poverty than in other countries and, hence, are able to care for their children at home. This type of assistance involves a relatively high level of expenditure on income transfers and a high rate of economic dependence among women (Perry 1991).

In 1989, 56 per cent of lone mothers were receiving social assistance. Lone mothers with young children are not required to enter the workforce in order to be eligible for benefits until all children are over the age of twelve. Rent assistance is available to low-income families with children and of the 85 per cent of lone parents who live in rental housing, 58 per cent are subsidized. Assistance covers rent over a certain level per month.[16]

In 1990, a lone mother without earnings living in rental housing with two children aged six to ten could be eligible for social assistance of Fl 1,450 (Can. $1,037) per month, a family allowance of Fl 284 (Can. $203.06) a month, average rental assistance up to Fl 192 (Can. $138), and a holiday allowance of Fl 83.42 (Can. $60) per month. This amounts to a total of Fl 2,009 (Can. $1,436.44) per month, which is 75 per cent of the net average production worker's wage (APWW). A lone mother would also receive education allowances for the children and an amount for health insurance (Perry 1991).

Widows with children under eighteen and widows over forty years old qualify for survivors' benefits at a taxable flat rate regardless of earnings. In 1990, 14 per cent of lone mothers were eligible for this benefit (ibid.).

Sweden

Social assistance in Sweden is based on income, assets, and willingness to work. Families with more than a certain amount of money in the bank are not granted assistance, nor are those who voluntarily reduce their working hours. To be eligible for social assistance in Sweden, parents are obliged to prove that they are looking for work, and this includes lone mothers with preschool children.

Eighty per cent of lone mothers receive a housing subsidy that covers 40 per cent of their rent, as well as a subsidized place in a child care facility (S. Gustafsson 1990). In 1991, a lone mother with two children between the ages of four and ten would receive the child allowance (worth SEK 1,500 or Can. $276), maintenance allowance (worth SEK 2,146 or Can. $395), subsistence allowance (worth SEK 4,375 or Can. $805) and a housing allowance (worth SEK 2,575 or Can. $474). This would give her a total monthly income of SEK 10,578 (Can. $1,946), which is 109 per cent of the 1990 net average production worker's wage (APWW) in Sweden (Perry 1991).

Municipal governments administer income security programs in Sweden (B. Gustafsson 1993a). The welfare system is decentralized, income thresholds are approved by local government, and criteria vary with the municipality. However, the municipalities are advised by the national Social Welfare Board (*Socialstyrelsen*) in their delivery of social welfare services (B. Gustafsson 1993a, 272).

Lone mothers in Sweden are eligible for child allowances, housing subsidies, subsidized child care, parental benefits, guaranteed child support payments, survivors' pensions (if widowed), and social assistance. A 1989 survey showed a number of reasons for lone mothers to claim social assistance. In most cases, the need was temporary, particularly following separation and divorce while they were waiting for a maintenance advance, seeking work or moving from part-time to full-time work, waiting for child care, or faced with unanticipated expenses (Perry 1991). Those who remained on social assistance for longer periods tended to be young unmarried mothers and women who had been out of the labour force or in low-status part-time work and had difficulty finding full-time work. In addition, long-term social assistance recipients tended to have fewer job skills or a pattern of multiple disadvantage – such as, for example, people with disabilities or visible minorities with language problems (ibid.).

Although most social assistance recipients are Swedish citizens, the rate has been several times higher among 'foreigners.' Immigrants and refugees used to be able to apply for social assistance if they were recently arrived in Sweden and lacked paid work as well as a resident permit. Without a resident permit, immigrants are not allowed to accept paid work, and many require public transfer payments while their permits are reviewed. Since 1988, refugees are no longer entitled to social assistance but are eligible for 'refugee assistance' (B. Gustafsson 1993a).

Sweden passed its first unemployment benefit legislation in 1934. Since 1956, unions have established and administered unemployment insurance programs, which are funded by contributions from employees, employers, and government. Eligibility for union-related unemployment insurance is based on twelve months' membership in the fund, including five months in the last twelve months prior to unemployment, registration at the public employment office, and availability for work. Benefits are paid for up to 300 days. Those ineligible for union-related programs (one-third of employees) are covered by labour market support programs (unemployment assistance), which are funded through employer payroll taxes and government funds. These benefits are means-tested according to family income and assets (U.S. Dept of HHS 1992, 270).

Sweden has one of the lowest salary differentials based on gender of industrialized countries, and any wage differential which remains is mainly due to occupational segregation. Unlike most other countries in this study, Sweden has developed a centralized organization of employers and unions which form a united bargaining group for wages and benefits. There are three national unions: the Swedish Confederation of Trade Unions (LO), the Central Organization of Salaried Employees (TCO), and the Swedish Employees Federation (SAF). The goal of all unions is to narrow the wage gap that exists between various occupations and to level out wage rates. As women have occupied most of the low-paid positions, they have benefited considerably from this policy (Goodwin 1984).

In 1960, SAF and LO (making up 90 per cent of blue-collar workers in Sweden) agreed to implement equal pay and removed any clauses in collective agreements which discriminated against women. This task was completed by 1965. In 1963, TCO (50 per cent of white-collar workers in Sweden) joined with LO to participate in a 'position classification' or job evaluation system. In the 1960s, a number of wage equalization measures were introduced, including a low-wage supplement, wage increase guarantees, and a social package which included improvements like accident insurance, pensions, and holidays (ibid.).

Each industry-wide collective agreement establishes its own standard of equal pay, which usually involves equal value as determined by a job evaluation plan. In 1979, the *Equal Treatment in Working Life Act* was enacted, covering the entire labour market. Gender discrimination is prohibited, and the law states that it is the employer's obligation actively to promote equality. The law also implemented new legal machinery – the equality ombudsman and the equality board. The equality ombudsman is a lawyer appointed for three years with the responsibility for ensuring that the law is implemented and assisting in other efforts to promote equality in working life. Employees, their representatives, or the equality ombudsman may make complaints to the equality board.

Two major factors have contributed to the success of pay equity in Sweden. Most blue-collar workers were already covered by job evaluation plans before 1960, and the attitude of the labour movement is favourable to equal pay (Goodwin 1984). Consequently, when women enter the labour force, they have a higher probability of comparable pay with men than women in any other country of this study. However, more than half of mothers with children under twelve work part time, including a high proportion of lone mothers (Perry 1991).

The United Kingdom

Industrialization and urbanization began early in Britain, generating the social conditions for the development of the welfare state. Ideologies allocated a marginal role for government in the economy, however, in accordance with the political philosophy of *laissez-faire* (Bolderson and Mabbett 1991, 55). Before 1908, the only government social security in Britain was provided by the 1834 Poor Law, which differentiated between the 'deserving' and the 'undeserving' poor, obligated employed persons to support other family members, and as a last resort provided a place in the 'workhouse' for the destitute. However, 'paupers' who were given a place to live were forced to give up their citizenship rights, which meant the right to vote as well as the right to raise their children and live as a family unit.

Until the 1900s, families and charitable organizations provided most assistance to the poor. In 1908, Britain introduced the old-age pension and in 1911 established national insurance for unemployment and sickness. After the First World War, unemployment insurance was expanded and spending on social housing increased. In 1934, a means-tested unemployment assistance scheme was introduced, funded through taxation. The Beveridge Report recommended in 1942 an expansion of the scope and coverage of the existing social insurance programs, the introduction of universal family allowances, and the creation of a national social assistance program. These recommendations were all implemented by 1948.

Except for family allowances, British social programs affirmed the principle of social insurance which covered all workers and provided benefits for their dependants. For those not covered by insurance, need had to be proven but benefits were not to be below subsistence (Bolderson and Mabbett 1991, 67). As in most countries of this study, social security programs expanded in the 1960s and 1970s. In 1966, national assistance became a two-tiered system with the introduction of the Supplementary Benefit for long-term recipients, but the able-bodied unemployed were paid at a lower rate.

The reforms in the 1986 *Social Security Act* developed three benefits: income support, family credit, and housing benefit, which were all based upon similar principles. This reform edged the social security system slowly in the direction of a negative income tax. Furthermore, it placed means-testing at the centre of the overall design for social security. The new act renamed the former Supplementary Benefit 'Income Support' and introduced a structure which discriminated less among different categories of claimants (disabled, old-age pensioners, or heads of lone-parent families).

The *Social Security Act* created a dual system of means-tested support: Income Support (or social assistance) for those not employed or working less than twenty-four hours per week, and Family Credit for families with dependent children in which parents are employed for twenty-four hours or more per week. Lone parents with children under sixteen, however, are not subject to a work test and may receive social assistance as well as the universal Child Benefit and the One Parent Benefit (which will be discussed later).

Welfare recipients in the United Kingdom are also entitled to housing benefits covering 100 per cent of public or private rental or interest on mortgage repayments, and Community Charge Benefit covering 80 per cent of the cost for municipal taxes (Perry 1991). The unit of assessment for means-testing is the family, and unmarried sexual partners of the opposite sex are treated as married spouses.[17] Most income, including insurance benefits, child benefit, severe disablement allowance, and invalid care allowance, is taken into account against Income Support entitlement. A certain portion of family income is disregarded, however.

This amounts to £5 (Can. $10) a week for individuals and £15 (Can. $30) for people who receive the lone-parent premium or have been unemployed for more than two years. The Income Support benefit is reduced pound for pound on earnings over £15 (Can. $29.48) a week. As the average hourly rate of pay of lone mothers on Income Support is £2.67 (Can. $5.25), this means that they can typically work only five and a half hours before they begin to lose the benefit (Bradshaw et al, 1992). In addition, if claimants and their partners or dependants own more than £6,000 (Can. $11,790) in capital, they are not entitled to social assistance (Michael Hill 1990). This amount is considerably lower than in Australia.

Family Credit is a means-tested benefit available to low-paid full-time workers with dependent children. Eligibility rules are similar to Income Support with some additional complexities. The maximum credit ensures that most families, where there is a full-time breadwinner, are better off than comparable families on Income Support. Above the Income Support level, Family Credit is withdrawn at the rate of 70 per cent: that is, for each £1 of income above that level, 70p of credit is lost (Michael Hill 1990). The maximum amount payable to mothers on Income Support and Family Credit is £100 (Can. $197) a week (in 1991–2), and even this is reduced on a pound-for-pound basis if capital exceeds £500 (Can. $983) (J. Brown 1992).

The housing benefit is means-tested and administered by local government but subsidized by the central government. It provides assistance for housing costs and municipal taxes (including rates and poll taxes). The benefit is designed to be compatible with the other two means-tested benefits (Income Support and Family Credit). Anyone at or below Income Support level is eligible for the full housing benefit, which is paid regardless of work status and covers full rent and 80 per cent of municipal taxes (Michael Hill 1990; Bolderson and Mabbett 1991).[18] Non-cash benefits, such as pharmaceuticals, health services, and free school meals and milk, are also available for low-income families (Perry 1991).

As I will discuss in chapter 4, parents also receive the universal Child Benefit (family allowance) and lone parents receive the One Parent Benefit.[19] The amount of the universal Child Benefit was frozen for three years from 1988 to 1991, and without indexation it did not recover its real value (J. Brown 1992). The Child Benefit and One Parent Benefit are paid to the parents or guardians of all children under sixteen and to students between sixteen and eighteen who meet the residence requirement (Michael Hill 1990).

By 1988, two main employment and training programs emerged from the central government – the Youth Training Scheme (YTS) for young people under eighteen, and the Employment Training Scheme (ETS) for people over that age. The government ruled that young single people under eighteen should normally receive a government allowance only if they participate in a training scheme. Exceptions were allowed for certain groups of vulnerable youth without parental support, however. For the majority of young people, refusal to participate in the Youth Training Scheme is followed by unemployment without income maintenance.

The Employment Training Scheme (ETS) was introduced in 1988 as a twelve-month training program targeted to the long-term unemployed, particularly those between the ages of eighteen and twenty-five. ETS involves a combination of training and private-sector employment. Each participant is offered advice and information about job training, and the aim is to agree on a course of practical action which will help the person get back to work. Participants receive basic income support with an extra £10 (Can. $20) per week. Some lone parents can receive up to £50 (Can. $98) per week for child care costs. Travelling, accommodation, and equipment costs may be met and bonuses may be payable upon completion (Michael Hill 1990). Since the end of 1991, unemployed people who previously refused training are required to attend courses or take a financial penalty (International Social Security Association 1992a).

The United Kingdom has had an unemployment insurance program since 1911, and the current law dates from 1975. The insurance, which is financed through contributions from employers, employees, and government, pays a flat-rate benefit plus an additional amount for a dependent spouse for employees who have contributed for a specified length of time. The benefit is payable for up to one year (U.S. Dept of HHS 1992).

In Britain, lone parents with dependent children (the majority of whom are female) may receive Income Support (social assistance) without registering for work. Ungenerous rules concerning part-time or occasional earnings tend to deter labour market participation, as does the lack of child care services. Consequently, Britain has a much lower rate of employment for lone mothers than most other countries in this study – 39 per cent in Britain in 1985 (Hardey and Glover 1991, 92) compared to about 50 per cent in Canada at that time (Lindsay 1992, 21). Lewis (1989) noted the low rate of lone mothers in the labour force in Britain compared to other countries, but argued that lone-parent families should not be treated as a separate policy sphere. Instead, policies should focus on employment opportunities for all women and provisions for young children.

Britain has a smaller percentage of lone mothers than married mothers in the workforce, as social assistance rules discourage part-time work (Ermisch 1991). In addition, lone mothers in poorer economic circumstances tend to remain lone parents longer than those with higher incomes. Increasing welfare benefits, however, could discourage people from working for low wages. This would increase dependency on a welfare system which already promotes dependence. Higher child support payments would be desirable but would not on their own reduce the poverty of lone mothers. Child care subsidies, education, and training would be the most effective policies to alleviate poverty and reduce dependency (Ermisch 1991).

One in seven families in the United Kingdom are headed by lone parents, 90 per cent of them by women. About 72 per cent of lone mothers are on social assistance, and the percentage of lone parents in the labour market has actually decreased in recent years (Bradshaw and Millar 1991). In Bradshaw and Millar's 1991 study, only 40 per cent were receiving any income in the form of earnings. Furthermore, there was little difference in disposable income between employed lone parents and those receiving only welfare, a fact that was attributed to benefit losses and the extra costs of working. Bradshaw and Millar found that many people were ignorant of the benefits to which they were entitled.

In Bradshaw and Millar's sample, one-half had no educational qualifications and 63 per cent had no vocational training. The women most likely to be economically active were divorced, older, had school-age children, and had some educational or vocational qualifications. About 57 per cent of the lone mothers on Income Support used it as a short-term emergency support when first becoming a lone parent. In addition, more than half of those on IS said they wanted to work or would enter the workforce if they had access to child care. The preferred employment rate for lone mothers was similar to the actual rate for married mothers. Most employed lone mothers worked in the service sector, but those working full time typically earned lower wages than all full-time female employees overall. Finding a job or increasing working hours was the main route off social assistance for these women.

Since 1979, the Conservative government in Britain has attempted to move social policy away from state welfare towards increased individual and family responsibility. Unemployment benefits fell between 1983 and 1988 relative to wages, child benefits were frozen, and the government unsuccessfully tried to eliminate the state earnings-related pension (SERP) and make it a flat-rate retirement benefit. Despite public support for universality, some British benefits have become more targeted, as they have in the other 'liberal' welfare states. However, the principle of social insurance has not been dislodged (Bolderson and Mabbett 1991, 179).

The United States

Aid to Families with Dependent Children (AFDC), commonly referred to as 'welfare,' had its origins in the *Social Security Act* in 1935 as part of President Roosevelt's 'New Deal,' to help the United States cope with the Great Depression. Originally called Aid to Children, the federal program provided cash payments for children, and it was not until 1950 that benefits were extended to mothers as well (Bolderson and Mabbett 1991, 71). Prior to 1935, state governments provided their own social security, including old-age assistance schemes, assistance to the blind, and widows' pensions. In addition, voluntary and charitable organizations provided most of the services to the poor and needy.

Initially, AFDC provided support for children with deceased fathers, but today it is primarily for children with an absent but living parent (usually the father) and whose custodial parent (usually the mother) has a very low income or none at all (Garfinkel and Wong 1990). AFDC provides cash benefits to families whose gross income is at or below 185 per cent of the state's 'needs' standard, which is set by individual states and therefore varies considerably (Bolderson and Mabbett 1991). The key feature of AFDC and other means-tested programs is the 'asset test,' which requires that the recipient have no more than minimal assets,[20] effectively prohibiting recipients from accumulating savings that would provide a buffer for financial emergencies (Sherraden 1991).

By the 1960s, the idea that welfare programs should enable lone mothers to stay home and raise their own children had begun to erode in the United States, although it was retained in some European countries (France, Germany, the Netherlands, and the United Kingdom). In 1967, the U.S. government tried to encourage mothers to enter the labour force by creating incentives within AFDC. When this failed, Congress passed legislation in 1972 which forced mothers to work when they had no children under six (Garfinkel and Wong 1990).

The *Omnibus Reconciliation Act* of 1981 (OBRA) established workfare on a widespread basis. Through this act, the Reagan government rejected mixed work and educational incentives and instead favoured a pure work requirement. OBRA was based on the view that the main issue in the welfare dilemma was dependency and not poverty (Evans 1993). After recipients had been employed for four months, they were no longer entitled to a standard earnings exemption and tax deductions were lowered. For many, these changes ended or reduced AFDC. OBRA specifed participation expectations, increased monitoring, imposed sanctions, and enlarged the pool of those participating in workfare.

Congress accepted some of these ideas in the 1988 *Family Support Act*, which contains work requirements, provision for child care, and some training services to facilitate employment. In 1988, 35 per cent of lone mothers received AFDC, and the average yearly amount for a mother with two children and no earnings was U.S.$4,617 (Can. $5,893.60) (Perry 1991). Under the new act, a mother receiving AFDC is obliged to regis- ter with the Job Opportunities (JOBS) training program. Lone parents are also entitled to health coverage under Medicaid and to food stamps, and about 20 per cent of AFDC recipients receive housing assistance. The combined annual value of these benefits in 1988 was about U.S. $7,939 (Can. $10,134) (Perry 1991). Unlike in other countries in this study, there is no national health insurance program for low-income families not on public assistance in the United States.

Public assistance recipients and other low-income persons are eligible for food stamp coupons with a designated cash value that may be used to purchase food at supermarkets. Started as a pilot project in 1961 as a way of deterring low-income people from spending money on 'non- essential' items, the program was enacted in 1964 under the *Food Stamp Act*. The costs have risen from U.S.$4.4 billion (Can. $5.6 billion) in 1975 to U.S.$22.3 billion (Can. $28.5 billion) in 1993 (Gilbert, Specht, and Terrell 1993). Food stamps (FS) are entirely federally funded and are nationally administered through the Department of Agriculture, although administrative costs are shared between the federal and state governments.

Unlike AFDC, the value of food stamps is indexed to the consumer price index, and the monthly amount of coupons is determined by household size and income. Households without earned income receive an amount equivalent to the monthly cost of a nutritionally adequate diet for their household size, as determined by the government. To qualify for food stamps, the household must have less than U.S.$2,000

(Can. $2,553) in disposable assets,[21] gross income below 130 per cent of the Office of Management and Budget guidelines (OMB), and net income below the poverty guidelines. One- and two-person households that meet the applicable standards receive a minimum of U.S.$10 (Can. $13) a month in food stamps (U.S. Dept of HHS 1991).

The U.S. federal poverty index is based on the cost of a 1963 subsistence food budget, multiplied by a factor of three, and updated annually for inflation. As an absolute rather than a relative measure of poverty, the poverty line is concrete and convenient to use but overlooks the existential quality of poverty as a condition of life (Gilbert, Specht, and Terrell 1993). The U.S. poverty index has been calculated at U.S.$12,675 (Can. $16,178) for a family of four in 1990 (ibid., 88) and is less generous than Canadian measures. In Canada, a family of four is considered to need $30,100 in a large city such as Toronto or Montreal.

AFDC has been said to encourage welfare dependency as it imposes high taxes on the earnings of welfare mothers and thereby discourages any attempt to supplement low earnings. It is designed to help the poor, and the benefits decrease as earnings increase. After four months at work, a woman faces a reduction of one dollar of benefits for every dollar she earns.

In addition to cash assistance and food stamps, the AFDC program provides special needs payments and emergency assistance to families with children. For example, states can make payments to recipients to help cover vital services, including heat in the winter, burial costs, and clothing. In 1989, thirty-two states provided special needs payments. The AFDC Emergency Assistance program provides one-time or short-term cash assistance to AFDC families to prevent evictions and utility shut-offs and cover first and last month's rent (Hess 1992a). The program is optional, and state governments that deliver it receive matching federal funds.

AFDC is funded jointly by federal and state governments, with the states paying on average 46 per cent of program costs (Hess 1992a). Benefits are not indexed to inflation, and in 1991 only eleven states raised benefits, while four adjusted for inflation. In 1991, state programs for the poor were cut sharply, and the greatest reductions were made to cash-assistance programs such as AFDC (ibid.). Benefits for AFDC continue to vary by state. In January 1992, for example, a family of three in Mississippi received U.S.$120 (Can. $153) a month, which was the lowest rate, while the same family received U.S.$924 (Can. $1,180) in Alaska (ibid.). The median benefit in 1991 for a family of three with no other income was U.S.$367 (Can. $468) a month, or just 42 per cent of the U.S. poverty line.

As we will see in chapter 4, low-income working parents with children at home may be eligible for the refundable Earned Income Tax Credit (EITC). This credit offsets the loss of AFDC and food stamps, but it does not provide 'base-level' assistance (Bolderson and Mabbett 1991).

The *Family Support Act* (1988), which became effective in October 1990, aimed to reduce welfare dependency by increasing economic self-sufficiency. The act is implemented through the JOBS program, which includes remedial education, job training, and supportive services. The target groups for JOBS are those who have been on welfare for more than six years and women whose youngest child is old enough to be within two years of losing eligibility for AFDC. Teen mothers are obliged to participate in JOBS if they are not high-school graduates but have left school, or if they have little work experience.

Mandatory provision for child care while mothers are in job training is a vital part of the act. The states receive matching federal funds which are not capped, unlike the JOBS program itself. The act also provides transitional child care services for up to twelve months for those who become employed, yet the shortage of quality child care undermines this provision. In addition, all AFDC recipients are eligible for free health services through Medicaid, and the act also provides a transitional one-year period for this benefit (Chilman 1992).

The act is complex and its requirements are numerous. Because it does not provide new resources for remedial education, job training, or placement, it places an administrative burden on the states. Problems arise in fund collection, as all funds must be administered through the state AFDC agency. The JOBS program requires that all trainees be present in 75 per cent of the sessions, and federal funding depends on this attendance, yet this is difficult both to monitor and to achieve (Chilman 1992).

The *Family Support Act* arose from prevalent sociocultural norms rejecting welfare recipients, from public policies that advocated 'work for relief,' and from attitudes that single mothers with children are deviants (ibid.). Although AFDC was originally designed to enable all mothers to care for their children at home, there was a shift in policy in 1967 and almost all mothers on AFDC were expected to be employed or in training programs. The 1980s also witnessed the strengthening of conservatism, in which free enterprise and the welfare backlash influenced ideas of personal achievement and materialism, thereby decreasing support for AFDC programs. While liberals saw the *Family Support Act* as offering opportunities for women to enter the workforce, conservatives sought to decrease welfare costs. By 1992, it was evident that states were facing a growing fiscal crisis and funding for the act was precarious (ibid.).

The *Budget Reconciliation Act* of October 1990 brightened the prospects of employed graduates of the JOBS program and their children, as well as of other 'working poor' families. In addition to the Earned Income Tax Credit, working poor families with children under one year old may receive an additional 5 per cent credit on their earned income, and in 1992, the maximum was U.S.$372 (Can. $475). In 1991, further health care assistance was extended to all children under six if they are members of low-income families (Chilman 1992).

The U.S. *Family Support Act* was a revision rather than a major reform. Benefits are still below the poverty line in every state, too much power is left to state governments, and local and state departments lack the resources and expertise to deal with the full range of their responsibilities. Like other U.S. anti-poverty schemes, the act is aimed at changing the social and psychological characteristics of people in poverty, instead of examining the inequities in the social, economic, and political systems. The act grew out of a combination of social, economic, and political trends that glorified the ideals of self-sufficiency and responsibility. At the same time, family life issues such as quality child care were often neglected (Chilman 1992).

Despite the lack of major policy change in the United States, there is considerable research on poverty and the conditions of mother-led families. Duncan and Rodgers (1990) indicated that between 1970 and 1985 the number of two-parent families dropped by 5 per cent while the number of lone-parent families more than doubled. Furthermore, one-third of all children and three-quarters of black children born between 1967 and 1969 did not live in intact two-parent families throughout childhood. Of those who spent time in lone-parent families, 54 per cent spent less than six years, while 10 per cent spent their entire childhood. Black children spend more time in lone-parent households than white children. In 1985, the proportion of families headed by mothers has been approximately three times higher for blacks (56.7 per cent) than for whites (17.8 per cent) and half of black children born into one-parent families remained there for their entire childhoods. Furthermore, children in two-parent families enjoy living standards more than 50 per cent higher and rates of poverty less than one-third as high as children in one-parent families.

For never-married mothers, economic status is lower than for divorced mothers, but in both cases low income is due to unemployment, low-paying jobs, and lack of child support (Duncan and Rodgers 1990). The economic status of mother-led families does not improve over time unless there is a remarriage or reconciliation. However, changes in family structure seemed to be less vital in leading women into poverty than the young age of motherhood.

Duncan and Rodgers (1990) argued that family structure is less important than labour market factors in accounting for the problems of children in lone-parent families. Lower income in lone-parent families can be explained by the reliance on a single income as well as the lower hourly wages for women and black workers. Furthermore, upon marriage dissolution, family income drops by about 40 per cent for women and their children, and economic problems account for many of the adverse effects of being raised in a lone-parent household. Duncan and Rodgers (1990) recommended transferring more of the absent father's income to children, increasing benefit levels of public transfer programs, and improving the wage rates of women who head lone-parent families.

Garfinkel and McLanahan (1986) examined the rising numbers of lone-parent families, the poorest of all demographic groups in the United States. One in every two lone-parent families is poor, and their poverty lasts longer and is more severe than in two-parent families. While many lone parents are dependent upon income transfer programs, many also work full time yet do not escape poverty. Garfinkel and McLanahan demonstrate that there is no significant correlation between raising welfare benefits and an increase in the number of lone mothers, as many U.S. critics have charged. During the Reagan era, cutbacks to public benefits reduced the incomes of mother-only families considerably in return for modest reductions in dependence and trivial reductions in the prevalence of lone mothers.

The 'War on Poverty' in the 1960s addressed issues like barriers to unemployment and community support but did not address the issue of adequate pay (Chilman, Cox, and Nunnally 1988). Later, the 1981 cuts by the Reagan administration caused hardship for many families, with little benefit to the government. The combination of work and welfare programs was not effective because of the lack of affordable child care, public health care, and adequate wages. At present, U.S. governments are focusing on enforcing child support payments; but this strategy is unlikely to decrease poverty, as most fathers of welfare-dependent children are living below the poverty line themselves.

Chilman, Cox, and Nunnally (1988) recommended that AFDC become a federal program with nation-wide standards for eligibility and benefit levels and that payments equal the poverty line. Work incentives rather than work requirements should be promoted, with allowance made for employment expenses and child care. Access to free or low-cost medical care is essential, as is improved access to affordable and regulated child care. Employment strategies must also be implemented at a national level. For the working poor, either minimum wages must rise or governments must provide wage subsidies and/or transfer payments (ibid.).

Early provisions of U.S. social welfare policy, such as protective labour laws and mothers' pensions, were designed to keep women out of the labour force and in a dependent position (Abramovitz 1989; Chilman 1992). The emergence of the modern welfare state involved government recognition of the responsibility to provide a minimum level of income for its citizens. Yet unemployment insurance and its employment programs focused primarily on male breadwinners and excluded most women. Eligibility requirements are still patterned after male labour force patterns, and benefits are determined by previous wages. The AFDC program was an attempt by government to replace the breadwinner role for women, but this program was funded at a lower level than all others. Many states developed eligibility requirements giving priority to one-parent families and 'suitable homes,' and classifying most mothers as 'employable' regardless of whether job opportunities were available (Abramovitz 1989). After considerable political pressure, many barriers to eligibility were removed in the 1960s and the numbers receiving aid rose significantly (ibid.). The 1981 cutbacks sent many women into low-paying and substandard jobs, reducing their standard of living. Over the years, AFDC has changed from an income support program to a mandatory work program.

Part of the poverty of lone mothers relates to discrimination in the labour market. The 1963 *Equal Pay Act* required employers to pay equal wages to men and women for work which demands equal skill, effort, and responsibility and is performed under similar working conditions. The law also prohibited wage reductions to create gender equality. Title VII of the *Civil Rights Act* (1964) prohibited discrimination in employment based on sex, race, colour, religion, or national origin for employers with twenty-five or more employees in the public and private sectors, employment agencies, labour unions, and organizations which administer apprenticeship programs.

In 1973, the *Equal Pay Act* was extended to cover professional and management employees, but a narrow interpretation has prevailed. Jobs had to be substantially equal, and the act did not allow the comparison of jobs of comparable worth. Since the 1970s, a number of unions and women's organizations have advocated equal pay for jobs of comparable worth (Goodwin 1984). Despite existing legislation, the U.S. labour force continues to be segregated, with women clustered in lower-paying and less secure positions.

The U.S. welfare system remains two-pronged: one prong is designed for labour force participants and another for those outside the labour force (Ellwood 1987). Furthermore, the best indicator of who will be poor in the United States is family structure. The poverty rate for two-parent families is not only considerably lower than for one-parent families, but their poverty is typically short-lived and closely tied to the state of the economy. Ellwood (1987) argued that governments should respond to this poverty through raising minimum wages, providing wage subsidies, initiating medical protection for all poor persons, and providing transitional support and job creation for the unemployed. On the other hand, poverty in one-parent families tends to be long-term, and 62 per cent of poor lone parents stay poor for their entire lives. While some measures mentioned above would help raise these families out of poverty, lone parents profit less from an upswing in the economy because family responsibilities interfere with full-time work. The current system of benefits provides two choices for lone mothers: to work full time or to remain on welfare. Part-time work, which could be a solution, is not economically feasible unless supplemented by government benefits. While the U.S. welfare system may prevent absolute poverty for some families, it does not address the underlying causes of poverty or resolve the problems of moving from welfare to employment. To do so would require increases to minimum wages, a refundable child tax credit, a uniform child support assurance system, and well-funded educational and training programs (Ellwood 1988).

In addition to a segregated labour force in which women tend to receive lower wages and benefits, lack of affordable child care, lack of statutory maternity benefits and unemployment insurance, and low unionization rates undermine women as earners. Furthermore, high divorce rates and poor enforcement mechanisms leave the onus of family support on mothers in many lone-parent families. As well, an ethos of equal opportunity rather than equality of outcomes and a philosophy of individualism work against improving the family policies and the economic status of women and their children in the United States.

CONCLUSION

Although all the countries studied provide social assistance to low-income parents, the eligibility requirements, benefit levels, administration, and basic philosophy behind the programs vary considerably. The main difference in eligibility relates to whether mothers with young children at home are considered to be 'employable.' Sweden and the United States are two examples of countries which encourage mothers with young children to enter the labour force; but while Sweden provides many supports to assist these mothers to combine work and family life, the United States does not. Britain and the Netherlands accept lower rates of labour force participation for mothers with preschool children precisely because they believe that these mothers provide important child care services at home.

While employment has increased for all women in Britain, it has not increased for lone mothers. Low labour force participation by lone mothers can be attributed to the availability of only marginal jobs, lack of day care facilities, and government programs that fail to offer any incentive to low-income lone mothers to supplement their incomes through employment (Hardey and Crow 1991). In comparison to Britain, lone parents in France are better off financially both in absolute and in relative terms. Eighty per cent of lone parents in France are in the labour force, although many work part time. A highly developed system of public day care, legislation which protects jobs during extended parental leave, and benefits which supplement rather than replace part-time work all facilitate labour force participation. In addition, France's history of left-wing parties, its Catholic background, and its long preoccupation with declining birth rates have encouraged more generous family programs (J. Baker 1986).

Comparing the generosity of benefits is not quite as simple as it seems, because low-income families may also be eligible for direct services (such as child care) and other social programs (unemployment or health insurance). Eligibility rules usually require recipients to retain low incomes and few assets, although the maximum level of capital varies substantially among countries. Germany is an example of a country which expects low-income parents to own very little, while Australia allows home ownership plus additional capital for recipients of the sole-parent benefit.

Expecting low-income parents to deplete their resources before qualifying for social assistance is a more punitive stance than allowing savings or home ownership. Parents who deplete their assets would clearly experience more difficulty in rebuilding capital after moving off social assistance. Allowing some savings would assist low-income parents to respond to financial emergencies with less stress and less dependence on government (Sherraden 1991).

One reason for the poverty of lone mothers relates to labour market discrimination and job segregation. Since the early 1950s, laws have been introduced in many jurisdictions requiring employers to give men and women equal pay for equal work. However, these laws were generally ineffective because the labour force remained segregated and men and women typically performed different kinds of jobs. In recent years, legislation has focused on equal pay for work of comparable value, and the principle implementation routes have been regulatory and administrative agencies, civil litigation, and collective bargaining. Yet enforcement mechanisms are not always adequate. For example, litigation is a complaint-based case-by-case approach, and is expensive, time-consuming, and subject to judicial discretion (Goodwin 1984).

Some researchers suggest that full employment is the single most important policy goal that has helped Swedish programs to alleviate women's dual burden of family earner and child care provider (C. Adams and Winston 1980). Swedish policies have been characterized by a simultaneous effort to promote parenting and full employment for both men and women. During the 1930s, declining birth rates and the 'population crisis' led to public policy encouraging families to procreate without economic burden. Unlike pronatalist policies in other countries, Sweden's policies did not confine women to the motherhood role. There has been a willingness to use social policy to advance economic goals. With relatively high social spending, social programs are financed through higher taxes on personal income, payrolls, and sales.

Sweden has also spent less on passive labour market polices such as unemployment insurance, and more on active programs such as job creation and retraining (Rehn 1985). Employment programs are coordinated through a National Labour Market Board, and both labour and management are represented. Sweden has been successful in keeping its level of unemployment low, but has been less successful in preventing inflation in the process. By the 1980s, 8 per cent of the Swedish government budget and 2 to 3 per cent of the gross domestic product were being spent on labour market measures, with the largest share going into retraining and relocation. No other country came close in terms of active labour market policy (Swenson 1989).

In the United States, policies have stressed the health and welfare of business before workers, and social policy tends to be reactive to distressful situations. U.S. policies have been based on the ideology that business is stimulated by tax cuts rather than increased spending. Furthermore, family policy remains a state responsibility, resulting in a fragmented system which inhibits reform (C. Adams and Winston 1980).

Families in Canada and the United States are far more likely than those in the European countries studied to be living in poverty, especially if there is only one parent present and that parent is the mother. Part of the differences in family poverty relate to the young age at which U.S. women become pregnant, often before they have completed their education and developed job skills or work experience. In addition, many unmarried mothers in the United States live alone rather than with the child's father; rates of cohabitation are higher in Sweden. However, none of these factors explains the differentials in poverty as well as the redistributive effect of government programs.

Australia is an example of a country which has provided a pension to sole parents living on low incomes, but this pension has had its opponents. Conservatives have argued that targeting sole parents for government support could discourage marriage and encourage separation and divorce. Sole parents are the fastest-growing family type in Australia, and 74 per cent are receiving income support (Lambert 1994). In the long run, conservatives have argued, increased marriage breakdown would disadvantage more children economically and would necessitate continued social assistance to these families. Consequently, redefining some mothers as 'employable' and moving them off social assistance has been one policy solution to rising rates of sole parents on welfare.

The European countries in our study are far more likely to target children and lone mothers for special government benefits. They have recognized that when mothers are abandoned to market forces without government protection, leave provisions, or subsidized child care services, these mothers often cannot compete with employees who do not become pregnant, have no family responsibilities, and are free to move to find a better position. In addition, several European countries have focused on policies to promote full employment and have provided relatively generous legislation for wage protection, benefits, and leave.

Parents are poor because they cannot find work or jobs with sufficient pay to support their children. In some cases, a parent's entry into the labour force is further complicated by the presence of young children, the lack of affordable child care, low minimum wages, high tax-back rates for government benefits if the parent takes on extra work, and little time off to deal with family responsibilities. In the next chapter, an examination of tax concessions and allowances for families with dependent children will further highlight the variations among these eight countries.

4

Child allowances and
family tax concessions

INTRODUCTION[1]

What political, social, and economic factors influence government decisions to provide child and family benefits and to choose different delivery mechanisms? Do countries with universal child allowances provide more generous benefits than those that focus on tax concessions? In this chapter, I attempt to answer these questions by examining the development of family or child allowances and various tax concessions for families with dependent children in Canada and the other countries in the study.

Most governments in this study provide a combination of child allowances and tax concessions to compensate parents partially for the financial costs of child-rearing. Some governments clearly prefer either universal allowances or targeted tax concessions. Canada is one example of a country that used to offer both tax concessions and a family allowance, but since January 1993 it has offered only tax concessions. In most Western countries, there has been a growing integration of tax and transfer systems over the past decade (McFate 1991, n4).

CHILD AND FAMILY ALLOWANCES

Child or family allowances are government payments usually delivered through weekly, bi-monthly, or monthly cheques to the mother or official guardian of dependent children. Eligibility is typically extended to all children of school age, although some countries prolong the age for students or children with disabilities. Other countries, such as France, offer this benefit only for the second and subsequent child. Benefits are usually tax free, although they often count as income for the purposes of other social programs.

A universal child allowance has many advantages not available to income-tested or means-tested allowances (such as social assistance). When universal benefits are provided for all children under a certain age (usually sixteen or eighteen), no needy children are missed. Administrative costs are lower for universal than for income-tested allowances, because a cheque is simply sent out to all families with dependent children without any investigation or monitoring of the family's financial circumstances. A universal benefit does not create the social stigma that is often associated with targeted welfare programs. Because benefits do not depend on earnings, income is supplemented rather than replaced, which means that there are no work disincentives and financial uncertainty is reduced for families near the poverty line (Garfinkel 1992). In addition, a universal child allowance indicates social or public support for child-bearing and child-rearing, which some governments wish to reinforce as fertility rates decline.

The practice of mailing the family allowance cheque to mothers has been praised by feminists, who note that full-time homemakers may not have control over any other household income. While policy makers have assumed that family income is shared by all family members regardless of who earns it, research has proven this assumption to be unwarranted (Pahl 1989; Hobson 1990). When men are sole breadwinners, they do not always share their earnings equally with other family members. Wives often complain that their husbands misspend 'family income' on their own activities, leaving insufficient money for food or children's clothing. Despite the fact that husbands tend to control the majority of the family income, wives have retained responsibility for buying food and children's clothing in most homes (Marshall 1993).

The main disadvantage of a universal child allowance is the higher cost of providing money for all children rather than only for those whose parents are in financial need (D. Meyer, Phillips, and Maritato 1991). Some governments have resolved this issue by taxing back a portion of the benefit from higher-income families, as Canada did before abolishing the family allowance. However, there may be political disadvantages to providing so-called 'universal' benefits and then quietly taxing them back, especially during periods of recession. It may appear to voters that the government either is giving with one hand and taking away with the other or is overspending by providing an allowance to non-needy families. Consequently, conservative governments, which tend to focus on using public money for the 'deserving poor,' may be tempted to use targeted tax benefits rather than universal allowances. Using tax benefits for children also has disadvantages, however, which will be discussed later in this chapter.

Countries which offer children's allowances usually do not provide tax deductions for children at the same time (Kamerman and Kahn 1983a; D. Meyer, Phillips, and Maritato 1991), although some countries offer both. Canada, for example, offered several different tax deductions and credits along with the family allowance until December 1992, when the family allowance was replaced by an income-tested tax benefit. France offers generous family allowances, and has also developed an income tax system in which larger families pay far less tax than smaller families.

Among the eight countries studied, six now provide a child allowance and in five countries it is universal. Although the United States provides tax deductions and welfare payments for low-income families, it has never developed a universal family allowance. Germany targeted its family allowance for second and subsequent children in 1982, and Australia began to target the benefit for all children in 1987. While all Canadian parents with children at home received a family allowance cheque from 1945 to 1992, it was replaced by a targeted tax benefit starting in January 1993.

Of the six countries that provide a child allowance, five finance it through general revenue (gained through various kinds of taxes). France has developed a different system, financing child allowances through payroll taxes paid by contributions from employers and employees regardless of parental status.

As Table 4.1 indicates, most of the countries studied developed family allowances during the 1940s, although France implemented its program as early as 1932. Some countries were responding to the decline in marriage and birth rates during the 1930s as well as the high death rates during the Second World War. In addition, the cost of living increased after the war, which led to a demand for higher wages or government income assistance to families. Table 4.1 also indicates that four of the five European countries provide higher amounts per child with increasing family size. In addition, most of the European countries continue to offer universal allowances despite the recession.

The value of child allowances varies considerably among the countries studied. According to Kamerman and Kahn (1988c), the value of a fam-

TABLE 4.1
Family allowances: initiation and 1993 eligibility in eight industrialized countries

Country	Date of first legislation	Universality (1993)	Variation by family size
Australia	1941, 1947	Not since 1987	Yes
Canada	1944, 1992	Not since 1993	No, except in Quebec
France	1932	Yes	Yes
Germany	1954	Not since 1982	Yes
Netherlands	1946, 1951	Yes	Yes
Sweden	1947	Yes	Yes
United Kingdom	1945	Yes	No
United States	None	—	—

SOURCES: Wennemo 1992, 206; Hohn 1987, 459–81; U.S. Dept of HHS 1992.

ily or child allowance for families with two children is usually in the range of 5 per cent to 10 per cent of the average production worker's wage. Oxley (1987) compared the provision of universal family assistance in sixteen industrialized countries, including Canada, using 1984 data. She found that most of the countries studied, with the exception of the United States and Denmark, provided universal cash assistance to families with children. Since, the time of Oxley's study, however, Denmark has revised its policy and now provides a universal child allowance, and Canada has eliminated its universal benefit. In 1984, Canada was also one of only two of the sixteen countries which taxed family allowances. There are differences among the countries in how a dependent child is defined, who is covered, the level of assistance, payment rates in relation to age, supplements, and taxation.

As one of several measures, Oxley calculated the value of universal family assistance for a two-child family as a proportion of the average production worker's wage. In this comparison, Canada ranked quite low, at 3.3 per cent, compared to the 9 per cent average. The other countries in the present study were rated as follows: Australia, 4.4 per cent; France, 9.7 per cent; Germany, 2.5 per cent; Netherlands, 13.1 per cent; Sweden, 10.7 per cent; the United Kingdom, 13.1 per cent; and the United States, 0 per cent. Oxley's study found that most family allowance payments are not indexed to the cost of living and, as a result, are declining in real value. Despite the importance of such a comparison,

Oxley advises that family allowance benefits alone are not a sufficient measure of the relative welfare of children; health services, education, and child care services should also be taken into account.

For the present study, the value of family allowances in 1975 and again in 1991 was calculated for each country, using the Canadian family allowance as a point of comparison.[2] Table 4.2 shows the national variations and how substantially the value has changed throughout those decades in most of the countries. The value of Canada's 1991 benefit appeared relatively low, with France's allowance more than six times higher and Sweden's more than four times higher than Canada's.

The increase in the value of the family allowance from 1975 to 1991 was slower in Canada than in the other jurisdictions. While the value of Canada's benefit doubled from 1975 to 1991, the United Kingdom's child allowance increased almost ten times during the same period, while Australia's increased nine times, and Germany's about seven times. Despite rapid inflation, Canada's family allowance declined in comparison to the benefit in all the other jurisdictions studied. In part, this can be explained by the introduction of the refundable Child Tax Credit, which I will discuss later in this chapter.

Since December 1992, Canada no longer provides a universal child benefit. For that reason, it is worth examining this recent policy change, as well as the original idea behind the family allowance and how it evolved over the years.

TABLE 4.2
Comparison of the annual value of family allowances in Canadian dollars, 1975 and 1991

Country	1975		1991	
	Family allowance (Can. $)	Ratio to Canadian FA	Family allowance (Can. $)	Ratio to Canadian FA
Australia	$ 103	21	$ 934	115
Canada	480	100	814	100
France	1,527	318	5,336	656
Germany	200	42	1,419	174
Netherlands	652	136	2,640	324
Sweden	702	146	3,785	465
United Kingdom	181	38	1,725	212
United States	n/a	n/a	n/a	n/a

SOURCE: Calculated for this study, based on figures from: U.S. Dept of HHS 1976 and 1992.

FAMILY ALLOWANCES IN CANADA

The family allowance (FA) was first paid in 1945 as a universal benefit to assist families with child-bearing costs. As the Second World War drew to an end, policy makers became concerned not only about disintegrating family life and low birth rates, but also about declining wages relative to the rising cost of living. At the end of the First World War, considerable social unrest and labour militancy had resulted from the unemployment and underemployment of returning soldiers, as well as from the rising cost of living (Cuneo 1979). In an attempt to avoid unrest after the Second World War, Parliament introduced the Family Allowance Program as an economic measure to help increase the spending power of Canadian families (Armitage 1988, 171). The design and philosophy of the Canadian family allowance was derived from social policy reviews such as the British Beveridge Report in 1942 and, especially, the Canadian Marsh Report[3] in 1943.

Ursel (1992, 195) further argues that family allowances were initiated by the federal Finance Department after years of wartime wage restraints, in order to curb labour's demand for wage increases and growing threats of unionization. The Canadian cabinet supported the bill when it became clear that if the government did not contribute some support to counteract rising family costs, the country would experience labour militancy and increasing wages. The bill passed unanimously in Parliament in August 1944.

Administered by the National Department of Health and Welfare, the Family Allowance Program delivered a monthly cheque to the main caregiver of the children, usually the mother. A set amount was paid for each child, initially under the age of sixteen and later under eighteen. When the allowance was first paid in 1945, it was worth 4.7 per cent of the average family income. This declined to 1.8 per cent in 1971, but after being tied to the consumer price index for much of the time between 1974 to 1986, the value increased to 3.2 per cent of the average family income by 1986 (Battle 1988). The amount per recipient family decreased as a percentage of average family income partly because the benefit was not always indexed to the rising cost of living while wages increased, but also because the number of children per family declined (ibid.). In addition, a larger amount used to be paid for older children.

In 1973, the *Family Allowance Act* was amended, and the new act was implemented in 1974. Benefits were increased significantly and were paid at a flat rate rather than varying with the age of the child. Immigrant families became eligible as soon as they were granted legal immigrant status instead of having to wait for one year.[4] The 1973 changes made FA taxable income and indexed the benefit level to the consumer price index. They also allowed the provinces to vary the amount of benefit according to the age of the children and/or the number of children in the family (Canada, Health and Welfare 1974).

Athough most Canadian families received about $35 a month for each child under eighteen in 1992, there were always several provincial variations in the amounts paid. For example, Alberta varied the amount by the age of the child, with parents receiving more money for an older child. Quebec supplemented the federal family allowance and provided higher amounts for older children, but also higher amounts for each subsequent child to a maximum of three. For example, in 1992, the FA rates in Quebec were $83.02 for a third or subsequent child under age eleven and $91.58 for a third or subsequent child aged twelve to seventeen (Hess 1992a, 28). When the federal government abolished the FA in December 1992, Quebec retained its own family allowance.

In 1979, the value of the Canadian family allowance was reduced with the introduction of the refundable Child Tax Credit, which will be discussed in more detail below. In 1986, the FA was partially de-indexed, meaning that an increase was given only if the rate of inflation was more than 3 per cent. Except in Quebec, the FA was treated as taxable income, and up to 40 per cent of the value of the benefit could be taxed back from higher-income earners. By 1989, however, the tax-back rate reached 100 per cent for families with net incomes over $50,000, which critics called 'the clawback' (National Council of Welfare 1992a). Although the FA cost the federal government $2.8 billion in 1991–2, one-third of this cost was recovered in federal and provincial taxes (Hess 1992a, 27).

In May 1992, the Conservative government under Brian Mulroney introduced Bill C-80, which created the new Child Tax Benefit. In order to finance this benefit, the government combined money from the former family allowance and the Child Tax Credits into a new benefit targeted to families with middle or lower incomes. The new benefit is non-taxable and partially indexed (when inflation is over 3 per cent) to the rising cost of living. In 1993, the maximum monthly payment was $85 per child under eighteen and was paid to families with a net income of $25,921 or less. Families with net incomes up to $70,981 receive partial benefits, while those with incomes over that amount do not receive any child benefit.

In addition to the monthly benefit, a supplement is paid to the 'working poor' of $500 per family each year, regardless of the number of children. This amount was not extended to welfare recipients because, the federal government argued, working poor families have greater expenses than those not in the workforce. It was assumed, however, that the real reason for withholding this amount from welfare recipients was an issue of jurisdiction. The federal government was worried that the provincial governments would view this new income as an opportunity to reduce social assistance payments. Over the past few years, the cost of social programs has gradually shifted from the federal to provincial governments (Hess 1992a), and provincial governments are examining all possible ways of reducing expenditures.

Although the Child Tax Benefit will undoubtedly save money for the government, many researchers have argued that it will do little in the short and long term to reduce child poverty (Battle 1992b; Kesselman 1993; M. Baker, 1994c). In order to create this benefit, no new money was added. Furthermore, it removed the recognition that child-bearing is a social responsibility, an assumption apparent in family policies from the European countries studied as well as from Australia (Kesselman 1993; Ontario Fair Tax Commission 1993).

Although the Canadian Family Allowance Program was abolished in 1993, Quebec retained its own family allowance program as well as a variety of other family-related policies. The most controversial is the allowance to parents of newborns, which provides $500 for the first child, $1,000 for the second child, and $8,000[5] for third and subsequent children (M. Baker 1994b). This allowance has been controversial for several reasons. In addition to helping parents with the cost of child-bearing, it apparently was inspired by nationalist sentiments concerning declining birth rates and the erosion of Quebec's power within the Canadian federation. The newborn allowance provides financial incentives to reproduce at the same time that unemployment rates remain higher in Quebec than in most other provinces and social assistance benefits have been severely cut. Many argue that this allowance does not counteract the forces inhibiting larger families: the shortage of child care services, the high cost of living, and the difficulty of combining paid work and child-rearing (Messier 1985; Le Bourdais and Marcil-Gratton 1994; M. Baker 1994b).

Universal family allowances were abolished in Canada while Canadians were preoccupied with concern over the potential separation of Quebec and the 1992 referendum on constitutional change. For this reason, political reaction was not as strong as some expected. Canada is not the only country which has eliminated universality from child allowances, however, as Germany and Australia have already made this change.

THE DELIVERY OF FAMILY BENEFITS: TAX BENEFITS VERSUS TRANSFERS

Most industrialized countries provide income tax concessions for parents with dependent children, for lone parents, or for working parents requiring child care services. In some countries these concessions are offered in the form of credits (which reduce the amount of income tax payable) and in others they are deductions (which lower taxable income). Credits are usually considered to be more beneficial to families because their relative value is higher for those with lower marginal tax rates. If tax credits are refundable, they can be used by those who pay no taxes because their income is either too low or comes from a source that is exempt from taxes. A tax exemption means that no income tax is payable on income from a particular source. In some jurisdictions, for example, family allowances are exempt from income tax.

Tax concessions, such as exemptions, deductions, and credits, are sometimes referred to as negative income tax. They are a way for the government to give back tax money to the people which cancels out income tax paid. Negative income tax transfers have become an important part of the social welfare system in a number of industrialized countries, including Canada (McFate 1991).

Although governments finance social programs through some form of taxation, an income tax system is more than a way to raise revenue. It also can be used to redistribute income from higher- to lower-income families, or from individuals or childless couples to families with dependent children. As the vast majority of residents are required to file an income tax form and most must pay tax, the government has access to personal information about income, expenses, and family status which easily can be used to target family benefits.

The choice of delivery mechanism for social benefits, which is derived from political philosophy, can be very consequential. For example, it can have significance for the objectives of the policy, the conditions under which people gain access to benefits, the number of eligible people claiming the benefit, the efficiency with which the policy is implemented, the roles of different agencies of the government, and the configuration of influence around the policy.

Tax concessions or expenditures compared to public transfers have a number of advantages and disadvantages from the government's viewpoint (OECD 1985). Tax expenditures are less visible to the public than transfers, as they do not appear on public accounts and are not as open to parliamentary scrutiny. When the Canadian government abolished the family allowance and created the new Child Tax Benefit, for example, the appearance was given that the federal budget had been cut by about $2 billion, and that the overall proportion of the economy taken up by government had decreased. In fact, both government expenditures and revenues decreased (M. Baker, Hunsley, and Michetti 1993).

Tax credits can be closely controlled and targeted when they are used for basic income supplement purposes. Income tests can be easily administered, and without the stigma of other application systems. Because the tax department tends to have the most extensive access to information of any government department, it can gain a more comprehensive picture of the income of individuals or families than departments which simply administer benefits. For similar reasons, these benefits can usually be administered at a cost savings, as the tax form is already used and processed. This mechanism also brings more people into the tax net, as a return is required for the benefit, although Canadians are not required by law to file an income tax form if they do not have taxable income.

The use of a tax mechanism also changes the dynamics of influence, both within and outside the government. In the Canadian case, the former family allowance was delivered by Health and Welfare Canada but the new Child Tax Benefit is delivered by Revenue Canada. Since tax policy is generally within the purview of the minister of finance, the relative power of that portfolio is increased over social policy. At the same time, tax accountants, lawyers, and business lobbyists now have a greater say in the social policy field. The Finance Department consults constantly with the private finance community, and the social policy tax credits now are more exposed to their scrutiny (M. Baker, Hunsley, and Michetti 1993).

COMPARING TAXATION SYSTEMS

It is difficult to compare the relative value of income tax concessions for families with dependent children without examining the entire tax system of each of the various countries. In addition, some governments offer generous child allowances or pensions for lone parents instead of tax concessions. In fact, we can roughly divide countries into two main categories: those which rely mainly on tax concessions and those which rely on social insurance programs to support families with children. Those using social insurance programs generally have lower rates of child poverty and a more equitable distribution of income (Kamerman and Kahn 1988c; McFate 1991). This suggests that using tax concessions to assist families with children is seen by governments as an alternative to major structural reform, which would more effectively redistribute income.

The unit of taxation varies among the countries in this study, with most using the individual as the unit, some the couple, and one the entire family. Top marginal and average tax rates also vary, as Table 4.3 indicates; but Canada's top marginal tax rates and average effective tax rate for a two-child family earning the average production worker's wage were moderate compared to those of the other countries studied.

Using both government taxation statistics and the Luxembourg Income Study data from the mid- to late 1980s, researchers have analysed the combined effect of government taxes and transfers and noted vast discrepancies among countries (McFate 1991; Smeeding, O'Higgins, and Rainwater 1990). In some European countries, tax concessions or allowances are so generous that families with dependent children may be

TABLE 4.3
Comparative income tax statistics

Country	Unit of taxation 1992	Top marginal income tax rate 1992	Average effective tax rate paid by 2-child family at APWW,* 1989
		%	%
Australia	Individual	47	13.3
Canada	Individual	51	6.3
France	Family	57	−7.2
Germany	Couple	53	5.7
Netherlands	Individual	60	−1.6
Sweden	Individual	54	20.3
United Kingdom	Individual	40	1.8
United States	Couple/ individual	31	7.3

* Combining the effect of taxes paid with benefits received, at the income of the average production worker, as a percentage of gross earnings
SOURCES: Adapted from Pechman and Engelhardt 1990; OECD 1992b, 44.

receiving more money from the government than they are paying in taxes. Even excluding transfers, the redistributional effect of the income tax system is considerably greater in Sweden than in Canada (Aguilar and Gustafsson 1987; Pechman and Engelhardt 1990).

Table 4.4 compares the income tax and social security contributions as a percentage of gross earnings paid by employees with two children and an average production worker's wage in each of the countries in 1991. From this table, we can conclude that Canada's income and payroll taxes are moderate compared to those of other countries. However, since these tables were compiled, some countries have created or expanded sales taxes, value-added taxes, and goods and services taxes, and such expenditure taxes are not included in these calculations. Table 4.4 also compares take-home pay plus cash transfers as a percentage of gross earnings in the eight countries, and indicates that Canada again appears moderate compared to the other countries. When we examine Table 4.5, however, we note that Canada's tax transfers are not as effective in reducing poverty as they are in most European countries.

Before examining these data, we need to look at the details of the development of tax concessions for families with children, first in Canada and then in the various countries included in the study.

TAX CONCESSIONS FOR FAMILIES IN CANADA

In Canada, the unit of taxation is the individual, and both federal and provincial governments require income taxes to be paid. Most provinces simply calculate their income tax as a percentage of federal tax, although they may offer provincial concessions (such as rent rebates). Residents of Quebec are required to file a separate Quebec tax form with different deductions and credits, as well as the federal form.

When it passed the *Income Tax Act* in 1918, the Canadian government built in several tax exemptions related to family status. These acknowledged that married breadwinners with dependants have additional expenses which unmarried employees do not have. Implicitly, the legislation recognized the social value of marriage and child-rearing, as well as the government's obligation to support these activities.

Before discussing the details of these family tax benefits, it is important to understand the difference between a tax exemption/deduction and a credit, and the difference between a refundable and a non-refundable credit. Canadian income tax calculations begin with total income, which could include employment income, interest income, business income,

TABLE 4.4

Cross-national comparison of taxation as a percentage of gross earnings, 1991 (for employees with two children and an income of an average production worker)*

Country	Personal income tax	Social security contributions	Take-home pay plus cash transfers
Australia	16.7	1.3	85.7
Canada	12.5	4.6	85.7
France	1.0	17.1	88.8
Germany	8.7	18.2	77.6
Netherlands	10.0	28.3	68.9
Sweden	28.0	0.0	83.0
United Kingdom	15.5	7.6	83.5
United States	11.3	7.7	81.0

* Excluding the effects of non-standard tax reliefs
SOURCE: OECD 1992b, Tables 1, 3, 4: 44, 46, 47

TABLE 4.5

Poverty rates of non-elderly families before and after taxes and transfers, mid-1980s

Country	Poverty rate* before taxes and transfers**	Poverty rate* after taxes and transfers**
Canada	17.4	13.9
France	20.4	9.9
West Germany	10.7	6.8
Netherlands	19.9	7.6
Sweden	15.3	8.6
United Kingdom	23.2	12.5
United States	18.0	18.1

* Percentage of all households with heads twenty to fifty-five years old who had incomes of less than 50 per cent of the adjusted national median income
** Includes all public assistance transfers
SOURCE: McFate 1991, Table 2 and Figure 1.

and taxable capital gains. From this total income, certain deductions are allowed, such as child care expenses, union dues, and moving expenses, to give the net income. From net income, further deductions are allowed, such as capital losses and capital gains deductions, to give the taxable income. When we know our taxable income, we can calculate the amount of federal tax we owe or look it up in the tax tables.[6]

There are three federal marginal tax rates which vary the rate of tax depending on annual income (OECD 1992b). In 1991, the first $28,784 was taxed at 17 per cent; anything between $28,784 and $57,568 was taxed at 26 per cent; and income above $57,568 was taxed at 29 per cent. Non-refundable credits are deducted from the amount of federal tax payable. Canadians are also expected to pay a federal surtax and provincial income tax.

In most provinces, the provincial tax payable is about half of the basic federal tax, but this varies by province (from a low of 45 per cent in the Northwest Territories to a high of 51 per cent in Quebec for the 1991 tax year) (Price Waterhouse 1992). In addition, there may also be a provincial income tax surcharge. From the total tax payable, refundable credits are calculated; these may be refunded to the tax filer even if he or she is not required to pay any income tax.

In conclusion, a tax deduction reduces taxable income, on which federal tax is calculated. The combined effect of the federal and provincial taxes and surtaxes means that as long as a person pays some taxes, a deduction is worth more when income is higher. On the other hand, a credit directly reduces the amount of tax payable. If the credit is refundable, the person may receive a refund from the government if no tax is owed. Most of the Canadian tax credits are calculated before the basic federal tax, so they reduce provincial tax payable as well (since provincial tax is usually calculated as a percentage of federal tax payable, except in Quebec).

The discussion of tax concessions in Canada is complicated because, in 1988, Canada converted a number of tax deductions to credits. While critics argued that the reform distributed benefits in a more progressive manner, most families suffered a substantial loss in benefits. Furthermore, the poorest of families were no better off, because family allowance benefits were only partially indexed (Battle 1988). Four years later, the same government combined all child tax credits with the family allowance to create the Child Tax Benefit, which is targeted to middle- and lower-income families.

The former non-refundable Child Tax Credit

In 1918 when the *Income Tax Act* was first introduced, a deduction for taxpayers with children under sixteen was built into the system. With tax reform in 1988, this deduction was changed to a credit, but it is worth discussing some details of the former deduction. Apart from the years 1942 to 1946, during which the deduction was abandoned, the value of this benefit increased sporadically with the cost of living. It is interesting to note that during the war years, when government money was tight, child benefits were eliminated. From 1974 until 1983, under mainly Liberal governments, the child tax deduction was fully indexed.

The former child tax deduction (CTD) used to consist of two parts: one for families with children under the age of eighteen and one for older children. In 1984, the CTD was worth $710 before it was gradually reduced by the Conservative government to $470 in 1988 and then to match the value of the family allowance in 1989. The CTD was reduced allegedly because it benefited higher-income earners, and the Conservative government favoured targeting most family benefits to middle- and lower-income earners.

In 1988, the CTD was converted to the non-refundable Child Tax Credit. In the 1991 tax year, the value of this benefit for children under eighteen was $69 for each of the first two children and $138 for third and subsequent children. The credit was available for older children only if they had disabilities. In the 1991 tax year, the value of the credit for older children with disabilities was $262 (Hess 1992b; Torjman 1994).

The Married Credit

In 1918, a tax deduction was also available for employees with dependent wives. Like the original child tax deduction, this concession rose sporadically with the cost of living and was converted to a non-refundable credit in 1988. Before tax reform in 1988, the deduction was worth $3,666 on federal income tax.

Changing the married benefit to a credit could have meant an improvement for lower-income earners, but the government reduced the actual value in the conversion (Battle 1988). The 1993 value for federal taxes was $915 compared to the former credit of $69 per child (OECD 1992b). If we combine provincial and federal tax savings, it was worth $1,418 (Torjman 1994, 71).

The question which remains in many people's minds is why the government considers a dependent spouse to be worth so much more than a dependent child. The Married Credit is not based on caregiving or even housework, but merely on financial dependency. Although many 'dependent' spouses (usually wives) provide useful services for their spouses (husbands) and children, few would argue that they are fulfilling an important function for the government or society unless they are caring for children or other dependants. Therefore, this tax concession could be viewed as a relic from the era of the male-as-sole-breadwinner family. Although a suggestion was made by a female cabinet minister (Judy Erola) to abolish this benefit in 1983, the reaction was strong and negative from conservative women's groups and politicians (M. Baker 1990b).

The Equivalent to Married Credit

As with the Married Credit, this benefit was designed as a deduction to equalize the benefits of one-parent and two-parent families, or to provide horizontal equity for families with equivalent incomes but different structures. Like the other deductions, it was converted to a credit in 1988.

The Equivalent to Married Credit was worth the same as the Married Credit in 1993, $915 in federal tax savings and $1,418 in combined provincial/federal tax savings, and is partially indexed to the cost of living (Torjman 1994, 71). New rules, in effect since 1993, attempt to treat common-law partners more like married couples, and prohibit lone parents from claiming the credit if they are in such a relationship (Townson 1993).

The former refundable Child Tax Credit

In 1978, this benefit was initiated by the federal Liberal government to assist lower- and middle-income families with the costs of child-rearing. During the 1970s, the cost of living was rising rapidly and concern was growing about poverty among young families.

Eligibility for the former refundable Child Tax Credit was based on net family income, and the amount varied by the number of children per family. For most families, it was paid once a year with income tax returns. For families with incomes under $16,810, it was paid in two instalments, to assist parents with the heavier expenses for the new school year and the coming winter. This benefit was administered by Revenue Canada and cost the government $2.1 billion in 1989 (Hess 1992b, 29).

In 1988, the income limit (net family income) for receiving the maximum benefit was reduced from $26,330 to $23,500. In this way, the government was targeting the benefit even more than it had in the past. In other words, fewer families became eligible for the maximum payment, which was $585 per child under the age of nineteen for the 1991 tax year (Hess 1992b, 30; OECD 1992b).

A supplement to the credit was available to families with children under the age of seven, provided that no child care expenses were claimed on income tax for that year. The amount of the supplement was $207 in 1991 (Hess 1992b, 30). This small supplement was granted after parents in one-income families complained that more tax concessions were being given to two-income families, and that parents who cared for their own children at home were being short-changed by government benefits. If both parents are in the labour force, they can deduct their child care expenses, and as we will discuss below, this deduction is relatively valuable.

The Child Care Expenses Deduction

For the 1993 tax year, child care expenses for working parents can be deducted up to a maximum of $5,000 per child under seven and $3,000 per child aged seven to fourteen (Townson 1993). Although most deductions were changed to credits in 1988, the Child Care Expenses Deduction remained a tax deduction more useful to middle-class than working-class families. However, subsidized child care spaces are set aside for low-income families, although there are more families that need them than spaces available (Burke, Crompton, Jones, and Nessner 1991).

Recent changes: the 1993 Child Tax Benefit

As I mentioned above, many tax deductions were changed to credits in 1988, including the former deduction for dependent children and dependent spouses, but not the Child Care Expenses Deduction. Despite these changes, the credit for a dependent spouse was still worth about fourteen times more than the credit for a dependent child (Baker 1992).

From 1988 to 1993, Canada retained both refundable and non-refundable tax credits for dependent children and a non-refundable credit for dependent spouses. In January 1993, however, the child tax credits and the family allowance were rolled into one income-tested credit, the Child Tax Benefit, which is not taxable and not fully indexed. It is worth a maximum of $85 per month and is administered by Revenue Canada (Townson 1993).

There are no special income tax benefits for lone parents in Canada except the Equivalent to Married Credit, and no federal allowance for lone parents. For low-income tax filers, the federal government provides a refundable Goods and Services Tax Credit. In addition, employees are required to contribute to social insurance programs (the Canada/Quebec Pension Plan and the Unemployment Insurance Fund). For the average production worker, this amounts to 4.6 per cent of gross earnings per year, as indicated in Table 4.4 (OECD 1992b, 46).

CHILD ALLOWANCES AND FAMILY TAX CONCESSIONS IN OTHER COUNTRIES

Australia

In 1941, Australia introduced a family allowance for families with two or more children. In 1947, this allowance was made universal and paid to all mothers with dependent children (Wennemo 1992), but universality ended in 1987.

Along with other OECD countries, Australia experienced slower economic growth, rising unemployment, and larger government deficits after the mid-1970s. Demands for social security increased with unemployment but also with changes in demographics, especially rising rates of divorce and increased claims by lone parents (Bolderson and Mabbett 1991, 87). At the same time, economic and fiscal difficulties led to contradictory pressures on the government both to increase and to cut back social security payments. In Australia, moves towards universality and more generous benefits were halted in 1975 with the defeat of the Whitlam Labor government. The new Fraser government tried to reduce social expenditures in order to bring down inflation (ibid.).

Before 1985, the family allowance program attempted to compensate for the higher costs which parents carry compared to childless couples. Since then, the program has adopted more of an anti-poverty strategy. In 1987, the Hawke Labor government, constrained by the deterioration of the balance of payments and external debt, introduced an income test for the family allowance to target it to lower- and middle-income families. In the same year, however, a more generous supplement was added for low-income families (Bolderson and Mabbett 1991, 89).

In 1992, the value of family allowances was A.$20.70 (or Can. $18.80) a fortnight for each of the first to third children and A.$26.70 (Can. $24.16) for the fourth and subsequent children or for a child living in an institution. This allowance is paid to mothers (or guardians) with at least one dependent child if the total family income is less than A.$64,167 (or Can. $58,264). An additional amount of income (A.$3,210 in 1992 [Can. $2,905]) is permitted for each child in the family (U.S. Dept of HHS 1992, 13).

Parents with a family income of less than A.$18,500 (Can. $16,743) and not receiving social assistance are eligible for the family allowance supplement. The amount varies by the age of the child and may be worth A.$53 to A.$77 per child every two weeks (Can. $48 to $70). The supplement is reduced by A.$1 for every A.$2 when income is greater than A.$18,500 (OECD 1992b). Low-income families may also qualify for rent assistance and pharmaceutical benefits (Perry 1991), and lone parents may be eligible for a pension as well as assistance with child support.

The individual is the unit of taxation in Australia. In 1976, the tax allowance for children and the existing child benefit were consolidated into a universal family allowance, along the same lines as the British universal benefit. Yet by 1987, the family allowance became income-tested and was supplemented by a more tightly targeted family allowance supplement (Bolderson and Mabbett 1991).

In Australia, there remains a tax credit worth A.$1,379 (Can. $1,252) a year for dependent children and a tax credit for dependent spouses worth A.$1,149 (Can. $1,043) per year (OECD 1992b, 108). Unlike in Canada, a child in Australia is worth slightly more than a dependent spouse in terms of tax concessions.

Lone parents are granted a tax credit of A.$1,105 (Can. $1,003), but Australia also provides a lone-parent's pension, which was instituted in 1989 and contains rental and child care assistance (OECD 1992b). For other parents, child care expenses are not tax deductible but fees are subsidized for low- and middle-income parents, as in Canada. There are also tax concessions for employers who provide child care services.

In Australia, income below A.$5,400 (Can. $4,903) is not taxed, and there are seven marginal tax rates varying from 20.5 per cent, to 47 per cent. There are no state or municipal income taxes, but there is a 1.3 per cent levy on taxable income imposed on residents to fund the National Health Scheme or medicare (Price Waterhouse 1992, 9,10)

France

France was one of the first countries to develop an explicit family policy, and there have been significant improvements to it in the postwar years (Gordon 1988). In 1932, a children's allowance program was initiated which operated as a social insurance program. It was financed through payroll taxes and provided family allowances for employees with dependent children. In 1939, the *Family Code* was introduced which discontinued the allowance for the first child and increased allowances for third and additional children, making the allowance explicitly pronatalist. At this time, France was deeply concerned about the declining birth rate aggravated by the 1930s Depression, as well as the rising population in Germany where the Nazis supported a high birth rate and encouraged mothers to remain at home to care for their children. In 1946, with additional concern about replenishing the population depleted from the Second World War (Smolowe 1992), French family allowances were extended to persons whose employment had been interrupted or who were not in the labour force. Furthermore, the French Constitution of 1958 (like that of 1946) confirmed the principle of the nation's duty towards the family (Commaille 1990, 70).

Social insurance, financed by contributions from both employees and employers, is also used in France to protect workers from lost wages due to illness, unemployment, and retirement in old age. In using social insurance to finance family allowances, however, France is unique among the countries in this study. It is especially interesting that although all employers and employees contribute to the fund, those receiving the allowance need not be employees themselves. The present family allowance is paid to all families with at least two children under seventeen years old, or under twenty years old if they are students. The amount is higher for each subsequent child, to a maximum of three children in a family. There is no income test for families to receive this benefit. As indicated in Table 4.2, the child allowance is worth more in France than in any other country in this study, and worth more than six times the former Canadian family allowance.

France also pays a supplement to the family allowance for low-income families. In addition to the allowance and its supplement, a universal young child's benefit is paid to both employees and homemakers for nine months, from five months before birth to three months after (Commaille 1990, 71). The idea behind this benefit is that families have greater expenses at the time of childbirth. For mothers who are also employees, the young child's allowance is combined with paid maternity leave of sixteen weeks (or twenty-six weeks for the birth of a third and subsequent child), at 90 per cent of previous earnings.

If a woman with three or more children (and at least one under three) wants to stay home to care for her children, the government may also provide a monthly parental education allowance (*allocation parentale d'éducation*). This allowance pays a maximum of about Can. $600 until the child is three years old, but is income-tested. A parent may also work part time and receive partial benefit. This allowance is adjusted annually for cost-of-living changes (U.S. Dept of HHS 1992). In addition, child care is both subsidized and provided by the government.

As I indicated in chapter 3, France also provides an allowance for lone parents, which is paid as a flat-rate benefit per child (Ray 1990). In addition, this allowance functions as an advance maintenance payment system for child support payments, as I will discuss in chapter 8.

The political and social consensus behind France's family policy has been influenced by Catholic-inspired political movements concerned with the birth rate and family values. But it has also been influenced by left-wing political parties and unions which promoted the reduction of social inequality, improved social programs, and women's labour market equality (Commaille 1990, 73). As in other industrialized countries, there have been recent pressures in France to reduce social security programs, but this has not yet had an impact on family benefits.

In 1945, France adopted a quotient system of taxation in which the unit of taxation is the family. Income is split not only between spouses but also among the children (Pechman 1987). Tax is calculated on a per-capita basis, with each spouse counting for one unit, the first two children for half a unit each, and third and subsequent children for one unit each. Unlike Canadian, German, or American taxpayers, the French substantially reduce their income tax burden when they have more children, which is a form of pronatalist policy. One-earner couples pay the same tax as two-earner couples (Pechman and Engelhardt 1990).

Unmarried children of eighteen and older are taxed separately. However, if they are students under twenty-five, suffer from disabilities, or are fulfilling their military obligations, they may choose to be taxed along with their parents using the quotient system. Unlike in other European countries, there is no significant move in France towards separate tax filing by spouses (Pechman 1987).

French parents do not begin to pay income tax until their income reaches almost 1.8 times the earnings of the average production worker. This is the result of a long-standing French policy to use the tax system to encourage higher birth rates. At lower income levels, married couples with children receive children's allowances from the government, resulting in 'negative taxes.' With earnings equivalent to the wages of the average production worker, a couple has an effective tax rate of minus

7.2 per cent, as shown in Table 4.3. The effective tax rate for a couple does not enter into the double digits until they achieve an income level 3.5 times the gross earnings of an average production worker (Pechman and Engelhardt 1990).

Most French family benefits are delivered through social insurance or direct state transfers rather than through the income tax system. The child allowance, which is universal and not considered taxable income for families, is financed through payroll taxes (Meyer, Phillips, and Maritato 1991). These payroll taxes or social insurance contributions also cover the cost of disability, maternity, unemployment, and illness, and represent about 17 per cent of an average production worker's wage, as Table 4.4 indicates (OECD 1992b, 46).

France has been identified as the industrial nation with the most generous benefit and tax relief system for families, particularly large families. Of the countries in the European Union, it also offers among the best provisions for child care for young children (Hantrais 1994).

Germany

In Germany, fertility rates were already below replacement levels in the early part of the twentieth century, and the Weimar Republic wrote pro-family statements into the Constitution in an attempt to counter declining fertility. In 1933, the Nazi government launched an explicit and racist population policy, designed to increase the birth rate and maintain 'racial purity.' This policy, however, was abolished by the Allies following the Second World War.

Present German family policies were developed under the Christian-democratic governments of the 1950s and 1960s and the social-liberal coalitions in the early 1970s (Hohn 1990, 81). In 1954–5, a universal child allowance was introduced when public concern increased over the low birth rate and high inflation after the war. Initially, the allowance was only for third and subsequent children, but in 1961 it was extended to the second child. In 1964, higher amounts were provided for larger families to a maximum of five children. The social-liberal government (1975–82) made the family allowance more generous and extended it to the first child. In 1982, however, when the Christian-liberal government came into power, the child allowance remained at a flat rate for the first child but became means-tested for the second child and subsequent children (Hantrais 1994). Yet higher amounts were still paid for larger families (Hohn 1990).

The value of family allowances now varies by family size and family income. For families with little or no taxable income, children's allowances are now worth between $22 and $101 (Canadian) per month for each child, depending on the number of children in the family (Brand 1989). Children's allowances are available for children under sixteen, although this is raised to age twenty-one if they are unemployed, and twenty-seven if they are students. There is no age limit for children with disabilities. German family allowances are funded through general revenue (U.S. Dept of HHS 1992).

In Germany, the unit of taxation is the couple, and couples are taxed at a much lower rate than unmarried individuals. Income splitting was adopted for married couples in 1958 after a Supreme Court decision required equality of tax treatment after marriage. This policy remains controversial, however, because the tax system provides more favourable rates for a husband who works overtime and claims his wife as a dependant than if she enters the workforce and he reduces his working hours (Hohn 1990). Yet married people with unequal earnings are treated more favourably than two single persons with the same income or a head of the household (an unmarried or separated person with dependants) (Pechman and Engelhardt 1990).

The German tax system assumes that the wife will stay at home and take care of the children while the husband is the provider. Tax credits for a financially dependent spouse compare generously to the other countries in this study, and may amount to the equivalent of about U.S.$10,000 a year (S. Gustafsson 1990).

Since 1986, lone mothers in Germany have been treated the same way as married couples by the tax system, in that they receive a double household deduction rather than merely one for a single person (S. Gustafsson 1990). This is similar to the idea behind the Equivalent to Married Credit in Canada. The child care deduction is primarily for working lone parents, and married couples can use this deduction only if one parent is sick or disabled. A German lone mother is taxed at a much lower rate than a Swedish lone mother, 10 per cent compared to 35 per cent of her income (S. Gustafsson 1990).

Tax benefits in Germany are more tied to marriage than to children. In 1975, West Germany enacted a child tax credit which was worth about one-quarter of the credit for a dependent spouse (Brand 1989). The credit has recently been changed to a deduction (OECD 1992b), which is opposite to the 1988 tax reform in Canada, in which deductions were changed to credits. German payroll taxes in 1991 amounted to

18.2 per cent of the average production worker's wage, as Table 4.4 indicates, a much higher percentage than in Canada (OECD 1992b, 46).

The Netherlands

In 1946, a family allowance was introduced that initially was employment based but was made universal in 1951 (Wennemo 1992). Since 1962, the Netherlands has provided a universal child allowance which varies by the age and number of children. For a family with two children between the ages of six and twelve, the total benefit amounted to Fl 3,693 (Can. $2,640) a year in 1991, more than three times the value of the former Canadian family allowance.

Although there are no special allowances for lone parents in the Netherlands, social assistance is relatively generous and does not require mothers with preschool children to enter the labour force (Perry 1991). Consequently, both lone and married mothers have low employment participation rates, particularly for full-time work. There is a strong tradition that women remain at home to care for their children, and mothers who choose this option are supported by high levels of benefits. As in the United Kingdom, the barriers to employment are high effective marginal tax rates and minimal child care support.

The tax unit in the Netherlands is the individual. After a basic personal exemption which is transferable to a spouse with no income, there are additional exemptions for low-income one-person households, lone parents, and working lone parents with children under twelve (OECD 1992b). The lone-parent supplement to the basic personal exemption amounts to Fl 3,728 (Can. $2,665) and any lone parent with dependent children under the age of twenty-seven is entitled to this benefit (OECD 1992b). A lone parent who works outside the household and has a child under twelve living at home is eligible for an additional supplement to the basic exemption. This is worth 6 per cent of the income earned outside the household to a maximum of Fl 3,728 or Can. $2,665 (OECD 1992b).

The marginal tax rates in the Netherlands are 13 per cent, 50 per cent, and 60 per cent, depending on income level, and there are no state or municipal taxes. One major change in the tax/benefit system implemented in 1992 was the decision not to adjust the tax brackets to the 3 per cent inflation rate (OECD 1992b). Compulsory social security contributions for a two-child family amounted to 28.3 per cent of gross earnings in 1991 (OECD 1992b, 46). As Table 4.4 indicates, this is by far the highest rate of payroll taxes paid by parents[7] in the countries in this study.

Sweden

Since 1947, Sweden has provided generous economic support for all families with children under sixteen through the non-taxable child allowance which is paid monthly to the mother or official guardian. Children are supported until age twenty if they are students or twenty-three if they have disabilities. Larger allowances are paid for third and subsequent children. The value of the child allowance was increased considerably in Sweden in 1982 and 1991, when some other countries in the study were cutting back on social benefits. According to Oxley (1987), the child allowance was worth 10.7 per cent of the average production worker's wage in 1984, compared to 3.3 per cent in Canada. By the calculations of the present study, the 1991 allowance for two children in Sweden was worth more than four and a half times Canada's former family allowance.

Sweden provides numerous additional family benefits and direct services for children in addition to a child allowance. Housing allowances are provided for low-income parents. Parental insurance, aside from providing parental benefits to new parents at childbirth, also compensates for income loss when parents need to provide occasional care of sick children, attend appointments with their children, or visit day care centres (Sundstrom and Stafford 1992). In addition, child care services are state funded and subsidized, and child support payments are guaranteed by government when parents divorce. As in France, Sweden's benefits for families are generous and pro-active, but they are based on a different philosophy. While France focuses on the family as a unit, Sweden has emphasized full employment, job training, employment equity, and individual rights.

In an attempt to increase female labour force participation, individual taxation was introduced on a voluntary basis in 1968 and by law in 1971 (Sundstrom and Stafford 1992). Both marginal and average tax rates are higher for for one-earner than two-earner families. The highly progressive tax system, which expects higher-income earners to pay a larger percentage of income tax, also makes it more favourable for a woman to go out to work than for her husband to work overtime (Lewis and Astrom 1992).

Most family benefits are delivered through social insurance or direct state transfers rather than tax concessions. For this reason there are no tax concessions for dependent spouses or children. Instead, as was mentioned earlier, there is a generous child allowance which is non-taxable and a system of guaranteed child support for one-parent families. The parent who receives the child allowance and child support does not pay taxes on this income, but maternity benefits are taxable and pensionable (Sundstrom and Stafford 1992). Although there used to be an income tax credit for lone parents for both national and municipal taxes (Perry 1991), it was abolished when the Social Democrats were voted out of office in 1991.

Relative to other countries in the study, Sweden's income taxes have been high, although they have been recently reduced. In 1982, the Swedish government reduced marginal tax rates to 50 per cent for most income earners and again in 1991 to 33 per cent (Sundstrom and Stafford 1992). Nevertheless, when combined with municipal taxes, the highest marginal tax rate is 54 per cent of gross earnings, as Table 4.3 indicates. There are both national and municipal income taxes, and municipal taxes average about 30 per cent of gross income (Price Waterhouse 1992, 303). National income tax begins at 5 per cent of gross income, increasing to 17 per cent for an average production worker. Furthermore, the average percentage of income paid in taxes tends to be higher in Sweden than in the other countries studied because a larger percentage of the population pays some income tax. In addition, there is a wealth tax.

Employees in Sweden do not make contributions to social security programs, as these are made by employers on their behalf. Employers pay about 33 per cent of total wages and salaries per year to cover the costs of the various pensions, health insurance, disability insurance, and guaranteed annual income (OECD 1992, 214,216).

The United Kingdom

In 1942, the Beveridge Report laid the foundation for universal children's allowances, as well as for unemployment and disability insurance, and the National Health Service in Britain (Guest 1985). The family allowance was introduced in Britain at the end of the Second World War (Lewis 1993, 19), at about the same time as in Australia, Canada, and Sweden. Since the 1940s, the universal allowance has been modified considerably although it was always meant to acknowledge the additional costs which parents incur when they raise children and to equalize the incomes of parents and childless individuals. The Child Benefit is now delivered weekly as an allowance to mothers or guardians. It is non-taxable, non-contributory, and not means-tested, and is financed from general revenue (Bolderson and Mabbett 1991).

In 1970, the Conservative government introduced the Family Income Supplement (FIS), which provided means-tested benefits for low-income earners with dependent children. The FIS was never integrated into the tax system, but in the late 1980s it was extended and amended to become a more targeted measure and renamed 'Family Credit.' It is now meant to supplement low wages of parents working more than twenty-four hours a week (Perry 1991), as was noted in chapter 3.

The major change to the British family allowance came in 1975, when the Labour government combined the original allowance and child tax deductions into the present Child Benefit. Although the previous tax deductions had been indexed to the rising cost of living, the present Child Benefit is not indexed and consequently has declined in value since it was initiated (Bolderson and Mabbett 1991).

In 1988, the value of the Child Benefit was frozen for three years and did not recover its former value when increases were announced in 1991–2 (Brown 1992). In 1988, there was some discussion about targeting the benefit or abolishing it, but this was not done. The government apparently listened to the arguments against means-testing benefits: that they are seen as demeaning by recipients, promote a poverty trap, and remove the only recognition given for the extra costs of raising children. Universal benefits can become a protection in times of insta-bility, such as marriage breakdown or unemployment, when there are changes in the level and regularity of family income. A universal benefit also protects the interests of children in families where income is dis-tributed unfairly among its members (Brown 1988).

Despite the Conservative government's attempts to cut back on social programs, the Child Benefit remains universal for children under sixteen (or nineteen, if the child is a student). A larger amount is paid to the first child on the grounds that he or she entailed the greatest expenditure (Hantrais 1994). As Table 4.2 indicates, the 1991 value of the Child Benefit for two children in the United Kingdom was about two times the value of Canada's former family allowance. However, it is now more similar in value to Canada's Child Tax Benefit.

Since 1989, the unit of taxation in the United Kingdom has been the individual (Lewis and Astrom 1992). All taxpayers are entitled to a basic exemption, and sole parents and sole breadwinners are entitled to additional exemptions which are comparable in value (OECD 1992b). Tax deductions for families with dependent children have been available in Britain since 1909 (Heitlinger 1993, 280), but were replaced by the universal Child Benefit in 1975. Unlike the French government, the British government does not assist women to combine employment and family life. Child care expenses cannot be deducted from income tax and, as we will see in chapter 6, the number of nurseries and preschool places is the lowest in Europe (Hantrais 1994).

The marginal tax rate for an average production worker in the United Kingdom is 25 per cent (Joshi 1990) and for higher income earners (those earning over £23,700) the rate is 40 per cent (OECD 1992b, 234). However, with the various exemptions and deductions, an average production worker with two children pays about 15 per cent of gross earnings in income tax, as Table 4.4 indicates. Social security contributions amount to 7.6 per cent of gross earnings, also shown in Table 4.4, but low-income employees are exempt from these contributions. There are no state or municipal income taxes in the United Kingdom (Perry 1991).

The United States

The United States is unique among industrialized countries in not providing a universal child allowance. Not coincidentally, American children fare considerably worse in terms of poverty rates than do their counterparts in Western Europe (Smeeding, Torrey, and Rein 1988). The United States relies mainly on a child tax deduction which is vertically inequitable, or more valuable to higher-income families. In addition, Aid to Families with Dependent Children (AFDC) provides cash benefits to low-income parents (Bolderson and Mabbett 1991), as described in chapter 3.

Meyer, Phillips, and Maritato (1991) illustrated that a child allowance would be more beneficial than the present tax deduction without being more costly. Using microsimulation methodology and 1984 data, they tested three proposals to improve the value of the 1989 tax deduction for children. The first simply converted the deduction into an allowance, which produces a benefit of U.S.$292 (Can. $373) per year or U.S.$24 (Can. $31) per month. The second added the share of AFDC money which would be saved from the programs, bringing the total amount to U.S.$312 (Can. $398) per year or U.S.$26 (Can. $33) per month. The third scenario used a figure of U.S.$1,000 which was what the tax deduction would have been worth in 1991 if it had retained its value over the years. The results of the simulation showed that the second model would result in a 2.8 per cent decrease in poverty and a 7.0 per cent decrease in the poverty gap, or the difference between the poverty line and the average income of poor families. The third model would result in a 14 per cent decrease in poverty and a 24 per cent decrease in the poverty gap, but for families currently on AFDC, there would be no financial difference. The authors argued that a children's allowance could be instituted that could decrease poverty and welfare participation, while not costing the U.S. government any additional expenditures. Yet the government has not acted on these recommendations. Instead, it has focused on moving parents from welfare to low-paid jobs and tightening up enforcement of child support orders.

In the United States, a married tax filer may choose whether to file as part of a couple, as an individual, or as the head of a household. Income splitting was adopted in 1948, and in an attempt to create vertical equity, married couples who file jointly use a schedule with more concessions than single filers. A head of household (unmarried or separated person with dependants) may file separately and thereby is treated more favourably than a single person but not better than a married couple (Pechman and Engelhardt 1990). However, high-income single persons or heads of households can reduce their tax liabilities substantially by marrying a person with little or no income and filing a joint tax return (ibid.; OECD 1992b).

The U.S. government provides tax deductions for dependants, including both children and adults, which amounted to U.S.$2,150 (Can. $2,744) for each person in 1991 (OECD 1992b). In addition, there is a deduction of U.S.$5,700 (Can. $7,276) for a married couple, U.S.$5,000 (Can. $6,382) for a head of the household, and U.S.$3,400 (Can. $4,340) for a single person. Because these tax concessions are deductions rather than refundable credits, families and individuals with higher marginal tax rates derive greater benefit from them than lower-income families (Bolderson and Mabbett 1991). Marginal tax rates were 15 per cent, 28 per cent, and 31 per cent in 1991, with separate income categories for single people and married couples (OECD 1992b, 239). As Table 4.3 indicates, the United States has the lowest marginal tax rates among the eight countries in this study.

Low-income working parents can take advantage of the Earned Income Tax Credit (EITC), introduced in 1976. In order to qualify for this re-fundable credit, at least half of income must come from earnings or private resources, and children must be under the age of nineteen. The maximum credit for one child, which is indexed over a five-year period, is U.S.$1,852 (Can. $2,364) and for two or more, U.S.$2,013 (Can. $2,570), which is intended to be spent on child care or other family expenses (Berrick 1991). Lone parents face relatively low effective marginal tax rates in the United States, except for those earning between 30 per cent and 60 per cent of the average production worker's wage (Perry 1991).

The United States also offers a Child and Dependent Care Tax Credit for parents who earn at least U.S.$10,000 (Can. $12,765) annually. Parents with incomes from U.S.$10,000 to U.S.$28,000 (Can. $12,765–$35,742) can claim 30 per cent of work-related child care expenses to a limit of U.S.$2,400 (Can. $3,064) per year for one dependent child, and up to U.S.$4,800 (Can. $6,127) for two or more. This results in a maximum non-refundable tax credit of U.S.$720 (Can. $919) and U.S.$1,440 (Can. $1,838). For taxpayers with gross incomes above U.S.$28,000, the Child and Dependent Care Tax Credit is 20 per cent of eligible expenses, resulting in a maximum credit of U.S.$960 (Can. $1,225) for families with two or more children. The main beneficiaries of this credit are middle-income families (Danziger 1990; Dunbar and Nordhauser 1991).

In some states, there are also municipal and state income taxes. Compared to tax rates in the other countries studied, however, U.S. tax rates are low, and couples with two children at the average production worker's wage (APWW) paid 7.3 per cent of their gross income in income taxes, as Table 4.3 indicates. Employees at the income level of the APWW contribute to social security programs at a rate of 7.7 per cent of gross earnings, as shown in Table 4.4 (OECD 1992b, 46). Again, this is relatively low in comparison to European countries, but higher than in Australia and Canada.

COMPARING THE VALUE OF TAX BENEFITS AND GOVERNMENT TRANSFERS

Unlike most of the European countries in the study, Canada has moved away from a universal family allowance towards an income-tested child tax benefit which pays about the same money to lower-income families as the previous benefit, and none to higher-income parents. This policy change, which took place under a Conservative government in 1992, is similar to reforms in Australia and Germany, although the Australian and German benefits are more generous. The United States remains the only country of the eight in the study that has never developed a universal child benefit but relies instead on tax concessions.

Britain moved in the opposite direction in 1975 under the influence of the Labour government, when it combined the family allowance and tax deductions for children into a more generous universal child benefit. Except for Germany, the European countries studied have retained universal child allowances, and in some cases made them more generous in recent years.

Nations using social insurance programs and universal measures rather than income-tested benefits have been more effective in keeping families with children above the poverty line. These conclusions are suggested by comparison of poverty rates before and after taxes and transfers, as Table 4.5 indicates. France, the Netherlands, and Sweden have been very effective in pulling families out of poverty by their tax and transfer systems. Despite Sweden's high tax rates, many studies have indicated that its government taxes and transfers are far more effective in pulling families out of poverty than those in Canada or the United States (McFate 1991). European countries are also more likely to provide generous direct services to low-income parents, such as housing subsidies, as well as support to all families with dependent children, such as preschool education and health care.

Numerous hypotheses have been put forward to explain why some countries have chosen universal child allowances while other countries have focused on tax concessions which are largely income-tested. Explanations usually focus on a combination of factors, including the ideology of governing parties; the influence of religious parties; and the effect of political alliances among governments, trade unions, and employer groups. The structure of government decision making has also been used as an explanation, especially the influence of federalism, corporatism,[8] and the input of advocacy groups. Demographic changes such as declining birth rates or an aging population have also been used to explain pressures on governments to provide family benefits. Nations seem to value children more when it is apparent that they will be needed to pay for future social policies. Also, changing economic and labour market trends, a large deficit, and high unemployment have led to pressure by labour to create or maintain social programs and by employers and bankers to reduce social programs.

Wennemo (1992) argued that once universal benefits are in place, they are difficult to abolish even when the government changes. Although this is the case for most of the countries studied, Australia, Germany, and Canada are exceptions. After eight years of Conservative government and growing public concern about the economy and the deficit, Canada abolished the family allowance that had been in place for nearly a half a century.

All countries use their tax systems to pursue objectives related to family policy. The structure of the tax system may attempt to promote marriage rather than cohabitation, may encourage women's labour force participation or make it difficult, may reward couples with children, and may encourage larger families. For example, Sweden has restructured the tax system to enhance women's labour force participation and reduce work-family conflicts (Sundstrom and Stafford 1992). Yet other countries, such as Germany, have developed tax structures which are more favourable to the presence of a homemaker parent than to children. This seems to imply that homemaker wives are more important to the state than are children, and that husbands need government relief from the financial burden of 'supporting' their wives. Such a policy overlooks the fact that most homemaker wives provide valuable services for their husbands (and children) in the home, and are a social and economic asset to husbands rather than merely a financial liability.

As we saw in Table 4.4, the average percentage of gross income paid as income tax in Canada is moderate compared to the average in European countries, while payroll taxes are relatively low in Canada. Yet other countries, such as the Netherlands, provide more valuable tax concessions for families, such as exemptions for one-person households, lone parents, and employed lone parents with young children. In addition, many European countries provide more generous, non-taxable child allowances and child support payments than Canada. Aguilar and Gustafsson (1987) showed that families with elderly 'heads' and lone parents in many European countries tend to receive more public sector transfers than they pay in taxes.

Although the average percentage of gross income paid in income taxes in Canada is relatively low in comparison to that in many European countries, Canadians *feel* overtaxed. Perhaps this is because they most often compare themselves to Americans, who have comparatively low marginal income tax rates (and moderately low payroll taxes). Yet in order to finance the more effective family and child benefits that are prevalent in the non-English-speaking European countries, the tax system in Canada may have to be substantially reformed. Implementing the type of tax system necessary to reduce income inequality and to support healthy family development will require a broad level of public understanding and support. A major barrier to high tax/high transfer policies in Canada is the degree of economic integration with the United States.

Yet more generous taxation policies for families could be achieved with no additional expenditures if fewer concessions were allowed for those with the highest incomes.[9]

Although it has been demonstrated that there is no relationship between the level of payroll taxes and national unemployment rates, there has been a widespread belief that high taxes lower productivity. Several nations with conservative governments (Sweden and the United States) have reduced marginal tax rates in recent years to appease the business community and attempt to stimulate the economy.

A number of countries, including Australia, Canada, Germany, Sweden, and the United Kingdom, have attempted to target or have successfully targeted family benefits to middle- or lower-income families. In targeting family benefits, however, Australia actually improved the total package for low-income families. This has not been the case in Canada, where low-income families receive about the same amount as before the 'reform' in child benefits, while middle- and upper-income families receive less or no benefit.

While both Australia and Canada recently targeted the child benefit or family allowance, Canada chose to deliver the benefit through the tax system while Australia retained the allowance. Some have interpreted Canada's move as 'harmonizing' its child benefit to make it more consistent with U.S. benefits for children (Banting 1993). Others have suggested that Canada's child benefit could be more easily targeted in the future as one tax benefit than as an allowance and several tax credits. It is also more firmly within federal jurisdiction, at a time when there are jurisdictional disputes over some Canadian social programs. Because the Commonwealth government in Australia delivers all income security benefits, it does not have the same concerns about overlapping jurisdiction.

While using the income tax system might be an efficient and effective way of delivering minimal family benefits, it is unlikely to improve benefit levels. Generally, countries that rely on tax concessions to assist families provide a *lower* level of benefits than countries using universal allowances, especially when the benefits are funded through social security programs.

5

Maternity/parental leave and benefits

A generation ago, most children were raised at home during their pre-school years by their mothers. In the last two decades, however, an increasing number of mothers with young children have been drawn into the labour force in many industrialized countries because one income can no longer purchase the same standard of living it did in the 1950s.

As was noted in chapter 2, the proportion of married women in the Canadian labour force has risen dramatically in the last twenty years while the proportion of married men has fallen slightly. Among married people aged thirty-five to forty-four, for example, 78.6 per cent of women and 93 per cent of men were working for pay in 1993. By contrast, only 43.9 per cent of married women and 92.8 per cent of married men between those ages were in the labour force in 1970 (Statistics Canada, annual(b)).

In Canada, unlike some other countries in this study, the percentage of lone mothers in the workforce is lower than the percentage of married mothers. In 1991, 52 per cent of lone mothers with children under sixteen worked outside the home compared to 65 per cent of mothers in two-parent families. Among lone fathers, 71 per cent worked outside the home compared to 87 per cent of dual-parent fathers (Lindsay 1992, 21). We might assume that lone mothers have more reason to be in the labour force than mothers in two-parent families. However, the lower participation rate of lone mothers may relate to lack of child care, lower employment qualifications, and social assistance policies which do not actively encourage entry into the labour force by mothers with pre-school children.

While 30 per cent of couples with children under nineteen were dual-earner families in 1970, this has increased to 70 per cent in 1990 (Marshall 1993). Since two incomes are increasingly needed to counteract the rising cost of living, it is not surprising that dual-earner families are more likely than traditional one-earner families to have higher incomes.

Several countries have accommodated or encouraged two-earner families by modifying the income tax system to create separate tax returns for both adults, as described in chapter 4. For example, Sweden introduced separate taxation for spouses which, combined with a progressive tax rate, allowed the spouse with the lower income (usually the wife) to pay income tax at a lower rate than if her income were combined with her husband's. Of the countries in this study, only the United States and Germany have retained the couple as the unit of taxation, while France taxes the family as a unit.

In addition to allowing parents to support their children and pay their bills, having two earners has altered authority patterns within families. Research on family decision making indicates that wives who work for pay increase their bargaining power in the marital relationship. Wives' money is often essential in determining whether or not couples can afford to buy a house, take a vacation, or clothe themselves and their children. Wives therefore feel they have a right to be involved in financial decisions. The relationship between family power and wives' earnings is not clear, however, partly because in Canada most husbands earn considerably more than their wives (Labour Canada, Women's Bureau 1990), as they do in the other countries studied. The gender gap in earnings is the smallest in Sweden, where policies have enforced employment equity.

Regardless of which factors influence family power and decision making, there has been a long-term trend in Canada towards social, legal, and economic equality between husband and wife. As women gained more education throughout the twentieth century and entered the labour force in increasing numbers, they fought for political rights and legal equality with men. With higher education, greater earning power, fewer children, and increased legal protection, women are achieving more personal and economic autonomy. At the same time, however, now that so many women are absent during the day and children are cared for by non-family members, Canadian women may have lost some of their former control over home and children (Armstrong and Armstrong 1988).

In the past fifty years, women's family roles have changed considerably while men's have changed more gradually, adapting to the changes in women's lives. Because some of the pressure has been taken off men to be the sole or major breadwinner in their family, they may be freer to remain in school longer, to change jobs, or develop their leisure interests. As gender roles change, men now have the opportunity to express their emotions more honestly and overtly and to develop closer relationships with their children and other adults. However, they may also be expected to do more housework and child care, as well as to consider their wives' employment when making career decisions.

Studies from countries where men are entitled to generous parental leave at the birth of a child (such as Sweden) indicate that men are far less likely than women to take paid leave from work (Haas 1990). Their reasons relate to concern about perceptions of lack of commitment by both employers and co-workers, and feelings that they cannot leave their work for extended periods without jeopardizing their positions (Widerberg 1990). Despite increased opportunities, men are less likely than women to pursue occupations and activities traditionally dominated by the opposite sex. This is not surprising, as women's work has historically been unpaid or underpaid, and undervalued.

DIVISION OF LABOUR: INSIDE AND OUTSIDE OF THE HOME

When women work full time in the home, some of the potential for conflict is reduced, as the division of labour is often firmly established (Armstrong and Armstrong 1988). Negotiations are most often needed when women work outside the home, and are most difficult for families when the wife is re-entering the labour force after many years as a homemaker. All other family members may be required to adapt to her working hours, and she is unlikely to be able or willing to continue doing all or most of the housework.

Despite the legal and labour force changes over the past forty years, studies still conclude that women are responsible for the bulk of household chores. For example, the 1990 General Social Survey sponsored by Statistics Canada contained questions on household chores, which included meal preparation and clean-up, indoor and outdoor cleaning, laundry, home repairs and maintenance, gardening, pet care, bill paying, and the travel required by these household chores. The survey concluded that the allocation of household tasks is far from equal. Although women employed full time have somewhat less responsibility for housework than women with part-time jobs or those at home full time, the majority of wives who are employed full time continue to have all or most of the responsibility for daily household tasks (Marshall 1993, 30). Sharing tends to be most common among younger, well-educated couples with few or no children. The likelihood of shared responsibility also increases as the wife's income level rises (ibid. 23).

In Canada, the husbands of women employed full time are slightly more likely to be involved in routine housework than the husbands of homemakers or part-time employees (Seccombe 1989; Asner and Livingstone 1990; Marshall 1993). In addition, employed wives are less likely than housewives to agree to relocate the household to accommodate their husband's job (Harrell 1985). Yet studies in other countries have also concluded that even when women work full time, they tend to do most of the housework and child care (Moss 1988; Bock and Thane 1991; L. Morris 1993; Bittman 1994). This domestic division of labour has serious implications for labour market segregation as well as for fertility.

Statistics Canada estimated that unpaid housework in Canada in 1992 was worth between $211 billion and $319 billion, which amounts to between 30 and 45 per cent of the gross domestic product. The lower estimate is based on the replacement cost, or the cost of purchasing these services. The higher estimate is based on the opportunity cost, or the amount that Canadians could have earned in the labour market if they had not been occupied with unpaid tasks (Theilheimer 1994). In Australia, Duncan Ironmonger (1994) calculated that in 1992, 380 million hours per week were spent on work outside the money economy, compared to 272 million hours per week on paid employment. Furthermore, the amount of unpaid work has increased far more than the amount of paid work since 1974.

Moss (1988) examined the loss of income experienced by women as a result of child-bearing in Britain. Only 30 per cent of women with children under age five were employed outside the home at the time of his study, but a significant number of these women worked part time. Moss suggested that barriers exist to full-time work, including lack of public child care and time factors relating to domestic responsibilities. British family policy focuses on cash transfers, but assumes and supports the idea that women will stay home and care for young children. Moss recommended more interventionist policies to minimize the income loss women experience due to child-bearing.

In a Canadian study of work inside and outside the home, Graham Lowe (1989) argued that women tend to be in more highly stressed jobs than men – that is, jobs with poor working conditions, a high work load, and/or little control over decisions. Women's 'double day' and gender inequality in the workplace further contribute to work stress. These findings differ from those of past research because previous studies often excluded women, used different measures of work stress for men and women, or failed to examine work done in the home. Lowe argued that problems of work stress should not require individuals to find new coping mechanisms; rather, work environments need to be modified. Other countries such as Norway and Sweden have more highly developed occupational health legislation than Canada, which could reduce work stress for employees of both genders. In addition, more generous leave for family responsibilities would alleviate stress for parents, especially mothers, and others with adult dependants.

Duxbury and Higgins (1994) argued that workplaces need to be restructured to accommodate the increase in the number of two-income families, especially with respect to the care of dependent children and frail elderly persons. There is a cost involved, socially and financially, if we continue to allow employees to resolve their own work-family conflicts. Workers who have difficulty balancing work and family are more likely to quit their jobs, to be less productive, to arrive late, to be absent from work, and to have physical and mental health problems. Unless governments and employers provide more assistance to these employees, Duxbury and Higgins claim, 'there will be no capable workers to carry on.'

With rising rates of female employment and declining birth rates, and with pressure from unions, employee associations, and feminist groups, the governments of most industrialized countries have developed maternity and/or parental leave and benefits. Governments differ considerably, however, in their basic philosophy and commitment to these programs; and the programs themselves are of varying derees of comprehensiveness. While maternity leave is viewed as protecting the health of pregnant women and unborn children in some countries, it is seen primarily as employment equity or an inducement for women to enter the labour force by other nations. Countries also differ in the way they fund maternity benefits, although most use social insurance programs involving employer and employee contributions. Countries also vary in the rate at which previous earnings are replaced by the insurance, from a low of 57 per cent in Canada to 100 per cent in the Netherlands and Germany. I will first discuss Canada's system of maternity and parental leave before comparing it with those of the other countries studied.

CANADA: MATERNITY/PARENTAL LEAVE AND BENEFITS

Qualifying for maternity leave and for cash benefits are two separate processes in Canada. Leave from employment is generally governed by provincial employment standards legislation, except where employees are under federal jurisdiction.[1] By the end of the 1970s, all provinces had passed laws entitling women employees to at least seventeen weeks of unpaid maternity leave. Saskatchewan now provides six weeks of unpaid paternity leave, and Newfoundland, Saskatchewan, Quebec, and Alberta provide adoption leave ranging from two days to seventeen weeks. Most jurisdictions have passed parental leave legislation for natural and adoptive parents; the exceptions are Alberta, Saskatchewan, and Yukon. Quebec allows thirty-four weeks of unpaid leave for each parent, while federal jurisdiction allows the mother or the father to take up to twenty-four weeks of unpaid leave or to share it between them (Canada, Government 1993).

The laws relating to maternity leave used to exclude most casual or temporary workers by requiring a period of continuous employment, the length of which varied by jurisdiction. Although women are no longer required to work for any specific length of time in British Columbia, New Brunswick, or Quebec to become eligible for maternity/parental leave, they must work for at least six months in federal jurisdiction and for twelve months in Alberta, Manitoba, Nova Scotia, Saskatchewan, the Northwest Territories, and Yukon. Ontario now requires thirteen weeks, and Newfoundland and Prince Edward Island require employees to work for twenty weeks in order to be eligible for a job-protected leave for pregnancy and childbirth (Canada, Government 1993). Until recently, the norm among the provinces was twelve months, which was similar to Australia but less than in the United Kingdom (Heitlinger 1993, 211).

When the *Unemployment Insurance Act* was amended in 1971, wage replacement benefits were first introduced on a national level for employees who were absent from work for pregnancy and childbirth. As was mentioned in chapter 3, unemployment insurance (UI) was established in 1940 as a social insurance program to provide income protection for workers suffering from temporary loss of employment income. Although many categories of workers were originally excluded from UI (such as government and white-collar employees, seasonal workers, and pregnant women [Cuneo 1979]), eligible workers may now obtain the following kinds of benefits: regular unemployment, sickness, maternity, or parental benefits.

In 1984, adoptive parents were allowed to receive UI benefits, and in 1990 another amendment created ten weeks of parental leave for either parent who qualifies. The 1990 amendment arose from a court challenge using the *Canadian Charter of Rights and Freedoms* to argue that biological fathers should have the same rights as adoptive fathers. Now both adoptive and biological parents are entitled to ten weeks of parental leave.

UI is administered by the federal government (Employment and Immigration Canada). Premiums are collected through payroll deductions or income tax, and about 3 per cent of earnings (up to a maximum) is deducted from pay slips of insurable employees and invested in the UI Fund. About 95 per cent of all workers in Canada are in 'ensurable employment' (Canada, Health and Welfare 1991, 180). Employers contribute about 1.4 times the amount that employees contribute to the fund (Hess 1992a, 37).

In order to be entitled to maternity benefits in Canada, a woman employee must have contributed to UI for twenty weeks in the last year (or since the start of the last claim) (ibid.). Maternity benefits are paid for fifteen weeks, from as early as eight weeks before the birth until up to seventeen weeks after (there is a two-week waiting period between stopping work and the start of benefits). As of 1984, adopting parents could receive benefits from UI if provincial labour laws permitted leave and employees met UI eligibility rules (Heitlinger 1993, 215). As of 1990, parental benefits also are paid from the UI fund for a maximum of ten weeks, but both spouses may not take maternity or parental leave at the same time. The value of maternity, adoption, and parental benefits depends on previous earnings. The maximum rate used to be 60 per cent of previous earnings, but was reduced to 57 per cent in 1993. However, some unionized and professional employees have their benefit level 'topped up' by their employers.

Despite recent changes, many women are ineligible for maternity leave because they have not worked continuously for a year and therefore cannot claim federal maternity benefits. Townson (1988) estimated that the take-up rate among employed women in 1981 was only 45 per cent. This rate has probably not improved much since then, as more women are working on short-term contracts or in temporary and/or part-time jobs and are therefore ineligible for both leave and benefits. Although Canada's system of maternity/parental leave and benefits is better than that in the United States, it appears ungenerous compared to those in the European countries, where the wage replacement rate is typically

80 per cent to 100 per cent and benefits are often provided for longer periods.

Canada and the English-speaking countries (or the 'liberal welfare states') have tended to view maternity and parental leave as an expense and irritant to employers or a deterrent to hiring women. On the other hand, the European countries studied seem to have viewed maternity and parental leave and benefits as a maternal and child health issue, a form of employment equity for women, an inducement to reproduction, and a citizenship right for every employed woman. Furthermore, some European countries have recently extended parental and child-rearing leave as a way of reducing unemployment, sharing jobs, and creating temporary positions for unemployed workers (Heitlinger 1993, 201).

As social insurance, cash maternity benefits for employed women are almost as old as sickness benefits. Maternity benefits were first established in Germany by Bismarck about a hundred years ago. By the First World War, several European countries, including France, Italy, and Britain, had already legislated some form of national maternity insurance for working women. The first and most influential international standard which recognized the needs of working mothers was the 1919 International Labor Organization Maternity Protection Convention. This convention laid down such basic principles as a woman's right to maternity leave, nursing breaks, wage compensation, and job protection (Heitlinger 1993, 190).

The motive behind such benefits partially arose from the overall concern with the health and well-being of children whose mothers worked in the labour force. However, the development of a cash benefit program within the social insurance system reflects the view that maternity contributes to the needs of society as well as of individual adults and families. In addition, it reflects the view that income loss at maternity is a social risk and that society as a whole should help to protect women against such loss (Kamerman and Kahn 1989b).

Maternity leave and parental leave policies differ in their focus and assumptions. Maternal leave policies are predicated on the assumption that childbirth is a physical ordeal for women that requires preparation and recuperation, as well as special protective legislation that is gender-specific. On the other hand, parental leave policies incorporate some concerns about the biology of childbirth with attention to the gender-neutral processes of nurturing and bonding (Garrett, Wenk, and Lubeck 1990). In some countries, the right to parental leave and benefits has been fought for on the principle of equal employment rights for men and women or for biological and adoptive fathers.

As female labour force participation has increased over the past three decades and birth rates have declined, governments have been pressured by social reformers, feminist groups, and unions to provide maternity and parental leave. The United States has not yet developed wage re-placement for childbirth, however, and the Australian maternity benefit is still provided by employers rather than government. Tables 5.1 and 5.2 compare maternity and parental benefits in the eight countries.

Australia

Historical studies of the Australian state have highlighted the role of the 'family wage' in influencing women's labour force participation. The idea of a family wage was initiated as early as 1907 by the union movement and, as Goodnow, Burns, and Russell (1989) state: 'Australia was one of the first societies to see the non-working wife as a desirable goal and a measure of adequacy and justice of men's wages ... Indeed, the position of the housewife in Australia was ensured and accentuated by the power and relative success of the trade union movement when organized labor was able to insist that more and more men were paid wages adequate for them to keep a wife at home.' Further policies strengthened the single-breadwinner family, as old age and sickness pensions were introduced in 1908, the mothers' allowance in 1912, the family allowance in 1941, and the widow's pension in 1942. These poli-cies implemented a 'concealed but systematic set of transfers maintain-ing women primarily as wives and mothers' (ibid.). In recent decades, however, the participation of women in the Australian labour force has increased and demands for maternity protection have followed. Yet, as was noted in chapter 1, women make up only 38 per cent of the workforce (compared to 44 per cent in Canada) and are largely situated in part-time temporary positions (Pixley 1993).

Maternity leave in Australia became available through national legis-lation as well as collective agreements negotiated by trade unions and employers, which were gradually extended to workers in other sectors. The 1973 *Maternity Leave Act for Australian Government Employees* gave federal public servants the right to maternity leave. As a result of the high rate of unionization in Australia, the union movement spearheaded the extension of maternity rights. In 1978, the Australian Council of Trade Unions (ACTU) and five unions brought an industrial test case before the Australian Conciliation and Arbitration Commission. It was agreed that any award granted in the case would benefit all employees. In 1979, the decision, which gave women employees the right to unpaid maternity leave, initially covered only six federal awards. The maternity clause accompanying the decision became a standard provision, however, and it now covers 94 per cent of female wage earners (Heitlinger 1993, 203).

The length of maternity leave and the benefit level vary by jurisdiction, occupation, and collective agreement. Federal public servants and those in the state of Victoria were awarded the right to twelve weeks' paid maternity leave in addition to a forty-week unpaid parental leave in 1985, which is the most generous of all the states. New South Wales offers six weeks with pay and six weeks with half-pay (as well as forty weeks of unpaid leave) to public servants (ibid.).

In 1989, ACTU presented a national test case for parental leave, claiming that the lack of parental and paternity leave discriminated against men. As of 1990, the Federal Industrial Relations Commission granted fathers the right to one week of unpaid paternity leave at the time of their wife's confinement and a total of fifty-two weeks of parental or adoption leave for men or women after twelve months' continuous service with the same employer (Heitlinger 1993, 208).

As in most other countries, both parents cannot take leave at the same time. Parents are also entitled to part-time employment, with the consent of the employer, up to the child's second birthday, and can thus combine leave entitlements with part-time work (Lamb, Sternberg, Hwang, and Broberg 1992). Maternity leave does not break the continuity of service, but it is not taken into account in calculating the length of service required to obtain other employment benefits (International Labor Office 1988b).

The ACTU and the Australian Conciliation and Arbitration Commission have played a major role in promoting women's rights. Among their successes are the commission's endorsement of equal pay in 1969, 1972, and 1974, as well as the recognition of the general principle of maternity leave in 1979, and the extension of maternity leave to adoptive mothers in 1985 and to home workers in the clothing industry in 1986 (Heitlinger 1993, 208). Women employees who work full time or part

TABLE 5.1
Paid maternity/parenting leave provisions

Country	Date of legislation	Length of leave and benefit
Australia (funded as an employer benefit)	• 1973 maternity leave • 1985 adoption leave for mothers • 1990 parental leave	• leave varies by jurisdiction and benefit comes from employer • maximum 12 weeks paid + 40 weeks unpaid in federal public service • 1 week paid paternity leave at birth + 52 weeks unpaid parental leave
Canada (funded as social insurance)	• 1971 maternity benefits • 1984 adoption benefits (both parents) • 1990 parental benefits	• 15 weeks paid maternity + 10 weeks paid parental leave at 57% wage replacement to a maximum benefit • 17–18 weeks unpaid leave (provincial jurisdiction)
France (funded as social insurance)	• 1909 maternity leave • 1913 maternity benefits • 1984 parental leave and parental education allowance	• 16 weeks maternity benefits at 84% of basic daily wage for 1st and 2nd child • 24 weeks maternity benefits at 84% for 3rd and subsequent child • up to 3 years unpaid job-protected leave (unless collective agreement adds pay) • 3 days paid paternity leave
West Germany (funded as social insurance)	• 1883 parental leave • 1927 maternity benefits • 1990 child-rearing allowance	• 14 weeks maternity benefits at 100% of previous wage • extended leave for 6 months at flat rate + 12 months flat rate (income-tested)
Netherlands (funded as social insurance)	• 1984	• 12 weeks at 100% of previous wage

TABLE 5.1 (*continued*)

Country	Date of legislation	Length of leave and benefit
Sweden (funded as social insurance)	• 1937 maternity benefits • 1974 parental benefits	• 12 months parental leave at 90% of previous wage + 6 months flat rate • right to reduced work day until child is 8
United Kingdom (funded as social insurance)	• 1975 maternity benefits	• 18 weeks paid (6 weeks paid at 90% + 12 weeks flat rate) • 40 weeks unpaid leave
United States (paid leave not required by law)	• 1993 right to unpaid maternity/ parental leave	• 12 weeks unpaid

SOURCES: Lewis, ed. 1993; U.S. Dept of HHS 1992; Kamerman and Kahn 1991a, 179–96

TABLE 5.2
Eligibility for maternity and parental benefits in eight industrialized countries, 1990–1993

Country	Eligibility
Australia	• 52 weeks continuous service with same employer
Canada	• 20 weeks continuous employment with same employer
France	• Entry into insurance 10 months before confinement plus 200 hours of employment in first 3 months of last 12; or 6 months contribution to insurance plan
Germany	• 12 weeks of insurance or continuous employment from 10th to 4th month before confinement
Netherlands	• No minimum contribution period
Sweden	• 240 days of insurance contributions before confinement
United Kingdom	• Employed continuously for 26 weeks by same employer at 15th week before confinement, average earnings £49 per week
United States	• One year with same employer for unpaid leave; no statutory maternity or parental benefits

SOURCE: U.S. Dept of HHS 1992.

time are now entitled to fifty-two weeks of job-protected leave after one year of continuous service to an employer. As in Canada, casual and seasonal workers are not entitled to maternity leave, which disqualifies about one-quarter of working women in Australia (Glezer 1988).

Maternity benefits vary by state, depend largely on collective agreements, and leave is paid only in some parts of the public sector and by large employers. In a 1984 study of women employees who gave birth in that year, only 21 per cent of those working in the private sector took maternity leave compared to 76 per cent of those in the public sector (ibid.). Many were not eligible because of having less than twelve months' continuous service, while others who were eligible planned to quit their jobs to stay home with their infants. Many employees and employers lacked information about maternity benefits.

In comparison to the United Kingdom (with forty weeks of maternity leave), Australia's leave provisions seem to be relatively generous and flexible. Aside from the extra twelve weeks which Australia provides, if a mother in the United Kingdom has a premature baby and has not taken the eleven weeks required prior to the birth, she is still entitled only to twenty-nine weeks after the birth (Heitlinger 1993, 204). In Australia, the only requirement is that six weeks of the fifty-two are to be taken after the birth. Australia also requires only twelve months of service as opposed to the two years required in the United Kingdom. More categories of employees in the United Kingdom are eligible for benefits during their leave, however.

Although more married women in Australia have entered the labour force, they tend to move into part-time or casual jobs. Even when they work full time, they tend to continue doing most of the housework. Australian men resist doing their share of domestic work, and their employment hours tend to increase just at the stage when their children are young (Pixley 1993; Bittman 1994).

France

Maternity leave was introduced as early as 1913 in France (Lewis, ed. 1993). Job-protected leave from work (*congé parental*) is now combined with a cash benefit that replaces lost earnings for a minimum of sixteen weeks, including six weeks before childbirth (Kamerman and Kahn 1989b). The length of leave and the generosity of benefits vary by the number of children in the family, with more generous benefits directed to larger families.

Parental leave is available to parents who have worked for more than one year in the last two years, and it may be taken as full-time leave or half-time work until the child is three years of age. The idea behind the *congé parental* is that at the end of the leave, the employee must be allowed to resume work or the employer will be forced to compensate the employee. Despite the gender-neutral name, the leave is rarely taken by fathers (Leprince 1991).

For the birth of the third child, twenty-six weeks are granted at 90 per cent of the mother's previous earnings for eight weeks before and eighteen weeks after confinement. For the first and second child, the maternity benefit is 84 per cent, payable for six weeks before and ten weeks after confinement. Fathers are permitted to take a three-day leave at birth. There are two additional weeks payable prior to confinement if complications arise, and two to twelve weeks in the case of multiple births.

The minimum cash maternity benefit in France is Fr 41.77 (Can. $10) per day and the maximum is Fr 317.52 (Can. $75) per day. Benefits are payable for both birth and adoption. The French government also requires employers to provide nursing breaks for employees, which consist of two thirty-minute breaks a day for up to one year after childbirth. Employers with more than 100 employees are required to instal nursing rooms in or near the workplace (International Labor Office 1988b). The French government also offers a monthly allowance for nursing mothers or milk coupons payable for four months (U.S. Dept of HHS 1992).

In 1984, a benefit entitled *allocation parentale d'éducation* (APE) was introduced for parents with more than three children and at least one child under the age of three. This benefit was designed to allow parents (usually mothers) with large families to receive partial compensation for lost earnings while raising their children at home (Leprince 1991). To be eligible, the parent had to be employed for twenty-four of the last thirty months, but in January 1987 this was amended to two years of work out of the last ten. The benefit was extended to allow parents to claim for three years, and in 1991 the flat rate was Fr 2,716 per month (or about Can. $632) (U.S. Dept of HHS 1992, 108).

Maternity and parental benefits are funded largely through a social insurance program which also covers sickness benefits. Employees contribute 6.8 per cent of their total earnings, while employers contribute 12.6 per cent of their total payroll per year. The French government also pays into the fund through proceeds from a 12 per cent surcharge on automobile insurance premiums plus proceeds from taxes on pharmaceutical advertising, alcohol, and tobacco (U.S. Dept of HHS 1992).

Germany

The social insurance system which now covers both sickness and maternity benefits in Germany dates from 1883. All wage earners, salaried employees, unemployment beneficiaries, and some categories of self-employed persons are covered by these benefits (U.S. Dept of HHS 1992, 113). Social insurance covering sickness and maternity benefits is funded through contributions from employers, employees, and government. More specifically, insured persons and employers both contribute premiums which average 6.4 per cent of insurable earnings and payroll, and the government also contributes to the cost of maternity leave and benefits (U.S. Dept of HHS 1992).

In order to qualify for cash maternity benefits in Germany, a woman must have contributed to the insurance program for twelve weeks, or must have been continuously employed from the tenth to the fourth month preceding confinement. In addition, she must be working or excused from work six weeks prior to expected confinement (ibid.). Fourteen weeks of maternity leave are provided at 100 per cent of previous covered earnings, paid six weeks before and eight weeks after confinement. In addition, a cash grant is provided for each birth, worth DM 150 (Can. $120) or more for each subsequent birth (ibid.).

Sickness funds provide paid leave for up to five days a year per sick child under age eight. If the insured employee or his or her spouse is hospitalized, the insurance will cover the cost of child care in the household for children under the age of eight (ibid.). Lone parents have complained about the inequity of this leave. While each working parent in a two-parent family is given five days of paid leave a year per sick child, lone parents are given only five (Brand 1989).

In addition to maternity leave, there has also been a program since 1986 in which one parent can take a job-protected leave for child-rearing. The amount of leave has been extended several times, from ten months in 1986 to thirty-six months in 1992. Typically, this benefit is also available to stay-at-home mothers and is not counted as income if they receive child support or social assistance. The child-rearing benefit (*Erziehungsgeld*) in Germany is quite generous by Canadian standards. It is worth about DM 600 (Can. $479) per month for the first six months, after which it is means-tested (Goldberg 1991). Although the benefit is earnings related, it is provided regardless of the occupational status of parents. Consequently, it is considered more of a 'housewife's wage' than the parental education benefit (APE) in France (Barbier 1990). Ninety-six per cent of young mothers receive this benefit (Brand 1989).

Although the child-rearing benefit is available to both parents, fathers made up only 1.3 per cent of claimants in 1987 (Goldberg 1991).

Germany, as well as other European countries, has used short-term withdrawals from the labour force as a form of temporary job creation for young people and the unemployed. One rationale for extending parental leave in 1988 was to decrease the unemployment rate. When leave was increased from ten months to twelve months, it was expected to create 200,000 one-year contracts for currently unemployed people (Docksey 1987; Heitlinger 1993, 201).

German reunification occurred in October 1990, and in order to understand present controversies over family policy in the united Germany, it is necessary to discuss the German Democratic Republic (GDR) or the former East Germany. This discussion will illustrate the two different political cultures and outline the family policies that the women of the GDR have had to relinquish. The GDR's 1949 Constitution was much like the Soviet one, in that it established juridical equality between the sexes, asserting women's right to work, to be educated, and to receive wages on an equal basis with men. In the 1980s, the GDR had the highest rate of female labour force participation in the world (85 per cent to 91 per cent), ranked the highest in female literacy rates, and ranked third, behind Canada and the United States in the number of women enrolled in higher education. Despite legal equality between the sexes, however, the standard of living and the quality of life were relatively low (Goldberg 1991).

East German women were entitled to a fully paid maternity leave for twenty-six weeks, and women usually took between three and four weeks before the birth. In 1986, a further seven months was introduced at 90 per cent of previous earnings, and either a parent or a grandmother could take the leave (Weigl and Weber 1991a). Women also were entitled to leave for housework of one day per month, a reduced work week for mothers with two or more children, and generous leave to take care of sick children (from four to thirteen weeks per year, depending on the number of children) (Goldberg 1991). Maternity benefits reimbursed 100 per cent net average earnings from the social insurance scheme, and there were two nursing breaks of forty-five minutes a day for all employed mothers with infants (International Labor Office 1988b). In the GDR, however, women were seen as solely responsible both for the care of children and for domestic work. Making benefits 'parental' did not change the take-up rate for men or even induce them to take on a greater proportion of domestic chores.

Female labour force participation in West Germany was about 30 per cent less than East Germany's at the time of unification. Unemployment rates among West German women have always been high, but the government chose not to support women's employment. Instead, it subsidized housewives by providing generous tax allowances for their spouses. Unification with West Germany in 1990 has left East German women without many of the benefits they once enjoyed. The unemployment rate has risen considerably. Reproductive freedom is restricted in the unified Germany, while women could have obtained an abortion under the health insurance program in the GDR. In addition, the almost universal child care system has been lost (Goldberg 1991). Nevertheless, compared to Canada and the English-speaking countries, the united Germany provides family benefits which appear relatively generous.

The Netherlands

As in Germany, maternity benefits in the Netherlands are provided with full wage replacement as part of the social insurance program, which also covers sickness benefits. Sixteen weeks' leave is available, but this may be extended to fifty-two weeks if the mother is unable to work for birth-related reasons. Part-time unpaid parental leave is also available for six months (Perry 1991).

Although the total fertility rate declined sharply from 3.2 in 1961 to 1.5 in 1987, population decline has not been perceived as a social problem, and there has not been the same concern about family policy in the Netherlands as in France. In fact, family policy is generally given a lower priority than other areas of social policy (Moors 1990). Increased female labour force participation is perceived to be one of the major causes of fertility decline, yet Dutch policies support both mothers who care for their children at home and employed mothers.

Religiosity seems to be slightly negatively correlated with the acceptance of government-directed family policies, and those who were politically left of centre were more in favour of government policies relating to families. Although people in the Netherlands generally feel that having children is a private affair for which couples themselves should take full responsibility (ibid.), this belief has not prevented the implementation of generous maternity leave and benefits.

Sweden

The social insurance program dealing with sickness and maternity benefits dates from 1891, but the present system of parental leave was introduced in 1974. Two main goals of the Swedish Social Democratic government have long been to strengthen both the role of women in the labour market and the role of men as fathers. Women's right to employment was established in the 1930s, and in 1937 the original maternity benefit system was implemented. The earnings-related benefit, which reimbursed 80 per cent of earnings, was initially payable to mothers only (Schwartz 1988). Aside from the equal-status goals of Swedish family policy, there was also concern about the low birth rate, or, as it became known in the 1930s, 'the population crisis' (Haas 1991). The declining birth rate was brought to the attention of society by sociologists Alva and Gunnar Myrdal in *The Population Crisis*, published in 1934. The Myrdals argued that the state should take steps to allow mothers to combine motherhood and labour force participation. The victory of the Social Democratic party in Parliament in 1934 set the stage for the reforms (Haas 1991).

In the 1960s, there was a dramatic jump in labour force participation rates which coincided with a shortage of male workers when the Swedish economy expanded. Since then, several reforms have aimed at combining the equal-status goals. These reforms include the introduction of parental insurance in 1974, recognition of the right of parents with infants to reduce their working day from eight hours to six at their own expense in 1979, and provision of pension credits for the care of children at home in 1982 (Schwartz 1988).

The more comprehensive parental insurance scheme which replaced maternity leave in 1974 demonstrated a new way of thinking about parental sharing of responsibilities for children. Women workers were needed by the expanding labour market and to maintain the family's living standard. For these reasons, the expansion of day care centres also was granted high priority by the Social Democratic government.

To qualify for cash parental benefits, each parent must have been insured for at least 240 days before confinement. The parents' cash benefit replaces 80 per cent of income loss for the first fourteen days and 90 per cent from the fifteenth day. Benefits are payable for up to 360 days until the child reaches the age of four and are taxable (U.S. Dept of HHS 1992, 269). Sickness and parental benefits are funded by contributions from employers and the Swedish government. The employer contributes 10.1 per cent of payroll, which covers about 85 per cent of the cost, while the government covers the remaining 15 per cent (ibid.). Parental benefits are administered through local social insurance offices.

Since 1974, parental leave can be used either full or part time at any point until the child is eight years old, and multiple births entitle a parent to six months of extra benefits for each child (Sündstrom and Stafford 1992). In 1978, parents obtained the legal right to unpaid leave of absence from work with full job security after the standard parental leave had ended and until the child was eighteen months old (ibid.). Those on parental leave from a full-time job in Sweden are still considered employees and do not lose seniority, which is important for qualifying for other benefits (ibid.).

Parents may divide parental leave between them as they desire, and may take it at any time up to the child's eighth birthday or the end of the first year of compulsory school. The mother may take six months' leave, and then for the following nine months both parents may work half time. Parents may also choose to reduce their working hours, until the child is eight years old, while retaining their jobs. Furthermore, parents are entitled to employment leave for children's illness: up to 60 working days a year for one child and 120 days for two or more children (Perry 1991). The Swedish parental leave act also includes two days per year to enable parents to spend time with their children in care facilities and to make contact with staff (Lamb, Sternberg, Hwang, and Broberg 1992).

The 'women as workers' policy and the decision to expand day care centres in 1976 were supported by the opposition parties as well as labour market organizations. Since 1970, however, there has been a division over family policy between the Conservative and Centre parties on the one hand and the Liberals, Social Democrats, and Communists on the other hand. The former favoured the breadwinner-housewife family, while the latter preferred the two-income family (Eduards 1991). The debate was crystallized in the 1988 election campaign. For the first time ever, the Centre, Liberal, and Conservative parties presented a specific joint proposal – one year of parental insurance plus a taxable child care allowance of SEK 15,000 (Can. $2,760) annually for all children between the ages of one and seven. The non-socialist bloc lost the election, however, and the Social Democrats, the Communists, and Green party were able to pass legislation for a gradual increase of parental insurance to fifteen and then eighteen months.[2] The labour movement had once again defined parents' interests in relation to the labour market rather than supporting child care allowances, which would have encouraged mothers to stay at home. Although the leave was extended, few men have taken advantage of parental insurance, which led the

Equal Opportunities minister to consider quotas. Parental insurance has, however, provided an incentive for women to secure gainful employment before they become pregnant (Eduards 1991).

Parental benefits are based on previous earnings; hence, the logic of the system demands that any woman contemplating motherhood secure a job before she has a baby. To some extent this imposes a middle-class pattern of delayed motherhood. Only 6 per cent of Swedish women do not conform to this pattern and pay the price by qualifying only for the low flat-rate benefit rather than parental benefits that replace earnings. Given the compensation principle, single mothers must be in the labour force and 87 per cent are in Sweden (compared with 52 per cent in Germany, 39 per cent in the United Kingdom, and 66 per cent in the United States) (Lewis and Astrom 1992).

All employed mothers in Sweden take advantage of the parental insurance benefit, and about 85 per cent return to work by the end of their paid leave or by the time the child reaches its first birthday. In 1987, 25 per cent of eligible fathers took the leave, but the average length of leave was 47 days for fathers and 265 days for mothers (Kamerman and Kahn 1991b). Men say that they fail to take advantage of the leave because their wives prefer to take it, because they are concerned about appearing uncommitted by their workmates and employers, and because many feel that their workloads do not permit more than a few days or weeks of leave (Widerberg 1990).

Justified by 'labour market necessity,' the ideology of equality has influenced all aspects of Swedish legislation, including that relating to wage work and rights for mothers. The government has recognized the 'production-reproduction' conflict inherent in a capitalist society where 'the male as a norm' lies behind the organization of the labour market. Parental leave is classified as a form of protective legislation to integrate women into the corporate structure (ibid.).

Although parental leave is a statutory right, Widerberg (1990) argues that a woman's work situation tends to deteriorate once she begins to claim her rights. The fact that women are far more likely than men to use parental leave creates a different working environment for women and further increases the tendency towards gender segregation in the labour market (ibid.). Swedish factory workers are placed in 'pools' when they take parental leave, and upon return they may be forced to take another job in a different department, with varying shifts. Sharing parental leave could further exacerbate women's difficulties on the job, as the short period of leave most fathers take could cause the mother to interrupt her labour force participation twice. Extended leave to care for sick children is also seldom taken, even though it is a statutory right. Many women say that they do not want to burden their workmates with the extra load and that they are under pressure to maintain good relations with their employers (Haas 1990).

Lone mothers with small children often cannot choose the option of reducing their working hours because they are concentrated in low-paying jobs and cannot support themselves on half-time wages. Furthermore, men are often in positions of power as supervisors and tend to design work schedules which are incompatible with working mothers' needs. In addition, having children is considered to be a personal matter, and questions regarding parental leave as it affects women are not considered 'traditional union questions.' As one woman in Widerberg's study said, 'If they [the local union branch] had brought these questions up, then all of us would probably have gone to their meetings' (Widerberg 1990).

Haas (1990) examined the effectiveness of parental leave in eliminating the gender-based division of labour. She studied whether the number of fathers taking parental leave equalized the position of the sexes in the labour market and in child care within the home once the leave ended. Based on 1986 data from 319 sets of new parents in Gothenberg, Sweden, she found that fathers who took parental leave were more likely to be involved in child care after the leave was over. As they gained an early start in becoming knowledgeable about their children, they tended to reduce their involvement in the labour force. Yet mothers retained primary responsibility for children and remained less involved and less satisfied in the labour market, whether or not their partners took up part of the leave.

In comparing the comprehensiveness of the Swedish welfare state and the somewhat less generous provisions of other industrialized countries, several reasons may be offered to explain the divergencies. Most important, the centralization of the labour movement and the unitary structure of the state facilitated collective bargaining and increased the speed of implementation. In addition, the Social Democratic party has been firmly in favour of women's employment equality. As well, unemployment rates during the period of expansion of parental leave provisions were much lower than in the other countries, and a shortage of male workers necessitated women's participation in the labour force (Schwartz 1988). Furthermore, Sweden has a small homogeneous population, a fact which reduces opposition to policies.

The United Kingdom

The social insurance program which covers sickness and maternity benefits in the United Kingdom was first introduced in 1911 (U.S. Dept of HHS 1992, 297). The legal right to maternity leave, however, was introduced in the 1975 *Employment Protection Act*, and certain rights were also included in amendments to this act in 1978 and 1980. This legislation allows the woman to cease work eleven weeks prior to the expected date of childbirth and, if the employee meets a number of qualifying conditions, to be reinstated twenty-nine weeks following the birth. There is no guarantee, however, that other employment benefits, such as occupational pension plans, will continue during this time away from work (Moss 1988).

To qualify for maternity benefits, a woman must be employed continuously for at least twenty-six weeks by the same employer at the fifteenth week before expected confinement. In addition, she must earn an average of at least £49 (Can. $96) per week in order to qualify (U.S. Dept of HHS 1992, 297), a provision that disqualifies many part-time workers. The basic statutory maternity benefit is £39.25 a week (Can. $77) for eighteen weeks. If the woman has worked for the same employer for two or more years, she may receive six weeks' leave at 90 per cent of average earnings, and then twelve weeks at the flat rate of £37.25 (Can. $73).

There is also a supplemental benefit or state maternity allowance for low-income women worth £35.70 a week (Can. $70) for an eighteen-week period starting at eleven weeks before the expected week of confinement (U.S. Dept of HHS 1992). In addition, the government provides a payment to very poor families to help them obtain such necessities as clothing, diapers, and medicine for the new baby (Bookman 1991).

Maternity benefits are funded as part of a social insurance program, with contributions from employees, employers, and government. Employees contribute a percentage of their earnings based on their income level,[3] while employers contribute between 5 and 10.45 per cent of their employee's wages, depending on the employee's wage bracket. The government contributes an amount equal to 5 per cent of gross contributions (U.S. Dept of HHS 1992).

After the election of the Thatcher government in 1979, statutory maternity benefits were eroded. The years of service required for protection against unfair dismissal increased from six months to two years. The 1980 *Employment Act* also allowed firms with fewer than six employees to refuse a request for maternity leave if they could illustrate its impracticality (Heitlinger 1993, 193). In 1986, the administration of parental leave benefits was shifted from the public sector – the Department of Health and Social Security – to the private sector. National insurance contributions pay for both maternity leave and unemployment benefits.

As in the United States, the emphasis on personal responsibility and individualism has led to negative responses by colleagues and employers towards those who wish to take extended maternity leave. These parents tend to be stigmatized in the same manner as those receiving social assistance. The Conservative government further promoted the idea that extending maternity and parental leave 'would add to employers' costs and could therefore affect their competitiveness, their willingness to recruit and promote young women and the total level of employment they could offer ... The compulsory introduction of parental leave would also damage competitiveness, undermine job prospects and ultimately be detrimental to the welfare of working parents and their children' (Central Office of Information 1987, as quoted in Heitlinger 1993, 196).

Many women who return to work after childbirth do so *before* the end of their leave, usually about four or five months after the birth. The return to work is necessitated by the fact that less than half of the leave period is covered by benefits and then mostly at a low flat rate rather than a rate related to previous earnings (Moss 1991).

Although the British system of maternity benefits appears to be universal, several problems have been identified. Many women do not have the employment history necessary to receive benefits, as the system assumes male work patterns. Another problem is reinstatement. Although jobs are legally protected, many women find it impossible or undesirable to return to their previous employment due to the shortage of adequate child care. Also, there is no maternity leave for adoptive mothers, and paternity leave is not officially endorsed (Marlow 1991).

The United States

Unlike all the other countries in this study, the United States has no national law requiring employers to provide maternity, paternity, or parental benefits. In 1993, the *Family and Medical Leave Act* finally became law under the Clinton administration, after fifteen years of controversy and three years after passing both houses of Congress. It had been vetoed twice by U.S. President Bush. This act requires employers with fifty or more workers to provide job guarantees in the event of medical emergency, childbirth, adoption, or the need for dependent care to employees who have worked for the employer for at least a year (Kamerman and Kahn, forthcoming). Like the state legislation, however, the twelve-week leave is unpaid, and for that reason many employees cannot afford to take advantage of it.

Although maternity benefits are unavailable to most U.S. employees, some employers provide short periods of paid leave as part of sickness or disability benefits. The decision to provide maternity leave or benefits generally lies in the hands of employers (Lubeck and Garrett 1991). Nevertheless, there has been a lengthy debate over these issues in the United States. Several earlier attempts to legislate maternity leave and benefits will be discussed.

In 1978, the federal *Pregnancy Discrimination Act* (PDA) defined pregnancy as a 'temporary disability' that should be covered by existing sickness and medical plans (Kamerman and Kahn 1991b). Working women in firms that offered disability and insurance policies had their coverage extended to pregnancy and maternity. The act itself did not obligate employers to establish such policies, however, despite the fact that most women worked in firms which did not offer disability benefits. The most important effect of the act was to require the five states which did have temporary disability insurance (TDI) to cover working women. Since 1978, no other states have mandated TDI (ibid.).

According to Bureau of Labor Statistics data of 1986, 93 per cent of all employees in medium-sized and large firms have some form of short-term disability coverage (although many U.S. women work in smaller firms). Five states and one territory have temporary disability laws that now include pregnancy: California, Hawaii, New Jersey, New York, Rhode Island, and Puerto Rico (Hayes, Palmer, and Zaslow 1990, 207–8). An Employee Benefits Survey in 1989 found that *unpaid* maternity leave was available to only 33 per cent of employees in medium-sized and large firms in the United States. Paid maternity provisions were rarely found, and paternity leave is not officially endorsed (Marlow 1991). Liberal policies, including paternity leave, tend to be confined to states with higher levels of unionization. In the state of New York, for example, collective bargaining agreements entitle either parent to infant care leave for seven months on a mandatory basis and two years on a discretionary basis (Hayes, Palmer, and Zaslow 1990).

In 1987, twenty-eight states *introduced* parental or family leave legislation, yet only four states *passed* the legislation – Connecticut, Rhode

Island, Oregon, and Minnesota. Family leave refers to a broader category than parental leave, including leave for the care of dependent adults such as spouses or elderly parents. Only in Connecticut was the legislation broadened to become family leave. In summarizing the four laws, the following conclusions could be drawn (Wisensale 1991, 70):

a) all were enacted at the state level without federal initiatives;
b) three of the four state laws apply only to the public sector;
c) all laws are gender neutral;
d) the length of leave varies from six weeks to twenty-four weeks;
e) small companies are exempt in all states (the size of the company required to conform varied from twenty-one to fifty employees);
f) all leave is unpaid.

Among companies that provide parental leave in the private sector, the average leave is two to three months. Large and medium-sized companies tend to provide some paid disability leave, either through disability insurance (production employees) or through paid sick leave (managerial, professional, and clerical employees). Federal employees may use annual or sick leave for post-partum recovery, at the discretion of supervisors.

At the state level, there is now a growing movement to establish parental leave (Lubeck and Garrett 1991, 197). Several states now provide unpaid leave of varying lengths covering mainly larger firms in the public sector, and numerous other states are considering some form of parental leave. In addition, parental or child-rearing leave is being negotiated in labour contracts (ibid.).

In U.S. debates over parental leave, a major objection has been the assumed high cost. In 1988, the General Accounting Office estimated that it would cost American businesses about U.S.$340 million (Can. $434 million) for an eighteen-week unpaid parental leave policy. The cost of extending the program to medical leave and leave for adoptive mothers and sick children was estimated at U.S.$160 million (Can. $205 million) annually (Kamerman and Kahn 1991b). However, the U.S. Chamber of Commerce came up with a much higher figure, estimating that the cost to business would be from U.S.$2.6 billion to U.S.$16.2 billion (Can. $3.3 billion to $20.7 billion) a year. Not surprisingly, the Chamber of Commerce organized a massive lobbying campaign against legislated leave, basing its arguments on opposition to government regulation rather than the principle of parental leave (Bravo 1991).

The debate about statutory maternity or parental leave in the United States is unique in several ways. First, most of the controversy has been over *unpaid* rather than *paid* leave, despite the fact that all the other countries studied have offered paid leave for years. Second, most of the proposals have suggested a system which is administered through private insurance companies rather than the public sector. And third, the legislation which finally passed covers a minority of larger companies and not the majority (Garrett, Wenk, and Lubeck 1990).

Small business and the U.S. Chamber of Commerce continue to argue that 'the market' should determine the level of wages and fringe benefits, including maternity and parental leave. This position, however, is based on several false assumptions (Trzcinski 1991). The first assumes that if women were valuable and productive employees, employers would provide high wages and benefits in order to retain them. The second assumes that if maternity and parental leave were important to employees, they would either find an employer that offers it or accept lower wages in order to acquire this benefit. Unfortunately, these arguments ignore the fact that discrimination is pervasive in hiring and pay (especially for black women), full employment does not exist, and because of family responsibilities it is not always possible for employees to relocate.

Arguing against the U.S. business opposition to statutory maternity benefits, Trzcinski (1991) found that female-dominated firms in the U.S. tended to offer fewer maternity provisions than male-dominated firms. In addition, male-dominated firms tended to provide both better fringe benefits and higher wages. However, unionized women were more likely to be eligible for disability and infant-care benefits than those who were not unionized. Trzcinski argued that the market has failed to provide adequate benefits for working parents (especially women) and that statutory leave, whether paid or unpaid, is necessary.

Although most discussions about creating statutory maternity or parental leave in the United States have focused on unpaid leave, a parental leave policy with wage replacement has also been proposed. Bookman (1991) argued that unpaid leave would tend to perpetuate the gendered division of child care and would benefit the mainly white, upper- and middle-class women who can afford to be absent from work temporarily without wages. If low-income or working-poor women were forced to accept unpaid leave, their families would fall below the poverty line and they would be forced to turn to the Aid to Families with Dependent Children program, which would be more costly to the government in the long term.

Two different philosophies underlie the question of pregnancy leave in U.S. federal and state policies: equal treatment for men and women and special treatment for women. Federal policy addresses pregnancy, childbirth, and post-partum recovery under the equal treatment approach by viewing them as temporary physical disabilities. The fact that men do not experience childbirth is seen as irrelevant because men experience other types of disabilities. The equal treatment idea is embodied in the *Family and Medical Leave Act* (*FMLA*), and the *Pregnancy Discrimination Act* which prohibited employment discrimination based on any physical ailment or disability, including pregnancy. In the 1987 'Cal Fed' case, in which the Supreme Court upheld a California law providing job security for up to four months for pregnant women, these women were viewed as 'disabled' by pregnancy. However, this job protection was not extended to other disabilities (Hayes, Palmer, and Zaslow 1990, 207–8).

In contrast to the equal treatment approach, the special treatment model argues that pregnancy is not a disability but a special circumstance which pertains only to women. Since the early 1900s, protective labour laws were designed for employed women, and some argue that these laws should be extended to pregnancy, childbirth, and post-partum recovery. Historically, however, some of these protective laws (such as exclusion from the night shift) disadvantaged working women by excluding them from more lucrative shifts or jobs. There has been a constant debate about the two legal models, and much of the argument concerns the Equal Rights Amendment in the American Constitution.

Liberal feminist groups strongly supported the *FMLA*, which combined the general disability proposals on a gender-neutral basis. Yet the female-only pregnancy disability approach is the most prevalent in state laws on mandatory leave. The major advantage of this approach is financial, since leave is given only to pregnant women rather than to fathers or adoptive parents. The major disadvantage is its narrow focus; it ignores all other workers with family-related problems, including problems related to child care or the care of dependants (Deller Ross 1991). The parental leave model debated in the United States would be an improvement over the pregnancy-disability model, since it would include fathers. But it too fails to provide sick leave for workers.

The *FMLA* model as it is followed in Connecticut, Maine, and Wisconsin provides both parental leave and medical leave (ibid.). The gender-neutral or equal treatment federal *FMLA* model recognizes workers' dual roles and includes fathers in child care. It ensures that workers will not be fired as a result of their medical condition, and it eliminates the potential sexual discrimination resulting from special treatment legislation (ibid.). Yet when the *FMLA* model was applied at the state level, the number of weeks it offers was reduced and the leave remains unpaid.

Researchers and advocates of parental leave have pointed to the developmental needs of children and parents, the need for women's equity in the workforce, and the need for labour force efficiency. They argue that extended paid leave would increase the number of mothers of newborns staying at home, thereby reducing the demand for public infant care. Paid leave would also encourage equal opportunity for women by increasing their attachment to the labour force and their job seniority. Greater equality of opportunity could perhaps lead to better promotions and higher wages (Hayes, Palmer, and Zaslow 1990). Those who oppose parental leave focus on the costs and loss of productivity assumed to be associated with it. Despite these arguments for and against, establishing unpaid medical leave and parental leave does not begin to satisfy the need for extraparental infant care. Instead, it merely raises the age at which child care is needed (Kamerman and Kahn 1991b).

Garrett, Wenk, and Lubeck (1990) noted that none of the legislation proposed or passed in the United States included wage replacement, and all of it placed the financing of maternity and parental leave on employers. Furthermore, all the legislation excluded employers with fewer than ten employees, even though three-quarters of work establishments employ fewer than ten people (Bookman 1991). The 1993 federal legislation concerns only employers with fifty or more employees.

Three traditions inhibit the United States from adopting a comprehensive family policy. The first is the importance historically placed on individualism and the lack of concern for the collectivity which would allow children to be seen as a shared resource. The second tradition relates to the suspicion of government, particularly in matters perceived to be 'private.' For example, small business has opposed a regulated parental leave policy because it objects to government 'interference' in private matters. The third tradition relates to the nature of the U.S. political process, which does not lend itself to building consensus on such principles as gender equality and child welfare. As in Canada, there is no legalized forum in the United States for including various interest groups in decision making. By contrast, Sweden's comprehensive family policy has come about as a result of its tradition of collective welfare, strong corporatist structures, and a system which promotes consensus building (Haas 1991).

Most of the other countries studied finance maternity and parental leave through social insurance programs, with contributions from employers, employees, and government. Clearly, the debate over maternity and parental leave and benefits will continue in the United States with little recognition of the fact that most industrialized countries have offered paid leave for years, without dire consequences to the economy.

CONCLUSION

Among the eight countries in this study, there is wide variation in the motivating philosophy behind maternity and parental leave and benefit programs, as well as in the duration of benefits and the level of compensation. Despite these variations, however, the underlying structure of the legislation remains essentially patriarchal and assumes male work characteristics as the norm. In most countries, entitlement is based on a lengthy employment record in standardized employment, despite the fact that many women have always worked on temporary contracts or in part-time positions with fewer than the required hours to qualify (Kaul 1991).

Furthermore, the gender-structured nature of the labour market and the differential use of parental leave by men and women preserve the unequal sharing of economic and practical parenting. When parenting is divided between the sexes, economic parenting is usually assumed by the father, who typically obtains full-time paid work more easily and receives higher wages. At the same time, women perpetuate their dependency through practical parenting, partly because it is still seen as 'women's work,' but also because women are less able to find high-paying and permanent full-time jobs. If only one parent is allowed to take parental leave at a time, the family is usually better able to survive on the father's higher wage. Because women have been socialized to be the caregivers of children (and to do most of the housework), they are perceived by both men and women to be the logical choice as recipients of leave.

Two trends are apparent in employment leave for pregnancy and parenting. One is the extension of unpaid parental leave, which is used to deal with several policy concerns. On the one hand, extended leave is an attempt to resolve the perpetual problems parents with infants face when they search for child care services. Second, extended leave allows mothers who want to care for their own children, and who can afford temporarily to forfeit employment income, to do so without giving up their job. Third, extended parental leave reduces absenteeism by temporarily replacing parents of infants or young children with employees who have fewer domestic responsibilities. And finally, extended leave helps reduce unemployment rates by offering short-term contracts as maternity replacements. This can provide invaluable job experience to otherwise unemployed or marginally employed people (Kaul 1991).

A second trend is the increased use of gender-neutral terminology within leave policies. In an attempt to create equal employment opportunities for males and females, parental leave has replaced gender-specific maternity leave in some jurisdictions and workplaces. In the United States, for example, maternity benefits have been perceived as discriminatory to fathers unless they are incorporated into sickness and disability insurance. This insistence on treating men and women exactly equally in terms of employment benefits is ironic considering the fact that women give birth and lactate while men do not. However, the U.S. Constitution may require equal treatment of men and women despite biological differences and the inequalities perpetuated by the present economic system. Radical feminists argue that this insistence on equal treatment of people who experience life differently is counterproductive for women and results from androcentric biases in social policy.

The introduction of maternity and parental leave legislation has served several interests. One relates to concerns about maternal and child health and welfare. Allowing pregnant women to obtain job-protected leave from work recognizes the health risks to the foetus and to the mother from overwork or exposure to certain work-related hazards. Permitting recovery time acknowledges that childbirth is physically and psychologically exhausting. Health and safety advocates have therefore argued in favour of gender-specific maternity leave.

A second interest served by maternity leave legislation relates to the need to secure and sustain the labour force participation of women. If, after working for a designated period of time, women are guaranteed paid leave while their positions are held open, they are more likely to enter the labour force and to ensure that they have met eligibility qualifications before becoming pregnant. Leaving the labour force completely for child-bearing and child-rearing and returning later was feasible for women only when the labour force was expanding, technological change was slower, men were paid a family wage, and divorce rates were lower. Now, women experience more difficulty in re-entering the labour force after five to ten years because of a shrinking market, increased competition, and rapid technological change. Furthermore, a smaller percentage of mothers can depend on another wage in the household.

Although women have always paid a heavy price in lifetime earnings for moving in and out of the labour force, maternity leave provisions have improved their economic status considerably. Consequently, most feminist groups and labour unions have fought for maternity leave.

Third, legislation promoting parental leave as opposed to maternity leave has been motivated by movements to increase the rights of fathers to care for their children. Although men have traditionally been required to place earning a living ahead of child care, new legislation acknowledges that some men want to play a larger role in their children's lives. Swedish research has indicated that fathers who take parental leave tend to spend more time caring for their children throughout the children's lives (Haas 1990). It may be, however, that these men are a self-selected group who are interested in nurturing. Other Swedish research indicates that men are far less likely than women to take parental leave even when it involves full or nearly full wage replacement (Widerberg 1990). In Canada, the expansion of parental leave resulted when a man went to court to argue that as a biological father he should be entitled to the same leave provisions as an adoptive parent.

Despite the different interests and origins of parental and maternity leave, the traditional division of labour has been maintained because legislation in all countries has been implemented within a gender-structured labour market. Although Sweden has allowed less gender inequality in wages and employment opportunities than other countries, inequalities continue. Women tend to take responsibility for 'kin-keeping,' child care, and housework in all countries of our study, and continue to be marginalized in the labour force.

Dalto (1989) found that the differential availability of maternity leave benefits is an important factor in determining the lifetime earnings attained by women. This study concluded that parental leave policies, along with the provision of adequate child care, are essential in order for widespread labour force participation to lead to significant gains in women's earnings. Dalto argues that intermittent labour force attachment, time spent at home, and lifetime earnings are partly dependent on the availability of maternity leave.

Policies which pay mothers to stay at home and care for their children for extended periods of time serve to reinforce patriarchal relations and further erode the position of women in the labour market. Some feminist researchers have suggested that extended parental leave should include a mechanism to ensure that both parents take part of the leave. One idea is that part of the leave would be forfeited if it were not shared between mother and father (Goldberg 1991). However, women and the family unit might suffer from such a policy by experiencing a reduction in the actual amount of leave taken.

Maternity or parental leave policies will not resolve the gender-based labour market or inequalities in the division of labour within the home. Social policies must also focus on improving women's labour market opportunities, raising girls' interest in occupational achievement, and increasing men's participation in child care (Haas 1990). In addition, changes need to be made to the structure of work to remove the assumption that it is separate from personal life. Similarly, the design of our social policies must consider that employment opportunities are not equal for men and women and that not all women are able to work in the standardized labour force. No matter what type of work they do, however, women need leave and financial assistance during childbirth. Any statutory maternity or parental benefits that are tied to a traditional male model of work will exclude a large minority of women.

6

Child care delivery and support

Non-family day care for preschool children originates from three traditions in the countries of this study. Since the nineteenth century, preschool or nursery school has been seen as a necessary and enriching part of early education, especially in Europe. Parents in all the countries have sent their children to kindergarten or preschool to develop the discipline and basic skills necessary for full-time school attendance and to enrich their early development. Private preschools have been especially valued in North America by middle- and upper-income parents.

The second tradition is day care developed for children from low-income inner-city families, especially in the United States, to give culturally deprived children a 'head start.' Researchers in the 1960s emphasized that children from these backgrounds performed below average in first grade and never caught up to other students from middle-class homes. Consequently, remedial preschool programs were designed to prepare 'at risk' children to enter school with less disadvantage than they would have experienced if they were cared for at home by their own mothers. State and national governments were willing to finance these programs to reduce the school drop-out rate, to prevent racial problems and urban unrest, to curb family violence, and to enable the children's mothers to move off welfare and enter the labour force.

The third tradition of child care relates to employment equity for women, and involves the recognition that without day care, mothers with preschool children could not enter or remain in the labour force. When women's labour was needed – for example, during the Second World War – governments provided subsidized child care services, even for middle-class families. Furthermore, governments with a socialist tradition (as in East Germany) or with a tradition of social democracy (as in Sweden) expected women to earn a living and contribute to the nation's economic productivity. To enable women to work for pay, these governments provided state-funded child care services, which came to be seen as a citizenship right.

Despite the availability of preschools and day care centres since the nineteenth century, prevalent ideologies in some countries supported the idea that mothers were best suited to care for preschool children. This ideology, which has been particularly strong in Canada and the English-speaking countries, in certain historical periods in Germany, and in the Netherlands, viewed non-family child care as a last resort. This belief, which appeared to be supported by 1950s research on maternal bonding and deprivation, as we will discuss later in this chapter, is implicit in the design of many social programs.

Prior to the Second World War, some governments legally restricted the employment of married women (especially in the public service) and established a family wage that would pay a man enough to support himself and 'his dependants.' After the war, however, the value of the family wage declined relative to the rising cost of living. Except in jurisdictions where the government provided a substantial allowance for children or homemakers (the Netherlands and Germany), married women began to enter the labour force during the 1950s and 1960s.

At first, mothers with school-aged children were used as a reserve labour force, working for pay only in peak times. Then a 'two-phase work cycle' developed, in which women worked before they had children and re-entered the labour force when all their children entered school or became self-sufficient. The development of part-time work in North America during the 1960s and 1970s further enabled mothers with young children to help increase or stabilize family income. As divorce rates soared in the 1970s and 1980s, the cost of living rose, ideologies supported paid employment for women, and more mothers entered the labour force on a full-time basis.

THE RISING COST OF CHILDREN

In modern urban societies, raising children is very expensive. The cost has been estimated over the life cycle and has been found to vary by country and region. A Canadian study found that two-child families in

Ontario spend at least 18 per cent of their gross income to meet child-rearing costs (Douthitt and Fedyk 1990, 29). Parents, as compared to child-free couples, cover these costs by taking on extra paid work and by refraining from using hired help or expensive labour-saving products. Income from other expenditures tends to be reallocated to child-related goods, and less tends to be spent on restaurant meals, recreation, tobacco and alcohol, adult clothing, and gifts. On average, families with children save less money than couples without children. For example, two-child families in Ontario save about 17 per cent of their gross income during the child-rearing years, compared to an average savings rate of 29 per cent by child-free couples over the same period (ibid.).

Calculations of the actual costs of raising children vary and quickly become meaningless as the cost of living rises. The Social Planning Council of Metropolitan Toronto estimated that the cost of raising a child from birth to age eighteen in the Toronto area was $94,500 in 1987 dollars. Yet this is a conservative estimate which assumes that the family rents an apartment, does not own a car, and does not pay for child care. If the researchers had added ten years of non-subsidized child care, the cost would have increased to about $140,100. Day care can more than double the annual cost of raising younger children and is usually the greatest single child-related expense a family incurs (A. Mitchell 1987). In 1992, the Manitoba government estimated that raising children to age eighteen in Winnipeg cost about $150,000 (Vanier Institute of the Family 1994, 94).

The two-income family, which is a major social innovation for middle-class families, became more prevalent as inflation increased in the 1970s and 1980s, as home ownership became more costly, and as raising children became almost unaffordable. Having a second income raises the standard of living in individual families but on a national level further augments the inequality between one-income and two-income families. In addition, two-income families create the need for new services, such as convenience foods, home cleaning companies, extended retail and business hours, and public child care facilities.

In chapter 5, the rise of labour force participation rates of mothers with young children over the past two decades was discussed. Only a few countries have provided sufficient financial support to families to slow the rate of women's exit from the home. In countries such as Australia, the growth of part-time work has enabled mothers to earn some money and retain their child care responsibilities. In others, women's entry into the labour force was assisted by an extensive state-funded child care system, financed through income taxes or payroll deductions.

Whether or not governments should be more involved in child care remains a contentious issue in most of the jurisdictions. Child care services are costly and require considerable public commitment to early childhood education and the goals of moving mothers off welfare and/or achieving equality in the labour force for women. Not all governments support these goals. Instead, some governments have preferred greater tax relief for one-income families as well as wages and pensions for homemakers who look after their own children.

Although lack of state-funded child care has not prevented many mothers from entering the labour force in Canada, it has clearly produced anxiety and reduced work productivity for those who are employed (Duxbury, Higgins, and Lee 1992). In addition, most Canadian mothers have been able to enter the labour force only through using unregulated child care, despite concerns about its quality and reliability.

MODELS OF CHILD CARE[1]

Three models of service delivery for child care predominate among the countries in this project. Although various labels have been used for them, in this study they are referred to as the social welfare model, the public responsibility model, and the mixed responsibility model.

Within the social welfare model of child care, the vast majority of services are provided by family members, neighbours, or private caregivers. Government assistance is very selective and subsidizes only the poorest and most disadvantaged children in order to keep parents off social assistance. Typically, only regulated, not-for-profit, or employer-sponsored services are subsidized by government. Furthermore, child care regulations and subsidies are usually established by provincial, state, or local governments and therefore vary considerably by jurisdiction. Enforcement is often erratic (Kamerman and Kahn 1991a). The social welfare model combines the two functions of early childhood education and social welfare. The United Kingdom and the United States follow this model, and several authors also include Canada in this category (Haskins 1992; Moss and Melhuish 1991).

Some countries, especially in Europe, view child care as a public responsibility and the right of every family living within the society, like the right to elementary school education. Preschool child care is seen as important for children's development and essential to enable mothers to participate equally in the labour force. Within this model, the government sets standards of education and care, and programs are heavily subsidized through taxes (Goelman 1992). If parents are expected to pay fees, these are charged on a sliding scale which considers family income and the number and ages of children in a family. Parents have a choice in the type of care they want, and extra services such as transportation and meals are often included (Perry 1991).

The public responsibility model has also been called 'universal day care' (Kamerman and Kahn 1991a), and European countries such as France and Sweden tend to favour this approach. Some analysts also place Germany (especially the former East Germany) in this category, while others place the former West Germany in the mixed responsibility category (A. Phillips and Moss 1989).

The mixed responsibility model falls between the other two, as child care services are provided by both the private and public sectors. Voluntary organizations, the private sector, and employers may be encouraged to develop services through capital grants or tax concessions. Certain categories of parents, such as lone-parent families or those with low incomes, may be given priority for subsidized spaces, and fees usually vary by family income. Governments may also provide income tax deductions or credits for child care, especially for parents who are employed or are full-time students (Perry 1991). More variation in quality of services, costs, and subsidies is apparent than in the public responsibility model, and there is generally a shortage of spaces and a high use of relatives as care providers. Australia and Canada follow this model, and the United States is moving towards it (Haskins 1992; Perry 1991).

TYPES OF CHILD CARE SERVICES

Licensed child care is offered in a variety of settings. To receive a licence, facilities must meet minimum government standards of health, safety, and programming (Lero, Goelman, et al. 1992). Different types of licensed care include day care centres, family day care homes, preschools or kindergartens, employer-sponsored care, before-school and after-school care, and vacation care. Many parents, however, rely on unlicensed and unregulated care by sitters, especially in Canada and the English-speaking countries (or the 'liberal welfare states').

Day care centres or nurseries, which could be sponsored by public or private organizations on a for-profit or not-for-profit[2] basis, provide licensed group care, usually for preschool children. To accommodate the needs of parents working full time, services are usually offered during regular business hours, although some centres offer part-time and occasional care. Centres are usually located in schools, community centres, workplaces, religious institutions, or separate buildings, but seldom in private homes (Herr 1989).

Family day care refers to paid care by a (female) non-relative, who is sometimes licensed by government to look after a maximum number of children (often three or four in addition to her own) in her home. Some of these women are trained, but most are mothers who stay home with their own children and wish to make money while doing so. Family day care is seen as an alternative to centre care, especially for infants and toddlers, because parents feel it offers a more home-like environment. It is not always licensed or regulated, however (Lubeck and Garrett 1991).

The nursery school or kindergarten model was developed by child psychologists in Germany in the nineteenth century and quickly spread to other countries. Such facilities offer preschool children disciplined but creative play in a group setting, and usually accept children aged three to five. The first public kindergarten opened in Ontario in 1883 (N. Sutherland 1976, 174), but it was not until the 1920s that kindergartens were accepted in Canada. They have been popular in Europe for many years, however, and France has the most extensive system of preschools in the world, called *écoles maternelles* (A.J. Frankel 1991). Rather than focusing on custodial care, nursery schools emphasize early childhood education and development. In Canada, private nursery schools (such as Montessori schools) are used mainly by higher-income families who are better able to pay the fees and often have strong opinions about the importance of certain educational philosophies. On the other hand, public kindergartens for five-year-olds are usually part of the education system, are located in school buildings, and follow the same hours as the school day, for either a half-day or a full day. Not all jurisdictions offer such programs, however. In Canada, for example, Prince Edward Island and Alberta do not offer public kindergarten classes (Friendly 1994).

Some employers sponsor child care services either at or near the workplace, and governments sometimes provide tax concessions or subsidies for capital costs. This type of facility is a relatively recent innovation designed to attract or retain female employees in certain industries, companies, or workplaces. To enrol their children in the program, employees are usually expected to pay fees, although this may be part of their employment benefits package.

Before-school and after-school programs provide school-aged children with supervised group activities from the end of the school day until parents arrive home from work. These programs are often recreational and are sponsored by community centres, school boards, other not-for-profit agencies, and day care centres. They are designed for children who would otherwise become 'latch-key' children (children who return to an empty home), because researchers and social workers have identified these children and adolescents as high risks for delinquent activities (Lero, Goelman et al. 1992).

Summer camps and vacation care schemes also provide day programs or residential programs lasting for several weeks during school vacation. These enable working parents to be assured that their children are supervised when school is out and allow homemakers to obtain a break from child-rearing. They may also provide enriched educational opportunities or specialized programs not available in the children's schools. For example, some summer camps include training or intensive courses in science, computers, music, specific sports, or outdoor skills, while others simply offer a variety of leisure pursuits.

Informal or sitter care consists of private arrangements made by parents for their children either inside the family home or in the caregiver's home. Care providers are often neighbours or female relatives, such as an aunt or grandmother (ibid.). Although some researchers note that most informal care is provided by the father of the children when mothers work (Herr 1989), the focus in this study is only on non-parental care; fathers will not be labelled 'sitters,' because they are parents.[3] Sitters may also be adolescent neighbours earning extra money or women unable to find other employment due to their immigration status, language problems, low education, or lack of job experience.

Parents often prefer informal child care for the lower cost, the convenience of having someone come to their home, or a wish for their child to spend time with a caring relative or friend. Culturally sensitive care or care for a child with special needs may be available only informally. On the other hand, parents may accept informal care because they are unable to secure regulated services within their community.

MODELS OF REGULATION AND SUPPORT

Child care services may be regulated in different ways, implying varying degrees of government involvement. Beginning with maximum government intervention, child care facilities may be inspected directly by government officials and approved only if they meet minimum standards. Alternatively, the government may contract out this inspection to trained professionals in early childhood development or to a child welfare agency. Governments may also not require government inspection unless there is a complaint, while establishing a registry of day care facilities with standards maintained through self-regulation and parental monitoring. In the resource and referral model, the government is not directly involved, but an independent agency compiles a list of resources and assists parents to find appropriate child care. The provider accreditation model, which is a way of distinguishing high standards on a voluntary basis, involves a professional organization which establishes rules and accredits day cares that meet the requirements. In the independent advocacy model, advocates conduct investigations when there is a complaint (Corsini et al. 1988).

In fact, in practice, a combination of all these models is often used within each jurisdiction (NAEYC 1987). In Canada, for example, provincial and municipal governments create day care regulations and are responsible for enforcing them, but professional associations are also involved in accrediting child care workers and monitoring services. In addition, the federal government commissions research and compiles statistics on provincial services, as well as sharing the cost of eligible services under the Canada Assistance Plan.

CHILD CARE IN CANADA

The history of child care in Canada[4]

The daytime care of children became a social issue in nineteenth century Canada following a noticeable increase in the number of 'neglected' and delinquent children in the industrialized cities. Poor, deserted, and widowed women were often unable to care for their young children because they needed to work for pay or because their incomes were too low. Children from these families were temporarily placed in institutions or children's homes, cared for by relatives or friends, or left to fend for themselves while their mothers worked as domestics or factory workers.

As middle-class women seldom worked outside the home (unless they were widowed or in serious financial need), child care for working mothers was generally seen as a welfare issue. Orphanages, foundling homes, and other children's homes were run by churches or charitable organizations and provided care for infants and children when their families were unable to look after them. These institutions were financed through donations and volunteer labour, and the children, when possible, worked for their board. Children were also placed with families by means of indenture and were expected to work for that family in return for their keep. As well, many poor or homeless children were brought from Britain to Canada in the nineteenth century and early decades of the twentieth in order both to give them homes and to provide labour for Canadian families. For example, the British philanthropist Thomas Barnardo organized the emigration of more than 25,000 British children between 1882 and 1915 (Corbett 1981).

The institutionalization of neglected and delinquent children declined considerably in Toronto in the early decades of the 1900s when it became clear that children benefited from a family environment. The Toronto Children's Aid began to place children in foster homes whenever possible, and after 1920 children's institutions became less prevalent in Ontario, although many still operated across the country. Settlement houses or community welfare centres provided some daytime care for welfare children, as well as programs to improve the health, morals, and education of the poor.

In the welfare tradition, one controversy had always been over whether to provide child care to enable poor women to work for a living or pay a mother welfare benefits to enable her to care for her children at home. Before federal or provincial support for social services, few municipalities or charitable organizations could afford to pay mothers to look after their children. When mothers were forced to work to support themselves and their children, they usually made private arrangements with neighbours or relatives for child care. It was not until 1916 that a Canadian province (Manitoba) initiated mothers' allowances, and these were only for 'morally upright women' with dependent children (Armitage 1988, 271). Federal universal mothers' allowances were introduced in 1945, as the Family Allowance Program.

While child care services originated from a welfare tradition, public kindergartens and nursery schools arose from developments in educational philosophy. Child psychologists from Europe encouraged conscientious parents to provide their preschool children with disciplined but creative play in a group setting. As mentioned earlier, the first public kindergarten opened in Ontario in 1883 (N. Sutherland, 1976, 174), but it was not until the 1920s that kindergartens began to be accepted in Canada.

After the First World War, birth rates were declining, but rates of infant mortality and maternal death were still high in Canada compared to rates in some European countries. Concern was expressed by doctors, journalists, members of the clergy, and social workers that mothers themselves were creating child health problems by their lack of knowledge of child care. During the 1920s and 1930s, strong criticism of the knowledge and expertise of mothers was expressed in magazines such as the *Canadian Home Journal* and *Maclean's*. Concern was voiced that the worldly ambitions of the 'new woman' (meaning the desire for education and paid work) would lead to the deterioration of family life (Strong-Boag 1982, 161).

In 1922, the federal government's new Division of Child Welfare produced a series of booklets providing practical child-rearing and domestic advice, and established clinics for expectant mothers and for babies as part of a campaign to reduce infant mortality. Popular magazines published a barrage of articles celebrating maternalism and recommending strict scheduling in infant and child care.

Within this social environment, nursery schools developed. In 1925, nursery schools were started for children of two to five years as part of the child study programs at McGill University and the University of Toronto (ibid.). All children enrolled were from middle-class families and had educated parents. They attended an enriched program of creative play and 'scientific child care,' grounded in behaviourist and Freudian psychology. Mothers occasionally assisted trained teachers but were not paid for their work.

Although the McGill nursery experiment lasted only until 1930, the University of Toronto program continued and became the model for settlement house and church nurseries. However, there was always a certain amount of opposition to the nursery school idea in Canada. From the 1930s to the 1950s, European and American research on early child development emphasized the importance of the bond between mother and child. Some parents, religious leaders, and policy makers feared that nursery school children would be deprived of that bond and would consequently develop abnormally.

Studies done in European orphanages showed that infants and children often became intellectually disadvantaged and emotionally disturbed over time. The results were interpreted as resulting from 'maternal deprivation.' However, these researchers (including John Bowlby and René Spitz) mistakenly confused the presence of the mother with nurturance, stability, and intellectual stimulation, and suggested that mothers who 'neglected' their children all day (meaning that they had them cared for by someone else) were voluntarily causing emotional and intellectual problems for them. No one studied the absence of the father during early childhood development, as it was assumed that only the mother could provide the nurturance a child needed. The studies also overlooked the fact that children who lived twenty-four hours a day in an orphanage were less likely to be emotionally stable than those who spent from eight to nine hours a day in a professionally run nursery.

Another reason why nursery schools did not become more popular in North America was the strength of the traditional idea that a married woman's proper 'career' was motherhood. If she was not caring for her children, some people felt that she was not fulfilling her duty. This was partly perpetuated by Freudian psychology, which was quite popular in North America in the 1930s and 1940s. Conservatives as well as trade unionists thought that nursery schools would encourage married women to work outside the home and compete with male breadwinners, leading to the dissolution of 'the family' (Pierson 1977).

Despite the prevailing attitude against employed married women, women's labour was needed during the Second World War in war industries and in many positions left vacant by men who had joined the armed forces. As part of a plan to draw women into the workforce, Prime Minister Mackenzie King revised the *Income Tax Act* to allow husbands to claim their wives as dependants regardless of how much money the wives earned. He also offered federal cost-sharing with provinces that provided day care centres for mothers working in war industries, a benefit which was later extended to all working women. Only Quebec and Ontario, however, made use of the *Dominion-Provincial Wartime Day Nurseries Act*. Furthermore, most of these nurseries were closed when the war was over and federal money was withdrawn (ibid.).

After the Second World War, kindergarten programs were expanded into the elementary school system in some provinces such as Ontario. These programs continued the nursery school philosophy, providing half-day enrichment programs for five-year-olds. Gradually, during the 1950s, some schools accepted four-year-olds. During the 1960s, when educational theories emphasized creative play, private preschools developed, including Montessori schools. Mothers also cooperatively developed play schools to provide intellectual and social stimulation for their preschoolers. When mothers' participation in the labour force continued to rise in the 1970s, child care centres were established both by private owners and by not-for-profit community organizations. While many private centres offered mainly custodial care, some provided educational services comparable to those available in nursery schools and kindergartens (Canada, Task Force on Child Care 1986).

Although child care was cost-shared during the Second World War by both federal and provincial governments, federal money was withdrawn immediately after the war. Not until 1966 was federal funding used again for child care in Canada. Since then, the demand for a national child care policy has increased with women's labour force participation and the growing strength of child care advocacy groups (Friendly 1994).

The growing demand for child care

Before the Second World War, most Canadian children were cared for at home by their mothers. In 1941, only 4.5 per cent of married women were working in the labour force (M. Baker, ed. 1990, 8). Even in the 1960s, women's labour force participation was influenced by marriage, the employment status and income of their husband, and the presence of children. If women were married, they were less likely to be working outside the home unless their husband was unemployed, sporadically employed, or a low-income earner. In addition, the presence of preschool children and the absence of non-family child care services kept mothers out of the labour force.

In the 1990s, on the other hand, younger women are more likely than older women to be employed, regardless of their marital status or the presence of children. By 1992, 61.4 per cent of all married women were in the labour force (Statistics Canada 1992b, B8). About three-quarters of mothers with children under twelve are now working for pay, compared to 35 per cent of all women aged forty-five and over. In addition, married women are at least as likely as separated, divorced, or widowed women to be working for pay (ibid.).

According to Statistics Canada and the Canadian National Child Care Study of 1988, two-thirds of women with children under sixteen were in the workforce. If we analyse these figures by the child's age, we find some variations. Where the youngest child was six to fifteen years of age, this figure rises to three-quarters. About 65 per cent of mothers were employed when the youngest child was three to five years of age (Lero, Goelman et al. 1992), while 61.6 per cent of women with children under three were employed in 1991, an increase from 32 per cent in

1976 (Statistics Canada 1992b, B19). Most employed mothers in Canada work on a full-time basis, or for more than thirty hours per week (Moss and Melhuish 1991).

In 1990, there were more than 1.3 million preschoolers (under age six) and 1.7 million school-age children (six to twelve) in Canada whose mothers were in the labour force. Therefore, as many as 3 million children may have been in need of alternative care arrangements. Yet in 1990, there were only 321,000 licensed spaces for children of those ages in the entire country. Only 18 per cent of preschool children with mothers in the labour force were enrolled in licensed family or centre day care full time, up from 4 per cent in 1981 (Burke, Crompton, Jones, and Nessner 1991).

In the 1980s, the political importance of child care increased in Canada with the rising numbers of employed mothers and the publicity granted to work-family conflicts. Two official commissions were formed to study child care, and the Canadian National Child Care Survey was initiated in 1983 (Lero, Goelman et al. 1992; Powell 1992). After considerable pressure from day care advocacy groups (especially the Canadian Day Care Advocacy Association), the Conservative government announced in 1987 a National Strategy on Child Care. This strategy contained increased tax deductions for working parents using child care services, research money for child care, and new legislation (the *Canada Child Care Act*), which proposed to alter the way child care is funded, taking it out of welfare legislation. However, as I will discuss in the next section, the tax reforms were implemented but the legislation never was, and child care is still funded as a welfare issue in Canada.

Funding child care in Canada

Although the licensing and regulation of child care services fall under provincial jurisdiction, the federal government made provision to share the cost of child care for low-income families in 1966, under the Canada Assistance Plan (CAP). To receive federal contributions, the provinces must spend the money first, then apply to the federal government to match eligible expenditures specified in the plan. For a limited number of families in financial need, subsidies are available, generally in not-for-profit government-regulated centres or family care homes. A criticism of this arrangement is that poorer provinces do not have the initial funds to spend on child care. Because of the shortage of licensed and subsidized child care spaces, most Canadian parents rely on unregulated sitters to care for their preschool children. Two-parent families whose incomes are above the provincially set level must pay the full cost of child care. In Ontario, infant care could cost as much as $10,000, while a high-quality preschool program costs about $6,000–$7,000 per child each year (Canada, House of Commons 1991).

In 1988, the federal government attempted to remove child care funding from CAP. However, the proposed *Child Care Act* caused considerable opposition from provincial governments, day care advocacy groups, feminist groups, unions, and conservative pro-family organizations. In fact, all witnesses who appeared before the parliamentary legislative committee (except the minister who proposed the legislation) opposed the bill, for the following reasons. First, it would have removed funding for day care from welfare legislation, but in doing so could have reduced the amount of federal money granted to some provinces by placing a ceiling on contributions instead of matching funding. Second, it proposed that public funding be extended to for-profit care, which many groups saw as an unnecessary subsidy to commercial enterprises and a waste of valuable tax dollars. The bill did not create national standards of care or nation-wide qualifications for day care workers, which day care advocates wanted but which the Quebec government refused to tolerate. Nor did it propose financial assistance to parents caring for their own children, which the conservative women's groups such as REAL Women of Canada requested. An election was called before the bill became law, and a new bill has not yet been introduced into the Canadian Parliament. In fact, the minister of health and welfare publicly announced in 1992 that there was insufficient public money both to expand child care services and to fight child poverty, abuse, and neglect, and that government priorities would focus on the latter.

The Canadian government also provides an income tax deduction for child care expenses of employed parents, which, because it is a deduction and not a credit, is most valuable to middle-income families. As part of the National Strategy on Child Care, the federal government raised the maximum tax deductions in 1988 from $2,000 per child under seven (with a family maximum of $8,000) to $4,000 a year for children under seven years and $2,000 for children seven to fourteen (with no family maximum). These amounts were again raised for the 1993 tax year to $5,000 and $3,000. In addition, the federal government allows parents to deduct a maximum of $8,000 per child from their income tax for children with special needs (Goelman 1992).

To be eligible for the child care expenses deduction, parents must be employed or studying full time and must show receipts for payment. However, the deduction is not used by a substantial minority of parents who pay for child care services but are unable to obtain receipts from care providers working informally within the underground economy (Canada, Senate 1988). Because the tax benefit for child care expenses is a deduction rather than a refundable credit, it is most beneficial for families with higher incomes and is of no use at all to those without a taxable income. In addition, it cannot be used by parents who care for their own children at home, a matter of great concern to groups representing homemakers (such as REAL Women of Canada).

The federal government further provides child care allowances for trainees in programs run by Employment and Immigration Canada. The Department of Indian and Northern Affairs also offers assistance for child care on some reserves in certain provinces. In total, federal day care expenditure is about $1 billion per year (Goelman 1992).

Canada's child care system ranks well below those of most of the countries studied in terms of level of funding, availability of spaces, cost to parents, and quality of care (Bronfenbrenner 1992; Goelman 1992; Lamb and Sternberg 1992). Critics have complained that the federal government has not created national standards, but others (especially lobby groups from Quebec) argue that this would violate the Canadian Constitution because the provision of child care services falls under provincial jurisdiction. The present situation, with different systems in each province, results in fragmented service and variable quality (Ochiltree 1992).

The most prevalent forms of child care

Informal care by relatives, neighbours, or hired sitters is the most prevalent form of day care in Canada. Most sitters operate outside provincial regulations, which means that care is unregulated by any level of government. In addition, sitters sometimes fail to report their earnings to the taxation office, and without official receipts, parents cannot claim the child care expenses deduction on their income tax.

Aside from informal care, most regulated care in Canada is centre-based. Day care centres provide care for infants and preschool or school-aged children, and may be run by commercial ventures or not-for-profit organizations such as community groups, religious associations, and trade unions. Although day care in Canada has retained a market focus, most centre-based care is not for profit, although this varies by province (Friendly 1994). Only in Ontario, Quebec, and Alberta have a small number of government-sponsored day cares been established (Goelman 1992).

The second most prevalent form of regulated child care is family day care, which is regulated in all provinces and territories except New Brunswick, Newfoundland, and the Northwest Territories. In 1989, family day care comprised 12.7 per cent of all licensed spaces and is increasing at a faster rate than centre care (ibid.). This type of care is often preferred by parents with children under three years because, typically, the staff-child ratio is more favourable to children, the homes are located within the neighbourhood, and they are run in a less institutional and bureaucratic way than centres (Ferguson 1991).

Kindergartens are provided for five-year-olds as part of the public education system in all provinces and territories except Prince Edward Island and Alberta (Friendly 1994). Private preschools also offer early childhood education in most provinces. Before-school and after-school programs are also available in most provinces, but in Quebec this service is provided by school boards (Ergas 1990).

As in other countries with a mixed responsibility model, a variety of day care services are available in Canada. Parents with able-bodied children between three and five, who live in cities, and who can afford to pay higher fees have the most options from which to choose.

Provincial regulation of child care

Although the federal government helps pay for child care services, the provincial, territorial, and municipal governments are responsible for licensing, regulation, and enforcement. Regulations, which vary considerably by province, tend to focus on physical conditions, but also deal with staff qualifications and staff-child ratios. Regulations are less stringent for family day care than for centres (Goelman 1992).

Provinces also differ in the proportion of not-for-profit and commercial child care spaces available to parents. Alberta and Newfoundland are the only provinces where commercial spaces exceed not-for-profit spaces (ibid.). About half of Ontario's day care spaces are in for-profit facilities and half are in not-for-profit centres. Saskatchewan has the fewest commercial spaces, only 1.5 per cent of its total (Ferguson 1991).

Ontario, which provides the most day care spaces of any province, has recently expanded spaces and subsidies under the New Democratic government, although subsidized spaces are still in short supply. The NDP government also announced a plan to convert private spaces into not-for-profit ones, to raise the wages and training opportunities of day care workers, to change the subsidy system from a flat rate to a sliding scale, and to create a publicly financed all-day kindergarten for three- to five-year-olds. These plans have not yet been implemented, however (Philp 1994).

In Quebec, almost half the not-for-profit spaces are operated by the Department of Education, giving the province the highest proportion of publicly sponsored day care spaces (33 per cent) as well as a high proportion of unionized day care workers (Goelman 1992). Rather than being part of social services, the agency that administers day care programs reports to the Quebec minister responsible for the status of women (Canada, Senate 1988).

Although Manitoba has moved towards a not-for-profit system of day care since 1982 (when it had an NDP government), Alberta (with a Conservative government) provides operating grants to help commercial centres meet government standards. In British Columbia, family day care providers are usually unlicensed, and government fee subsidies for low-income parents may involve unregulated services (Goelman 1992). Nova Scotia, Newfoundland, and New Brunswick offer minimal services, and as of 1988 the Northwest Territories was not regulating child care at all (Canada, Senate 1988).

The many provincial variations create a system which lacks unity, consistency, and sometimes quality. Most not-for-profit centres maintain long waiting lists, since the number of families who need child care far exceeds the availability of spaces. With several levels of government involved in record-keeping and regulation, research on ,child care is difficult (Ferguson 1991). The National Child Care Information Office in Ottawa relies on provincial reports that vary in the way statistics are compiled (Goelman 1992).

Child care concerns

The quality of care both in regulated centres and in private homes by sitters continues to concern many parents. Centre employees in some provinces and sitters in all provinces are not required to have any special training. These jobs generally pay the minimum wage or below and attract more females than males, and employers have difficulty attracting and retaining committed and trained employees. The quality of care received by most children of working parents can be monitored only by parents, who seldom have the opportunity or time to investigate conditions fully. Because parents often cannot find alternatives within their neighbourhood, they are forced to accept whatever care is available.

A number of interest groups have formed around child care issues, most notably the Canadian Day Care Advocacy Association, which is an amalgam of provincial organizations. Numerous advocacy groups have requested increased federal funding and more subsidized spaces; national child care standards; and better training, fringe benefits, and pay for child care workers. There is a wide discrepancy between the qualifications and salaries of child care workers and kindergarten teachers, for example. Although both types of employees are typically women, kindergarten teachers are under the jurisdiction of the Ministry of Education and are frequently unionized. On the other hand, day care employees who work in the private sector or are partially funded through the Ministry of Community and Social Services typically receive low wages and are seldom unionized.

Parents of children with 'special needs' have not had an easy time finding suitable day care in Canada. Before institutions and hospitals were built in the 1960s, mothers were the main caregivers of children with disabilities. As policies of deinstitutionalization are used to reduce health care costs, this traditional source of unpaid labour is being increasingly called upon once again. But adequate attention is not always given to the fact that most mothers are now employed. Without remuneration and community assistance, these mothers are unable to supervise their children because they must work for pay. Furthermore, many parents now expect children with disabilities to be integrated into the local day care centre or public school so that they can receive the same education as other children. In fact, court cases using the equality clause of the *Canadian Charter of Rights and Freedoms* have been fought over this issue.

Child care problems have encouraged some mothers to remain at home with their children. Few centres accept children under the age of two unless they are toilet-trained. Even if space is available, mothers sometimes feel that they can provide higher quality care than anyone else. Some are also concerned about the spread of infectious diseases among infants in centre care. Finding a qualified sitter to come to the child's home or who will welcome an extra child in her home is also difficult. Despite parental concerns about the qualifications of sitters, their dependability, their cultural and moral values, and their potential for child abuse, most parents with young children need to work for pay. Therefore, informal care remains the typical form of day care.

Increasingly, employers are allowing parents extended unpaid leave for up to five years to care for their children at home. Only some employers offer such leave programs, however, and typically only mothers use it. Fathers often feel that they would be unable to leave their workplace for an extended period or to forfeit their earnings, which are usually higher than their wife's. Few families can survive on one income, and the parent who stays at home may experience difficulty in re-entering the labour force.

The nature of the funding mechanism has created a two-tiered system of child care in Canada. Preschools or nannies are used by wealthier children, while government-subsidized day care is provided for the needy. While kindergartens are funded as part of the education system, day care is usually funded as part of social services, thereby perpetuating the artificial distinction between education and social welfare (Kamerman and Kahn 1989b). Those with middle-class incomes are forced to pay the entire cost of day care, although the government offers valuable tax deductions for those who can obtain receipts.

Child care is considered to be a family matter by many conservatives in Canada, and some still feel that mothers with preschool children should stay at home unless their labour or income is necessary, either to the government or to the family unit. As more mothers have entered the labour force and advocacy groups have mobilized to demand change, however, child care has been placed higher on the political agenda (Powell 1992).

A CROSS-NATIONAL COMPARISON OF CHILD CARE SERVICES

Australia

As in Canada, the model of child care delivery in Australia is mixed responsibility. Services are operated by not-for-profit organizations, commercial enterprises, and state and local governments (Perry 1991), but most children with employed mothers are cared for informally by relatives (Ochiltree 1992). The main types of licensed care in Australia are day care centres, family day care, and preschool services (Ergas 1990).

About 14 per cent of preschoolers attend day care centres which provide either full-time or part-time care (Perry 1991). Extended, emergency, or occasional day care may also be available from centres (Ergas 1990). Family day care, which is licensed and coordinated by an authorized agency, provides full-day, occasional, emergency, and outside-school care for up to four children in a private home (ibid.). In addition, half-day education for children aged three to five may be provided by public or private preschools. State governments operate and regulate public kindergartens and after-school programs, usually in schools (Ochiltree 1992). Vacation care is also provided by community groups, but there are few employment-based child care facilities in Australia (Ergas 1990).

The labour force participation of mothers is increasing in Australia with the decline of the family wage, rising unemployment, and inflation. In June 1990, 46 per cent of adult women were in the labour force compared to 77 per cent of adult men. Among mothers with children aged five to fourteen, 69.5 per cent were in the workforce although more than half worked part time (Ochiltree 1992, 298). As in Canada, the greatest increase in labour force participation has been among women age twenty-five to forty-four (Goodnow, Burns, and Russell 1989). The participation rates of women and mothers in the labour force are lower in Australia than in Canada (E.A. Anderson 1991).

Since the *Child Care Act* in 1972, the Australian government has played a major role in the direct funding of licensed family day care facilities. As in Canada, the state and local governments administer and regulate child care services, but different government departments are responsible for child care in each state (Ergas 1990). There is some variation among states, although differences are kept to a minimum by federal policies, and public and private child care in Australia is considered to be of high quality. There is more variation in quality among private centres than in public facilities (Ochiltree 1992).

New public day care centres are funded through federal-state-local government cost-sharing arrangements, with the federal government covering the majority of expenses. The Commonwealth government pays an operation grant of A.$16 (Can. $14.48) for each approved place for children under three years old and A.$11 (Can. $9.96) for each place for children aged three and over. Special needs subsidies are also available. Since November 1988, fee subsidies have been extended to eligible private centres (Perry 1991), and state governments also fund after-school care, occasional care, vacation care, and some family day care (Ergas 1990).

Although parents must pay fees for child care services, subsidies are available to low-income and middle-income families using public and eligible private centres and employer-provided services (Ochiltree 1992). Subsidies to families vary with the number of children and family income. For example, a family with one dependent child and an income below A.$19,300 (Can. $17,467) (69 per cent of the mean income) pays A.$15 (Can. $13.58) per week. The cut-off point for a day care subsidy for a family with one child is a family income of A.$56,286 (Can. $50,939) (double the average income) (Perry 1991).

As in the United Kingdom, child care is not tax deductible by parents, but the Australian government provides tax deductions to companies providing services, to encourage employer-sponsored child care. Until recently, mothers paid income tax on any child care assistance they received from employers (Ochiltree 1992).

A shortage of child care spaces exists in Australia as in Canada, and lone parents who are employed or looking for work are given priority. The number of private day care centres has increased since November 1988, when they became eligible for government assistance. Tax concessions have also increased employer-provided child care services, although they are still few in number (Perry 1991). Child care and early childhood education programs are available within government social services for children from low-income families, Aboriginal children, and children with disabilities. However, there is a degree of stigma attached to these targeted programs (R.G. Brown 1989).

Although the *Child Care Act* initially focused on children 'in need,' a policy of universal access to child care was established in Australia in 1983. Nevertheless, priority is still given to two-income families, employed lone parents, and children with special needs (Ergas 1990). Funding increased steadily through the 1980s, and child care has become a political priority since women's work has become more important (Goodnow, Burns, and Russell 1989; Ochiltree 1992). In September 1994, a new Home Child Care Allowance was introduced, which will be merged with the Parenting Allowance in 1995 (for the spouses of low-income and unemployed persons caring for children under sixteen) (Australian Government 1994).

Despite these initiatives, Australians have been slow to accept non-family child care. Personal independence is still highly valued, traditional gender-segregated views persist, and despite women's labour force participation, mothers have retained the major responsibility for housework and child care (Goodnow, Burns, and Russell 1989). Any trend towards convergence in the time spent by men and women in housework and child care since 1987 has occurred because women are spending less time and not because men are spending more. This trend has been labelled the 'masculinisation of women's housework' because women's patterns are looking more like men's (Bittman 1994).

France

France is often viewed as the prime example of the public responsibility model of child care delivery (Perry 1991). Although informal care by relatives was once prevalent, it is now typical only for children under the age of three. Most preschool children are now enrolled in a nursery or day care facility. For example, about 20 per cent to 25 per cent of children aged two and under and more than 95 per cent of children aged three to five were in some form of public day care or preschool (Stork 1992).

France is well known for its *écoles maternelles*, which are preschools mainly for children aged three to six years, established and operated by the Ministry of Education. Ninety-four per cent of children aged three to six attend, making this the most extensive preschool system in the world (Kamerman and Kahn 1991a). These preschools operate according to the school day (six and a half hours per day) and are tuition-free. Most close for lunch and on Wednesday afternoons, as do the public schools (Bronfenbrenner 1992). Because so many mothers are now in the labour force, preschools may also provide before-school and after-school programs (Ergas 1990).

Ecoles maternelles are funded through payroll deductions from all employees and employers in France, rather than through parental fees, which makes them unique in the world (Kamerman and Kahn 1991a). There are a number of criticisms of these preschools, however. The major one relates to overcrowding. For example, there may be one teacher and one assistant for twenty-five four-year-olds, and classes can be as large as thirty-five children (Stork 1992). Another criticism relates to their hours of operation, which coincide with the school day rather than regular business hours. Working parents may have to hire someone to fetch their children from preschool and to care for them for the remainder of the workday. Yet most parents send their children to these non-compulsory schools because they already pay for them with their taxes. Private kindergartens are also available for children aged three to six.

Day care centres (*crèches*) exist in a variety of forms and usually cater to children under the age of three (Ergas 1990). *Crèches* are publicly funded and operated, and usually are open from eight to twelve hours a day, Monday to Friday. If they are affiliated with a workplace involving shift work, the hours may be extended (Leprince 1991). The *crèche collective*, or group day care, usually involves thirty to sixty children, and is often locally based or affiliated with a workplace. *Mini-crèches* are smaller with an average of sixteen children, and may be part of an apartment or community building. *Crèches parentales* are established and operated by mothers with the assistance of professional staff (Ergas 1990). Family day care or *crèche familiale* is located in the caregiver's home for between one and three children. Family day care is becoming more popular and less expensive, but not all facilities are regulated by government (Leprince 1991).

Occasional-care centres (*haltes-garderies*) also provide part-time care for children up to six years of age. Before-school and after-school care is also arranged by municipal or regional governments, and special vacation programs are sponsored by private organizations or municipalities (ibid.).

While *écoles maternelles* are part of the public education system, *crèches* are administered by the Ministry of Social Affairs. Both are financed from payroll taxes through the National Family Allowance Fund (Caisse Nationale d'Allocations Familiales). This fund contributes to the construction and 50 per cent of the operating costs of new facilities. Funding for employer-sponsored services and parent-initiated facilities is at a lower level than for public centres (A. Phillips and Moss 1989). The cost of day care is shared by local authorities and parents. About one-quarter of the actual costs are paid by parents, while the municipal governments pay the remainder (Leprince 1991). Lack of coordination among the various levels of government and the two ministries (Education and Social Affairs) is considered to be a problem affecting the administration of day care and preschools (ibid.). Both ministries recruit, train, supervise, and pay staff for public and private facilities (Kamerman and Kahn 1991a).

Middle-class parents are much more likely than other parents to have a mother's helper or nanny in their home. While this is the child care of choice for many parents, it is quite expensive (Stork 1992). In-home care in France is unregulated and unsubsidized, but parents may receive tax concessions or apply for government financial assistance if they cannot afford these services but have a proven need (A. Phillips and Moss 1989).

TABLE 6.1
Child care funding and services in eight industrialized countries, 1990–1993

Country	Model of responsibility	Funding	% of preschoolers in day care	Tax deduction	Parental wage
Australia	Mixed	Subsidies for low-income parents + parental fees	14%	No	No, except for single parents
Canada	Mixed	Subsidies for low-income parents + fees	18% in licensed care	Yes	No
France	Public	Payroll taxes + general revenue + parental fees	25% under 3 years; 95% 3–5 years	Yes	Yes (*allocation parentale d'éducation*)
Germany	Mixed/public	90% taxes; 10% parental fees	2% under 3 years; 75% 3–5 years	Yes	Yes (*Erziehungs-geld*)
Netherlands	Mixed	Subsidies for low-income families + fees	11% under 3 years; 50% 3 years; 90% 4 years	No	No
Sweden	Public	Payroll taxes + income taxes + minimal fees	73% under 6 years	No	No

TABLE 6.1 (continued)

Country	Model of responsibility	Funding	% of preschoolers in day care	Tax deduction	Parental wage
United Kingdom	Social welfare model/private	Subsidies for low-income families + fees	1% in public centres; 5% in family day care	No	No, except for welfare mothers
United States	Private/mixed	Subsidies for low-income families + fees	23% in centre care; 70% 3–5 years	Yes, in 50% of states; EITC for poor	No

SOURCE: Compiled for this project from the many articles and books cited in this chapter.

Although the child care system is not always coordinated with regular business hours (Dewar 1988), there is a relatively high rate of labour force participation among women in France (Stork 1992). In 1988, 66 per cent of married mothers and 85 per cent of unmarried mothers were in the labour force (Kamerman and Kahn 1991a). Of mothers with only one child where that child is under three years old, 69 per cent are employed (Leprince 1991). Most mothers work thirty or more hours a week (Moss and Melhuish 1991).

Fr 10,000 can be deducted from taxable income for each child under seven in public day care if both parents are employed. Parents may also receive tax concessions if they employ a person in their home to look after their children (Leprince 1991).

As discussed in chapter 5, France also provides an allowance to parents who cease work or work part time in order to care for their children at home. For parents with three or more children and at least one under the age of three, this benefit allows parents (usually mothers) to receive partial compensation for lost earnings while raising children at home (Leprince 1991). To be eligible, the parent has to have been employed for two years out of the last ten. In 1991, the maximum benefit was Fr 2,716 per month, adjusted to the rising cost of living and paid for a maximum of three years (U.S. Dept of HHS 1992, 108).

Despite the unique and extensive child care system in France, spaces are insufficient, waiting lists are long, and regional differences are apparent in availability. In Paris, for example, there is one space for every nine eligible children; in half the provinces there is one for every fifty eligible infants (Ergas 1990). Many parents who use relatives and family day care would prefer regulated care (Leprince 1991).

Originally, child care in France was based on the welfare model, but over the last twenty-five years it has developed into a universal service. A widespread assumption exists that child care is good for children and that it equalizes learning opportunities (Balleyguier 1991). Although pronatalist concerns have influenced decisions to support parenting in France (Hayes, Palmer, and Zaslow 1990), there are still concerns that lack of choice in day care services could reduce the birth rate (Leprince 1991).

Germany

Although the model of day care in Germany could be classified as mixed responsibility, there is a basic orientation towards universal child care (A. Phillips and Moss 1989; Perry 1991). Germany, like France, offers a broad range of services. Day care centres (*Krippen*) look after children under three, while preschool programs (*Kindergarten*) cater to children from three years of age until they enter compulsory schooling at six (Weigl and Weber 1991b).

Kindergarten, which is attended by three-quarters of children aged three to five and about 2 per cent of children under three (Kamerman and Kahn 1989b), is financed through public taxes. It is either tuition-free or requires low fees (Bronfenbrenner 1992). Most kindergartens offer half-day classes, but one-fifth offer classes for a full school day (Kamerman and Kahn 1991a).

About 98 per cent of German day care is not-for-profit and is heavily subsidized by government (Ergas 1990, 187). Ninety per cent of costs are paid equally by state, regional, and local governments, while parents are expected to pay 10 per cent (Kamerman and Kahn 1991a). Some government funding is also available for parent-initiated services (A. Phillips and Moss 1989). Subsidies increased in West Germany between 1970 and 1980, but decreased between 1980 and 1983. Even with an increase in 1984, subsidies remained lower than in 1980 (Ergas 1990).

In Germany, staff members of public and private operators are recruited, trained, supervised, and paid by the municipal child care or local social service administrators (Kamerman and Kahn 1991a). Before reunification, East German nurseries were the responsibility of the Ministry of Health, and regional offices made decisions about the provision of local services, staffing, and the allocation of resources. Parents were not charged fees for education or care, but contributed to the cost of food (Weigl and Weber 1991b).

Until recently, the former West Germany has done little to develop public child care, as most children under three used to be cared for by relatives, neighbours, cooperatives, and providers of family day care (Stork 1992). In the 1970s, the government began to support Family Day Care (*Tagesmutter*), which is less bureaucratized than kindergarten (A. Phillips and Moss 1989). Weekly foster-family care for children under three was also developed in which the children spend the week with the foster family and return home on weekends (Ergas 1990). In addition, before-school and after-school programs and lunch-time programs are available for children under twelve or fourteen. These programs are mainly publicly run but involve only 3 per cent of school children (ibid.).

One of the most serious criticisms of child care in the former West Germany was the shortage of spaces. In the 1980s, one-third of employed women did not return to work after the birth of their child because of the lack of child care services (Kamerman and Kahn 1991a). Since most child care is still part time, many women are forced to leave the workforce or use several different child care arrangements to cover the day (A. Phillips and Moss 1989). However, there are many state (Länder) variations in the provision of child care services (Hantrais 1994).

In contrast, the former East Germany had the highest rate of day care use in Eastern Europe at 90 per cent of three to five-year-olds and 60 per cent of children under three (Kamerman and Kahn 1991a). For children aged five months to two years, nurseries were developed in which 89 per cent were community based and 11 per cent were attached to workplaces. Nurseries usually share a building with kindergartens (for children aged three to six). In 1987, there were enough nursery places for 81 per cent of eligible children, with 90 per cent coverage predicted for 1990. In the same year, kindergartens provided spaces for 94 per cent of children (Weigl and Weber 1991b). East German parents also hire childminders (*Pflegemutter*) to care for their children, but these women are not registered, regulated, or publicly paid (ibid.). Following reunification, however, West German policies and standards were imposed on East Germany, much to the concern of feminists (Hantrais 1994).

In both parts of Germany, preschool is not geared to the needs of working mothers, and there is an assumption that it is beneficial for children regardless of whether or not mothers are employed (ibid.). For many years, East German society saw nursery care and kindergarten as an educational supplement for the family, important for children's social and independent experiences and as the first stage in a child's education. At the same time, it enabled mothers to work for pay (ibid.).

As was noted in chapter 2, the labour force participation of married mothers has been kept relatively low in the former West Germany by high tax deductions for dependent spouses in one-earner families and the child-rearing benefit. The child-rearing benefit is quite generous by Canadian standards and is provided for a maximum of three years. It is worth about Can. $480 per month for the first six months, after which it is means-tested (Goldberg 1991). Although the benefit was initially earnings related, it is now provided regardless of the occupational status of the parent.

In January 1991, the new *Child Care Act* came into effect, stating that every young person has the right to develop his or her potential fully with the support of society through private and public organizations and minimal state interference (Lorenz 1991). One section of the act makes particular reference to preschool children, acknowledging the changing role of mothers in the labour market. Social problems are no longer qualifying criteria for such programs, and all types of child care facilities are expected to demonstrate an educational rather than a custodial mandate (ibid.).

The Netherlands

Compared to the other European countries in this study, women's labour force participation in the Netherlands is low and the government does not provide the same level of public support for child care (A. Phillips and Moss 1989; Stork 1992). In 1989, only 26 per cent of mothers with children under four years old and 22 per cent of mothers with children aged five to nine were in the labour force, and the vast majority worked part time (Pierrehumbert 1992). Less than 3 per cent of mothers with preschool children were employed more than half time (A. Phillips and Moss 1989). As in Canada, lone mothers have a *lower* participation rate than married mothers, with 18 per cent of those with children under four and 20 per cent of those with children aged five to nine in the labour force (ibid.). As in other countries, women's employment rate tends to decline when they have more children (ibid.).

Group child care in the Netherlands may be sponsored by governments, not-for-profit organizations, or commercial ventures. Government day care tends to be reserved for low-income families, and less than 2 per cent of children under four are enrolled in government centres (Lamb and Sternberg 1992). Commercial and employer-initiated day care are the fastest growing types in the Netherlands, with the number of centres doubling between 1986 and 1989 (Clerkx and Van Ijzendoorn 1992). However, only 1 per cent of children under three are cared for in employer-sponsored centres (A. Phillips and Moss 1989).

Part-time parent-run play centres, which are popular in the Netherlands, are intended mainly for children under four and provide care for 8 per cent of children under three and 50 per cent of three-year-olds (Clerkx and Van Ijzendoorn 1992). Employees in play centres need only minimal training, but 25 per cent have education in early childhood development. Play centres are typically open only two or three hours per day for two days a week, and are not intended to assist working women. Ninety per cent of play centres are subsidized by the government for about 45 per cent of their costs (A. Phillips and Moss 1989).

About half of children aged three and 90 per cent of four-year-olds attend government preschools, which operate for five to seven hours during the school day (Stork 1992). The goal of preschool is early childhood development and school preparation. Preschools or kindergartens have continued to increase in popularity and have recently begun to attract more middle- and upper-class children since they have been portrayed as an educational rather than a welfare service (Lamb and Sternberg 1992).

School begins at age five in the Netherlands, and parents are obliged to send their children for a minimum of twelve hours a week the first year and full time after that. One per cent of school-aged children attend public day care before or after school hours and are integrated with the younger children (Clerkx and Van Ijzendoorn, 1992).

Child-minding, which is a recent development in the Netherlands, is privately funded, unsubsidized, and not supervised by government, and sitters are used by families for times when other care is unavailable. In addition, a small number of the younger children are enrolled in subsidized family day care homes, although upper- and middle-class parents often employ nannies or send their children to private preschools (Lamb and Sternberg 1992).

The child care system in the Netherlands is influenced by the segregation which permeates the entire society, based on religion and political philosophy (Clerkx and Van Ijzendoorn 1992). The main divisions are between liberals and socialists and Roman Catholics and Protestants, but the Protestant tradition is particularly strong (Stork 1992). Each group retains its own political parties, unions, media support, and schools, and these institutions serve to maintain segregation. Social issues become entwined with political agendas, which means that new social programs are slow to develop. There is also a tradition of social differences between regions and a preference for decentralization in decision making (Clerkx and Van Ijzendoorn 1992).

Traditionally, employed mothers in the Netherlands worked at home or at a job where they could take their children. If wet nurses or child care was needed, in-home care was the method of choice (ibid.). Out-of-home child care was initially a welfare function to help mothers who could not adequately care for their children (Sigel 1992). Early child care centres were established in the 1870s by upper-class women for the purpose of socializing poor lower-class children and providing them with religious and moral training (Pierrehumbert 1992). Since the 1970s, child care has been perceived more as an educational than a welfare service (Lamb and Sternberg 1992).

Attitudes in the Netherlands still favour women's role in the home, however, and this traditon is encouraged through government policies (Sigel 1992). Employed mothers with preschool children are sometimes viewed as 'selfish' by society and government authorities (Clerkx and Van Ijzendoorn 1992). Yet mixed messages about child care are given; while mothers are expected to care for their children at home, considerable research has been aimed at developing child care programs (Sigel 1992).

In the Netherlands, there is limited tax relief for parents using out-of-home child care, but it is regressive and favours higher-income families. Single parents are entitled to an additional tax deduction if child care costs more than 10 per cent of their income (A. Phillips and Moss 1989).

Because many facilities offer only part-time care, families often must rely on a combination of child care arrangements in the Netherlands. Little organization or funding is available for family day care, and access to state subsidized care remains limited to the poorest families. Day care services have not kept pace with the increased need, a lack which has forced many mothers to remain out of the labour force (ibid.; Clerkx and Van Ijzendoorn 1992).

Sweden

The Swedish day care system is often viewed as the epitome of public responsibility (Perry 1991). Compared to that in other industrialized countries, women's labour force participation has been high in Sweden since the late 1960s (Lewis, ed. 1993, 19), and the development of child care services has facilitated this high rate of participation. In 1988, 89 per cent of mothers with children under sixteen were in the labour force (Kamerman and Kahn 1991a) although 43 per cent worked part-time (Broberg and Hwang 1991).

In 1988, 73 per cent of children under six were enrolled in day care and 55 per cent of these were in full-time care (Kamerman and Kahn 1991a). Child care in Sweden is varied, provided by centres, parents' clubs, leisure centres, kindergartens, and family day care. All children are eligible for child care services (either full time or part time) between the ages of six months and seven years (Stork 1992). Before-school and after-school care is available until children reach the age of twelve (Kamerman and Kahn 1991a). About 60 per cent of all preschool children (85 per cent of the children of lone parents) are enrolled in public day care, while 13 per cent of Swedish preschool children are enrolled in private facilities (Perry 1991).

Day care centres, which offer the most prevalent form of care, are autonomous from schools, and their operating hours coincide with the work day. Most facilities are publicly managed and financed (Hwang and Broberg 1992). In most municipalities, day care centres accept children only on a full-time basis, as most mothers work full time. However, centres are also required to offer part-time care places (Ergas 1990). A unique feature of the Swedish system is that child care groups are not segregated by age, which means that siblings can remain together (Kamerman and Kahn 1991).

The second most prevalent form of child care is family day care, which is available for both full-time and occasional care (Ergas 1990). The 'day mother,' caring for up to four children in her home, is paid by the municipality and is supervised by the municipal social service department. While day care centres are most popular in urban centres, family day care is more prevalent in rural areas (Nelson 1990; Broberg and Hwang 1991).

Kindergartens, which focus on education rather than custodial care, are designed for children to attend half days for one or two years before they start school (Hwang and Broberg 1992). In addition, child care cooperatives are available for parents (usually mothers) who care for their children at home. Facilities and preschool teachers are provided by the municipality, but parents are required to participate (Broberg and Hwang 1991). Also, publicly funded recreation centres provide before-school and after-school care for children under the age of ten or twelve. While sitters and nannies are preferred by some parents, others choose care by relatives. Parent cooperatives, not-for-profit facilities run by religious or other community organizations, and a few private day care centres also exist in Sweden (Hwang and Broberg 1992).

Unlike in other countries in this study, family, taxation, and labour market policies in Sweden encourage maximum labour force participation for both men and women. In addition, government policies promote gender equality and the redistribution of income to families with children from those without and from higher- to lower-income families (Kamerman and Kahn 1989b; Lamb and Sternberg 1992). Child care policy is designed to establish an educational program for all children, to ensure safe child care, to take special responsibility for children with special needs, and to promote gender equality (Hwang and Broberg 1992). In 1982, the *Social Services Act* consolidated Sweden's public commitment to universal child care services. However, although the act emphasizes direct provision of services, a secondary government objective is to assist private day care (Ergas 1990).

Swedish law requires that municipalities provide kindergarten places for all six-year-olds for 525 hours per year during the year before they start school (Perry 1991). While kindergarten is part of the Swedish education system, there has also been a move to expand child care spaces. In 1985, a government resolution stated that by 1991 all children over eighteen months of age should be entitled to attend a day nursery, family day care, parental cooperative, play school, or preschool (Ergas 1990). This date, however, has been deferred several times (Kamerman and Kahn 1991a).

Day care standards for children are issued by the National Board of Health and Welfare and are rigorously and strictly enforced (Hwang and Broberg 1992). During the 1980s, however, state regulation shifted towards the local municipal level, with increased support for research and development. Staff are recruited, trained, supervised, and paid by municipal child care administrators or local social service administrators (Kamerman and Kahn 1991a). In many municipalities, fifty to one hundred hours of training are mandatory for centre staff and day mothers before they are allowed to operate (Hwang and Broberg 1992).

Municipal centres and family day care are financed through minimal user fees and government grants obtained from payroll taxes. All employers (but not employees) contribute 2.2 per cent of total salary budgets towards child care services (Broberg and Hwang 1991). State grants are provided directly to day care centres run by parent cooperatives and other not-for-profit centres. Municipalities also receive grants from the National Board of Health and Welfare to contribute to their costs (Hwang and Broberg 1992). In 1987, the Swedish government paid 47 per cent, the municipalities 43 per cent, and parents 10 per cent of the cost of day care centres. The cost of family day care, however, is covered more by municipalities and parents (Broberg and Hwang 1991).

Although not-for-profit organizations receive government grants, commercial day cares cannot (Perry 1991). Public subsidies are also provided for three or four families to share the costs of a caregiver in a private home (Kamerman and Kahn 1991a). Since the 1970s, funding for child care has been increasing, and all families who need it are entitled to public support to obtain child care (Stork 1992). Fees are heavily subsidized and determined locally according to a formula that considers income, number of children, and hours spent in day care. On average, parents pay 10 to 15 per cent of the actual cost of child care; fees are income related and cost less than 10 per cent of the average female wage (Perry 1991).

A unique feature of the Swedish day care system is that it is a free-standing program independent of public education, social services, or health care (Kamerman and Kahn 1991a). The National Board of Health and Welfare, however, sets standards for the design of premises, staffing and staff training, the size of groups, and ratios of staff to children (Hwang and Broberg 1992). Municipalities are responsible for building, operating and developing programs in accordance with the *Social Services Act* (Perry 1991).

Although Sweden's child care system is comprehensive, well integrated, and of high quality, the demand for public care exceeds the supply (Lamb and Sternberg 1992). Priority is granted to the children of single parents, working parents, and immigrants, and to children with physical disabilities, but the need is greatest for children under three years of age (Kamerman and Kahn 1991). An urban-rural split is also apparent in the conceptualization and provision of services. Urban municipalities seem to favour day care centres, while rural areas provide more family day care (Broberg and Hwang 1991). Within government, the debate continues about the state's role in family day care. Some municipalities have argued in favour of more choice for parents and more personalized care for children with special needs. However, the national government has considered family day care too expensive and too diverse to manage (ibid.).

Despite the fact that the Swedish system of child care has been held up as a model, it has been criticized as costly and biased towards centre and non-family care (Lamb and Sternberg 1992). Parents who look after their own children at home receive no assistance. Poorer rural children and immigrant children are underrepresented in municipal day care, as more than three-quarters of immigrants care for their own children and are reported to prefer this option.

Some critics feel that Swedish day care has become too professional, which weakens family and cultural roots (Broberg and Hwang 1991). They argue that forcing both parents to work for a living means that they have too little time to spend with their children, which does not benefit children (Wolfe 1989). These concerns were partially answered when parental leave was extended to eighteen months and parents with preschoolers were allowed to reduce their working hours without loss of seniority. Nevertheless, such policies tend to maintain the gendered division of labour in both the home and the labour force.

Despite such criticisms, Sweden's child care system is renowned for its educational value, its strong public support, and the opportunities it provides mothers to enter the labour force. As was mentioned in chapter 5, parental leave policies allow employed parents a job-protected leave for up to eighteen months after birth or adoption. The leave can be taken at any time up to the child's eighth birthday or the end of the first year of compulsory school. Parents may also choose to reduce their working hours while retaining their job until their child is eight years old. In addition, employed parents are entitled to up to 60 days' leave per year for one child and 120 for two or more to enable them to stay at home during a child's illness (Perry 1991). Two days per year are also provided to enable parents to spend time with their children in day care facilities, to familiarize themselves with activities, and get to know the staff (Lamb and Sternberg 1992). The Swedish school system accommodates employed parents by offering children a free cooked meal at lunchtime and by providing longer school days (S. Gustafsson 1990). The combination of direct child care services, fee subsidies, leave policies, and school lunch programs makes Sweden one of the most generous in terms of policies for children.

The United Kingdom

The model of child care in the United Kingdom is private responsibility (Perry 1991). As in the Netherlands, the rates of labour force participation in the United Kingdom for mothers with preschool children are among the lowest in Europe. In 1990, for example, only 23 per cent of mothers with children under three were in the workforce and most were employed for fewer than thirty hours a week (Bronfenbrenner 1992). As in Canada, the percentage of lone mothers in the labour force is lower than for married mothers. Participation rates for lone mothers are kept low by social assistance rules which do not encourage them to enter the labour force, high marginal tax rates, low wages for women, public housing regulations, and lack of public child care services (Joshi 1990). As in the other countries, mothers' rate of paid employment in the United Kingdom tends to decline with the number of children and the presence of preschool children. Consequently, while 43 to 50 per cent of three- and four-year-olds are enrolled in day care, this figure declines to less than 2 per cent of children under three (Perry 1991).

Most preschool children in the United Kingdom are cared for by their mothers, their fathers, or other relatives (Ochiltree 1992). Five per cent are cared for in family day care homes by child-minders (Perry 1991; Moss 1991). Child-minders, who are subject to regulation and are expected to register with local authorities, are paid directly by parents, although subsidies are available to some low-income parents (Melhuish and Moss 1992).

The largest category of formal care for three- and four-year-olds is independent playgroups, which operate five hours per week and were originally run by mothers (Ochiltree 1992). Five to 10 per cent of children under two attend and 40 to 45 per cent of three- to four-year-olds. Playgroups, which are staffed by a leader, an assistant, and parents, are registered by local authorities and affiliated with the Pre-School Playgroups Association (PPA), which provides training and support (Ergas 1990). Yet British playgroups tend to be underfunded. More than half of all children attend before they reach school age, but because of their part-time nature playgroups do nothing to meet working parents' needs (Melhuish and Moss 1992).

Government-sponsored day care centres are rare and are set aside for children considered to be 'at risk' (Melhuish 1991). Although there was an increase in the late 1980s, government-provided places were available for only 1 per cent of children under five in 1988 (Melhuish and Moss 1992). Day care centres run by local councils operate under the auspices of the Department of Health and Social Security and there tends to be a stigma attached to their use (Ochiltree 1992).

Publicly funded preschools or kindergartens are used by only 10 per cent of children in Britain (Haskins 1992). Three- and four-year-olds are enrolled for three or four terms for several hours a day (Moss 1991). Public facilities are run by the Department of Education and Science and are usually located in schools. Out-of-school care is also affiliated with schools (Ergas 1990). Private preschools provided spaces for only 1 to 4 per cent of eligible children in 1988 and are used mainly by higher-income families (Haskins 1992). A small number of employer-sponsored day cares also exist in Britain (Moss 1991).

The middle and upper classes in the United Kingdom have always preferred nannies, governesses, and nursemaids to out-of-home care because of their greater convenience. To some extent, these are still the preferred form of child care for those who can afford the cost and have the space to provide accommodation for the caregiver in their home (Melhuish and Moss 1992).

Traditionally, there has been considerable opposition in Britain to employment for married women and mothers (Haskins 1992; Ochiltree 1992). When women's labour was needed during the Second World War, however, this value was set aside and temporary expansions of public day care facilitated women's work. Recently, because of declining real wages and rising costs, women are again needed in the workforce, and day care is again becoming a priority for government (Melhuish and Moss 1992).

For centuries, wealthier families in the United Kingdom have hired non-family members to care for their children. Despite this upper-class pattern, the prevalent ideology in Britain is that day care has harmful effects on children and should be limited to disadvantaged children (Melhuish 1991). Some researchers have argued that this prejudice extends to preschool educational programs as well (Haskins 1992). Raising children is considered to be a private responsibility, and parents are expected to care for their own children. If parents need non-family child care, they are expected to arrange for and purchase it themselves and to rely on market forces to provide the necessary services (Lamb and Sternberg 1992).

In Britain, the government holds that its role is not to provide child care services directly, but to draw the need for day care to the attention of employers and to encourage them to act. The 1989 *Children Act* provided a limited tightening of regulations covering private nurseries, child-minders, and other child care centres, although these regulations are still minimal (Melhuish and Moss 1992).

The United Kingdom is the only country in this study that does not give priority for child care to the children of working parents (A. Phillips and Moss 1989). Neither has the British government been willing to initiate national regulations or universal entitlement programs for funding (Haskins 1992). As in Canada, there is a two-tiered system of day care in which the government subsidizes services for disadvantaged, disabled, and troubled children while wealthier parents pay for part-day, educational nursery schools or hire nannies (Kamerman and Kahn 1991a). Although generally committed to social programs and the provision of universal benefits, the government of the United Kingdom has been reluctant to become involved with child care, choosing instead to leave it to local governments (Ochiltree 1992).

Responsibility for child care remains divided between the Departments of Education and of Health and Social Security. The Department of Education oversees kindergartens, which are tuition-free. The Department of Health and Social Security regulates and registers private day care centres, play groups, and child-minders and the small number of public facilities (Melhuish and Moss 1992). The National Childminders Association supervises child-minders, but site visits tend to be much less than recommended. One study found that 59 per cent of homes were visited every six months and 21 per cent had not been visited in a year (Moss 1991). As in Canada, kindergarten teachers are paid the highest wages, while playgroup workers and child-minders are paid the lowest wages (Melhuish and Moss 1992).

Employed parents who send their children to employer-sponsored child care used to pay taxes on the government subsidies to employers, as they were treated as taxable fringe benefits (A. Phillips and Moss 1989). The government removed these tax barriers in April 1990 to encourage more employer-sponsored child care (Haskins 1992). Limited funding is also available for parent-initiated facilities (A. Phillips and Moss 1989).

As a consequence of the prevailing ideology about the importance of child care by mothers at home, relatively few infants and toddlers are cared for by non-family members. Only about 6 per cent of children under the age of one, 10 per cent of one-year-olds, and 26 per cent of two-year-olds are in child care facilities in Britain, but this rises to 75 per cent for three-year-olds and 90 per cent for children aged four and over (Haskins 1992). The child care system depends on voluntary and private for-profit services, and there is a shortage of places, especially for children under three years old (Melhuish and Moss 1992).

As parents juggle care arrangements, children are taken from one caregiver to another, which causes instability for children. There has been a recent and rapid expansion of private centres as a response to government inaction about creating more public facilities (Moss 1991). The number of registered child-minders increased by 28 per cent between 1985 and 1988, and the number of day care centres increased by 49 per cent (Haskins 1992). Child-minding is the government's preferred method of care because it is inexpensive and close to the ideal of children being raised at home (Moss 1991).

Many researchers consider the child care system in Britain, unlike the welfare and public education systems, to be inadequate and fragmented

(Bronfenbrenner 1992; Goelman 1992; Haskins 1992; Kamerman and Kahn 1991a; Lamb and Sternberg, 1992; Melhuish and Moss 1992; Ochiltree 1992). Staff are poorly trained and underpaid, the turnover among staff is high, and staff-child ratios are unfavourable to children. Because local councils retain responsibility for child care services, there are large variations in political commitment, supervision, and regulation in different regions.

Child care facilities are not evenly distributed throughout Great Britain, but rather reflect the needs of women in the labour force (Moss 1991). For example, while Wales, Northern Ireland, and Scotland have few facilities and lower female labour force participation rates, England has the majority of child care facilities and the highest labour force participation rates. Although the difference among regions is less pronounced for child-minders, lack of child care has an impact on the labour force participation of mothers. In the 1980s, for example, one-third of employed women did not return to their jobs after giving birth because of a lack of child care (Kamerman and Kahn 1991a).

The United States

Although child care delivery in the United States could be classified under the social welfare model, some researchers have suggested that it is moving towards mixed responsibility (Perry 1991). Like Canada, the United States offered federal child care subsidies during the Second World War to encourage women to contribute to the war effort, but withdrew them once the war was over. Direct federal subsidies did not begin again until 1962. In 1964, the Head Start Program was initiated to provide early educational services for children from impoverished and culturally deprived families (Ergas 1990). Yet, like Canada, the United States still has no national system of child care.

As with other aspects of family policy, child care is a state responsibility in the United States. Most services are unregulated and unsupervised, the quality of care is often low, and more for-profit centres have been developed in the United States than in any other country (G.C. Adams and Johnson 1991; Kisker and Maynard 1991; Ochiltree 1992). About 53 per cent of U.S. child care is for-profit, and private care initiatives continue to increase (A.J. Frankel 1991). Although the diversity of services is interpreted positively by private day care operators in that it gives parents many options and choices, most researchers agree that the United States lags behind other industrialized countries with respect to out-of-home child care (Bronfenbrenner 1992; Goelman 1992; Haskins 1992; Kamerman and Kahn 1991a).

Depending on the ages of their children, between 57 per cent and 66 per cent of mothers in the United States are in the labour force, and three-quarters work full time (Haskins 1992). By 1995, it is projected that the mothers of three-quarters of school-aged children and of two-thirds of preschoolers will be in the workforce (Hofferth and Phillips 1987).

In 1990, about 35 per cent of children under four and 70 per cent of children aged three to five were enrolled in full- or part-time day care (Lamb, Sternberg, and Ketterlinus 1992). Nine million out of fourteen million preschool children were cared for informally (Hofferth and Phillips 1991). Since the 1960s, however, the proportion of children in informal care has been decreasing steadily with the expansion of regulated care (Lubeck and Garrett 1991).

Apart from informal care, one-quarter of American parents use family day care, especially for infants (A.J. Frankel 1991). Family day care is mostly unregulated, although to what extent is debatable. Estimates vary from 50 per cent to more than 90 per cent (Kontos 1991; Kisker and Maynard 1991), a variation which illustrates the lack of national child care statistics. Most states regulate family day care through licensing, registration, or both, but the rules are extremely variable. In 1988, twenty-seven states required some sort of licensing and thirteen offered voluntary registration, but homes with fewer than four or five children are usually exempt. Yet the average number of children per family day care home (in addition to the caregiver's children) is only two (G.C. Adams and Johnson 1991). This means that most family day care homes are exempt from state regulations.

There are several reasons why family day care remains essentially unlicensed in the United States. Regulations vary by state and municipality, there is a lack of financial support for enforcement, problems with compliance are difficult to resolve, and rules are often viewed as unreasonable, a perception which drives operators underground. Many families turn to unregulated family day care as a response to an inadequate number of licensed spaces, but also because they tend to assume that informal arrangements are more 'home-like' and therefore better for children. In reality, this may not always be the case (Nelson 1991).

Day care centres, which are regulated in all states, offer group care and are gaining in prominence, especially for older preschoolers (J.R.

Walker 1991). Most centre-based care is privately owned and run as a commercial enterprise (Ochiltree 1992). Recently, government funding has increased, although children with disabilities and children from low-income families are given priority (Ergas 1990). In 1988, centre care was available to one-quarter of poor families and 23 per cent of preschoolers with working mothers (Perry 1991). Few day care facilities operate during extended hours, a fact which contributes to the problem of unsupervised children (Flynn and Rodman 1991).

A small number of employer-sponsored day cares operate primarily in service industries that employ mainly women (Lubeck and Garrett 1991). Since 1986, employers have been granted tax exemptions for child care provided through employee benefit plans (Ergas 1990). Only 1 to 2 per cent of private enterprises sponsor child care, however, although their numbers are increasing (Hayes, Palmer, and Zaslow 1990).

More than half of the American states provide kindergarten classes for five-year-olds, and when they do, approximately 95 per cent of eligible children attend. Twenty-four states also offer pre-kindergarten for four-year-olds. These programs are operated by the school system and are therefore exempt from day care licensing requirements (ibid.). Until recently, educationally focused preschool was available only to neglected and abused children, but the criteria have been expanded to cover children with disabilities and those from low-income families (Kamerman and Kahn, 1991).

Because nannies and in-home sitters are unregulated, little information is available about these options. After-school programs are legislated in twelve states and operate in schools and community centres (Hayes, Palmer, and Zaslow 1990). However, little government support has been forthcoming for after-school programming, even though the negative effects of leaving children unsupervised have been acknowledged. Government resource and referral programs help link parents and care providers, and supply training and support to staff (Ergas 1990).

As in the United Kingdom, the U.S. government has been reluctant to become directly involved in either funding or providing day care, which has been considered a family matter and a mother's obligation (Getis and Vinovskis 1992). Yet when women's labour force participation is needed or when the reduction of welfare dependency is deemed desirable, these values are put aside and child care becomes a policy priority (Haskins 1992). The intent of child care in the United States seems to be to protect the health and safety of disadvantaged children rather than to promote high quality care or early childhood education (Lamb, Sternberg, and Ketterlinus 1992) or to encourage employment equity for women. Group care is believed by some conservatives to be damaging to children, especially toddlers (Zigler 1989).

Many Americans also believe that child care is best dealt with by local or state governments, and that federal involvement is redundant, interfering, and unnecessary (Bronfenbrenner 1992; P.R. Thompson and Molyneaux 1992). However, decentralization has resulted in inconsistency in services even within the same state. The obtaining of child care services is also viewed as a transaction between consumers and providers; when the demand increases, it is assumed that day cares will be established to take advantage of the new market. However, care for certain kinds of children, especially for infants or children with disabilities, is seldom profitable and will therefore always be in short supply. Furthermore, many parents and educators believe that entrepreneurs should not be allowed to make a profit from children (Hofferth and Phillips 1991).

Current U.S. policy places child care within a social welfare context, targeting services to poor and problem families (Kagan, 1991). Under the conservative Reagan government, direct federal support was reduced, private sector incentives were increased, and the use of informal child care was promoted (Tuominen 1992). In other words, child care services were further decentralized, deregulated, and privatized (Nelson 1990).

Although there is no nationally mandated comprehensive system of child care in the United States, the federal government does establish some regulations and provides funding to states and indirect subsidies to consumers. Norms are set at the federal, state, and local government levels (P.R. Thompson and Molyneaux 1992). Until recently, direct federal government involvement in day care has been small, limited to the Head Start Program and day care for military dependants (Bronfenbrenner 1992). Now, however, there are twenty-two federal programs, although assistance remains targeted to specific groups or individuals (Herr 1989). As women's participation in the labour force becomes more prevalent, child care is becoming a more important item on the political agenda (Ochiltree 1992). For example, the JOBS Program requires states to provide child care assistance for parents who are required to work (Offner 1991).

Although federal funding was increased recently to help low-income families pay for child care, some parents pay a substantial portion of their income for this service. The average expenditure is 11 per cent of family income, but high-income families pay less than 5 per cent while low-income families pay between 20 and 25 per cent (Hofferth and Phillips 1991).

In 1988, the *Family Support Act* shifted the focus from the question of whether the government should become more involved in child care to what this role should be and how much it would cost. Further legislation passed in October 1990 provided increased grants to states to develop direct services and established refundable tax credits for low-income lone working parents (Robins 1991). Nevertheless, the cost of child care remains a predominant concern (Blau 1991).

Just over half the states allow tax credits or deductions for child care expenses at a lower rate than the federal tax system (Clifford and Russell 1989). Yet the federal government is a major funder of day care and spent U.S.$8 billion (Can. $10.2 billion) on it in 1991 (Hofferth and Phillips 1991). Half of this funding was for the Earned Income Tax Credit (EITC), discussed in chapter 3, that could increase parents' ability to purchase child care. The U.S. government also offers a Dependent Care Tax Credit, for which families can reduce their income tax by up to U.S.$2,400 (Can. $3,064) for one child and U.S.$4800 (Can. $6,127) for two or more children for child care expenses (A.J. Frankel 1991). The tax credit is not refundable, however, which makes it worthless for low-income families paying no tax (Prosser 1991). If child care is unlicensed, parents cannot take advantage of federal tax benefits and providers cannot receive subsidies. Furthermore, assistance is not available to parents who leave children with neighbours or relatives (G.C. Adams and Johnson 1991).

In addition to tax benefits, the next largest recipient of federal child care money is Head Start, the early intervention program for at-risk children (Leik et al. 1991). Next is the Social Services Block Grant passed in 1990 to increase resources to low-income families for purchasing child care. The Child Care Food Program also received more than U.S.$602 million (Can. $768 million) of federal money in 1988 for meals and snacks for children enrolled in day care centres (Lamb, Sternberg, and Ketterlinus 1992).

Mothers participating in Assistance to Families with Dependent Children (AFDC) are allowed to deduct from their income the amount paid for child care up to a limit of U.S.$175 (Can. $223) a month per child over two and U.S.$200 (Can. $255) a month for each child aged two and under (Hayes, Palmer, and Zaslow 1990). Projected spending from 1991 to 1995 is U.S.$114.4 billion (Can. $146 billion) for all programs (Haskins

1992). The Department of Education also provides support for certain programs targeted to high-risk children (Clifford and Russell 1989).

The number of child care spaces in the United States is increasing and is expected to keep increasing in the near future (Hayes, Palmer, and Zaslow 1990). Yet many researchers argue that there is a serious shortage, especially for children under three, school-age children, children living in rural areas, and children with special needs (Kisker and Maynard 1991). This shortage means that parents' child care decisions do not always reflect their preferences (Flynn and Rodman 1991).

Increasingly, children are being recognized as a 'resource' in the United States, and this is reflected in changes in policy (Hayes, Palmer, and Zaslow 1990). With the new child care legislation, some researchers believe that the United States has crossed the line from using day care as a protective service for deprived children to viewing it as a supportive, educational, and developmental service for all children (Bronfenbrenner 1992; Kamerman and Kahn 1989a). Yet the system remains highly diversified, with a distinction between educational pre-schools and programs for needy children, and wide variations in price and quality among the various programs (Hofferth and Phillips 1991). As in Canada, U.S. parents often must use several resources to meet their child care needs. Because they also lack information about programs, they do not always make informed choices (G.C. Adams and Johnson 1991). Market forces which keep staff salaries low and turn-over high adversely affect the quality of care. Lack of enforcement is also a problem (Lamb, Sternberg, and Ketterlinus 1992; NAEYC 1987).

Until recently, work and family were assumed to be completely separate in the United States, and conflicts between them were considered to be a women's issue. Increased acknowledgment of the extent and cost of work-family conflicts has led to some initiatives, such as flextime policies, family leave and benefits, and dependant care policies. Although these programs are growing, as yet few employees have access to them (Galinsky, Hughes, and David 1990).

Employment remains essential not only for income security and as a status symbol, but also because access to social benefits often depends on it. Yet the government has failed to put into place the necessary programs or benefits to meet either existing or new needs of working families. Instead, any response has come from trade unions, industry initiatives, the women's movement, or the environmental protection movement (Kurzman 1988).

The U.S. system of child care differs from those of the other countries in this study in its diversity, its high percentage of for-profit care, and its market orientation. Nevertheless, it is moving in the direction of mixed responsibility, with more tax concessions for the child care costs of employers and families.

CONCLUSION

The philosophical differences in the various approaches to child care among the countries in this study are exemplified in differences in levels of government intervention and in funding mechanisms. Government assistance for child care can be provided through tax relief to families or employers, cash allowances to families, subsidies to operators, or the provision of direct child care services. In addition, countries also differ over who pays for child care. Is it the user, employers (through payroll taxes), or the taxpayer (through payroll or income taxes)? While some governments try to encourage the development of child care services in the private sector, others focus on providing services directly or on subsidizing not-for-profit spaces. Finally, governments differ in their approach to regulation and enforcement, although these usually fall to state or local governments.

Generally, the child care policies of the European countries can be contrasted with the policies of Canada and the English-speaking countries, although there are differences within these two broad categories (Haskins 1992; Kamerman and Kahn 1989b; Lesemann and Nicol, 1994). In Europe, preschool child care is typically viewed as a citizenship right, as part of early childhood development, and as important for preschool children regardless of the employment status of their mother. Because child care is viewed as a social responsibility, services are publicly funded. Although parents pay a small fee in some countries, in others there are no user fees because services are financed through payroll taxes or from general revenue.

In most of the European countries except Sweden, there is a division between day care for children under three and education for children between three and five years old. In most countries in this study, child care services for infants and toddlers usually fall within the jurisdiction of social services, while kindergartens and preschools are part of the education system. In Sweden, there is one public system of preschool care and education, which includes infants, toddlers, and preschoolers and remains separate from the elementary school system.

The English-speaking countries, on the other hand, typically provide a two-tiered child care system, although this may be less true for Canada.[5] Wealthier families tend to use part-day preschools that emphasize educational development and offer an enriched program. Government subsidies are made available only to low-income families and single parents, and these are usually restricted to regulated and licensed premises. Consequently, there is a shortage of subsidized spaces, especially for infants, school-aged children, and those with special needs. In order to afford child care services, middle- and lower-income families are sometimes forced to use lower-quality unregulated care that is mainly custodial (Kamerman and Kahn 1989b). While the two-tiered system may provide better care for the rich than in the Swedish public child care system, the quality of care in Canada and the English-speaking countries depends largely on the family's financial resources, the age of the child, and where the family lives.

In Canada and the English-speaking countries, regulations are usually established by state or local governments, with inadequate enforcement mechanisms. In addition, controversy continues over whether the government should subsidize for-profit facilities or fund only not-for-profit ones. The quality of care in for-profit facilities tends to vary widely, from better than average to much worse; in general, however, staff-child ratios tend to be higher and wages lower. For-profit providers may need to scrimp on some aspects of services or on facilities in order to make a profit, and the care provider often subsidizes the private facility through low wages (Hayes, Palmer, and Zaslow 1990; A. Phillips and Moss 1989).

Most researchers have argued that public care is preferable to private care (Ergas 1990; Corsini et al. 1988; Lamb and Sternberg 1992; Leavitt 1991; A. Phillips and Moss 1989). The main argument for public care concerns licensing and regulation. When public money is spent, services become visible and can be monitored and improved. Licensing can also lead to better training and higher wages for staff, greater job satisfaction, staff-child ratios more favourable to children, a greater educational component in the program, and more stimulating activities for children (J.R. Walker 1991; Pence and Goelman 1991).

Private operators and *laissez-faire* conservatives believe that there are drawbacks to government licensed and regulated child care. Certain providers argue that regulation can deter providers from entering the market, thus reducing the number of spaces, increasing prices, reducing parents' options, and encouraging underground operations. Furthermore, municipal governments argue that they could not afford the increased resources needed for enforcement. Child care regulations certainly increase the public cost, which some jurisdictions, especially in the United States, are unable or unwilling to pay (Hayes, Palmer and Zaslow 1990; J.R. Walker 1991).

National child care data are often lacking, especially in jurisdictions where day care is private or under state or provincial jurisdiction. In fact, most countries (except Sweden) lack statistical information on child care services and facilities (Hwang et al. 1991), which makes comparative research difficult. Research is especially needed on informal and unlicensed child care because it is the most prevalent form in many countries (Ochiltree 1992).

With the rise in the labour force participation of mothers, non-family child care services have expanded and increased in acceptance over the past decade in all the countries studied (Kamerman and Kahn 1991a). Despite this expansion, all countries experience a shortage of licensed spaces for infants, for children with disabilities, for cultural minorities, for rural dwellers, and for the children of shift workers (Ergas 1990). In many countries, parents are concerned about high staff turnover and inadequate caregiver qualifications, and want maximum flexibility in operating hours and activities. Although both parents and non-parents tend to feel that child care services deserve more public support (Hayes, Palmer and Zaslow 1990; A. Phillips and Moss 1989), the conservative 'pro-family movement' in Canada and the English-speaking countries views non-maternal child care as a last resort.

In all countries, the debate continues about whether child care should serve the needs of children or the needs of employed mothers (Lamb and Sternberg 1992; P.R. Thompson and Molyneux 1992). Early childhood educators, some religious organizations, and the pro-family groups emphasize children's needs, while feminists and trade unions tend to focus on women's employment equity. Many researchers have identified the connection between affordable child care services and gender equality in the labour market (Lamb and Sternberg 1992; A. Phillips and Moss 1989). Despite some change over the past twenty years, in all the countries studied women have retained responsibility for housework and child care. These responsibilities accompany them into the workforce (Ergas 1990). Only through a combination of labour market and family policies such as those found in Sweden has greater equality for employed mothers been created.

7

Child protection, family violence, and substitute care

THE CHANGING STATUS OF CHILDREN

Historians disagree about the treatment of European and North American children in previous centuries because the available evidence is scarce and comes mainly from art, the history of costume, literature, and religious writings. Parents appear to have altered the way they interacted with children over time with the evolution of religious ideas, demographic trends, and the importance of children's labour to the economy (M. Baker 1993b, 168). The period between childhood and adulthood appears to have been lengthened with industrialization, as child labour was abolished and workers were expected to acquire more formal schooling. In addition, ideas have changed about when a 'child' should be considered an adult before the law.

One trend is clear, however. The power that parents held over their children has been gradually restricted over the past century. In many countries, children were once considered the property of parents. The Romans went further than any other legal system in placing the liberty and lives of children within the power of the father (ibid. 170). Early Roman law included the right of fathers to give their children away or to have them put to death. Under English medieval law, a new concept became accepted whereby parents had an obligation to exercise guardianship over legal minors. By the eighteenth century, children were regarded as chattels or property under English common law. Parents had three duties towards their children at that time: maintenance, protection, and education and, because of these obligations, parents could claim authority over their children (Bala and Clarke 1981, 2–4).

As a result of the work of social critics, including writers such as Charles Dickens, who described the fate of children in institutions in

Oliver Twist, the nineteenth century was a period of social reform in Great Britain, Australia, the United States, and Canada (Bala, 1991b, 2). The first legal challenge to the absolute rights of parents occurred in New York in 1870, when a social worker who was horrified at the neglect of a child sought legal assistance and finally turned to the American Association for the Prevention of Cruelty to Animals as a means of obtaining legal sanction. Soon after this, the American Society for the Prevention of Cruelty to Children was established. Twenty years later, in 1891, the first such organization was founded in Canada, called the Children's Aid Society.

From this beginning, legislation was created in all jurisdictions of North America to protect children under a certain age from neglect and abuse. In 1893, for example, reformers persuaded the Ontario legislature to enact the *Children's Protection Act*, which gave Children's Aid societies the right to remove neglected or abused children from their homes and become their legal guardians (Bala 1991b, 3). Such actions demonstrated a concern by the state for the well-being of children and an acknowledgment that parents did not have sole authority over their offspring. From this evolved the idea that children are citizens in their own right and that the state has an obligation to enable minors to exercise these rights (M. Baker 1993b, 170).

Four main concepts underlie and shape the socio-legal status of children in the English-speaking countries. The first is *patria potestas*, paternal power or the integrity and power of the family. The second is *parens patria*, the state as parent, or the authority of the courts to make decisions on behalf of those unable to act for themselves. The third is the *best interests of the child*, a concept used to justify state intervention in child neglect and delinquency cases and to make custody decisions after divorce. The fourth is *the child as person before the law*, which is a relatively recent concept in Canadian law (Ayim 1987, 4; M. Baker 1993b, 171).

During the 1970s and 1980s, children's rights became an issue of public concern and North American laws underwent extensive reform. In Canada, children's rights are protected by both federal and provincial legislation. For example, the *Criminal Code* contains sections requiring parents to provide children with the necessities of life and protecting children from physical and sexual abuse. The federal government also shares with the provinces the cost of health and welfare services and provides direct grants for research and education on child abuse. The provinces, however, create and amend their own child welfare legislation and have jurisdiction over child protection agencies (M. Baker 1993b, 171).

CHILD WELFARE AND CHILD PROTECTION

Any child welfare system must try to achieve a balance between child protection and family preservation (Rains 1991). This is a difficult task because, while the public expects action and investigation, there is increasing intolerance for inaccurate allegations and unnecessary interventions (Downing et al. 1990). The delivery of child welfare services is plagued by similar problems in Canada and the English-speaking countries or 'liberal welfare states': inadequate finances, staff shortages, difficulties in coordinating a variety of service-delivery mechanisms, unclear responsibilities, and problems reconciling statutory and supportive systems (De'Ath 1989).

In Canada and the English-speaking countries, child protection is the major focus of the child welfare system. Mandatory reporting of child abuse (defined mainly as physical and sexual abuse) was one of the major legislative reponses to the publicity arising from American medical research on child abuse in the 1960s. With these new laws, the caseloads of child protection workers have risen to overwhelming levels.

Although many child welfare systems acknowledge that most of their clients are women and children living on low incomes, not all systems have questioned the theoretical connections among poverty, abuse, gender, and 'inadequate parenting.' For example, in North America, the practice of apprehending children and placing them in foster care because their parents (or mothers) have been accused of 'child neglect' has been criticized because mothers are unable to respond to their children's needs until their own are met (Kadushin and Martin 1988; Callahan 1993a). Yet, unlike some of the European countries in this study, most jurisdictions in North America and Australia provide only minimal financial assistance to low-income families and little respite care for the children of mothers who are experiencing temporary stress or abuse from an intimate partner.

Models of child protection

Within the eight countries in this study, three main models of child protection are apparent: voluntary service, involuntary service, and prevention. The differences among them imply major differences in priorities. While some countries clearly adopt a residual view of child welfare, others focus mainly on prevention and other pro-active measures.

The first model of child protection involves a voluntary request by the child, parent, or family for assistance from the government or child welfare agency. This method is preferred in most agencies because clients who seek assistance are more likely to take the advice of professionals and to attempt to resolve their own problems (Besharov 1990b). This effort could involve joining a self-help group; accepting group, individual, or couple counselling or therapy; leaving an abusive partner; or being referred to other services such as legal, financial, home-making, or child care assistance.

The second model of intervention is involuntary and is initiated by a complaint, often from another professional such as a social worker, teacher, doctor, or day care worker (Kadushin and Martin 1988). The basis of the complaint could be physical or sexual abuse, or neglect. 'Neglect' has always been more difficult to define and prove than physical abuse, and usually means that the child's basic needs for life, including medical or health needs, are not being met. Emotional abuse may be even more difficult to define and prove, but usually means that the child's self-esteem is undermined through scapegoating, rejection, ridicule, humiliation and ostracism (ibid.). In North American jurisdictions, social service workers are expected to notify the police in cases of suspected abuse. When the police become involved, parents may be required by the courts to seek services from child welfare agencies (Marsh 1990). Parents cannot refuse an intervention, and once a social service agency is involved, it cannot withdraw until the child is considered to be safe (Kadushin and Martin 1988).

The third model of intervention in child protection involves prevention programs, which may be available to all parents and children, or may focus on families considered to be 'at risk' of abuse, neglect, or behavioural problems because of their poverty and previous associations with the police and social agencies. These programs include giving training in effective parenting and providing visiting homemakers, parenting surrogates, support groups, and access to drop-in centres and day care centres. Programs may be operated by government or voluntary social service agencies, but are usually financed and regulated by government (ibid.).

CHILD WELFARE AND FAMILY VIOLENCE IN CANADA

Child and family protection services are provided by provincial, territorial, and municipal governments: services are also established and run by First Nations peoples and voluntary organizations. In most jurisdictions, mandated services emphasize the protection of children rather than of other family members such as women or elders from abuse or neglect. Largely for this reason, I will deal mainly with children in this chapter.[1] Child welfare agencies are required by provincial legislation to provide voluntary and involuntary services to children and their families, including temporary care for children in protection cases. In some jurisdictions, these agencies also regulate and supervise adoptions (Barnhorst and Walter 1991). Child welfare agencies generally serve all children in the province, but some cater to specific religious or cultural populations. In Ontario, for example, separate Children's Aid services are available for Catholics and Protestants. In Manitoba and several other provinces, child welfare services for some First Nations people are provided within their communities.

Divisions of race and social class are also apparent within Canadian child protection systems. Interveners are often white, well-educated, and middle class, while clients are usually poorly educated, living in poverty or near-poverty, and often are part of a mother-led family. A number of racial minorities are overrepresented in the Canadian child welfare system, but the most pervasive problems have been with Native children, who have been apprehended and taken into care at more than three times the rate of other children (Bala 1991b).

About 70 per cent of Canadian child welfare workers are women, and 60 per cent have undergraduate university degrees in general arts or social work. The average age is about thirty-five years old. Because of the stressful nature and low pay of child protection work, there is a high turnover rate, with an average job tenure from eighteen months to three years (Callahan 1993b, 67).

In Canada (as in the United States), the child welfare agency has two functions: child protection and child care. The law presumes that parents are capable of raising their own children without state interference and clearly places the burden on protection agencies to establish the need for intervention.

Child protection in Canada

Child protection organizations and legislation began in the 1890s with the establishment of private Children's Aid societies (CASs). In 1893, Ontario gave CASs the right to remove neglected or abused children from their homes and become their legal guardians until they reached the legal age of adulthood. Child protection agencies were established throughout Canada by the early years of this century and child protection legislation was enacted in each province. Within the last thirty years, however, the field has grown enormously and its activities have become increasingly intertwined with legal procedures.

Until the early 1960s, agencies dealt largely with obvious cases of physical abuse and neglect, the placement and adoption of illegitimate children, adolescent 'unmanageability,' and delinquent youth (Bala 1991b, 3). In practice, the system tended to operate informally with little thought given to children's rights. The 1960s saw the beginning of mandatory reporting by professionals of suspected cases of physical abuse, while the 1970s and 1980s were characterized by a recognition of sexual abuse as a problem. This awareness led to an increase in reporting.

One of the major challenges now facing the child welfare system is the dramatic increase in the number of allegations of child abuse in Canada. Between 1985 and 1990, for example, Ontario experienced a 65 per cent increase; while between 1984 and 1992, the number of child protection service referrals in Newfoundland increased 734 per cent. While much of this increase is attributed to growing public awareness of child abuse and mandatory reporting laws, some social workers also suggest that there is an actual increase in the abuse and neglect of children (Scarth 1993, 5). However, no longitudinal data are available to substantiate this claim.

During the last twenty-five years, the child welfare system has undergone a legal revolution (Bala 1991b). At the federal level, the 1982 *Canadian Charter of Rights and Freedoms* ensured that parents whose children are apprehended from their care are entitled to a judicial hearing within a 'reasonable' time. It also restricted the authority of child protection workers to apprehend children without prior judicial authorization. A trend is apparent towards clearly defined decision making to allow for less discretion by judges and social workers. An example of this evolution is the *Young Offenders Act* (1984), which placed more emphasis on rights and responsibilities than its predecessor (Thomlison and Foote 1987). This act has provoked much controversy, however, for treating adolescent offenders more leniently than adults, even when they commit serious offences.

Because child protection agencies are funded by government, they are agents of the state with significant legal powers to search for children who may be in need of protection and if necessary to force parents to surrender custody (Bala 1991b). Some critics have argued that the investigation of child abuse and the apprehension of children should be the responsibility of the criminal justice system rather than of social service workers. Apprehending children from their parents compromises the ability of workers to establish a supportive relationship with client families, an abilitiy that is important in doing social work (Callahan 1993a).

The age at which a 'child' becomes an 'adult' in the eyes of the law can vary from age sixteen to age nineteen, depending on the province (Vogl 1991, 37). Provincial legislation also defines a child 'in need of protection,' and many provinces include statements of basic philosophy. For example, British Columbia and Prince Edward Island have short statements that decisions should be based on 'the best interests of children.' Quebec, Manitoba, Alberta, New Brunswick, and Ontario have longer statements of principles about family autonomy, choice of the least disruptive or detrimental alternative, continuity, prevention and family support, and about special considerations for Native families. Definitions used in child abuse legislation and practice are not always focused and specific, however, and consequently are open to a wide range of interpretations (Barnhorst and Walter 1991).

There are two basic approaches to child protection in Canada: the interventionist and the family autonomy approaches. The interventionist approach places considerable discretion in the hands of social workers and judges by using relatively vague language that is open to interpretation. Language does not focus on harm to the child, but rather on home conditions and parental behaviour. All provinces except Ontario and Alberta use this approach.

The family autonomy approach used by Ontario and Alberta employs more precise language which is more likely to be interpreted in a consistent manner. It attempts to limit discretion and to restrict intervention to relatively well-defined situations, consistent with the notion of due process. This approach links harm to the child with acts or omissions by parents. It also is oriented more towards 'permanency planning,' requiring case plans in court and specific provisions for care at key stages in the child's life. This approach allows narrower grounds for state intervention, includes more specific definitions, and emphasizes parental rights more than the interventionist approach (Bala 1991b).

In most jurisdictions of Canada, the law places a duty on the public to inform child protection authorities if there are 'reasonable grounds' to suspect the abuse or neglect of children (Vogl 1991). What constitutes reasonable grounds is, of course, debatable. All jurisdictions require physical and sexual abuse to be reported, while requirements related to other types of situations may vary. Because emotional abuse is difficult to prove, it is not usually dealt with by the court (Genereux 1991).

The person who reports a case of suspected child abuse is offered immunity from civil liability unless the report is made maliciously or without reasonable grounds. There is also some degree of liability for failure to report, but few lawsuits brought against child protection agencies in Canada for overzealous or incomplete investigations have succeeded. Some jurisdictions require that names of informants be kept confidential (Vogl 1991).

In all provinces, social service agencies have the authority to apprehend children and place them in substitute care on the basis of a social worker's judgment. In Ontario and Alberta, a social worker must obtain a warrant from a judge and can apprehend without a warrant only if the child would be at 'substantial risk' during the time it takes to obtain the warrant (Barnhorst and Walter 1991). But there is always some judgment involved in these cases.

The Quebec *Youth Protection Act of 1977* was the first to introduce the notion of rights for children in care,[2] including the right to be informed of appeal mechanisms and to consult a lawyer. In 1984, Ontario went even farther, with an outline of concrete rights for children in care, such as the right not to be subjected to punishment. The idea of independent status for the child has been accepted in Quebec and Ontario but acknowledged in only a few procedural ways in other jurisdictions (Vogl 1991).

Child abuse registers, or centralized data banks of accused or convicted abusers, are in use in Ontario and Manitoba. There have always been controversies about whether the names of convicted or accused persons should be entered on the register. In addition, issues about who should have access to this information, how long names should remain in the register, and how the data should be used have also been contentious (Genereux 1991).

Although child abuse is a criminal offence in Canada, both civil and criminal courts are involved in dealing with child protection. Abuse and neglect are generally dealt with through civil proceedings, although civil and criminal proceedings may occur simultaneously (Bala 1991b). Legally, the burden lies with the child protection agency to prove that parents are incapable of protecting the child, and the agency remains involved throughout the court process (Vogl 1991). In September 1990, Manitoba established the first Family Violence Court in Canada in response to developments in the criminalization of child abuse. This court, which handles all cases involving child victims, from first appearance to final disposition, is victim-centred and designed to reduce delays (McGillivray 1990).

Historically, the use of the criminal law has been avoided in family situations. However, in 1988 the *Criminal Code* and the *Canada Evidence Act* were amended in Bill C-15, which has been praised by some as a victory for child protection and children's rights. Others argue that the legislation is an infringement of the rights of accused persons under the *Canadian Charter of Rights and Freedoms* and an open invitation to malicious accusations (ibid.). Bill C-15 abolished the corroboration requirement in child abuse cases for children's testimony and allowed it to be screened from the accused or videotaped in advance. Also, cases could no longer be routinely diverted from the criminal justice system. Despite these legal changes, prosecutorial discretion has caused uneven dispositions, sentences are criticized for being too lenient, conviction rates remain low, and some argue that judges do not understand issues of sexual abuse (ibid.).

Soon after a child is taken into agency care, an interim custody hearing takes place. In Alberta and Ontario, the agency is required to provide a written case plan for the court to consider. Three types of orders are possible: supervision, temporary wardship, or permanent wardship. In a supervision order, the child returns home, is supervised by the agency, and may be required to undergo certain treatment. Temporary wardship, which varies from twelve to thirty-six months depending on jurisdiction, places the child in a foster home or residential care facility with the agency as guardian. Permanent wardship terminates the legal relationship with the biological parents, and the child may either be placed for adoption without the consent of the birth parents or may remain a permanent ward without being adopted. If children are not adopted, their wardship is reviewed every twelve months in most jurisdictions, but in others, reviews are possible only if circumstances change (Cruickshank 1991).

Voluntary care agreements between the parents and the agency specify when a short-term placement (six months to two years) will end and the child will be returned home (Barnhorst and Walter 1991). Maximum limits are designed to force social workers and judges to make decisions regarding a child's future. However, voluntary care agreements are not always truly voluntary, tend to be underregulated, and may be used to avoid a court hearing (ibid.).

When a child is in the care of a child protection agency, access by the birth parents varies by jurisdiction. In Alberta, British Columbia, Manitoba, and Ontario, the courts have the authority to make a restraining order in a protection case and prevent the parents from seeing the child. The court in most provinces also has the authority to order a parent to pay child support to the agency (Genereux 1991).

The recent philosophy in Canadian child welfare is to emphasize 'family autonomy and preservation,' support programs, and the 'best interest of the child' (Barnhorst and Walter 1991), although these concepts are difficult to apply. Children are not supposed to be removed from their homes unless parental care poses a significant threat. Permanency planning or planning for continuity and stability is considered essential for children, and adoption is designed to provide a permanent home (Horne-Roberts 1991).

The recognition of due process has resulted in an expanded legal aid system but more time delays and, some argue, a more adversarial system (Bala 1991b). Court proceedings are slow, cumbersome, and subject to many adjournments. Although clients of child welfare have always felt a level of hostility towards the system, new laws now provide a forum in which they can challenge decisions that profoundly affect their lives (Vogl 1991). In most cases, parents are left to make their own decisions about the best way to care for their children according to their own values, beliefs, and experience (Bala 1991b).

A fundamental premise underlying Canadian laws is that coercive government intervention in family life should be kept to a minimum and direct interference is justified only when care falls below the minimum standards that society will tolerate. The child welfare system, however, has been criticized for ignoring the larger structural issues of poverty, unemployment, racial discrimination, one-parent families, and community and family violence (Bala 1991a; Wharf 1993). Furthermore, individual psychological solutions are often sought for social problems. In most jurisdictions, the child welfare system is still focusing on removing children from their parents' home, teaching parenting skills, and providing family therapy rather than addressing the causes of income disparities, family violence, and lack of jobs which propel people into the child welfare system.

Substitute care

If children are apprehended by child welfare workers, they may be placed in three categories of substitute care: foster homes, group homes, and large institutions. Although the number of children in care has been declining as agencies focus on assisting children within their families, there are increases in some areas, likely due to the recession and related family breakdown (Scarth 1993, 6). Furthermore, the number of children in care varies considerably by province, as Table 7.1 indicates. The rates in Manitoba, Yukon, and the Northwest Territories are influenced by high numbers of placements of Native children, and this will be discussed in a later section.

Although the majority of children in care are in foster homes, there has been a dramatic reduction in the number of homes in all provinces (Scarth 1993, 7). Although foster care has proven successful for younger children, there are greater difficulties for those who enter a home later in their childhood or during adolescence. In addition, there have always been concerns that stereotypes about social class and culture influence decisions about which children end up in care, who are selected as foster parents, and which homes are chosen for specific categories of children. The shortage of homes is chronic because foster parents receive little remuneration for their efforts and the number of mothers who can afford to remain outside the paid labour force is declining. Specialized education or training is not required for Canadian foster parents, who receive a minimal payment designed to cover expenses. Foster homes are subject to few legislative guidelines, although they must be approved and regulated by child welfare authorities (Cruickshank 1991).

The second type of substitute care is the group home, which is licensed by the province for five to ten children and is more structured and accountable than family foster care. Because group homes hire paid staff and experience high staff turnover rates, they are more expensive to run than foster homes. The third kind of substitute care is the large institution, which is on the decline in Canada. Institutions are recommended in only the most serious cases, such as those involving children and adolescents who commit criminal offences or suffer from persistent psychiatric disabilities.

Substitute care in Canada is chronically underfunded, and in many areas there is a real shortage of facilities. Front-line employees often have little or no training to deal with troubled children or violent adolescents. Frequently, children are moved from one placement or social worker to another when workers cannot handle them or when facilities close. Although this would be undesirable for any child, it is especially so for those whose backgrounds are characterized by financial and emotional instability, violence, racial discrimination, or cultural disintegra-

TABLE 7.1
Children in substitute care in Canada, per 1,000 children, 1992

Province	Rate per 1,000 children
Newfoundland	4.9
Prince Edward Island	5.9
Nova Scotia	7.4
New Brunswick	6.3
Quebec (1991)	5.2
Ontario	4.3
Manitoba	18.7
Saskatchewan	8.7
Alberta	5.8
British Columbia	7.6
Yukon	20.0
Northwest Territories	20.2

SOURCE: Scarth 1993, 5–8.

tion. In some regions and cities, a disproportionate number of child apprehensions involve black or Native children, many of whom become involved with the child welfare system at an early age and experience multiple foster placements.

Child welfare and Native children[3]

Prior to the 1960s, most Native people lived within extended families in isolated regions, and children in need of care were looked after by other members of the extended family. Elders were also involved in child care and instructed young children in language and traditions. In some cases, the Indian agent (the local representative of the federal government) would place a child with another family on the reserve. Often, however, children were sent away to Indian residential schools which discouraged the use of Native languages and cultural traditions (P. Johnston 1983). Since the establishment of Canada in 1867, legislation regarding Native people has remained a federal responsibility, while child welfare issues for other Canadians fall under provincial jurisdiction.

In 1947, the Canadian Council of Welfare and the Canadian Association of Social Workers presented a brief to a parliamentary committee that was considering changes to the *Indian Act*. They argued that Native people were not being provided with services comparable to those for non-Natives, that Indian agents were generally not qualified to make child welfare decisions, and that no legal or social protection was being provided for Native children or their families. They condemned the practice of placing neglected children in residential schools and recommended an extension of the provincial services of health, welfare, and education to residents of reserves. In 1951, the federal government made major changes to the *Indian Act*, including extending provincial welfare services, but no additional funding accompanied these legal changes. Consequently, only some provinces actually extended child welfare programs, and jurisdictional disputes continued (ibid.).

When the profession of social work developed and expanded after the Second World War, attention was focused on the absence of welfare services among Native children but no major changes were made. During the 1960s, a high percentage of Native children were removed from their families and placed in substitute care by social service workers. This pattern, which has been called the 'Sixties Scoop' (P. Johnston 1983, 23), emerged for several reasons. Colonialist policies required English-speaking education for Native children, and population was so low in remote areas that children were sent to centralized residential schools. If these children experienced problems at school, the authorities found them non-Native foster families whom they believed would provide a stable family environment. Alcohol abuse and widespread poverty among Native people, cultural misunderstandings, jurisdictional disputes, and paternalistic policies also encouraged the removal of Native children from their cultural environment to be cared for by non-Native families. In recent years, First Nations people have protested against policies such as residential schools and non-Native foster care for Native children, and have attempted to take control of their own child welfare services (P. Johnston 1983; Warry 1991).

The demand for child care services has generally increased with women's rising labour force participation as well as with rising rates of poverty and family disintegration. Native women, especially those living on reserves, have experienced extremely high unemployment rates and lower labour force participation rates than non-Native women. In addition, Native families have suffered from severe social and economic problems that require a variety of social services, including substitute child care, treatment for substance abuse, counselling for the victims and the perpetrators of violence, and family support programs.

The Native population is growing at a rapid rate (Muir 1988), which means that the demand for child care and child welfare services may increase faster among Native people than in the rest of the Canadian population. Furthermore, a large percentage of Native women head one-parent families (Siggner 1986; Warry 1991) and require child care services while they work, study, or look for employment. A major focus in discussions of Native child care has been on past practices which have allowed so many people to become alienated from their culture through placement in non-Native foster homes. In addition, finding ways to provide and pay for day care services which are culturally sensitive remains a concern in Native communities.

Native people now expect child care and child welfare services in their own language, controlled by their own people, and based on traditional values such as the importance of the extended family and elders (Native Women's Association 1986; McEvoy 1991). Some First Nations groups, such as those in Manitoba, have negotiated tripartite agreements with the provincial and federal governments which allow them to control their own child welfare and child care services with money from both levels of government.

The quantity and quality of child welfare services provided to Native children on reserves across Canada have varied greatly. A number of court decisions have indicated that unequal provision of services to Native Indian people would not be tolerated. This has led to the establishment of bilateral and tripartite agreements. In a bilateral agreement, the federal government pays the costs of services provided by the province, while a tripartite agreement is negotiated among the Indian band and the provincial and federal governments. The province usually agrees to address the needs of Native children and communities by establishing child welfare agencies mandated under provincial legislation, while the federal government provides full or partial funding. Yet this arrangement does not permit Native people to define how their lives are to be governed and controlled.

Spousal violence and child welfare [4]

As with child abuse, the incidence of marital violence and abuse reported to authorities has grown dramatically throughout North America. Canadian research in the early 1980s estimated that one in ten women in Canada is psychologically, physically, or sexually abused by her husband or live-in partner (MacLeod 1980), even though many of these incidents are not reported to the police. Depending on how 'wife battering' or 'wife abuse' is defined and whether cohabiting partners are included, estimates have varied. However, the one-in-ten figure is thought to be conservative by people who work with battered women (MacLeod 1989).

Some researchers have tried to relate the apparent increase in family violence to changes in bargaining power within marriage, as well as to higher levels of unemployment, financial stress, and substance abuse. A large part of the apparent increase, however, has been caused by 1983 reforms to the *Criminal Code* ending spousal immunity from charges of sexual assault and by the enactment of laws requiring professionals and ordinary citizens to report abusive behaviour. Previously, wives were expected to tolerate abuse and keep it behind closed doors, especially if it was sexual in nature, but laws and attitudes have now changed. Feminists in the shelter movement have encouraged social service workers to become more cognizant of the long-term consequences of living within an abusive family.

Partners charged with family violence are now more likely to be arrested and convicted than in the past, when police and the courts saw marital violence as a private family matter. In turn, better enforcement of the law encourages reporting. These factors have increased the visibility of all forms of family violence. Whether there is actually more abuse and violence than in the past remains under dispute, however.

The vast majority of reported marital violence and abuse cases (95 per cent) involve a male perpetrator and a female victim. Some studies claim that women are also heavily involved in abusing their partners, although this behaviour is less likely to be reported to police or social workers (Strauss and Gelles 1990; Brinkerhoff and Lupri 1988). Some acknowledge that female-to-male violence is less consequential in terms of physical harm and more often occurs as acts of self-defence. On the other hand, feminists tend to highlight the fact that 95 per cent of victims are women with men as the perpetrators and to argue that the term 'family violence' is misleading and ideologically based, as it implies that violent behaviour is evenly distributed among family members. Consequently, feminists tend to prefer the term 'violence against women and children.'

The Canadian Victimization Survey (part of the General Social Survey of 1988) found that, in general, men were more likely than women to be victims of assault and robbery, and that young men were at the greatest risk of violent victimization (Sacco and Johnson 1994). Among people aged twenty-five to forty-four, however, women were more likely than men to be victims of violence. This survey indicated that while single men are in the highest risk group for violent victimization among men, separated and divorced women have higher rates of assault than single or married women. Fewer than half of these cases are reported to the police, however. In most cases of 'spousal violence,' physical abuse is not an isolated event (H. Johnson 1990). Some abused women are assaulted on numerous occasions by their male partners or former partners and have sought help many times from neighbours, friends, social workers, and police.

Although there has been considerable publicity about female victims of homicide, most victims as well as suspects are men. However, women are more likely than men to be killed by an immediate family member: 57 per cent of women compared to 24 per cent of men. Furthermore, Canadian homicide statistics indicate that husbands are more likely than wives to murder their spouses. In 1988, seventy women were killed by their husbands compared to twenty-one men killed by their wives. The survey also indicates that homicide rates are not rising in Canada at present, although there had been a steady upward trend from 1961 to 1975 (Canadian Centre for Justice Statistics 1994).

Despite the higher rates of male victimization in the larger society, several factors work together to maintain women's vulnerability within intimate relationships. Men's aggression against women is maintained by patriarchal ideas that men should be in control of a relationship. Although relations between the sexes are changing, some men have retained traditional ideas. Women who overstep their man's definition of acceptable behaviour may be subject to abuse, especially if the man feels insecure about his own status and also abuses alcohol or drugs. In addition, the prevalence of violence in the media makes it seem socially acceptable to want to maintain control and to use violence to achieve this goal.

Feminism, changing social values, and new laws have encouraged women to redefine 'abuse' to include forced sexual encounters, verbal putdowns, and psychological attacks as well as physical violence. Yet, despite the unwillingness to tolerate abuse, many women cannot support themselves and their children without their husband's paycheque. Even with transitional housing and temporary financial assistance, they feel that they would not be able to provide their children with adequate economic or emotional security if they left their home and partner.

Until recently, police did not seriously respond to calls about domestic violence against women because they perceived that women did not want charges laid or would later withdraw them (MacLeod 1989, ii; H. Johnson 1990). There is now a nation-wide policy for police to charge men who batter. Yet shortage of temporary and low-income housing, lack of knowledge about where to turn for assistance, inability to support themselves and their children on their own wages, and fear of losing their children prevent many wives from leaving an abusive home. Some women continue to tolerate abuse because of a feeling that it may somehow be their fault. Those abused as children are especially likely to suffer from low self-esteem and feel that they are not worthy of better treatment. Many more women, however, fear reprisal from a spouse or former spouse who has threatened to kill them if they go to the police. Considering the number of women killed by their partners, fear of reprisal may be entirely justified.

Although the impetus for change came from the feminist movement, policy makers, social service agencies, women's groups, police, and researchers have developed new ways of dealing with violence against women. Many of the programs provide crisis intervention for the women and their children. When social workers intervene in an incident of domestic violence, the woman is usually encouraged to develop a protection plan that could involve hiring a lawyer, laying charges against her spouse or ex-spouse, finding transitional housing for herself and her children, and, if necessary, acquiring social assistance benefits to cover her living costs. Through either individual counselling or group therapy, battered wives are helped to restructure their thinking about violence and to view it as unacceptable regardless of their own behaviour.

Increasingly, the male batterer is charged with an offence, and is also provided with opportunities for counselling. The aim of counselling is to help him explicitly accept responsibility for his acts of violence instead of blaming his partner, learn to control his emotions, develop better communication skills, and learn non-violent behaviour from male role models. There remains a controversy between feminist groups and male batterers' groups over how scarce resources should best be used. Feminists argue that women's shelters should receive the bulk of public resources because women are most often the victim. Men's groups, some social workers, and many policy makers argue that funding services for victims to the neglect of services for perpetrators deals only with the symptoms.

Action against family violence, including elder abuse, child abuse, and spousal abuse, has involved public education for social workers as well as for some lawyers and judges. For example, sensitization workshops are being provided for judges to increase their knowledge of program options and the implications of this form of violence for women, their families, men who batter, and the wider society (MacLeod 1989, ii). In addition, some support services have been provided for families who are perceived to be 'at risk' of violence because of their stressful circumstances. However, preventive measures have not been widespread in North America.

Although governments at all levels have voiced their concern about family violence, and specifically about violence against women and children, financial constraints are a major impediment to establishing new programs and transitional housing. Until recently, many transition houses for battered women have been funded by private donations and staffed by volunteers, and operated on the verge of closing because of lack of funds. Governments are now providing more money for operating costs. Follow-up therapy and counselling may also be necessary for the entire family, but these services also cost money to establish and maintain. Despite the serious nature of family violence, new program funding for the rising number of reported victims and their abusers is difficult to find.

Recent research has noted the prevalence of physical and sexual violence in dating and courtship, and suggested that there is a relationship between courtship violence and marital violence. For example, in a Canadian study of 202 male college students by Barnes, Greenwood, and Sommer (1991), 42 per cent of the sample reported that they engaged in some form of courtship violence. An American study by O'Leary and colleagues (1989) found that the chance of spouse abuse was more than three times as great if violence had also occurred during courtship. Research has also found that adults who batter their spouse or children have often come from families where their parents engaged in similar behaviour.

These studies have led to three major theories about marital violence. The intergenerational theory suggests that solving conflicts through physical or verbal violence is learned from previous family or interpersonal experiences. The patriarchal theory adds that the prevalence of violence against wives is symptomatic of the low status of women, the social acceptability of violence towards those considered most vulnerable, and the way in which family life has previously been protected from intrusion by the law. Now that women are encouraged to object to abuse by their partners, and social services are available to assist them, this kind of behaviour, which always existed, appears to be more prevalent. A third theory originates from systems theory and views marital violence as a misguided way of resolving conflict used by families under crisis or by people with personality disorders. This theory is not necessarily incompatible with the intergenerational and patriarchal theories; not everyone who has witnessed spousal abuse or who lives in a society that condones violence against women becomes abusive. Each theory contributes to the explanation of the perpetuation of violence.

The solution to the problem within the systems framework is to offer men or couples therapy sessions to help them improve their communication skills and learn to control their emotions and express their feelings and needs without resorting to violence. Yet some feminists argue that valuable resources should not be used to counsel perpetrators when services are unavailable for victims. Furthermore, they argue that couples counselling could provide an unnecessary risk to women, who are forced into therapy and negotiations with someone who has harmed them in the past and could continue to do so. Feminists tend to recommend pressing charges against the perpetrator and providing support groups for 'survivors' of abuse, transitional housing for women and their children, practical advice about living outside abusive relationships and dealing with abused children, and assertiveness training for women.

As divorce laws become more liberal, women become better able to support themselves, and enforcement of child support laws improves, an increasing number of women are leaving abusive relationships. Yet, some battered women remain in abusive relationships for many years, despite the emotional and physical risk to themselves and their children. For some, the risks of poverty and loneliness and the fear of reprisal are greater than the risks of living with abuse, and our governments have offered these women and children few alternatives.

ADOPTION ISSUES[5]

Adoption is a legal transaction extinguishing one family, transferring parental rights and responsibilities, and creating a parent-child relationship between non-biologically related persons (Katarynych 1991). The legal adoption of children is sometimes a response to child abuse, parental neglect, extreme poverty, or war, although many adoptions in Canada and the United States involve the formal adoption of the spouse's children by a step-parent. In the past few decades, numerous changes have taken place in the availability of children, in adoption regulations, and in agency practices. These changes have important implications for public policy.

Adoption trends

Over the last four decades, the family structures of children available for adoption have changed in many countries. While most adopted children in the 1950s were the 'illegitimate' children of unmarried mothers, 65 per cent of adoptions in the United States in 1984 and 60 per cent in Canada in 1992 were by relatives or step-parents (Hersov 1990; Daly and Sobol 1993). This North American pattern has resulted from high divorce and remarriage rates and an increase in blended families. The remaining adoptions occur when infants or children cannot be cared for by their biological parent as a result of death, abuse, neglect, or lack of resources.

In all industrialized countries, the number of infants and children available for adoption dropped in the 1970s and 1980s with the decline in birth rates and the improvement of social services for one-parent families. In many European countries, and to a lesser extent in North America and Australia, prospective parents are turning to war-torn or less-developed countries as the main source of adoptive children both for humanitarian reasons and because there are too few infants and young children available for adoption within their own country. Some argue that the shortage of infants and children has led to a more child-focused attitude in adoption and a reduced emphasis on parental needs (Hall 1986). The current trend towards international adoptions, which are predominant in Europe and subject to fewer regulations in many countries, may reverse this focus.

Although adoption is governed by legislation in all the countries in this study, decisions are also influenced by the ratio of infants, older children, and special needs children to parents willing to adopt children. The rising numbers of unmarried couples, single parents, minority parents, and parents of modest means willing to serve as adoptive families in North America has changed agency practices. In selecting adoptive parents for 'hard-to-place' or 'special needs children,' agencies are under pressure to expand traditional notions about 'suitable' adoptive families (J.A. Rosenthal and Groze 1990; Speirs and Baker 1994). In fact, financial subsidies from public funds now make it easier for low-income foster parents in some jurisdictions to adopt a child who has been living with them (Hill and Triseliotis 1991).

Adoption decisions are also influenced by the agency's mandate, whether it is public or private, and whether the private agency is not-for-profit or for-profit. Many public agencies have seen their workloads increase with rising reports of child abuse and budget cuts, leaving fewer social workers to deal with more work. Within this climate, adoption issues tend to receive a low priority and workers have time only for home studies and urgent placements (Upham 1989). Other factors influencing adoption decisions are the trend to allow birth mothers a role in selecting suitable parents and the search and reunion movement, in which adoptees are gaining the right to seek knowledge of their biological origins (Katarynych 1991, 153; Speirs and Baker 1994).

Models of adoption

Adoption involves varying degrees of government intervention in the different jurisdictions studied. In some, professionals or private agencies arrange all or most adoptions, while in other jurisdictions, governments or government-sponsored agencies regulate adoptions. The disclosure of information about birth parents also varies by jurisdiction.

Private adoptions, which are usually arranged between birth and adoptive families by private professionals or agencies, may be arranged without government intervention, but most are monitored by a social service agency operating under government guidelines. There are three kinds of private adoptions. The first type is arranged by a private practitioner for a social service agency, is monitored by the agency, and requires no parental fees (Wells and Reshotko 1986, 177–8). The second type of private adoption is arranged either by the birth mother herself or by an intermediary (often a lawyer or physician), and fees cover any medical and legal services rendered. These fees could total $5,000–$6,000, as in the province of Ontario (Gooderham 1994). The third type bypasses government regulations, involves large fees, and sometimes uses fraudulent practices (N.C. Baker 1978).

About two-thirds of U.S. adoptions are carried out by private professionals or agencies. Some agencies are for-profit while others are not-for-profit; some are licensed while others are not (Flango 1990). In Canada, the National Adoption Study shows a similar pattern, as well as a steady decline in domestic private adoptions from 4,436 in 1981 to 1,725 in 1990 (Daly and Sobol 1993). Prospective adoptive parents turn to the private sector to avoid the stress of a lengthy home study, to shorten the time they have to wait for a child, and especially when adopting stepchildren. There may also be advantages for government, as expenditures for adoption may be reduced when parents pay a third party to find them a child and social service workers have more time to devote to child protection cases. However, private adoption allows wealthier parents an edge over those with lower incomes.

All adoptions must follow legislation regarding procedures. Although private adoptions may require a social work evaluation before they are finalized, this step is often perfunctory. Most social workers conclude that once a child is placed, the arrangements should be disrupted only for very good reasons (Meezan, Katz, and Russo, 1978, 26–7). There may be no counselling for birth mothers, a lack of confidentiality, unclear legal entitlement, and the intermediary may not share important and relevant information (Kadushin and Martin 1988). Parents who are turned down by public agencies as 'unsuitable' tend to have more success with private adoptions (Ricketts and Achtenberg 1989).

In the public model, adoptions are arranged and monitored by government departments or accredited agencies with professional social work staff. Ideally, this allows careful control over which families are allowed to adopt, pre-adoption counselling for both birth and adoptive families, home studies before adoption, and follow-up services (Speirs and Baker 1994).

With a steady decline in the number of adoptions in the last decade, the public sector both in Canada and the United States has been left to provide permanence for hard-to-place children, while the private sector often arranges infant adoptions and adoptions by step-parents. This already occurs in Canada in provinces which permit private adoptions, such as Ontario. Some provinces which do not allow private adoptions may be leaning in this direction; for example, a recent amendment in Quebec permits private home studies for intercountry adoptions (ibid.).

Open adoptions are sometimes preferred for older children who already have an established relationship with their birth family (Cook 1991–2). In closed or confidential adoptions, the most conservative form, there is no contact between adoptive and birth families, and identities are kept secret. Adoptive parents are offered limited information about the birth parents, usually only basic medical information or a brief biographical sketch (McRoy 1991). Closed adoption is based on the assumption that secrecy facilitates relinquishment, promotes unity in the new family, and protects against the stigma of illegitimacy.

Selecting adoptive parents

The discretion that has been allowed in interpreting adoption laws and standards has resulted in a wide variation in agency practices in North America. Studies reveal that workers evaluating the same adoption applicants often differ in decisions to accept or reject, as well as in assessments of the specific strengths or weaknesses of the applicant (Brieland 1984; Sachdev 1984, 84; Westhues and Cohen 1988). Despite variations, however, couples who adopt infants from agencies tend to be slightly older and to have higher incomes and levels of education than biological parents. About one-quarter are childless (Bachrach 1983; J. Cohen and Westhues 1990). These applicants may be preferred because they are perceived to be better able to support a child financially and because they tend to be articulate, assertive, and able to make a favourable impression on white middle-class social workers. Parents who adopt special-needs children, however, tend not to be economically privileged. Many were foster parents before adopting, and fewer are childless (Speirs and Baker 1994).

White middle-class social workers have often failed to recognize cultural differences in lifestyle, child-rearing practices, extended family caregiving, and the validity of traditional sources of assistance (C.P. Christensen 1989; Gibbs 1990). Although North American agencies usually have a policy of placing children in same-race homes, this may not occur because it requires considerable cooperation and extensive communication with culturally based adoption agencies. In European countries, where the population is more homogeneous, questions about the racial and religious matching of adoptive children and their prospective parents are less relevant (L.J. Schwartz 1991).

Although the law stipulates that decisions about adoption should be 'in the best interests of the child,' the parties may not always agree on what is best for the child. Although it might be more effective and less costly for an agency to maintain a child at home with family support programs or to follow the principle of 'family preservation,' North American agencies have tended to place children in substitute care. Private agencies have sometimes been more concerned with finding children for adoptive parents (especially if there are fees involved) than with assisting the birth family. In other situations, if a child has proven difficult to place, social workers may be pressured to place a child with any family that fits the minimum requirements (Speirs and Baker 1994).

Adoption in Canada

As the structure of most families has changed, the institution of adoption has evolved considerably over the years. Legal adoption has a long history in some Canadian provinces, with the earliest law in New Brunswick in 1873 (Katarynych 1991).[6] All legislation deals with the same basic issues, including relinquishment of the child, placement, the finalizing of adoption, and the possibility of reunification. Children become available for adoption under the following circumstances:

1. when a court order is obtained to terminate the rights of parents and make the child a permanent ward of the province;
2. when parents voluntarily surrender their child to a welfare agency or the police;
3. when parents leave their child permanently with a relative; and
4. when parents remarry and want their new spouse to be the legal parent of their child.

The statutes of most provinces give the child protection agency the exclusive right and duty to determine the best interests of permanent wards and to assess a child's suitability for adoption. In some provinces, private agencies have been established to deal with the heavy demand for relative and international adoption, and provincial governments are moving towards legislative regulation of the procedure and cost. All Canadian provinces have rules around revocation of consent, and all allow the court to waive or dispense with consent if the inability to obtain it is barring an adoption that would otherwise be 'in the child's best interests,' although courts are usually reluctant to do so (ibid.).

Adoption decisions are based on rules about who can adopt which emanate from laws, accreditation boards, and social agencies. The rules are intended to provide guidelines about what constitutes a suitable family environment, appropriate family structures, and acceptable parental attitudes in order to ensure that the child's best interests are served. Canadian agencies must abide by provincial legislation, but they also use the adoption standards of the Child Welfare League of America. In addition, the agencies themselves devise their own rules based on the availability of adoptive parents and children needing adoption and on local circumstances (Speirs and Baker 1994).

Some provinces specify who are eligible to adopt according to the age, marital status, residency, and other attributes of the potential parent. Most statutes permit the child to be present at the adoption hearing, and some require the court to satisfy itself that the child understands and appreciates the nature and consequences of adoption. Except in Ontario (where the statutory age is seven), all children aged twelve and over who are the subject of adoption proceedings have the right to give or withhold consent unless the court removes the right. Adoption results in a change of the child's name and status.

Estimates of the number and type of adoptions in Canada have varied considerably over the past fifty years. In 1939, about 2,000 children were adopted. By 1971, this figure rose to 20,500 before the figures began to decline (Hepworth 1980, 3,132). Data from the National Adoption Study show a steady decline between 1981 and 1990 from more than 5,000 to fewer than 3,000 domestic adoptions, excluding relative and custom adoptions[7] (Daly and Sobol 1993).

Improved contraception, legalized abortion, and the increasing desire of unmarried mothers to raise their own babies have led to the dramatic decline of infant adoption placements (J. Cohen and Westhues 1990, xi). In addition, child welfare staff are required to make a greater commitment to keeping families intact as a result of the permanency planning movement and the emphasis on family preservation. Couples routinely wait from three to seven years, and up to ten years or more in certain jurisdictions, before having a child placed with them, and few receive healthy Caucasian babies (R. Walker 1987; Westhues and Cohen 1988, 12).

As the total number of infants placed for adoption has declined, the average age of children at adoption has increased (Daly and Sobol 1993). Furthermore, the proportion of children with behavioural problems and physical and mental disabilities has also increased, as a result of improved reporting of abuse and neglect, greater emphasis on youth protection, the deinstitutionalization of children with disabilities, and initiatives to find permanent homes for all children taken into care (J. Cohen and Westhues 1990, xii).

Despite the rhetoric of 'the best interests of the child,' placement decisions are often made to solve short-term public policy problems. One such problem is what to do about the growing numbers of older and disabled children in foster care. Another is the time and public expense of providing pre- and post-adoption services during budget cuts. Placement decisions must also consider the vested interests of certain groups (such as birth mothers, infertile couples, and gays and lesbians) that wish to change adoption legislation and practices to incorporate new models of family and changing moral values. Although agencies can afford to be highly selective with infant adoptions because there are so few infants available, they have tended to expand their notions of a 'suitable' adoptive family for older children who are considered more difficult to place (Speirs and Baker 1994).

CHALLENGES FOR CANADIAN CHILD WELFARE SYSTEMS

Canadian child welfare agencies clearly face a number of challenges. Funding freezes and cutbacks by the federal government have placed more financial pressure on provincial governments and the voluntary sector, causing some agencies to pare down prevention programs, especially in rural and remote areas (Scarth 1993, 7). At the same time, the cultural and racial backgrounds of the client group are changing, requiring new culturally sensitive programming. Yet change in the child welfare system has been slow to occur for several reasons.

Children and poor women, the main recipients of services, do not have a strong political power base. Furthermore, child protection workers are often over-extended and lack training and support. As a result, they are vulnerable to stress and errors in judgment, and have little opportunity to push for reform. There is also a lack of national data and the longitudinal research that could be used to enlighten and improve services. Even gathering statistics is difficult, as child welfare and social services fall under provincial jurisdiction, record keeping differs across jurisdictions, and the provinces control the release of information (ibid.).

Despite these criticisms, there have been improvements. In 1991, British Columbia undertook a community review of its child welfare legislation and services and produced a government policy paper proposing changes to strengthen support to families and introduce more community participation. Several provinces are providing training and increased remuneration for foster parents. Numerous projects are connecting professional mainstream agencies to informal helping networks and support systems (Scarth 1993, 8). Other jurisdictions are introducing early intervention programs for families that are considered to be at risk for wife abuse and child abuse and neglect. In addition, more Native communities are controlling their own child welfare services. One of the most important initiatives, however, involves redefining the mandate of child welfare from a crisis intervention model to one which emphasizes community development and family support (ibid.).

Like the English-speaking countries in this study, Canada's child welfare system is based on a residual philosophy of social welfare. In contrast, the European countries have adopted a more pro-active and preventive model. In the next section, the child welfare systems of the other countries will be outlined and discussed.

CHILD WELFARE: A CROSS-NATIONAL COMPARISON OF CHILD
PROTECTION AND ADOPTION

Australia

Child protection

The child welfare system in Australia, as in the other English-speaking countries and Canada, is based on a residual role for the state in family life – the idea that the state should intervene only when the family cannot cope. Most Australian children in substitute care come from socially disadvantaged, mother-headed families, and most foster mothers are upper-working-class women (B. Smith 1991), as in Canada. The current foster-care system has been criticized for focusing on mothering skills and for making invidious comparisons between 'good' mothers and 'bad' mothers rather than dealing with the poverty in which many of these families live (Aitken 1991).

The states and territories have jurisdiction over both family law and child welfare programs, and therefore laws and procedures to address these issues vary (Morfuni 1991). Casework is organized within the social security administration following general guidelines in the Australian Constitution (Finlay and Bailey-Harris 1989). The *Family Law Act 1975* and the *Family Law Amendment Act 1987* are the two pieces of legislation dealing with child welfare matters. The main change in the 1987 legislation was the introduction of a separate Family Court of Australia to deal with marital matters, including divorce and custody.

With the dual court system, both state family courts and the Family Court of Australia could be involved with a family at the same time. If child abuse is disclosed while dealing with divorce, for example, the case must be referred to the state court, which deals primarily with child protection and child care (Morfuni 1991). State courts have been encouraged to take on federal responsibilities to help simplify the system, to avoid fragmentation, and to minimize trauma to families (Finlay and Bailey-Harris 1989). Yet the provision in the *Family Law Act* that allows states to establish their own family courts has been criticized for allowing fragmentation of the system. Each state could have different rules and procedures, leading to varying results, inequalities among states, delays, and lack of clear lines of responsibility and protocol (Morfuni 1991).

Since 1983, the *Family Law Act* has granted children the right to separate representation in family court (Finlay and Bailey-Harris 1989). In most Australian states, the Legal Aid Commission pays for this representation; in the remainder it is paid by the Department of Community Services. The child's lawyer acts in 'the best interest of the child,' not as instructed by the child. Family court is a civil court and handles abuse cases differently from criminal court, which relies on proof beyond reasonable doubt (Morfuni 1991).

If counselling ordered by family court reveals abuse, it is not always clear whether the counsellor is legally obliged to report the abuse. Reporting is mandatory in some states, but state laws take precedence over federal laws. It is generally accepted that abuse should be reported to state authorities, but the *Family Law Act* precludes counsellors from revealing the content of sessions in court. Consequently, in states with no mandatory reporting law, there may be procedural problems (ibid.).

In 1989, Australia's highest appellate court held that the resolution of an allegation of child sexual abuse is subservient to the court's determination as to what is best for the child's welfare, as provided by legislation (Bates 1990–1). The courts are required to strike a balance between risk of harm to the child through sexual abuse and the possibility of benefit to the child through parental access. Nevertheless, the courts are not supposed to award custody or access to a parent if it would expose the child to an 'unacceptable risk' of sexual abuse. Two questions that remain unanswered are: 'What is an "acceptable" risk?' and 'Acceptable to whom?' (ibid.).

Adoption

The goal of adoption in Australia is to provide a permanent home for the child, not to find children for suitable parents (Horne-Roberts 1991). As in other industrialized countries, the numbers of infants available for adoption have been declining, although step-parent adoptions have been increasing with rising rates of divorce and remarriage (Hall 1986). The role of adoption in step-families is under review, however. The concept of guardianship is becoming preferred over adoption, as the relationship between the child and the birth parent is seen as taking precedence (Finlay and Bailey-Harris 1989).

Adoption is a state responsibility in Australia, and both legislation and practice vary by state. The court makes adoption orders in every state except Queensland, where they are made by the director of children's services. Placements are arranged through the adoption branches of the state welfare department or by private agencies approved by that department. Potential adoptive parents are selected by the Department of Community Welfare (ibid.). Adoptive parents must be heterosexual and, except in exceptional circumstances, married. In South Australia, a common-law relationship of five years is considered equivalent to legal marriage. The adoptive parents must also be at least eighteen years old, with the father eighteen years and the mother sixteen years older than the child (ibid.). Foster parents who have established a stable relationship with a child may apply to adopt that child.

In order to be eligible for adoption, children must be under eighteen in most states. Guardianship is favoured over adoption for stepchildren and Aboriginal children in Victoria, and other states are expected to follow this practice (ibid.). There is a provision for subsidized adoption in Australia, which means that low family income is not always a barrier to becoming adoptive parents (Hill and Triseliotis 1991).

If birth parents are married, both need to give their consent to the adoption. If they are not, only the mother's consent is required, although this is beginning to be challenged in certain Australian jurisdictions. If children are over twelve years old, their consent is also needed (except in the state of Victoria, where the wishes of children must be considered regardless of age). Parental consent may be revoked within a specified period if the order was obtained by fraud, duress, or other improper means, or for some other exceptional reason (Finlay and Bailey-Harris 1989). Birth parents in Australia have had little or no control over the decision-making process in placements. Adoptions were traditionally closed and any agreements made between birth and adoptive parents have been informal and unenforceable, except in the state of Victoria. In recent years, however, secrecy in adoption has been reduced (Horne-Roberts 1991; Van Keppel 1991).

In several Australian states, adoption registers have been developed to facilitate contacts. In Victoria, an adult adoptee has been permitted since 1984 to receive identifying file information on request without a birth parent's consent. A birth parent may apply for information as well, but will receive identifying information only if the adult adoptee consents (Finlay and Bailey-Harris 1989). In Western Australia, an adult adoptee may now apply for an original birth certificate unless there is a negative entry by the parent in the Contact Register.

In recent years, as birth rates have fallen and more unmarried mothers have been raising their own children, there has been growing interest in international adoption. Most children adopted from outside the country come from South-East Asian countries. Originally, these adoptions were unregulated and privately arranged, but because of concern about how children were actually obtained, a Joint Committee on Intercountry Adoptions prepared recommendations in 1986 that have been accepted in all Australian jurisdictions. Overseas adoptions must now be supervised by the Ministry of Social Welfare to assure that there is compliance with the laws and regulations of the country of origin, that applicant parents have been assessed, that relinquishing parents have consented, and that children meet health requirements. The placement is supervised for up to twelve months (ibid.).

In Australia, the family is seen as the natural and fundamental unit of society, the best place for children, and an institution which should be protected and supported (B. Smith 1991). At the same time, domestic violence and child abuse have become more apparent, and female victims are overwhelmingly those in traditional housewife roles who are economically dependent on their partners (Pixley 1994). High divorce rates, increasing unemployment, and the growth of low-wage work are creating larger case loads for social workers but fewer opportunities for parents to become self-supporting. Yet welfare services tend to focus on crisis management, especially on protecting children from abuse, rather than on resolving the underlying causes of poverty and unemployment.

France

Child protection

The child welfare system in France differs from those in Australia and Canada in four ways: France focuses more on prevention, retains a closer link between social services and health care, spends more money on children's services, and has developed a more explicit family policy.

Both parents are financially responsible for their children and have joint authority over 'legitimate' children. If children are found to be in need of care or protection, several possibilities exist. A guardian may be delegated by court order if parents have not demonstrated interest in their child for more than a year or if the child was taken into substitute care without parental involvement. This guardianship often involves placement within the extended family. A second type of intervention is to appoint a sponsor who provides hospitality, financial assistance, and communication through letter writing, but has no legal authority over the child. A third alternative for an abused or neglected child is adoption (Verdier 1988), which will be discussed in more detail later.

One example of the preventive focus of French family policy is that regular medical, psychological, and social examinations of children have been a government requirement for receiving family allowances since 1980. This link between social services and health care is a unique feature of the French system, in which 25 per cent of social workers have a public health background (Schorr 1989). A second example of the preventive focus of French child welfare policy is that the government maintains and subsidizes family holiday homes for low-income families as a way of preventing family problems (Kadushin and Martin 1988). Additional examples are the provision of child-rearing allowances and state-run child care centres, as discussed in chapter 5 and 6. All these social supports help reduce family stress and the need for foster care and adoption. In the 1980s, although the French social service system underwent severe budget cuts, the principles behind child welfare do not appear to have changed (ibid.).

Adoption

There are two types of adoption possible in France: full adoption and limited adoption. Full adoption (*adoption plenière*) is a complete legal and physical transfer of a child to another family (Horne-Roberts 1991). Only children under fifteen years of age can undergo a full adoption, and there are about 4,000 a year (Verdier 1988). The second type is a limited adoption (*adoption simple*), which is partial and reversible. The child remains with the natural family and maintains hereditary rights and the family name, while the adoptive family acquires parental authority and responsibility for supporting the child. The natural parents retain secondary responsibility for supporting the child but forfeit parental authority. A limited adoption ends with a repeal initiated by the adoptive family or child, or with a full adoption. There are about 2,000 limited adoptions a year, mostly of older children (Horne-Roberts 1991).

There is no provision for subsidized adoption in France (Hill and Triseliotis 1991).

Germany

Child protection

Germany is among the least generous of the European countries with respect to child welfare (Schorr 1989). The state is allowed to intervene in the family only as a last resort, for it is assumed that families are competent to care for their members (Lorenz 1991). There is more state intervention with children born outside marriage, however, as a guardian from the local welfare office is assigned to the child at birth to assist the mother (Kadushin and Martin 1988).

Child welfare policies are designed to promote the welfare of children within their families (Lorenz 1991). If a child is in danger, the youth office may intervene and place the child in care. Parents or guardians must be notified immediately, and the case must be brought before a court by the end of the day. If necessary, police must act under the guidance of the youth department (ibid.).

Since 1973, permanent orders without parental consent have been possible through guardianship court, which can replace parental consent with that of an agency if there has been gross and continuous neglect of parenting duties (Baer 1986). The youth office must actively attempt to locate the parent for three months before proceeding. If the parent is available, the office must provide counselling about guardianship replacement and after three months may apply to guardianship court. Guardianship can also be replaced if a parent is permanently and seriously mentally handicapped to the point where care for the child is impossible. When guardianship is suspended, contact and all legal relationships between the child and the birth family end (Kuehl and Winter-Stettin 1986). The child may be placed in a licensed foster home, which must have passed an inspection by the youth office (Lorenz 1991).

The German Child Protection Federation, established in 1898, operates crisis lines and shelters for abused children. As in France, the German government maintains family holiday homes, subsidized for low-income families, as a preventive measure. A unique medical specialty called 'social pediatrics' has been developed to teach parents better child care in the family environment (Kadushin and Martin 1988). The

Child Care Act 1991 gives local youth offices responsibility for looking after the needs of children and youth in their geographic area. Private and public organizations deliver services coordinated by the youth office (Lorenz 1991).

Adoption

In Germany, the family is considered to be the most important unit of society, the normal place for a child, and adoption is allowed only when it serves the 'welfare of the child' (Grandke 1989–90). Prior to 1977, children could not be adopted without parental consent, but in that year the adoption law was reformed, more children were freed for adoption, and they could be placed earlier and in more appropriate homes. Adoptions declined in the 1980s in Germany as in all industrialized countries, although step-parent adoptions and the number of applicant parents have increased (Textor 1991, 1992).

In Germany, all adoptions must be approved by the state. Public youth welfare offices are mandated to provide adoption services, but other state-recognized agencies, such as those connected with the Lutheran or Catholic churches, may also offer these services (Kuehl and Winter-Stettin 1986). Applicants must be evaluated and screened by social workers from government-approved agencies, who counsel both the birth mother and the adoptive parents (Textor 1992). Among married couples, one adoptive parent must be twenty-five years old and the other twenty-one years old, with an upper age limit of thirty-five years recommended. A single adoptive parent must be twenty-five and a step-parent twenty-one years old (Kuehl and Winter-Stettin 1986). Foster parents may apply to adopt foster children if the child has been integrated into the family for a specified length of time (Textor 1992).

The consent of both married parents or of an unmarried mother is required unless an agency has acquired guardianship of the child (Kuehl and Winter-Stettin 1986). Children fourteen years and over must consent to adoption, and they may revoke consent at any time until finalization one year after placement. In addition, an adoption may be revoked if there were legal or procedural irregularities or lack of consent by parents (ibid.). Nearly all German adoptions have been closed, although some exchange of information has become popular with social workers since the 1980s. There is no provision for subsidized adoption (Hill and Triseliotis 1991).

Germany has considerable experience with international adoptions, as the birth rate has been declining for years and few German infants are available (Kadushin and Martin 1988). One in seven adopted children is 'foreign,' and certain agencies specialize in arranging these adoptions (Baer 1986). Parents who adopt foreign-born children are typically middle and upper class, and most are university educated (Kuehl and Winter-Stettin 1986). Critics argue that foreign adoptions technically are illegal in Germany because private adoptions are not allowed, yet ways are found to import 1,100 children a year, mainly from developing countries (Textor 1992).

Adoptions must be finalized in accordance with German law even if they have already been finalized in another country. Post-adoption services are available, and birth and adoption records are no longer sealed (Kuehl and Winter-Stettin 1986). Adoptees aged sixteen or older are allowed access to public records, including the names of birth parents, without the permission of adoptive parents (Textor 1992).

The Netherlands

Child protection

In the Netherlands, child protection services are carried out by the Councils for Child Welfare, which are government-mandated agencies (Rood-de Boer, 1988–9). As an alternative to reporting to the government agency, however, child abuse may also be disclosed to a 'confidential doctor' who provides services without reporting the abuse to child protection authorities (Kadushin and Martin 1988).

Several values underlie the Dutch child welfare system. The 'best interests of the child' are considered a priority, and parental authority can be put aside by government in order to protect children. Second, it is felt that children belong in their own families if at all possible, and should not be removed without justification. Third, a mother always has a legal relationship with her child, but a father must acknowledge paternity if the child is born outside marriage (Hoksbergen and Bunjes 1986).

There is a strong focus on prevention and family support as a solution to child welfare problems in the Netherlands. Visiting homemakers, trained for eighteen months, come into the home to assist parents with child care and are a major part of treatment plans. In addition, special villages known as 're-education centres' are established for families experiencing problems, in which employment is obtained nearby for the father and the children attend the village school. Social workers teach parenting skills and model behaviours for the family (Kadushin and Martin 1988).

Many delinquent children are placed under the supervision of a volunteer 'family guardian' who works with one or two families. This individual does not perform casework but rather models appropriate behaviour as well as facilitating liaison with the child welfare system. Institutions and foster care are used equally in the Netherlands (ibid.).

The child welfare system is funded through taxes, but part of the funding for children's services comes from the post office. A special set of children's stamps is issued each year and a portion of the income goes to the Dutch Foundation for the Child (ibid.). Since the mid-1980s, government policy has focused on reducing expenditures, and child protection has been affected by budget cuts. In addition, deregulation of the child welfare system has become an aim, which some believe contradicts the stated commitments to the best interests of the child and the welfare of families (Rood-de Boer 1988–9).

Adoption

The present adoption law in the Netherlands was enacted in 1956, and step-parents have been permitted to adopt since 1979 (Hoksbergen and Bunjes 1986). As in all the countries in our study, the number of Dutch infants available for adoption has declined in recent years, as a result of falling birth rates and improved social services for single mothers.

There are two basic types of adoption in the Netherlands. In-country adoptions are further sub-classified into relative adoptions (mainly step-parent) and non-relative adoptions. The second type is intercountry adoption, which will be discussed below. Waiting lists of parents wanting to adopt are long, fees are high, and there is no provision for subsidized adoption (Hill and Triseliotis 1991).

A relinquishing mother must be at least sixteen years old and unmarried. After birth, the baby is placed with a foster family or in a children's home for three months while the birth mother receives counselling. Adoption regulations require applicant parents to have been married for at least five years. The age difference between child and applicant parent must be at least eighteen years, and applicants must not be over forty. However, age and marriage requirements do not apply to relative adoptions. To be eligible for adoption, the child must be under the legal age, but most are under six. The consent of children over twelve must be sought and their wishes heard by a judge (Hoksbergen and Bunjes 1986).

Adoptive applicants are approved following an assessment by the Child Welfare Board. Before placement, they are permitted supervised visits with the child in the foster family. Upon placement, the adoptive parents receive guardianship of the child, but there is a one-year period before the legal adoption is granted. During this time, a social worker supervises the adopting family (ibid.).

Adoptions in the Netherlands are usually closed, but the concept of more openness is gaining popularity (ibid.). Because of the small size of the country, it is relatively easy to trace natural mothers, and social workers usually act as intermediaries. Adoption files are kept for thirty years for the purpose of search and are then destroyed, but there is no legislation covering post-adoption services (Rood-de Boer 1988–9).

Adoptions are arranged by the Councils for Child Welfare and finalized by the district court. When the adoption is finalized, the child acquires the status of legitimate child of the adoptive parents, and all legal relations between the child and the birth family are severed. Adoptions cannot be annulled for any reason, even if there has been an error in procedure (Hoksbergen and Bunjes 1986).

Because there are very few Dutch infants available for adoption, babies are actively recruited from abroad, especially by higher-income parents who can afford the cost. International adoptions are arranged by not-for-profit organizations, and may be a physical or a financial adoption. Physical adoption means that the child comes to live with the adoptive family, but parents may also support a child in its own country in exchange for contact and information (ibid.). Usually only children under school age are allowed into the country for physical adoption, but an exception may be made if the child is adopted with a younger sibling. Once a child is physically adopted in the Netherlands, he or she becomes a citizen (Hill and Triseliotis 1991). As there is no legislation covering international adoptions, anyone can act as intermediary for the adoption of foreign children and there are no pre- or post-adoptive services for parents (Hoksbergen and Bunjes 1986).

Sweden

Child protection

Like France, Sweden has developed a wide range of programs designed to prevent poverty, abuse, and neglect, and as a result has the lowest infant mortality in the world (Ziegert 1987). These programs include comprehensive health and education systems, a universal child allowance, a means-tested housing allowance, government advances on child support payments for children of divorce, a comprehensive day care scheme, study loans, a children's ombudsperson, and a statutory right to grow up in an environment free of violence. This supportive legislation appears to be more effective than a reactive child welfare system (such as Australia's or Canada's) designed to intervene after problems arise and in which decision making is directed by court rulings with judicial discretion.

Swedish child welfare is governed by the *Compulsory Care of Young Persons Act* and the *Social Services Act* which regulate the circumstances under which children are taken into care if their health or development is endangered at home (Andersson 1992). An effort is made to promote children's inclusion within their families, homes, and communities, and services are operated entirely by government with no voluntary organizations involved (ibid.). Because municipalities provide their own social services, there is considerable variation by region. Child welfare boards are advocacy-oriented and take responsibility for major services in the community. These boards have two basic functions: client-centred support and treatment, and social control and intervention (Kadushin and Martin 1988).

Family members may enter the child welfare system voluntarily or involuntarily. If a child is placed without parental consent, the social worker has to defend the placement in the County Administrative Court and the Administrative Court of Appeal (Andersson 1992). It is the practice, however, to retain children's involvement with their parents, and 80 per cent of children in care are placed with relatives or foster families (Hessle 1989). Although institutions are used as a last resort in substitute care, they involve interventions for the entire family rather than for the child only (Kadushin and Martin 1988).

As in other countries, most Swedish children in care were raised in working-class homes and 83.4 per cent come from one-parent families. Parents are typically female with low levels of formal education. Most are unemployed and unskilled, and in 40 per cent of the cases, at least one parent is an immigrant. Twenty per cent of cases arise from parent-adolescent conflict. Of children taken into substitute care, about half stay for more than two years (Hessle 1989).

Adoption

Because birth rates in Sweden have been low for decades, there are few children available for adoption and the number has been declining since 1965. For example, there were only fifteen to twenty Swedish children available for adoption in 1986, excluding step-parent adoptions. Yet about 1,500 children are imported each year for adoption, about half of whom are Asian (Andersson 1986).

The Swedish National Board for Intercountry Adoption assists applicants and acts as a liaison with the children's countries of origin (Kadushin and Martin 1988). A couple wishing to adopt applies to the local Social Welfare Committee that carries out a home study of the applicant family. If the report is favourable, the family applies through one of the six organizations authorized under the *Act of Intercountry Adoption Assistance* and supervised by the board (Andersson 1986). When the child arrives and is placed with the family, the social welfare board supervises the placement until the adoption is finalized by the district court. Parents can then apply for citizenship on behalf of the child, which is promptly granted. Step-parent and other adoptions basically follow the same procedure, without the involvement of the international agencies.

Open adoptions are favoured in Sweden (Andersson 1986). Although there is no provision for subsidized adoption (Hill and Triseliotis 1991), this is made unnecessary by the Swedish social welfare system, which is based on the principle of universal entitlements.

Child welfare practice is designed to reduce the need for individual intervention by developing structural measures aimed at improving the social environment (Andersson 1992). Welfare policies emphasize prevention and focus on helping children within their families. For example, all children are monitored regularly at child welfare centres throughout the first two years and then at age four. An out-of-wedlock child is assigned a child welfare guardian at birth to assist the mother (Kadushin and Martin 1988). Another measure aimed at preventing child abuse is the operation of holiday homes for low-income families and mothers at home, with visiting homemakers to care for the children while mothers are away (ibid.). Compared to the other countries in this study, Sweden provides generous programs for all children, not only those in need of protection (Schorr 1989).

The United Kingdom

Child protection

Until the Second World War, Britain provided services mainly for families in dire need and distress, while reinforcing the values of hard work, thrift, temperance, and moral virtue (Langan 1985). Despite the postwar reorganization of health, education, and welfare services, problems of poor housing, low income, and delinquency persisted throughout the 1950s and 1960s. Instead of acknowledging the social and political reasons for these problems, governments focused on individual responsibility and 'the problem family.' By the later 1960s, however, the reorganization of National Assistance as Supplementary Benefits in 1966 reflected the government's recognition that the poor were not going to disappear and required continuing government support. Beginning in the late 1960s, social work was reorganized and expanded in Britain, state intervention in the economy became more extensive, and the government began to provide family and community services instead of just social security benefits (ibid.).

In 1968, the Seebohm Report led to a major rationalization of the services provided by local government and charitable organizations. The *Children and Young Persons Act 1969* and the *Children Act 1975* extended and solidified the social work professions, integrating a range of activities from dealing with child abuse to community organizing. However, social work theory and practice continued to favour such traditions as the patriarchal family and the ideology of motherhood and women's caring (ibid.).

Throughout the 1980s, the Conservative government under Prime Minister Thatcher was committed to New Right ideologies, including the belief that public expenditure was too high, that the welfare state was wasteful and dominated by a self-serving bureaucracy, and that help should be concentrated where it was needed most. The Fowler Review of Social Security (1985), which was designed to ensure that the cost of social security did not continue to rise, differentiated more emphatically between the 'deserving' and the 'undeserving' poor. The *So-*

cial Security Act which followed in 1986 attempted to target benefits to low-income families with children (Abbott and Wallace 1992, 124).

Despite government aspirations and rhetoric, the social security system remained relatively intact because widespread popular support exists for universal health services, education, and indexed social security benefits (Mishra 1990; Bradshaw 1993). However, there have been cutbacks to public housing, school lunch programs, and clothing grants (Abbott and Wallace 1992, 123). As well, some social services have been privatized, and user fees have been added for certain health and social services (Mishra 1990, 23). Child welfare services remain targeted to children who have been abused or neglected or are in need of protection.

Child welfare legislation in the United Kingdom is enacted by the central government and administered by local governments and voluntary organizations. Local authorities receive funding from the central government but retain some discretion on how to spend it (Hill and Triseliotis 1991). Family Service units provide local services under the *Children Act 1989*, including training for families at risk, residential care, and the health visitor system, which is a universal outreach service. Nurses trained in child development and family dynamics work with families from childbirth until children enter school (S. Cohen and Warren 1990).

The *Children Act 1989* set a new agenda for child welfare by expanding the definition of 'children in need' to disabled and hospitalized children and by attempting to make the system fairer and more efficient (Ryburn 1991). For children in care, the legislation requires formal plans and frequent reviews of these plans to reduce multiple placements. Children placed outside the home voluntarily are said to be provided 'accommodation,' the parents retain legal responsibility, and the authority of local government is specific and limited. Parents or legal guardians may remove a child from accommodation at any time. The term 'in care' is used only for placements without parental consent (Ward and Jackson 1991).

A child might come to the attention of child welfare authorities through parents' voluntary request if they cannot control or care for the child or if a parent fears abuse by the partner. In addition, a child or adolescent who commits a criminal offence might be apprehended by police and turned over to the child welfare agency. Social workers may also use a 'place of safety order' to apprehend children or adolescents considered to be in danger or inadequately cared for (McCarthy 1991).

One-third of all children in care are apprehended under place of safety orders (Packman and Jordan 1991).

As in North America, reports of child abuse and neglect have increased in recent decades. When abuse or neglect is suspected, the case is added to the local register. These child abuse registers have been criticized for inaccuracies, and research has not found many differences between children and families who are on the registry and those who are not (Campbell 1991). Once abuse is reported, the court may remove the child from the home and may issue an order for interim care or supervision for a temporary period. A care order may be made only if the court is satisfied that the child is maltreated or beyond parental control. In Family Court, a child has the right to legal representation, and the guardian, solicitor, and child may all make representations.

Before local authorities make a decision about a child, they must consult the child, parents or guardian, and any other significant adult in the child's life (such as a grandparent) (Rains 1991). If the child is allowed to remain at home, supportive services and treatment are prescribed; these are often provided by volunteers supervised by professionals (S. Cohen and Warren 1990). The child welfare worker must review the family resources and advise both child and family of their legal rights. Race, language, religion, and culture must be taken into account in placement decisions (Ryburn 1991). If a child is placed in care, the parents, guardian, or child may apply for a discharge order at any time, and parents may also apply for access (Burrows 1991).

The *Children Act 1989* replaced parental rights with parental responsibilities, and children are no longer considered the property of parents. With greater acceptance of the concept of due process, parents gained more rights as compared to social workers. Now, a voluntary agreement between parents and the agency is attempted before court action is initiated. If a child is admitted to care, the law makes it more difficult to terminate parental rights (Thoburn 1991). The main consequences of the *Children Act* have been to allow local authorities and voluntary agencies to provide more supportive services, with the idea of reducing the number of care orders and the need for criminal proceedings (Gibbons 1991). However, there have been complaints that local authorities do not all interpret the act in the same way (Bebbington and Miles 1989).

The majority of children spend a short time in foster care, and are usually placed with an unrelated family. Placement with relatives is declining as procedures become more legalistic (M.I. Lowe 1991). There are two categories of long-term care arrangements: substitute care and supplemental care. Substitute parents take on the entire parenting role, while supplemental parents share it with the birth parents (Thoburn 1991).

In the United Kingdom, foster care may be public or private. Public fostering is initiated by an agency, and the home must be approved and regulated. Parents may also arrange fostering privately for children who are not necessarily child welfare risks. Apart from a requirement that the local government be notified of the intention to place a child in a foster home, legislation regarding private foster homes is minimal. Homes are not assessed or licensed, although local authorities do monitor them.

The *Foster Care Charter* of 1988 represents care as a partnership between family and agency. It states that all children should have the right to live in a family, that the interests of the child must be safeguarded, and that culture and religion must be respected. Fostering is viewed as different from, but not a replacement for, other parenting (McFadden 1991).

If a child in care cannot return home, the agency may apply for a 'freeing order' which allows for adoption (Burrows 1991). If no one adopts the child within a year, the parent must be notified and given an opportunity to apply for a revoking order. As much as possible, it is considered desirable to find a permanent home for foster children. Despite an emphasis on 'permanency planning,' priority often is given to adoption without adequate consideration of family support services (Hall 1986).

The recent focus on prevention and family support has led to the development of family centres, which grew out of day care centres. These centres focus on preventive work with families in the community and respite care as alternatives to residential or foster care for children. In addition, self-help groups have been developed for parents and relatives of children in care (Tunnard 1989).

Although social workers are still used as gatekeepers and case managers in the British child welfare system, they can no longer unilaterally terminate contact between child and parent and place children in alternative care. They must confer with local authorities before acting, which leads to greater accountability (Thoburn 1991). In addition, parents have the right to be given information and to receive a hearing, and more respect is now granted to due process (Rains 1991).

Despite these improvements, there is growing concern about the high number of cultural minority children in care. In London, for example, more than half of the children in care are from cultural minority families (Bebbington and Miles 1989). Although many children in private foster homes are of West African origin, most foster families are white. There is some suggestion that West African families choose private fostering in British families to enable their children to learn the English language and British culture (M.I. Lowe 1991). Whether or not this is the case, private fostering is monitored by the African Family Advisory Board and local authorities. In addition, the National Foster Care Association, a voluntary organization of social workers and caregivers, monitors foster care (ibid.).

As with the child welfare systems in Canada and the English-speaking countries of this study, a potential conflict exists in the United Kingdom between protecting children and supporting families. Social workers are expected to remove children from their parents in cases of suspected abuse, but at the same time to gain the confidence of clients and offer supportive services (Rains 1991).

Adoption

As in the other countries in this study, the number of adoptions in the United Kingdom has been declining since the late 1960s. From 1968 until 1984, for example, the number fell from about 25,000 to 8,000 (Hall 1986). Despite the rise in divorce and in numbers of reconstituted families, step-parent adoptions have been discouraged in the United Kingdom, in contrast to practice in the United States (ibid.).

Although Britain had a tradition before 1982 of having voluntary organizations arrange adoptions, now only government-approved agencies may do so, except for placements with a close relative. Adoptive parents are selected according to the child's needs, and suitable parents come from a variety of family structures and socio-economic backgrounds. Since 1982 when subsidized adoptions were first available, low income has not been a barrier to becoming an adoptive parent (ibid.). In particular, groups of siblings and children with disabilities benefit from subsidies, and 80 per cent of subsidized adopters were foster parents (Hill and Triseliotis 1991). Relative adoptions are rarely subsidized, although assistance with legal costs may be available through other means. As a response to the shortage of appropriate homes for children with special needs and racial minority children, adoption agencies have been using a variety of recruitment techniques, including television and catalogues (Hall 1986).

A professional assessment of adoption applicants is required by a government-approved agency or professional in the United Kingdom. Efforts are made to match the racial background of children with adoptive parents, and birth mothers may state a religious preference for adoptive parents (Kadushin and Martin 1988). The child must be legally free for adoption by parental consent or a court order dispensing with consent. Regulations stipulate that the child must be at least nineteen weeks old and must have lived with at least one of the applicants for three months before a court application can be made. Adoption applications must be heard by the high court, county court, or magistrates court (ibid.). In a relative adoption, the child must have lived with at least one of the applicants for twelve months. If children are old enough, they must agree to the adoption (Hall 1986). Legally, adopted children become members of the adoptive family and acquire all the rights of membership in that family. At the same time, birth parents lose all rights to the child, and contact between the child and the birth family is terminated (Horne-Roberts 1991).

In the United Kingdom, no one agency specializes in intercountry adoptions. Couples make private arrangements, apply for a six-month entry permit for the child, and then apply to a British court for adoption. After this point, the process for domestic adoption is followed. A foreign child will automatically receive British citizenship upon adoption (Kadushin and Martin 1988).

Increasingly, more open forms of adoption are preferred by British social workers, and the *Children Act 1989* established a post-adoption register to facilitate contact between adopted persons and birth families (Textor 1992). At age eighteen, children adopted after 1975 are entitled to a copy of their original birth record, but those adopted before 1975 must undergo counselling before receiving it. The right of access to birth records has been controversial because of the fear that adopted children might try to blackmail or harm their original family (LeSueur 1991).

Although the United Kingdom is committed to protecting children, this value has been upheld largely through the removal of children from their homes. Prevention and permanency planning are relatively recent goals, but there is now more concern about supporting parents to enable them to care for their children (Pritchard 1992).

The Barclay Report (1982) on the role and task of social workers advocated a form of 'community social work' that would mobilize informal caring networks and operate in partnership with them. There was little recognition in this report, however, that much of social work and caring work is provided by women (Brook and Davis 1985). Cutbacks to the welfare state are encouraging greater reliance on 'home care,' 'community care,' or 'informal networks' rather than more costly government services. In many cases, this means that women are once again being expected to perform some of the caregiving work that had been provided by institutions and agencies during the 1960s and 1970s. Furthermore, women social workers are expected to encourage women clients to put the interests of their handicapped children, elderly relatives, or abused friends before their own interests. In this way, 'women social workers are aiding their own oppression by oppressing women clients' (Miles 1981).

Increasingly, social workers are seen as hasty, controlling, and adversarial – no doubt because they are burdened with growing numbers of child abuse and family violence cases in a system with shrinking resources (Packman and Jordan 1991). In addition, government social service departments are turning to a private sector style of management, emphasizing cost-effectiveness and contracting out services to private agencies. Social workers are also increasingly subject to performance pay and fixed-term contracts. These structural changes will undoubtedly influence social service delivery, creating a more pluralist social welfare system. However, the values and practices of the competitive market may prevail to the detriment of the effectiveness of the services (Pinker 1994).

The United States

Child protection

State legislation governs child welfare and family services in the United States, and services are delivered both by government and by private agencies that are largely or completely funded by state governments (Denny et al. 1989). Child protection agencies are granted the legal authority to act for the state to protect children from abuse, neglect, and exploitation (Rappaport 1991).

Child abuse and neglect are crimes in all states, but each has its own reporting laws (Rains 1991). In the past fourteen years there has been a 300 per cent increase in reports of child maltreatment, since laws began to require mandatory reporting (Gustavsson and Kopels 1992). However, there is no national policy regarding child welfare, and definitions of abuse and neglect vary (Scales and Brunk 1990).

Who is required to report child abuse also differs by state. In some states, only professionals must report and they can be held civilly or criminally liable for not doing so. Other states require any person to report who has reasonable cause to believe that a child is being maltreated, with the assurance that the reporter's identity will be kept confidential (Sailor 1990–1). Depending on state laws, reports of child abuse must be made to child protection and/or law enforcement agencies. In most states, police are required to report suspected cases to child welfare agencies, and in more than forty states, child welfare agencies also must notify law enforcement officials of abuse cases (Besharov 1990a, 1990b). Even though reporting suspected abuse is mandatory for professionals, only 20 per cent of cases encountered by professionals are actually reported. Many professionals are unfamiliar with procedures and laws, mandatory reporting laws tend to focus on physical and sexual abuse rather than neglect and emotional maltreatment, and prosecutions are rare (Kadushin and Martin 1988).

The U.S. federal *Child Abuse Protection and Treatment Act*, passed in 1974, provides financial assistance to states meeting the following requirements: they must protect all children under eighteen from mental and physical injury and sexual abuse, must require abuse and neglect reports, must guarantee confidentiality of records and legal immunity for reporters, and must provide a guardian for children whose cases come to court. Although this act prompted many states to revise their legislation, for constitutional reasons the federal government cannot interfere with state statutes regarding child abuse (C.C. Young 1990–1).

If children or adolescents are apprehended, they have the right to due process (Sailor 1990–1). A preliminary hearing follows in two to three weeks, in which parents indicate whether they will contest the petition. An adjudicatory hearing follows to determine whether abuse has occurred according to state law, followed by a dispositional hearing in which the placement and treatment plan is established. At each stage of the process, the case may be terminated (Kadushin and Martin 1988). In family court, the child has the right to separate representation (Morfuni 1991).

Many states also provide procedural protection for child witnesses in abuse trials. In some jurisdictions, children may testify on videotape or by closed-circuit television, or may use anatomically correct dolls (Rains

1991). However, the fact that family court is still based on an adversarial system designed by legal experts can intimidate children, families, and social workers. Contrary to social work principles of cooperation and negotiation, the court system is based on conflict, evidence, and legal proof (van Wormer 1992).

Several outcomes are possible in family court, as the judge may order temporary guardianship, permit the child to stay at home with court supervision, or terminate parental rights. Secondary punishments include prohibitions on visits or certain types of employment with children (Kadushin and Martin 1988). Once in court, the role of the social worker is restricted to suggestions and influence, while the judge retains the legal right to make demands on the family and child (van Wormer 1992). Twenty per cent of U.S. child abuse cases lead to alternate placement of the child, usually in foster care, group homes, or institutional placements. Eighty per cent of treatment is in the form of casework counselling (Kadushin and Martin 1988; Gustavsson and Kopels 1992).

In 1978, the United States enacted the *Indian Child Welfare Act* which recognized the importance of providing culturally appropriate child welfare services. Native American tribal governments gained jurisdiction over child protection proceedings involving Native American children living on reservations, and state courts and governments are required to respect their decisions. The Native American tribes also obtained the right to intervene with off-reservation children who may be subject to foster care placements or termination of parental rights (Kadushin and Martin 1988).

The U.S. child welfare system is designed to prevent hasty action and assure due process, but is a two-tiered civil-criminal system. Criminal proceedings, which are difficult to prosecute, are rarely initiated with maltreating parents, as social services are the preferred avenue for intervention. Sexual abuse cases are the most likely to involve both civil and criminal actions, and to use foster care as part of treatment (ibid.).

The system is based on the assumption that parents do not want to hurt their children, and are able and willing to change their behaviour (ibid.). Furthermore, there is a historical bias against government involvement in family matters, which is seen as an unnecessary intrusion (Gustavsson and Kopels 1992). Americans value independence, autonomy, individualism, self-reliance, and self-fulfilment, and parental rights still take precedence over children's rights (Sailor 1990–1). There is no national family policy, and most legislators would not be supportive of a national policy if tax increases were involved (Granger 1989).

Adoption

While adoptions in the United States increased from the 1950s to 1970, they have been decreasing ever since (Kadushin and Martin 1988, 538). The 1980 *Adoption Assistance and Child Welfare Act* was a step towards reinforcing the value of family preservation rather than removing children from their homes to provide services. The federal act required states that expected federal funding to develop case plans, to carry out six-month reviews, to require judicial hearings within eighteen months of a child's being taken into care, and to implement a state-wide information system (A.A. O'Donnell 1992).

Adoption is governed by state legislation and agency practices. All states forbid payment to pregnant women in connection with adoption, but most states allow private adoptions. With the high rates of divorce and remarriage, about two-thirds of adoptions are by step-parents (Hersov 1990). Over the years, however, a two-tiered system has developed in the United States. Healthy infants are placed privately with middle-class white couples, while minority, older children, children with disabilities, and sibling groups tend to be placed through public agencies. The percentage of older children placed for adoption is increasing, and black, Hispanic, and Native American children are overrepresented among those available for adoption (Kadushin and Martin 1988).

In any adoption, a child welfare agency is required to investigate the circumstances and make a recommendation to the court. If the child and the adoptive parents do not reside in the same state, the legal process occurs in the parents' state. Cross-border adoptions can be complicated, since adoption laws differ, although most states have recently enacted interstate legislation to address and coordinate adoption activities.

A hearing is held and the court makes a decision based on 'the best interests of the child.' After a trial period of six to twelve months, the adoption is finalized, the child takes the surname of the adoptive parents and receives a new birth certificate, and the adoption record is usually sealed. Adoptive parents acquire all legal rights and obligations towards the child (ibid.).

Most adoptive applicants are married infertile couples, although couples with children, gay couples and single persons may also adopt according to law and regulations (Speirs and Baker 1994). However, agencies can easily find reasons to refuse applicants. There must be a home study that considers the applicants' age, health, race, religion, length and quality of marriage, and 'personal suitability.' Home studies have been criticized as subjective, since social workers may use personal standards and biases in making decisions (Kadushin and Martin 1988). Most agencies prefer applicants under forty years old, and some states require religious matching and efforts to place racial minority children in similar homes (ibid.). The value of matching adoptive children and parents for religion and race, however, is sometimes given priority over the 'best interests' of the child (L.J. Schwartz 1991).

Foster parents may apply to adopt children who have lived with them for an extended period of time (Kadushin and Martin 1988). Subsidies are also available for parents adopting children with special needs through the Federal Adoption Opportunities Program, which makes subsidized adoption mandatory in each state and matches state funds (L.J. Schwartz 1991). The goal is to eliminate significant barriers to the adoption of children with special needs, and, in particular, to facilitate intraracial adoption of minority children (LeMay 1988–9). Typically, children in subsidized adoption are older, have special needs, are part of a sibling group, or are from a cultural minority (Kadushin and Martin 1988). Eighty per cent of subsidized adoptions are by foster parents, but three-quarters of relative adoptions are also subsidized (Hill and Triseliotis 1991).

Closed adoptions are the traditional norm in the United States, but open ones may be allowed in step-parent adoptions or if both birth and adoptive parents agree (L.J. Schwartz 1991). Most states have recently passed laws permitting adult adoptees to obtain information about birth parents. However, access to records is typically granted only for medical or genetic reasons, the process is slow, and applicants may have to wait years for their request to be heard (Kadushin and Martin 1988).

Foreign adoptions have increased since the Second World War, but especially with the shortage of American babies in the past fifteen years. Two-thirds of foreign adoptees are now Asian, and most of the rest are from South or Central America. Each country that allows its children to be adopted has its own rules and procedures, as does the United States, and social service agencies work with international organizations in these adoptions. Because of the high demand, however, there is a black market in adopted children from other countries (ibid.).

As with all aspects of child welfare, the *Indian Child Welfare Act* gives U.S. Indian tribes control over adoption within their communities. The law requires efforts to place children first with relatives, second intraracially, and then interracially only if prior efforts fail (L.J. Schwartz 1991).

The number of healthy babies available for adoption has been declining while the number of 'hard-to-place babies' has been increasing. To help place children in permanent homes, the *Adoption Reform Act* of 1987 provided for a federally sponsored national adoption information exchange. In addition, many states have developed their own information exchange systems (Kadushin and Martin 1988).

American parents are guaranteed constitutional rights to the companionship, care, custody, and management of their children (Cook 1991–2). If a child cannot remain with the family, however, adoption is thought to be the most desirable form of permanent substitute care. Nevertheless, biological relationships are considered more important than social relationships, which is reflected in prejudice against adoptive families as 'unnatural' (Kadushin and Martin 1988).

Over the last twenty-five years, state governments have become more involved in child welfare issues in the United States. The number of purchase-of-service contracts between government and not-for-profit child welfare agencies has been increasing. Although not-for-profit agencies disguise government's role in service delivery, this restructuring has led to greater government influence and intervention in the child welfare system (S.R. Smith 1989). In addition, in 1989 thirty-seven states developed a government children's commission and forty developed advocacy groups for children coordinated by the National Association of Child Advocates (Scales and Brunk 1990).

Despite the official policy of preserving families, the rate of child placement in the United States has not decreased since the early part of the twentieth century (Pelton 1991). The foster care system has become a huge revolving door. Agencies have not been provided with resources other than foster care and are unable to address the problems of poverty. The main reason for placement seems to be lack of concrete and supportive services to families, inadequate levels of income security, and parents' inability to cope with the stress of poverty without government assistance. Yet few monies are directed to preventive services. In addition, the high value placed on 'family privacy' inhibits social workers from doing any preventive work (ibid.).

During the 1980s, there was a growing concern in the United States about the effects of abuse and neglect, family breakdown, increasing child poverty, child health problems, and high school drop-out rates. Numerous researchers noted that maltreated children grow into maladjusted adults and become a further burden on society (Cook 1991–2; Granger 1989; Kadushin and Martin 1988). As the percentage of children in the population has decreased due to low fertility and delayed child-bearing, the argument that children are an important societal resource has been strengthened. Despite international concern about child poverty, however, social service expenditures for children were reduced during the Reagan years and little is now spent on prevention (Kamerman 1989; Smith 1989).

CONCLUSION

All countries in the study have developed laws which establish the rights and duties of parents, which protect vulnerable family members from neglect and violence, and which mandate services to deal with family problems. However, these laws and services tend to focus on the most vulnerable – children under a specified age. In comparison to European countries, Canada and the English-speaking countries (especially the United States) have developed reactive child welfare and family service policies that focus on protecting children from abuse after it has occurred and been substantiated. Once children have reached a designated age in a particular child welfare system, family services are no longer available.

Historically, most social security programs and welfare services have focused on the needs of children (especially their need for protection from parental abuse and neglect) and on fathers as family 'breadwinners.' Priority is still placed on 'family preservation,' even at the expense of mothers (Brook and Davis 1985). Mothers rather than fathers are expected to provide daily child care despite their need to earn a living or their desire to develop their skills and education. Low-income mothers with family problems are taught home-making and child-rearing skills by middle-class (usually female) social workers and nurses, but their employment and financial needs are not always adequately addressed through social assistance programs or employment programs. Mothers tend to be blamed for 'neglecting' their children, even when the father is absent (Swift 1995), for not protecting children from sexual abuse (Krane 1994), or for their children's unruly behaviour. Although women are no longer expected to take the children's father to court to obtain court-awarded child support in most jurisdictions, they are still expected to provide home care for family members with disabilities or special needs, especially in those jurisdictions which have implemented deinstitutionalization programs.

Although an increasing number of government programs are recognizing women's needs to become and remain self-supporting after they become mothers, governments have not always provided the necessary social supports to allow this to happen. These supports would include enforceable employment equity programs, subsidized child care services, visiting homemaker programs, respite care, marriage counselling, government health services, statutory family leave, extended parental leave with pay, or opportunities to work part time while retaining social assistance. As we have seen both here and in earlier chapters, social supports of this type are provided in such countries as Sweden and France.

Children and adolescents from single-parent, visible minority, and low-income families are overrepresented in the child welfare systems of all countries, yet few policies in Canada and the English-speaking countries focus on reducing family poverty, stress, and cultural/racial discrimination. Instead, policies and programs concentrate on resolving the symptoms of child abuse, delinquency, and family violence on the assumption that clients are experiencing mainly psychological or interpersonal problems (Kamerman 1989; L.J. Schwartz 1991; A.A. O'Donnell 1992). Children with behavioural problems or child victims of violence are counselled, encouraged to accept group therapy, or provided with substitute care. Parents who neglect or abuse their children or each other are taught parenting skills, money management, and conflict resolution skills. In recent years, governments have provided short-term funding for crisis housing and the development of self-help groups, but these services are not always part of the regular budget for family services.

There is little public recognition in Canada and the English-speaking countries that raising children while living in poverty and experiencing racial/cultural discrimination leads to anxiety, anger, and resentment and increases the probability that children will exhibit behavioural problems. There is little public recognition that unemployment and low income reduce parents' ability to deal amicably with each other and to cope with problem children. Furthermore, there is little public recognition that poverty and unemployment limit women's opportunities to leave violent partners and to support their children on their own. If these structural barriers were acknowledged, substantial policy reform would have to be initiated at considerable public cost.

As in other aspects of family policy, the United States exemplifies an underfunded and punitive child welfare system, which is also wracked with problems of divided jurisdiction and racial inequality (Kadushin and Martin 1988). With mandatory reporting laws, child welfare agencies are often overburdened and are forced to direct most of their limited resources towards dealing with child abuse, even though neglect and accidents may be more prevalent (Gustavsson and Kopels 1992). In a litigious society oriented towards individual rather than collective rights, the conflicting claims of parents' rights, family rights, children's rights, and state rights can be hard to resolve (Rappaport 1991).

New laws requiring mandatory reporting of child abuse have solved some problems but created others. In Canada and the English-speaking countries, the conflicting demands placed on social workers as apprehenders of children and providers of family support contribute to high turnover and 'burnout' (Gustavsson and Kopels 1992). Furthermore, in some jurisdictions (such as Quebec), financial cutbacks and the reorganization of social services have eroded the mandate of social workers dealing with child and youth protection to deal with other pressing concerns in the family. In the United States, social workers are also vulnerable to malpractice suits. New laws about child abuse give social workers in many countries less discretion and more paperwork, even though such laws may provide a fairer system for children and parents (A.A. O'Donnell 1992).

The United States is one of the few countries in the world that has not signed the United Nations Convention on the Rights of the Child (1989), although it was active in drafting it. The United States was unwilling to ban the death penalty for persons under eighteen, a requirement for signatories to the convention. In other respects, while federal and state laws may already be in compliance with the convention (C.P. Cohen and Miljeteig-Olssen 1991), there is often a large discrepancy between what the law says and how it is enforced.

While Canada signed the convention and the prime minister publicly committed the government to reducing child poverty and family violence, more effort has gone into child protection and research on family violence than into dealing with family poverty. Canadian child welfare systems have been reformed to emphasize due process and legal change, but the causes of abuse and neglect have not received comparable attention. Social assistance levels and minimum wages have remained low while unemployment rates have remained high. Cost sharing for provincial child welfare systems continues to be reserved mainly for crisis intervention, and little money is set aside for prevention work within families and communities.

In many countries, residential treatment for children is becoming increasingly short term, and many programs are closing or are losing funding. This partly reflects policies of 'family preservation' or the importance given to maintaining children in their own family environment or finding permanent adoptive parents. Yet in North America, few resources are spent on prevention within families, and resources tend to be mandated for child protection. The removal of children from the home and the provision of substitute care continue despite principles of family preservation. Consequently, the real motivation for closing residential programs appears to be to reduce costs rather than to improve service. With the economic slow-down of the 1980s, child welfare systems have been eroded, with preventive programs in countries with essentially reactive systems being the most vulnerable (Schorr 1989).

France and Sweden stand out among the countries in this study for their preventive and pro-active approach to family problems and child welfare. Government cash benefits in these countries reduce child and family poverty more effectively than in Canada. Direct services (such as public child care, school nurses, and holiday programs for low-income families) prevent or dramatically reduce neglect and violence and the subsequent need for reactive child welfare services and substitute care. In France and Sweden, for example, family or child allowances are more generous, parental leave is longer and better funded, public child care is provided or subsidized, child support after divorce is enforced by the government, and some form of guaranteed annual income is securely in place.

Despite the more generous income security programs in the European countries, lone mothers and low-income families are the main recipients of the child welfare system in Europe, as in North America and Australia. In the European countries, however, family supports and prevention programs are used more often than substitute care. For example, adoption is sometimes partial and supportive to the birth family, without necessarily requiring them to relinquish parental rights totally and irrevocably. Respite care, visiting homemakers, surrogate parents, and subsidized holiday homes are used more frequently than in Canada and the English-speaking countries. Public child care services provide daytime care and education to children, and also reduce the number of unsupervised or 'latch-key' children.

In the European countries, child and family poverty are directly addressed through such income security programs as lone mothers' allowances, child allowances, and child-rearing benefits. As was discussed in chapter 3, such government transfer programs counteract low incomes more effectively than similar programs in Australia, Canada, and the United States. In addition, unemployment rates have been lower in most of the European countries than in Canada, allowing more parents to support their own children. Furthermore, public consensus has been high in many European countries that children are a social responsibility and that public taxes should finance family benefits and services, allowing these countries to focus more on prevention and voluntary family support and less on involuntary reactive services.

8

Divorce laws, child custody, and child support

MARRIAGE, DIVORCE, AND MATRIMONIAL PROPERTY

Changing gender roles, the rise of dual-earner families, and greater expectations of personal fufilment in marriage have heightened the stresses on modern marriage. The demand for easier divorce led to legislative change in many countries, but policies concerning spousal support, division of matrimonial property, and child support have remained contentious. In this chapter, the focus will be on the determination of child support amounts and the enforcement of court-awarded child support awards. First, however, I examine some trends in marriage and divorce laws, the division of matrimonial property, and child custody, both in Canada and in the other countries studied.

The patriarchal family and women's rights

When European settlers first came to Canada, they brought their marriage customs and legal traditions with them. In Quebec, the French Napoleonic Code formed the basis of the legal system, while the rest of Canada adopted English common law. Under both systems, husbands and fathers had legal authority over their wives and children, and wives had the legal status of a minor child. In addition to having no political rights, women could not sell or acquire property but had to depend on their husbands to control it on their behalf.

The Married Women's Property Act, which was first passed in England in 1870, was introduced gradually to the anglophone Canadian provinces after Ontario first passed such legislation in 1872 (Dranoff 1977, 48). This legal change was seen as a milestone by advocates of women's rights because it allowed married women to retain their own wages, income, or property. However, this legislation was more important for middle- or upper-class women who inherited property than for the vast majority of women who owned little. In the same historical period, women's rights advocates and trade unionists were also demanding access for women to higher education and the professions, the right to participate in politics, and the right to protection from dangerous or unhealthy working conditions (M. Baker 1993b, 116).

In the long fight over women's rights, conservative opponents used the construct of the patriarchal family to deny women both political and legal rights. They argued that 'the family' was the basic unit of society and men as 'family heads' voted and controlled property on behalf of their wives. Giving married women the vote was tantamount to giving families two votes. Women's rights advocates fought this family construct for many decades before it began to be made more egalitarian after 1870. Yet some of the battles are still being fought, among them disputes over the division of matrimonial property, spousal support, and child support after divorce.

Prior to the twentieth century, in the rare cases where the couple separated and there was a dispute about the custody of the children, the husband was granted legal custody. Although the right to maternal custody was granted in England in 1839, it was not until after 1917 that Canadian provinces allowed mothers equal rights with fathers in guardianship or custody of their children. British Columbia was the first province to pass such legislation, but Quebec did not amend its *Civil Code* until 1964 (Dranoff 1977, 39).

Until the 1960s, the marital roles of men and women in Canada differed by law. A woman promised during the wedding ceremony to 'love, honour and obey' her husband while he promised to 'love, honour and cherish' her. He could establish their domicile or legal residence, and she was expected to live wherever he lived, to maintain their household, care for their children, and be sexually available. In return, she was entitled to 'dower rights,' or the right to one-third of his property should the marriage dissolve, in recognition of these services. During the marriage, the husband was expected to provide her with the 'necessities of life,' but *he* decided what was necessary (Dranoff 1977, 25, 26).

In Canada, family law and divorce law are regulated by two separate and completely independent levels of government. The federal government has jurisdiction over divorce, including the legal right to remarry and those areas of 'corollary relief' restricted to issues of child custody, access, and financial support. The provinces have jurisdiction over marriage, the division of matrimonial property upon the separation of spouses, and laws pertaining to child custody, access, child support, and spousal support (Syrtash 1992). These powers are 'collateral' to those powers enjoyed by the federal government, however. If a spouse goes to court and invokes the federal *Divorce Act*, the laws of the federal government override similar provisions passed under provincial laws, unless a court orders otherwise.

Prior to the 1970s, when a divorce was granted in Canada, the former husband could be required by the courts to pay alimony, or life-long financial support, to his former wife if she had not committed a 'matrimonial fault.' Interestingly, the most serious 'matrimonial fault' or reason to forfeit financial support was having sexual intercourse with another man. In other words, support was contingent upon the good behaviour of the wife at the time of separation (and subsequently), rather than on her unpaid domestic services or child-rearing during marriage. If she deserted her husband, 'committed adultery,' or remarried, she lost her right to support.

If a wife had not committed a matrimonial fault, she could be awarded a portion of the matrimonial property or alimony (spousal support payments), depending on her husband's economic circumstances and judicial discretion. Enforcement procedures, however, were always a problem. If the former husband did not pay or was late in his payment, she had to take him to court after each offence in an attempt to retrieve her money. Because the enforcement of alimony fell under provincial jurisdiction, a former husband could easily avoid payment by moving out of the province (M. Baker 1993b, 117).

After a series of court cases in the 1970s which left divorced women badly off financially, advocacy groups lobbied for changes in the division of matrimonial property. Feminist groups felt that women were receiving a smaller share than they deserved because their unpaid contributions to households were not being considered. In 1971, for example, the much-publicized Murdoch case went to the Supreme Court of Canada and led to increased concern about the consequences of marriage breakdown for women. In this court case, Irene Murdoch ran the Alberta family farm for several months of each year while her husband worked out of town at a wage-labour job. The twenty-five-year marriage broke up after he physically assaulted her, but the Alberta court gave the farm to the husband because his name was on the deed and most of the money used to purchase it had come from his earnings. The wife was awarded alimony of $200 a month and the right to continue living in the farmhouse (Dranoff 1977, 52). This case went to the Supreme Court of Canada, where the decision not to grant Irene Murdoch a share in the ranch was upheld because her farm labour was considered to be 'normal for a rancher's wife' (ibid.). Reaction to this decision precipitated considerable controversy and protest, especially from feminist groups.

Since the 1970s, when Canadian family law began to be reformed, most provinces have changed their laws in an attempt to equalize the property, custody, and support rights of husbands and wives. In most provinces, the family home and any property which the family jointly uses (called 'family assets' or 'matrimonial property') are divided equally between former spouses after divorce. It may no longer matter whose name is on the deed of ownership or whose money made the purchase. In addition, public pension credits may be split upon divorce (M. Baker 1993b, 117). However, it is possible for a spouse to argue that his assets belong to his business rather than to the family unit, and court cases have been fought over this distinction. Furthermore, if the husband has business debts or declares bankruptcy, his ex-wife could end up owing money to his creditors rather than receiving spousal support (M.E. Morton 1988).

The expectation of self-sufficiency shortly after divorce is built into the new Canadian divorce law of 1985 (Diduck 1990). Former wives are no longer awarded life-long 'alimony,' but only temporary 'spousal support' based on financial need rather than moral conduct or domestic services during marriage. Both partners are now expected to work to support themselves (Payne 1994). While the old law was based on the principle that men were breadwinners and women were dependants, the amended laws imply that both have equal opportunity to become self-supporting after marriage (M.E. Morton 1988). However, the new law still contains some judicial discretion with respect to spousal support, especially for older women who would be unable to find work and long-term homemakers with few job skills. The trend towards fixed-term support is most difficult for young women who are deemed 'employable' (Diduck 1990).

Bala and Bailey (1990–1) noted that Canadian courts are showing greater flexibility in insisting on a connection between the need for support by a former spouse and the marriage itself. In 1989, for example, the Nova Scotia Court of Appeal concluded that in long-term traditional marriages, the wife's realistic chances of achieving self-sufficiency must be considered, and the economic disadvantages incurred by the wife should be redressed upon dissolution of the marriage. The court concluded that in modern marriages, the standard of living that would have been attained had the marriage not interfered with the career development of the wife needs to be addressed. In long-term traditional marriages, the law recognizes that there should be some relationship between the partners' standard of living before and after the marriage dissolution. In practice, however, this principle has not always been applied by the courts.

Prior to 1989, there was little judicial discretion in the division of matrimonial property in Quebec. Couples signed a marriage contract either to keep their property separate during marriage (which meant that neither could claim the other's property upon divorce) or to share it equally under the control of the husband during the marriage. In 1989, Quebec introduced a new law on marital property division which provides for mandatory division of the 'family patrimony' when a marriage is ended by divorce, annulment, separation, or death. Couples who had married prior to July 1989 were given eighteen months to opt out if they so desired. The category of assets to be divided is relatively narrow and includes residences, furnishings, family cars, and pension rights. However, the law also states that the court may divide assets unequally if equal division would result in injustice. One spouse could be asked to provide a 'compensatory allowance' to compensate the other for goods or services that enriched the other's property. Factors which are considered include the brevity of the marriage, the waste of certain property by one spouse, and/or 'bad faith' by one spouse (ibid.). This new element of judicial discretion in Quebec's *Civil Code* brings it closer to the English common law that is used in the rest of Canada (M. Morton 1990). In many cases, however, judges have proven unwilling to make use of the compensatory allowance (Rayle 1988).

Because Canadian family law is written to be gender neutral, many judges have implied equal access to earned income in their divorce decisions. Yet the vast majority of North American husbands have higher earning power than their wives. Taking time off work to bear and raise children appears to place women at a permanent economic disadvantage (M.E. Morton 1988). Evidence of this appears in numerous studies both in Canada and the United States which indicate that women and children tend to live on reduced incomes after marriage breakdown, while men tend to acquire a higher personal standard of living (M. Baker 1983; National Council of Welfare 1990b; Weitzman

1985). For these reasons, the division of matrimonial property and payment of spousal support remain contentious areas of policy reform in both countries.

Swan (1986) examined the political economy of American family policy from 1945 to 1985, focusing on the implications of the intrafamilial division of labour on divorce. He concluded that the typical division of labour within the home, in which household tasks and child care are primarily women's responsibility, works to the disadvantage of women but to the advantage of the primary breadwinner when the marriage ends. Without public policies to reduce income inequalities between husbands and wives and to help women combine work and family life, women will continue to be disadvantaged. At present, both child-bearing and household labour contribute to significant income loss for women, and Swan saw no indication that U.S. public policy will resolve these issues in the near future.

Amendments to U.S. and Canadian divorce laws which focus on self-sufficiency for divorced women have a negative impact on women, whose unpaid caregiving and housework are not always recognized (National Council of Welfare 1990b). Furthermore, judgments in child support appear to focus on how much the father can afford to pay rather than on what the child needs to maintain his or her standard of living. Not surprisingly, the poverty rates among female-headed families reflect these policies and practices.

TRENDS IN DIVORCE LAWS

As was noted in chapter 2, divorce rates have risen throughout the twentieth century in many industrialized countries. In Canada, they sharply increased after 1968 when the grounds for divorce were liberalized after years of lobbying for such reform by civil liberties organizations and legal advocates and for more restrictive laws by religious groups. Before 1925, legal divorce in Canada was very restricted, expensive, and easier for men to obtain than for women. A new ground was created for divorce in 1968 called 'marriage breakdown,' which was strictly defined as separation for three years for a deserted partner or five years for the spouse who left the marriage. The law retained the notion of 'fault,' as separation was added to existing grounds of adultery and physical cruelty, which required one partner to establish proof of the other's 'matrimonial fault.'

The adversarial system of divorce has been strongly criticized for making divorce more acrimonious, complex and expensive than it needs to be. With the 1985 legal changes, however, 'marriage breakdown' has been even more liberally defined as a one-year separation with no attempt to assign fault to either partner. Although Canada moved towards a 'no-fault' divorce system with the 1985 reform, it is technically not such a system because marriage breakdown was added to, rather than substituted for, existing fault-based grounds (Glendon 1987).

In an international study of OECD countries, Maclean (1990) noted that the rapid increase in rates of divorce has been accompanied by a widespread reluctance to attach blame to either party for the breakdown of marriage. In Sweden, for example, fault-based divorce is no longer available. In France, fault is only one of several grounds for divorce; and in the United States, at least twenty-nine states had accepted no-fault divorce by 1987 compared to one state in 1970.

Yet not all divorce legislation prior to the 1960s was entirely fault-based (Glendon 1987). Australia and a few American states permitted divorce after a period of separation on the grounds of 'incompatibility' as well as on fault grounds. Since 1915, Sweden has permitted divorce on the ground that the marriage has 'broken down,' in addition to fault grounds. Nevertheless, while these options may have existed within legislation, until recently obtaining a divorce using no-fault grounds was difficult and often required a lengthy period of separation (ibid.).

The 1960s saw a growing dissatisfaction with fault-based divorce, and between 1969 and 1985 divorce law in nearly every Western country was reformed. Like Canada, most countries added a no-fault ground but did not remove the concept of fault from legislation. In 1969, California became the first Western jurisdiction to eliminate completely any fault ground for divorce (ibid.). However, studies by Weitzman (1985), indicated that this reform had negative consequences for women and children, as I discuss later.

In Australia, the *Family Law Act 1975* changed divorce legislation from a fault-based to a no-fault regime (Smart and Sevenhuijsen 1989). Under this act, the single ground for divorce is 'irretrievable breakdown of the marriage' evidenced by twelve months of separation. Like Canada, Australia is a federation, and although under the constitution the federal government has only limited power over family law, that power does extend to laws about marriage and divorce and laws which deal with the children of those marriages. In 1988, after lengthy negotiations, a majority of states referred some of their powers over family matters to the Commonwealth (or federal) government. The *Family Law*

Act also legislated a counselling service within a nationwide Family Court (Burrett 1988).

In France, legislation was revised in 1975, and divorce is now available through three categories of grounds: fault-based, mutual consent, and unilateral no-fault (Glendon 1987). About 58 per cent of divorces are granted using fault-based grounds and 40 per cent using mutual consent. Only 2 per cent use the unilateral no-fault ground because the criteria are fairly stringent. For example, the couple must be separated for a period of six years or the petitioner's partner must have suffered for six years from a serious mental illness from which recovery is unlikely, with substantiating diagnoses from three experts. Judges retain the right to reject requests for a no-fault divorce if it will cause the other spouse financial hardship or will have a negative impact on the spouse's mental or physical health (Ravelet 1987).

In 1973, Sweden replaced a system accepting both fault and no-fault divorce with a new system of only no-fault divorce. Unlike some other countries, there is no judicial discretion to deny a divorce in Sweden (Glendon 1987). In the United States, divorce falls under state jurisdiction, which means that regulations vary by state. Eighteen states and the District of Columbia had eliminated fault grounds entirely from their divorce legislation by 1987. Twenty-two states permitted unilateral no-fault divorce after a waiting period of one year or less, and eight states required a waiting period of more than one year. Two states required mutual consent for no-fault divorce (ibid.).

When California eliminated all fault grounds and permitted divorce only upon showing incurable insanity or irreconcilable differences in 1969, the concept of alimony was also altered. It became temporary spousal support, and the ex-spouse was expected to become self-sufficient within an established period of time (Jacob 1988). This change has also occurred in Canada, and has been the source of much contention because many former wives have been unable to become self-supporting, especially if they had remained at home raising children during the marriage.

CHILD CUSTODY

From the beginnings of Canada as a nation, married fathers were generally awarded legal custody of their children if the couple separated. In 1877, Ontario authorized the courts to grant custody to the mother if the father died, even if he had by will appointed someone else. In 1917,

British Columbia was the first province to recognize the equal right of both parents to custody and guardianship of their children (Dranoff 1977, 36). By the 1940s, judges came to agree that children in their 'tender years' required the care of their mothers more than their fathers. If all other factors were equal, mothers were given custody of young children.

By the 1970s, Canada, the United States, and several European countries began to move away from the presumption of maternal custody to decisions based on the 'best interests of the child' or the child's welfare rather than the property right of either parent. This concept, however, has been criticized for being vague and open to interpretation as evidenced by the wide variety of practices (Smart and Sevenhuijsen 1989). Despite laws requiring custody decisions based on the child's welfare, the majority of children in North America and Europe still reside with their mother after marital separation and divorce. Yet joint custody is becoming more popular, and some jurisdictions have entrenched the presumption of joint custody in law.

As divorce rates have increased in the United States and Canada, so has controversy over how custody decisions are made and the amount of judicial discretion involved in these decisions. However, the courts are not always involved in custody decisions, as some parents make their own decisions about who will live with the children after divorce. When decisions have been made in court, judges have tended to grant sole custody to one parent, while the other parent has been given specified visiting rights or limited access. Some parents voluntarily shared parenting, but the courts did not necessarily sanction these private arrangements.

Although joint custody was seldom awarded by Canadian courts prior to 1986, statistics now indicate that there has been a rise in joint custody. Figures from the Department of Justice, shown in Table 8.1, and figures from Statistics Canada[1] disagree about whether this rise in joint custody has come at the expense of sole custody for fathers or mothers.

In Canada, joint custody means that both parents share *decision making* about the child even when the child lives primarily with one parent. A distinction should therefore be made between joint physical custody (sometimes called shared parenting), in which both parents share the physical care of the child, and the legal term 'joint custody.' Because 'custody' refers to legal decision making rather than residence, the term 'residential parent' is sometimes used instead of 'custodial parent' to denote the parent providing daily care for the child. Because shared

TABLE 8.1
Custody of children involved in divorce in Canada, 1986 and 1990

Custody awarded to:	1986	1990
	%	%
Mother	72.0	73.3
Father	15.3	12.2
Both parents (joint custody)	11.6	14.3
Another person	1.0	0.2

SOURCES: Canada, Federal/Provincial/Territorial Family Law Committee 1991;
Canada, Department of Justice 1993.

parenting arrangements require considerable post-divorce cooperation, they are not very prevalent (Ambert 1990b).

In most states of the United States, joint legal custody is presumed to be the normal arrangement unless it is demonstrated that it would be harmful for the child (Pearson and Thoennes 1990). Yet despite this presumption, shared parenting or joint physical custody made up less than 2 per cent of custody arrangements in California in 1988. In 95 per cent of joint legal custody arrangements, children lived with their mother most of the time (Coller 1988).

Studies of the impact of joint custody on children note the importance of cordial relations between divorced parents and frequent positive contact with the child. Furthermore, parents and children involved in court-ordered joint custody are less satisfied with the arrangement than those who agreed to it voluntarily (Irving, Benjamin, and Troeme 1984). Especially when parents are involved in custody and visitation disputes, joint legal custody can also lead to emotional and behavioural problems in the children (Johnston, Kline, and Tschann 1989). Children's lives are least disrupted if divorced parents live in the same neighbourhood, if they can provide their children with a room in each of their homes, and if they are both concerned about their child's welfare and can cooperate over child-rearing issues. Because these conditions are difficult to meet as well as costly, this form of custody is an option considered by a minority of couples, who tend to be from the educated middle class (Ambert 1988b).

Joint custody is now being promoted in Canada by fathers' rights groups representing fathers who want more involvement in decisions relating to their children's lives and may also wish to share physical care. Some liberal feminists have also seen joint custody as a more egalitarian division of parental roles, and a number of child welfare professionals view it as beneficial for children to continue to be cared for by both parents after divorce, as long as the care is loving and consistent.

Involuntary or court-ordered joint custody, however, has been opposed by more radical feminist groups who argue that it often works against the interests of divorced women. Even when the children live with their mother most of the time, joint custody allows the father veto power over her decisions concerning the children (Drakich 1988). This power could be misused in contentious divorce cases. Feminists also argue that joint custody tends to reduce the amount of child support which judges award to mothers, because they assume that fathers are also sharing costs, even though the fact that a child spends some time in the father's home does not mean that the mother's costs are noticeably reduced. There appears to be little statistical evidence for the argument about reduced child support, however. Government statistics indicate that fathers who remain in contact with their children are more likely to make their child support payments and that fathers with joint custody tend to pay higher amounts of support than those without custody (Canada, Department of Justice 1990, 82; Pulkingham, 1994).

Increasingly, feminists argue that joint custody is being used as a means of controlling women and weakening their already precarious position after marital separation. Women who have been victims of spousal abuse often want to sever all connection with their former husband and may fear for the safety of their children. Consequently, many feminists are advocating that the deciding factor in custody awards should be the question of which parent was the 'primary caregiver' of the children during marriage. This 'primary caregiver principle' provides the most continuity for the children, is relatively easy to define, and avoids the threat posed to women in unequal joint custody situations (Smart and Sevenhuijsen 1989). On the other hand, the principle may reinforce women's traditional role as mothers and the gendered division of labour both inside and outside the home (Pulkingham, 1994).

The state of West Virginia has legislated a 'primary caregiver presumption' in its divorce and custody legislation, if a minimum objective standard of 'fit parenting' is met (Smart and Sevenhuijsen 1989). The primary caregiver is defined as the person who prepared and planned meals; bathed, groomed, and dressed the children; purchased, cleaned, and cared for their clothes; sought medical care; arranged social interaction among peers; arranged alternative care; put the child to bed; disciplined the child (a category that includes the teaching of manners and toilet training); educated the child in the religious, cultural, and social spheres; and taught elementary skills such as reading. Although the primary caregiver is granted custody if children are under six, older children have the opportunity to voice their opinions. Joint custody is not encouraged, although parents may agree to it voluntarily.

Critics of the 'primary caregiver presumption' charge that it is the same as the 'tender years doctrine' and unfairly favours mothers (Wadlington 1990–1). Yet the legislation is written to be gender neutral and would equally favour custody for a father who had performed these duties. As few fathers perform these duties, however, the primary caregiver presumption would essentially be a return to the pre-1980 reforms and would reinforce the gendered division of labour.

Divorce mediation has increased in response to the failure of North American legal systems to respond to changes in marriage and to deal with the consequences of marriage breakdown (Richardson 1988b). Research from four Canadian projects in Saskatoon, Montreal, St John's, and Winnipeg indicated that mediation generally results in higher maintenance awards, has a higher incidence of joint custody arrangements, and results in clearer and more specific access arrangements. The research found no significant differences between mediated and non-mediated cases with regard to compliance with court orders, post-divorce relationships, or legal costs. In these areas, mediation had no apparent negative effects but was not dramatically different in results from non-mediated cases.

Receiving custody of children may soften the initial blow of marital separation because the children are a source of affection and companionship. Nevertheless, divorced women with custody often report a difficult readjustment to single life because children require continual supervision and financial support. They also require considerable emotional support, especially at the time of parental separation, if they witness parental disputes or violence, were unprepared for the breakup, or blame themselves for the divorce. In addition, the presence of children constantly reminds separated women of their family status and former married life and therefore lengthens the transition period from married to single life (M. Baker 1983). Attempting to provide children with a stable environment on a low income may occupy much of the time and energy of separated and divorced parents, especially mothers.

LONE PARENTING[2]

Although living with children can be fulfilling and rewarding, having no other adults to talk to, especially about child-rearing issues, can be isolating. Loneliness can be aggravated if you cannot afford to hire a sitter in order to search for a job or go out with friends. Work overload and role strain are problems for lone parents of either gender, who may be attempting to fulfil the role of both mother and father, to earn a living, and to perform household and child care tasks that are often done by two people. The demands of paid work, parenting, and care of a home can be exhausting (Hanson and Sporakowski 1986; G. Lowe 1989). In addition, many lone parents are involved in custody or child support disputes, even years after the separation or divorce occurred.

Lone parenting, even when it is a personal choice, can be very challenging, bringing financial problems, social isolation, role conflict, and physical and emotional exhaustion. But custody is granted to the mother in about three-quarters of Canadian divorce cases, and most never-married lone parents are mothers. Therefore, discussions about the problems of lone parents are really discussions about lone mothers in most cases. Furthermore, the problems experienced by any lone parent are aggravated by the gendered division of labour both in the workplace and within the home, a division which tends to be reinforced by social policies.

Numerous studies have indicated that divorced women and female family heads are more likely to be poor than their male counterparts (Hardey and Crow 1991; National Council of Welfare 1990b). Not only do women tend to earn lower wages when they enter the full-time labour force, but female family heads are less likely to be working full time than male heads of lone-parent families. As was discussed in chapter 3, social assistance programs in some jurisdictions consider mothers with preschool children to be 'unemployable,' especially if child care services are unavailable or unaffordable.

Increasingly, two incomes are necessary to maintain the same standard of living which one wage could maintain in the 1950s, yet many lone parents are underemployed or unemployed. In countries with private support enforcement, many non-custodial parents (usually fathers) do not regularly pay child support even when the court has ordered them to do so (Richardson 1988b; Galarneau 1992). Lack of child support payments and high rates of unemployment and underemployment among lone parents increase the probability of dependence on social assistance.

There is growing recognition in Canada and the English-speaking countries that allowing children to live in poverty may have unanticipated consequences more costly than the various schemes to improve the economic status of one-parent families (M. Baker 1992). There is considerable public acceptance in North America of the idea of 'making fathers pay.' For example, Canadian newspapers have referred derogatorily to fathers who default on their child support payments as 'deadbeat dads' (Mackie 1994). Yet for both ideological and logistical reasons, there is far less public support for solutions to high unemployment, lack of child care, equal pay for work of equal value, or low minimum wages – solutions that could prove to be more effective than the pursuit of defaulting fathers in raising lone mothers out of poverty.

Low incomes of lone mothers

Numerous studies have indicated that lone mothers typically experience low incomes from underemployment, low levels of social assistance and child benefits, and lack of child support from the children's father. Lenore Weitzman of Stanford University, whose 1985 study became very influential for future research and policy analysis in both Canada and the United States, found that divorced mothers and their children experienced a 73 per cent decline in household income one year after marriage dissolution, while divorced men's household income increased by an average of 42 per cent (Weitzman 1985, 323). From an analysis of American divorce settlements over a number of years, Weitzman concluded that 'no fault' divorce laws have led to greater inequality than before family law reform. Prior to these changes, women could have been awarded alimony and could have delayed the divorce hearing until they negotiated a higher settlement. Weitzman argued that new American divorce laws, which abolished alimony in favour of temporary spousal support, are based on the false assumption of gender equality in the labour force.

Canadian studies have also indicated that divorced women, especially lone mothers, tend to be worse off financially than men or fathers after divorce. Using Canadian tax files from 1982 to 1986, Finnie (1993) found that women's family income dropped by roughly one-half in the first year after divorce while men's declined by about one-quarter. Using income-to-needs ratios to adjust for family size, however, Finnie found a small rise in economic well-being for men and a 40 per cent drop for women.

Canadians, Americans, and Australians have all argued that private procedures for enforcing support payments are inadequate because they leave the onus on the financially dependent spouse to take the other to court. This usually meant that women had to hire lawyers to take their ex-husbands to court. Although fathers might pay child support temporarily, the woman had to repeat the exhausting and expensive procedure each time the father failed to pay (Canada, Federal/Provincial/ Territorial Family Law Committee 1991). Most provinces, including Manitoba and Ontario, have begun to devise new enforcement systems in which the government pays child support directly to the custodial parent and automatically retrieves the money from the other parent. This system has increased the likelihood that the custodial parent will receive payment.

As we saw in chapter 3 (Table 3.1), mother-led one-parent families in Canada (and most other countries in our study) are much more likely than two-parent families to be living in poverty. Although poverty rates have fluctuated over time, the rates for lone mothers were higher in 1991 than throughout the last decade. From 1981 to 1991, the gulf between the rich and the poor in Canada widened, a fact which underscores the need to improve income security policies (Lochhead 1993, 24).

Since most lone-parent families now originate from separation and divorce, policy makers have focused on improving enforcement procedures for child support payments in an attempt to bring these families out of poverty. Yet the typical amount of child support paid is relatively small, less than $200 per month in the United States (Seltzer 1991) and about $250 in Canada (Galarneau 1992). This suggests that most lone parents would still be poor even if court-awarded payments were regularly made.

A more effective solution to the poverty of lone-parent families would be to take systematic action to improve women's position in the labour force, since women head most of these families. Pay equity laws would need to be enforced so that 'pink-collar' jobs were not paid less than the jobs that men normally do. Women could be assisted to find better-paying positions through continuing education and retraining programs. These programs could provide on-site child care to enable women to attend classes without worrying about their children. More subsidized child care spaces would also be needed throughout the community and in the workplace to encourage lone parents to enter the labour force or to continue working. Expanding child care services would cost additional money, yet welfare is also costly to governments. Accepting welfare is certainly detrimental to the self-esteem and opportunities of lone mothers, but the consequences might be even greater for their children.

The enforcement of child support

In Canada and the English-speaking countries, governments have focused on the enforcement of court-awarded child support as the main policy initiative to reduce the poverty of mother-led families. With the rise in one-parent families living on social assistance over the past two decades, the cost of defaulting to governments is considered to be too high and an unnecessary expense.

Enforcement of child support, however, is a political issue only in countries which leave enforcement to custodial parents. In many European countries, the state guarantees child support to the custodial parent and later retrieves the money from the non-custodial parent. Failure to pay by the non-custodial parent is either less frequent because of the efficiency of the retrieval system or of less concern because of the ideology that child support is a social responsibility. Consequently, the time and money spent by North American governments in trying to 'make fathers pay' could be viewed as a politically conservative or even somewhat misguided policy initiative.

Three major types of enforcement models are used in the countries studied in this project: private enforcement, limited advance maintenance, and advance maintenance (see Table 8.2). Private enforcement requires the custodial parent to take the initiative and pay the expense of establishing how much money the non-custodial parent should pay to support his[3] children. Then she must take the children's father to court to obtain a court order for payment, and every time there is non-payment, she must bring a civil contempt charge against him. Increments are also initiated through the court system and involve judicial discretion. Until recently, this system was used in the United States and Australia and is still the predominant method in most Canadian provinces. It is not used in any of the European countries studied, however.

Limited advance maintenance provides direct government enforcement for custodial parents on social assistance or for individuals who have difficulty dealing with defaulters on their own (Garfinkel 1988). This model has also been called 'quasi-judicial' and has been used in some Canadian provinces, U.S. states, and European countries. This

TABLE 8.2
Child support enforcement in eight industrialized countries, 1991

Country	Enforcement model
Australia	• limited advance maintenance (since 1988)
Canada	• private enforcement in most provinces (Ontario and Manitoba have limited advance maintenance)
France	• advance maintenance
Germany	• limited advance maintenance
Netherlands	• limited advance maintenance
Sweden	• advance maintenance
United Kingdom	• private enforcement
United States	• limited advance maintenance in some states

SOURCES: Compiled from numerous articles cited in this chapter.

model was also used in Australia while the system was in transition to advance maintenance in the late 1980s.

In the advance-maintenance model, a public agency pays child support to custodial parents and collects the money from non-custodial parents (Kamerman and Kahn 1989c). All custodial parents qualify for child support and are paid directly by a government agency mandated to garnish earnings automatically from the paycheques or income tax refunds of non-custodial parents. If the custodial parent is on public assistance and the amount of child support is less than the amount of social assistance, the difference is made up by the agency (Chambers 1988). The payment is designed to supplement rather than replace the earnings of custodial parents and is not intended to be seen as welfare (Nichols-Casebolt and Garfinkel 1987).

Advance maintenance, best exemplified in Sweden, is the most effective model of child support enforcement in terms of guaranteeing a regular and minimum level of payment. Not surprisingly, it is the preferred method in most of Europe, where there is a growing trend to provide a guaranteed minimum payment (Dopffel 1988; Garfinkel 1988; Garfinkel and Wong 1990; Kamerman and Kahn 1989c).

Models of calculating child support

Although there are many ways to calculate how much separated parents should be required to pay for child support, four models will be discussed below: (1) the income-sharing model, (2) the Melson formula, (3) the percentage-of-income model, and (4) the equalization-of-standards-of-living model. In practice, many jurisdictions use a combination of these models.

The basic principle behind income sharing is that a child should receive the same amount of parental income before and after divorce (Thoennes et al. 1991). The formula prorates the incomes of both parents in calculating how much the non-residential parent should pay. For example, if one parent earns twice as much as the other, the parent earning more would be expected to contribute twice as much. This means that the amount of child support received by a mother could decrease if her income increased relative to the father's (Garfinkel and Melli 1990). There may also be some adjustment depending on the child's age or the frequency and length of visits to the non-residential parent (Thoennes et al. 1991). Some European countries use elaborate support tables designed to capture these elements (Maclean 1990).

The Melson (Delaware) formula was first developed by Judge Elwood F. Melson in the United States in 1979 and revised in Delaware in 1990. Within this model, parents are allowed a self-support exemption set at the poverty level before child support calculations are made. After this exemption, the net income of both parents is combined, a primary support amount per month for each child is established, and then adjustments are made for other expenses. The award is increased by a standard-of-living allowance, and further adjustments are made for other dependants, current spouses, and extended visits of the children (Thoennes et al. 1991). This model is similar to the traditional system of establishing child support, when children received what was left over after parents' needs were met (Garfinkel and Melli 1990).

The percentage-of-income (Wisconsin) model is the simplest of all. Regardless of income, a fixed percentage of the non-residential parent's income is required for child support, with the percentage varying only by the number and age of children. The percentages are 17 per cent for one child, 25 per cent for two, 29 per cent for three, 31 per cent for four, and 34 per cent for five or more. The formula does not include the income of the residential parent, because she is assumed to be providing care as well as her own income for child support.

Equalization of standards of living is a resource-sharing model, since the main objective is to redistribute resources between two households (Kamerman and Kahn 1988b). The formula exempts a poverty level of support for members of both households, and the remaining income is redistributed proportionally according to the numbers of persons in each household. Incomes of new spouses may be considered to ensure equivalent standards of living for both households (Goldfarb 1987).

The next sections look at the actual enforcement and calculation procedures used in Canada, and then compare all the countries of the study.

CALCULATION AND ENFORCEMENT OF CHILD SUPPORT IN CANADA

Traditionally, child support has been enforced privately in Canada through an adversarial court process (Richardson 1988). Although federal law covers issues relating to divorce, custody, and support, the provinces are responsible for enforcing custody and support orders. Children are eligible for court-awarded support until age sixteen or older if they are still financially dependent (M. Morton 1990). Although enforcement procedures vary by province, social work and legal officials have had the discretion to decide whether or not to enforce court-awarded child support in most provinces (Garfinkel and Wong 1990).

The federal *Divorce Act, 1985* contained two child support objectives. One recognized that both spouses have an obligation to support their child, and in some provinces this obligation is extended to step-parents. The second objective was that child support should be divided between spouses according to their abilities, although property can substitute for regular support (Galarneau 1992). Since 1987, provinces have been able to track defaulting parents by using federal tax files and have been allowed to garnish federal money owing to the parent, such as income tax refunds (M. Morton 1990). Since this change, the amounts paid have increased slightly (Sev'er 1992).

A joint federal-provincial-territorial project is currently working towards rules to standardize child support awards across Canada, as well as to address other weaknesses in the current system (ibid.). In Manitoba, there has been a Maintenance Enforcement Office since 1980 that monitors all support accounts. Payments are made directly to the office and then forwarded to the recipient. Because the system is computerized, a default is immediately noticed and action is taken (ibid.).

Ontario has recently instituted an automated system of recording payment that initiates an enforcement procedure if the payer defaults (Galarneau 1992). The Ontario *Family Law Act* (1986) had stated a preference for a systemic approach to child support over judicial discretion and the *Support and Custody Orders Enforcement Act* (July 1987) established a Support and Custody Enforcement Branch to process payments.

Failure to pay leads to prompt garnishment of wages, seizure of assets, and possibly imprisonment. As of March 1992, Ontario employers are obligated to withhold support payments from the wages of employees who are delinquent in their payments (ibid.).

In 1988, Quebec passed legislation for a similar system of child support enforcement, but it was never implemented. In August 1994, six weeks before the provincial election, the Quebec Liberal government announced that it would implement a new system for collecting support payments. At that time, federal-provincial talks were being held about new ways to limit defaulting parents from moving out of province to avoid child support payments (Mackie 1994). However, the initiative ended when the Liberals were voted out of office in September 1994.

In Canada, the level of child support has depended on judicial discretion and effective advocacy. When deciding on an award, judges have considered any economic advantages or disadvantages arising from marriage breakdown, the financial consequences to the children, the length of the relationship, functions performed by the spouse during cohabitation, and any other order or agreement relating to child support (Galarneau 1992). However, assessment formulas and periodic updating have not been used (Garfinkel and Wong 1990).

As legal separations fall under provincial jurisdiction, not all marriage breakdowns are included in federal divorce statistics. Furthermore, many couples separate with no official notice, which means that they cannot be tracked using federal or provincial government records (Richardson 1988a). Traditionally, the majority of child support cases are settled out of court but formalized in a hearing (ibid.). Yet this system has resulted in very low awards with very high default rates (ibid.).

While amounts increase with non-custodial parents' income, the percentage of income tends to decrease (Stewart and McFadyen 1992). In 1988, child support payments formed 7 per cent of the payers' median income and 9 per cent of mean income (Galarneau 1992). Support payments represent a significant portion of income for many lone-parent families, as child support constitutes 12 per cent of lone parents' median income and 15 per cent of mean income (ibid.). On average, Quebec has awarded the most generous support, while the four Atlantic provinces have had the lowest awards (ibid.).

Increasingly, spousal support is granted for a fixed term, intended to motivate the recipient to become financially independent as quickly as possible and influenced by the 'clean break' philosophy of divorce (ibid.).

The *Divorce Act, 1985* states that fixed-term support is to promote self-sufficiency 'as far as practicable.' Reasons for remaining dependent on spousal support might include illness, lack of marketable skills, or advanced age. In Manitoba, having custody of preschool children is seen as a legitimate reason for lack of self-sufficiency. Canadian legislation typically states that both parents are legally responsible for their children and makes no gender distinctions with respect to responsibilities or rights (Stewart and McFadyen 1992). Yet, there are vast differences between what the law says should happen and what actually happens.

In Canada, both child and spousal support paid are tax deductible, while support received is considered to be taxable income. There has been considerable controversy about these taxation requirements. A Quebec woman, Suzanne Thibaudeau, argued before the courts that the federal government requirement that custodial parents pay tax on child support payments received is a violation of the equality clause in the constitution. In May 1994, the Federal Court of Appeal ruled unconstitutional, under the *Canadian Charter of Rights and Freedoms*, the law requiring custodial parents who receive child support to pay income tax on these payments while non-custodial parents enjoy a tax deduction on their payments. In the same month, the federal government established a Task Group on the Tax Treatment of Child Support to seek opinions from a wide range of Canadians and to advise the government on possible options for change. Meanwhile feminist groups, such as the Women's Legal Education Action Fund (LEAF), argued that a married mother is not required to pay income tax on money her husband provides for the child, so why should a separated or divorced mother be expected to pay tax on the same sort of income transfer? They argued further that the income of divorced fathers tends to be much higher than that of divorced mothers, yet the fathers are given the tax 'break.' In May 1995, the Supreme Court of Canada heard a federal government appeal, and overturned the previous decision. This means that the taxation of child support received will continue.

A CROSS-NATIONAL COMPARISON OF SYSTEMS OF CHILD SUPPORT ENFORCEMENT

Australia

Until 1988, child support in Australia was determined by the courts and orders were made in accordance with the financial resources of both parents (Harrison 1991). As entitlement to the sole-parent pension did not require the recipient to seek child support from the other parent, few orders were sought by low-income custodial parents. Prior to the reform, only 24 per cent of potentially eligible lone parents and 37 per cent of those covered by a judicial support order received any child support payments (Harrison et al. 1991).

Since 1988, Australia has been in the process of changing from private enforcement to an advance-maintenance model of child support enforcement. In 1988, the *Child Support Registration and Collection Act* established a Child Support Agency within the Australian Taxation Office to manage court-ordered support payments. Participation in the scheme is compulsory for those on social assistance, but other recipients may opt out after registration (Harrison 1991). Children of separated, divorced, and unmarried parents are covered by the new scheme, but unmarried mothers are expected to cooperate with the paternity determination process (Garfinkel and Wong 1990; Maclean 1990).

The Australian Child Support Scheme was implemented in two stages. Stage one established the Child Support Agency, registered support orders, and began collecting money which was owed following a court order. A Child Support Registrar, who deals with unpaid support, was given the means to trace and locate liable parents, involve employers in the payment process, and have support payments deducted from employment income. Payments are now either made to the Child Support Agency directly by the non-residential parent or deducted automatically from his paycheque. Money is paid into a trust fund and then paid monthly to the custodial parent's bank account (Harrison et al. 1991).

The scheme has integrated the social security, taxation, and family law systems by amending the *Family Law Act* and the *Social Security Act*. The amendments to the *Family Law Act* removed the provision that social security entitlements should be considered in setting the level of support. In addition, child support was given priority over other financial commitments, and regular payments were favoured over lump-sum settlements. Amendments to the *Social Security Act* treated support payments separately from other income, yet included them as income for purposes of determining social assistance.

In 1989, the second stage of the reform involved a formal approach to maintenance assessment. The intention was to remove the calculation of child support from the court and base it on a formula which would be consistently applied (Garfinkel and Wong 1990). The formula, which combines aspects of American income sharing, the percentage-of-income model, and the Melson formula, takes into account both parents' incomes and the child's needs (Bates 1989–90). Calculations are based on the taxable income of one or both parents, but the custodial parent's income is included only if it is above average. Before calculations are made, the non-custodial parent is allowed a self-support exemption which may be adjusted according to the number of dependent children.[4] The remaining income is multiplied by a percentage according to the number of children – 18 per cent for one child, 27 per cent for two children, and up to 36 per cent for five or more children. There is a ceiling of about A.$65,000 (Can. $58,825) per year on the non-residential parent's income above which he pays no more. In the case of shared care, the number of children attributed to each parent is 0.5 and the amounts are offset against each other. The formula of child support applies to all couples whether or not they were legally married, but parents may opt out of the program if they both consent to make private arrangements.

The level of child support is reviewed annually using information from income tax returns and is automatically calculated to cover changes in parental income or major life events such as the birth of a new child. Before the implementation of this program, research showed that the level of support tended to remain constant despite the impact of inflation or changes in income (Harrison et al. 1991).

The reform of the Australian child support system grew out of both monetary and social concerns similar to those in Canada and the United States. Only 30 to 40 per cent of non-custodial parents paid any support prior to reform, and when support was paid, it was insufficient to pull the lone-parent family out of poverty. Awards varied throughout the country as a result of judicial discretion (Bates 1989–90). As well, the boundaries between child support and social security were unclear before the reform. Social security benefits were taken into account when support was determined by the courts, and child support was viewed as a 'top up' to social assistance. This resulted in high social security payments for the government and lower child support awards for non-residential parents (Harrison 1991).

Inherent in the new scheme is the idea that parents, regardless of marital status, have a duty to support their children and that first and second families should be considered equal (Bates 1989–90). The scheme was designed to separate child support from the issue of visitation rights, to require parental support for children in lone-parent families, and to ensure regular payments and family privacy. In addition, the government was determined to increase the amount of private child support in order to use fewer government resources (Harrison 1991; Maclean 1990).

Stage one reforms have been evaluated by the Australian Institute of Family Studies and proven cost-effective. Through the scheme, the Department of Social Security saved A.$19.1 million (Can. $17.3 million) in 1988–9, support orders were higher, and more families were receiving money. After a year and a half, 24 per cent of registered custodial parents who had not been receiving payments prior to the scheme were receiving them. In addition, recipients generally expressed satisfaction with the new system. In stage two, the new formula raised the average award of child support. There were fewer appeals than anticipated, and public antagonism was only minimal. Some mothers resented not being eligible for stage two because they did not have separation agreements prior to the legislation (Harrison et al. 1991).

Implementation has been slow because of transitional procedures, and this has caused some frustration to recipients. In addition, registration does not guarantee receipt of child support and, by December 1990, just over half of registered parents were receiving payments through the agency. Apparently, there was a long delay between initial registration and first payment (ibid.). Many parents still pay directly to the agency without automatic wage withholding. In some cases, employers and employees may have colluded against payroll deductions, although most employers have not reported being inconvenienced. Payers (fathers) are generally dissatisfied with the system, but complaints had to do mostly with making adjustments to a new system (Harrison 1991).

Despite reform, there is still inequality within the Australian child support system. Compared to parents and children who are benefiting from the legislation, ineligible parents and children receive lower awards and no annual adjustments. Parents who registered under stage one, between 1988 and 1990, receive only half as much money as those registered under stage two (Harrison et al. 1991). Some critics also believe that the formula is not sensitive enough to individual and regional circumstances and costs, and should not have retained a ceiling for high-income parents. In addition, the scheme has been criticized for the practice of waiting until tax time to adjust the amount, even when circumstances change in the middle of the fiscal year. A concern has also been raised by feminist groups that the new scheme may provoke violent men to react against their former wives. Some critics feel that custody and access disputes will increase, while others suggest that the opposite will happen and that relationships will improve (Harrison 1991).

France

Until recently, court-awarded child support payments were enforced through civil proceedings. If unsuccessful, the custodial parent could request garnishment of wages or tax refunds. As a final resort, a defaulting parent could be charged with neglect and given a fine or suspended sentence (Maclean 1990). In 1985, a limited advance-maintenance system was initiated which transferred the collection of child support to the tax offices (Kahn and Kamerman 1988). Child support is now paid to an insurance company which then disperses it to the custodial parent on a monthly and/or lump-sum basis. Children are eligible for support until the age of eighteen (Dopffel 1988).

The calculation of child support is based on private arrangement and judicial discretion. The amount is usually established by parents and ratified in court, where the judge acts as an adviser and mediator. Although each judge may set different standards, a lower and upper limit for support is established and some earnings are protected for the paying parent (ibid.). Often, indexation clauses are part of the initial award and further adjustments are made by judicial review (Garfinkel and Wong 1990). Increases could relate to child-rearing costs, an increase in wages for the paying parent, changing economic conditions, or anything else deemed relevant to the situation (Kahn and Kamerman 1988).

When a parent defaults, advance maintenance is paid by the agency, which then recovers the money from the non-residential parent. In France, the National Family Allowance Fund (Caisse Nationale d'Allocations Familiales) actively pursues maintenance defaulters using the power of the *Code de la Sécurité Sociale* (1988). A minimum level of child support is established by law, and is based on the couple's income and the number of dependent children under twenty-five (Rubellin-Devichi 1990–1).

For unmarried parents, determining paternity is not considered to be worth the cost and effort, as unmarried parents are not a large category in France (Kahn and Kamerman 1988). French law is traditionally based on the Napoleonic Code, which did not recognize illegitimate children. Consequently, establishing paternity has more to do with inheritance than child support in France (Dopffel 1988).

Child support payments are the main source of income for 10 per cent of households where the mother is employed and 50 to 70 per cent of households in which she is a homemaker. Yet the compliance rate is only about 60 per cent for all orders (Maclean 1990). The French system is said to favour non-custodial parents by basing the amount and subsequent increases of support on their financial circumstances rather than the needs of the children and the lone-parent household (Garfinkel and Wong 1990). Standardized support has been rejected as a concept and judicial discretion is permitted, which creates an inequitable system for children. For example, advance maintenance for children without established paternity tends to be lower than for those with established paternity (Dopffel 1988). There are also concerns among conservative and religious groups that advance maintenance could encourage cohabitation and divorce (Maclean 1990).

As was discussed in earlier chapters, French family policy provides generous child allowances and child-rearing allowances to all families with young children, providing mothers with the option of staying home. Although this payment is unrelated to child support, it improves the economic status of all children, regardless of the family income or marital status of parents (Kamerman and Kahn 1989c).

Germany

Before reunification, the West German child support system, developed in 1980, was based mainly on judicial discretion with a limited advance-maintenance program (Kahn and Kamerman 1988). If a custodial parent on welfare was having difficulty collecting, she could request assistance from the appropriate public agency and the court would comply (Garfinkel and Wong 1990). The basic guaranteed amount of child support used to be equal to social assistance, but children of unmarried parents did not have the right to support from the non-residential parent (ibid.). Child support payments were not indexed because it was believed that this would fuel inflation, but payments were increased every few years at the discretion of government, doubling between 1970 and 1988. Non-custodial parents were expected to support their children until they turned eighteen or completed university (Frank 1987–8).

Children of unmarried parents did not have the same rights as children of divorced parents. They were socially considered 'separate but equal,' but in reality were expected to make do with less. A curator or public trustee was automatically involved to determine paternity and regulate payments. A voluntary recognition of paternity was acceptable, but medical determination procedures could be used (Dopffel 1988).

In 1986, the West German system was reformed with the *Law Amending Maintenance, Procedural and Other Provisions*. The new law stated that a divorced spouse has the right to claim maintenance if she is unable to be self-supporting after divorce and if she has a child to care for from the marriage. Child support was increased above the level of social assistance and considered to be separate from it. Support was also extended to never-married women. The new rules state that the child of divorced parents is to be maintained as before (Grandke 1989–90). When the child reaches the age of majority but is still enrolled in secondary education, child support is reduced by half. Although child support is usually paid monthly, a lump-sum supplement might be warranted if there are special needs and judicial ratification is obtained (Dopffel 1988).

Germany now follows an income-sharing formula where both parents are held proportionally responsible for supporting the child, depending on their means and the child's age (Dopffel 1988). Although there is some degree of standardization, the initial amount of child support and subsequent increments are based on judicial discretion (Garfinkel and Wong 1990). Some earnings, appropriate to the parties' 'station in life,' are protected for the parent, and a 'saturation limit' above which support is not paid is assumed rather than legislated (Dopffel 1988). The system for determining the level of child support in Germany has been criticized for being discretionary and unequal, as judges in different jurisdictions tend to award different levels of support (ibid.).

In the former East Germany, a system of support tables was used, based on parental income and the number and ages of children. The level of payment was relatively low. The *Family Code* of 1966 made both spouses equally responsible for their children (Grandke 1989–90). Living together before marriage was neither socially acceptable nor seen as equivalent to marriage, but rather was viewed as a step towards marriage. After divorce, the goal was to assist the wife's transition into paid work and self-sufficiency, but a man's second family, if any, was given priority in law (Dopffel 1988).

Advance maintenance in West Germany is limited to a maximum of three years for children under six years of age and ends when the custodial parent remarries (Garfinkel and Wong 1990). Only when children are very young is it considered appropriate for a lone mother to remain at home with her children. When they reach school age, she is expected to enter the job market (Kahn and Kamerman 1988).

The Netherlands

Although custodial parents in the Netherlands must first sue the non-residential parent for child support through the courts, there is a system of limited advance maintenance (Kahn and Kamerman 1988). The local Council of Child Protection, which is a public agency, is responsible for the enforcement of court-ordered child support payments (Garfinkel and Wong 1990). After the council sends a copy of the support order to the debtor's employer, earnings may be garnished and employers can be charged with non-compliance if they do not cooperate. For self-employed parents, property may also be confiscated (Wiebrens 1988). This enforcement system applies to children from divorced parents and unmarried relationships if paternity is declared. Private agreements may also be enforceable after examination in court (Dopffel 1988).

The level of child support is established by private arrangement or judicial discretion, and is related to parents' financial circumstances rather than the level of public benefits (Garfinkel and Wong 1990). Before calculation of support, an amount of income is set aside for personal use by the non-residential parent (equal to the minimum upon which all social benefits are based). The remainder is divided equally among all claimants, with child support taking priority over spousal support. Acknowledgment of paternity means responsibility for support, and lump-sum payments are allowed for non-marital children. Yet paternity tests are rarely used, and paternity outside marriage is established by voluntary recognition (Wiebrens 1988).

The cost of raising children is established through budget survey data. The family allowance (which was more than three times the value of the Canadian family allowance in 1991) is intended to pay 40 per cent of the cost of raising a child, and parents are expected to pay the remaining 60 per cent. The cost of child-rearing is expected to be shared by both parents, and once the amount is set, it is indexed to the cost of living (Garfinkel and Wong 1990). Unless the recipient wishes to receive payment directly, payments are made through automatic bank account transfers, as Dutch banks share a central registry to track payers' accounts (Wiebrens 1988). If the paying account has insufficient funds, the agency forwards money to the custodial parent and the payer is charged interest on the overdraft. As in Canada, child support paid is tax deductible, but support received is taxable.

Support is not influenced by the remarriage of the absent parent, although it may be readjusted with the birth of additional children, and step-parents may be liable for child support. Normally, support is paid until the child is age sixteen, but this is raised to twenty-one if the child is still in school. Standardization of support has been under active discussion in recent years (Dopffel 1988; Wiebrens 1988).

Child support claims may be transferred to other jurisdictions if the father works in a country with which the Netherlands government has a reciprocal agreement. In addition, renewal of passports of Dutch citizens living abroad can be refused if they have not made their child support payments. Imprisonment is the final penalty for non-supporters (Wiebrens 1988).

Compared to other countries in our study, the Netherlands has developed a strong administrative structure and an efficient collection system for court-awarded child support (Garfinkel and Wong 1990). The percentage of unpaid support is less than 8 per cent (Wiebrens 1988). In many cases, however, the amount of support is inadequate to reach the minimum income determined by government, or the guaranteed annual income, and the custodial parent is entitled to an extra allowance. Since 1981, there has been a provision that supplements all incomes to a minimum level, and low-income families receiving child support would also benefit from this guaranteed income (ibid.). All social benefits in the Netherlands are paid from social insurance, funded by employers, employees, and government contributions.

As Dutch society values the breadwinner-homemaker family, the minimum wage is set high enough to support this family structure. Rather than encouraging mothers into the workforce, as in Sweden, social policy in the Netherlands is designed to support mothers at home (Wiebrens 1988). The Netherlands also has a low rate of single parenthood and the lowest rate of out-of-wedlock births in Europe. Only 7 per cent of Dutch families have one parent, most of whom are women, and 5 per cent of children live in one-parent families. Only 1 per cent of family heads have never married (Kamerman and Kahn 1988a).

In terms of general family policies, the Netherlands is less generous than many other European countries (Kamerman and Kahn 1989c). Child support awards are influenced considerably by judicial discretion (though there are government guidelines), and there is no automatic advance-maintenance system (Garfinkel and Wong 1990).

Sweden

Sweden's Advance Maintenance Program, initiated in 1937, has been used as a model for many countries. The program began with legislation allowing lone mothers living with children to apply for advance maintenance payments if the father failed to pay support. In 1947, eligibility became independent of the custodial parent's income, and in 1957 a guaranteed minimum level of support for a child was established by the government. If the non-custodial parent could not pay this minimum, the government guaranteed it.

The national government assumes responsibility for collection for public assistance recipients when fathers fail to pay, and for those voluntarily enrolled in the program (Garfinkel and Wong 1990). Divorced persons may opt out, and unmarried parents may apply to enrol in the program (Chambers 1988). A child support case is first referred to the Crown bailiff for collection, and if necessary, wages are withheld or the amount owing is deducted from income tax refunds. There is a five-year statute of limitations on these debts, but about 75 per cent of child support is eventually collected. Enforcement by criminal proceedings has long ago been abolished (Kindlund 1988).

All calculations of support are determined by the social security system and there is a minimum amount guaranteed by the government (Garfinkel and Wong 1990). The minimum child support payment is set at 40 per cent of the basic needs assessment for children (Kahn and Kamerman 1988). A standard formula considers the after-tax incomes of both parents and step-parents, as well as the age and needs of the children. This formula is used for families on public assistance, but may vary for others. Before calculations are made, parents are allowed to reserve a portion of the base amount for themselves, a dependent spouse, any other dependent children, and for housing. Normally, 60 per cent of a parent's income is considered in calculation of child support (Maclean 1990). Payments are tax deductible to a limit, but unlike in Canada, child support received is not taxable. Furthermore, child support and advance maintenance are not deducted from social assistance (Kamerman and Kahn 1989b).

Parents are expected to pay child support until the child finishes high school or reaches the age of twenty-one. Support is paid monthly unless a lump sum is requested. Amounts are indexed annually by seven-tenths of the rise in the consumer price index, but if parents' financial circumstances change, they can apply to the courts for a review. Otherwise, the award is reviewed and revised after six years. Deductions are made if the child visits the non-custodial parent for extended periods. In cases of joint custody, no support allowance is fixed, but joint custody can be terminated at the request of either parent (Garfinkel and Wong 1990).

Child support is paid to the Social Insurance Office, which administers the program (Kindlund 1988). Whether or not the non-residential parent makes the payment, a portion of the basic amount of child support is paid as advance support by the office to the residential parent. Private agreements are accepted, but can be amended through the court system (Dopffel 1988). Step-parents, married or cohabiting, may be held responsible for their stepchildren's support if the new couple have at least one child together (ibid.).

Only 35 per cent of all advance maintenance is eventually collected from non-custodial parents (Kindlund 1988). Despite the low collection rate, establishment of paternity is not considered to be a major issue in Sweden's child support system, although residential mothers are expected to cooperate with the paternity determination process (Dopffel 1988). Paternity determination is the responsibility of municipal social welfare departments, and paternity is established more than 95 per cent of the time, either by voluntary consent or by the local social committee. The mother receives advance maintenance whether or not paternity is established (Kahn and Kamerman 1988).

The Swedish system is not without problems. Critics have argued that the revision of support levels is not always sensitive to changes in the family's economic circumstances, and there is concern by religious groups and conservatives that some well-off parents are receiving public child support benefits. Although means-testing has been suggested, this would probably not be cost-effective, since most lone-parent families are not wealthy (Kindlund 1988). Another criticism is that court-awarded child support is too low and too highly supplemented by public funds. Non-custodial parents typically pay somewhat less than the actual award, and the Social Insurance Office makes up the difference. This means that mothers have less incentive to apply for increases than they would if the awards were greater than advance maintenance. In addition, the real value of support awards has declined in recent years due to partial indexation. However, men's groups argue that higher support awards would generate non-payment and increase administrative costs for collection (Kindlund 1988).

Another concern is that additional personal and social problems, including a disincentive to remarriage, are created from child support debts, since a new partner's income is taken into account in calculating the level of child support. Also, when support is combined with the lone-mother's allowance, lone-parent families are better off than poor two-parent families, as the allowance is not diminished by child support payments (Maclean 1990). As well, the need to improve the economic circumstances of the father's second family places more responsibility for the support of first families on society (Kahn and Kamerman 1988).

In Sweden, nearly 30 per cent of families are headed by lone parents, but both parents are held legally responsible for their children. The child support program is based on the assumption that mother-led families are economically weak and that advance maintenance is therefore an essential service (Krause 1988). Lone-parent families are better off in Sweden than in many industrialized countries because custodial parents become eligible for various benefits and training programs when they apply for advance maintenance (Lundstrom 1989).

The United Kingdom

Despite the New Right policies of the Conservative government in the United Kingdom since 1979, until the changes to child support laws in 1993, little was done to reform the 'permissive' social legislation of the 1960s and 1970s. Divorce has become simpler, available since 1984 after a one-year rather than a three-year wait. Furthermore, the divorce rate has been rising steadily for the past decade, and more mothers have entered the labour force in low-paid part-time jobs (Abbott and Wallace 1992, 120).

In the later 1980s, concern about family breakdown, the poverty of lone-parent families, and the implications of these trends for social unrest and welfare dependency increased under the third Thatcher government. The percentage of lone parents relying on social assistance rose from 38 per cent in 1979 to 70 per cent in 1992. Yet by 1989, only 23 per cent of lone parents were receiving child support payments, compared to 50 per cent ten years earlier (Lister 1994). Although lone parents have been encouraged to enter full-time work, they have not been required to do so, and child care services have not been made available. Despite the fact that many other countries have required lone parents to enter the workforce, many Conservatives in the United Kingdom oppose such a policy because they feel that it goes against the interests of 'the family' (ibid.). At the same time, the Conservatives have expressed concern that young women become pregnant in order to obtain subsidized housing and social benefits, despite a lack of evidence to support this belief.

In October 1990, the government's proposals for reforming child support laws came out in a White Paper entitled *Children Come First*. The *Child Support Act*, which was partially modelled on the Australian scheme and took effect in 1993, has been described as 'the most far-reaching social reform in forty years' (ibid.). This act involves a determined attempt to enforce the financial responsibility of absent parents in order to reduce the financial responsibility of the state. Despite the outcry from middle-class men, absent fathers will pay higher support payments. Yet although this reform was introduced with the government rhetoric that 'children come first,' most children will not be better off (ibid.). The household incomes of children may not rise and could fall because mothers' social benefits will be reduced to compensate for increased child support income. As in the United States, the primary motivation of child support reforms appears to be to reduce government expenditures.

The *Child Support Act* transferred the responsibility for assessment and enforcement of child support from the courts to a new executive agency called the Child Support Agency (CSA). This responsibility will be phased in between 1993 and 1997. The courts will retain responsibility for property settlements, paternity disputes, and visiting arrangements (ibid.).

Prior to 1993, there was no advance-maintenance system in the United Kingdom, although the government helped collect child support for mothers on social assistance if they applied for this service. Only people on social assistance received advances, and then the support was diverted through the Department of Health and Social Security. There was no concept of standardized support, and awards have been widely discretionary (Eekelaar 1988). Court-awarded child support has been paid monthly, weekly, in a lump sum, or in a combination of forms, until the child turns eighteen (Dopffel 1988).

Judges have tended to base the level of support on children's needs and the financial means or earning capacity of parents, who are allowed some protected income of their own (Weitzman 1988). Levels were set or ratified in court, and the maximum award was equivalent to the level of Social Benefits plus one-quarter of the father's net income. Defaulters could have earnings or property garnished, and serious defaulting could have led to imprisonment (Eekelaar 1988). In the setting of child support awards, the second family was given priority over the first, a policy which led to considerable controversy (Maclean 1990).

The *Children Act, 1989*, effective October 1991, stated that the welfare of the child should be of 'paramount consideration' after divorce. Parental rights and duties were replaced by the new concept of 'parental responsibility,' and both parents were held responsible for children. For the first time, joint custody was possible. However, the act also ended affiliation proceedings, the formal mechanism used to make unmarried fathers pay child support (Freeman 1990–1).

In 1984, divorce legislation promoted the 'clean break' philosophy and self-sufficiency for divorcing partners (Eekelar 1988). A divorce, however, cannot be finalized until the courts are satisfied with the arrangements for the children (Maclean 1990). Private agreements are permitted, but the courts have a right to intervene if the amounts are deemed inadequate or inappropriate (Dopffel 1988).

Children of unmarried parents have few rights even if paternity has been established, but step-parents may be expected to help support the child even after the termination of marriage (ibid.). No pressure has been placed on mothers to enter the labour force if they have preschool children. In fact, the expectation is that they will stay home (Kamerman and Kahn 1989b). Mothers who work outside the home lose their benefits, and it is therefore not worth their entering the labour force except in a high-paying position.

In the United Kingdom, there are a number of universal benefits, such as child allowances, medical benefits, housing supplements, and school meal programs. Yet most one-parent families are poor, and the situation is worse for divorced mothers than for widows (Eekelaar 1988). Most one-parent families are supported by social assistance, and only 7 per cent of households are dependent on child support payments as the main income (Maclean 1990). Yet before the 1993 reform, fewer than two-thirds of non-custodial parents paid their court-awarded child support and only 12 per cent of unpaid support was recovered from liable parents by government (Dopffel 1988). There was a reluctance to enforce child support awards in Britain because it was assumed that most fathers do not have the means to pay and that it would therefore not be worth the money and effort to try to make them (Eekelaar 1988).

Prior to 1993, policies regarding families were designed only to meet basic needs and were seen as an anti-poverty strategy (Kamerman and Kahn 1989b). As child support directly reduced social assistance benefits, there was no incentive for mothers to pursue it (Maclean 1990). Neither did social policies encourage lone parents to look for employment, for they were better off on public assistance. While the new *Child Support Act* will reduce lone mothers' reliance on social assistance by placing a greater onus on fathers to pay, it may not improve the incomes of lone parents and their children. The new act also perpetuates and reinforces women's economic dependence on men (Lister 1994).

The United States

Historically, the American states relied on the private enforcement model of child support. Although new federal requirements are now propelling states to move in the direction of a limited advance-maintenance model, child support enforcement remains the responsibility of state governments (Krause 1990).

In 1984, Congress passed a set of amendments to the *Social Security Act* aimed at enhancing the enforcement of child support payments by noncustodial parents (Glass 1990). The legislation required the states to establish guidelines to assess the level of support, a collection procedure for all lone-parent families, and an enforcement procedure which included wage garnishment, interception of tax refunds, liens, credit-bureau notification, and other measures when payments are not made. All states were expected to establish guidelines for child support awards by October 1987 (Christensen et al. 1990).

In 1988, further federal legislation threatened a reduction in federal support to those states which did not comply. Not surprisingly, there has been considerable variation among states in their progress towards reform. In New York State, for example, all support awards should be automatically withheld from wages by 1994, and by 1995 collection should be fully automated (Glass 1990). But other states have not moved so far in this direction.

Under the influence of the New Right, the enforcement of court-awarded child support is now viewed in the United States as the strategy of choice for reducing public assistance expenditures. As more public money is spent on lone-parent families, attempts to enforce parental support are gaining public acceptance. This attitude is consistent with public pressure against raising taxes and towards privatization (Danzinger and Nichols-Casebolt 1990).

Traditionally, the level of child support was established by private agreement or by judges in court on a case-by-case basis (Garfinkel 1988).

Judicial discretion in assessing child support has been extensively criticized for several reasons. First, the typical level of support did not allow lone parents to live independently of government benefits, and many mothers received either no support at all or small and erratic payments which forced them onto welfare. Second, awards were inconsistent even within the same state. Third, public funds were being used to support children who could be supported by their non-resident parents. Fourth, serious delays in processing awards caused hardships for the families. In order to collect overdue awards, custodial parents had to initiate court action and pay for it themselves. Finally, lax enforcement condoned and encouraged non-custodial parents to default on payments (Garfinkel and Wong 1990; Garfinkel and Melli 1990; McLindon 1987; Thoennes et al. 1991).

In 1984, the state of Wisconsin first developed guidelines for calculating child support levels, but since then each state has developed its own method of assessment. Although the most popular model is income sharing, sixteen states determine support by the percentage-of-income (Wisconsin) model, and three states follow the Melson formula. States may choose their own formula, but must consider the needs of children and the parent's ability to pay (Lima and Harris 1988). In many states, payments are now sent through a state agency that manages the account and forwards money to the custodial parent. Awards are usually updated every three years (Krause 1990).

Under the new system, responsibilities are divided between federal and state jurisdictions, which is a departure from the traditional approach of family policy as a state obligation (Chambers 1988). The federal government prescribes the obligations and guidelines, reimburses states for a percentage of the administrative and collection costs, and enforces payment (Krause 1990). The federal Office of Child Support Enforcement (OCSE) in the Department of Health and Human Services helps the states develop and manage their programs and provides technical assistance (Kahn and Kamerman 1988). States are required to establish a State Commission on Child Support, which is a system for automatic wage deductions and for compelling employers to honour wage assignments (Garfinkel and Wong 1990). The states keep detailed records of each case, are connected by a central computer system, and are expected to cooperate in locating an absent parent (Krause 1990).

State and federal governments have also strengthened legislation related to establishing paternity, which is also a state responsibility. Statutes of limitations, previously from two to six years, have been dropped, and now paternity can be established up to the child's eighteenth birthday. Paternity establishment is compulsory before unmarried mothers are eligible for child support (Danzinger and Nichols-Casebolt 1990).

Considerable research has attempted to ascertain which method of calculating child support leads to higher awards. For example, Thoennes, Tjaden, and Pearson (1991) compared three states using three different models of calculating child support: Colorado (income-sharing model), Hawaii (Melson formula), and Illinois (percentage-of-income model). They found that case processing was more efficient than before the reform and award levels increased in all three states, especially Hawaii, which had the lowest pre-guideline levels. Relative to non-residential parent's income, awards increased significantly in Hawaii and Illinois, where there were also fewer zero-dollar awards after the guidelines. In comparing pre- and post-guideline awards by income level of recipient families, the researchers found that the income-sharing model was most beneficial to low-income families, the Melson formula to middle-income families, and the percentage-of-income model to upper-income families.

Garfinkel, Oellerich, and Robins (1991) also compared three models of calculating awards: the Wisconsin (percentage-of-income) model, the Colorado (income-sharing) model, and the Delaware (Melson) model. They found that the amount of child support increases with net income under the Wisconsin model while the amount decreases under the other models. Except at low levels of net income, the Wisconsin guidelines result in higher awards. In comparison with the old system of award setting, however, the new guidelines all fare better. They noted that the problem with the old guidelines was that they often failed to provide for the need to update the award (for exmaple, to keep pace with inflation). The authors expressed concern, however, that while the new guidelines will increase the level of child support awards, they may not increase compliance. Furthermore, a system to update awards is crucial.

Child support enforcement services are now available to all families, including those not on Aid to Families with Dependent Children (AFDC). Families on AFDC, however, may keep only U.S.$50 (Can. $64) a month of the support collected on their behalf (Kahn and Kamerman 1988). This indicates that the main purpose of the new enforcement system is to move families off welfare rather than improve their economic situation. Enforcement services also include locating absent parents, establishing paternity, setting and enforcing support obligations, and collecting payments (Garfinkel and McLanahan 1986; Glass 1990).

If all or most of the court-awarded child support is collected, the new American program has been calculated to save the government considerable amounts of money (Garfinkel and McLanahan 1986). Since the new legislation began, collections are increasing. Although there are differences among states, combined AFDC and non-AFDC collections compared to administration costs yielded $3.31 collected for every $1 spent in 1985. From a cost-benefit perspective, the program has been more successful for AFDC cases (Glass, 1990). Nevertheless, the average child support payment is only about U.S.$2,000 (Can. $2,553) per year and awards are still inconsistent (Maclean 1990).

A number of criticisms have been made of the U.S. reform in child support enforcement. Unmarried mothers tend to receive the least out of the reform and their cases are not viewed as cost-effective. Paternity can be difficult and expensive to establish, and unmarried fathers are assumed to be young, unstable, and unwilling (and often unable) to pay. The system is most effective for those who become eligible as a result of divorce proceedings (Nichols-Casebolt and Klawitter 1990).

The 1984 legislation has also been criticized for using guidelines rather than clearly standardizing the process for setting awards (Garfinkel and McLanahan 1986). In all models, variability is highest for upper-income families, particularly where attorneys are involved, which suggests that discretion is still present and influenced by legal representation. The equalization-of-standards-of-living model has not been accepted anywhere in the United States. The reason given by Garfinkel and Melli (1990) is that it would benefit the custodial parent (mother) and child to the disadvantage of the non-custodial parent (father). Aside from criticisms about various formulas, feminist concerns have also been expressed that the new program might force abusive fathers to remain involved with their children, possibly with traumatic consequences to both children and their mothers. In addition, conservative men have argued that public enforcement invades the privacy of fathers and children (Krause 1988).

Historically, U.S. social policy has followed a residual model, providing minimal assistance for those most in need (Lundstrom 1989). Recently, there has been a change in the social climate towards more social responsibility for children and a conviction that all parents are responsible for to their children (Fletcher 1989). In addition, lack of financial support from an absent parent is believed to be a major factor in child poverty (Kahn and Kamerman 1988). However, behind these values and the new child support enforcement rules lie the desire to keep public expenditures low by making parents instead of taxpayers finance child support (Glass 1990).

CONCLUSION

In the past two decades, all the countries in this study have experienced rising rates of marriage dissolution, female-headed households, and children born outside marriage. Yet not all governments have responded to these trends in the same way. Most have reformed their divorce laws to add the no-fault clause of 'marriage breakdown' to the existing grounds based on fault. Most jurisdictions have also amended laws to make them gender neutral and to equalize the division of matrimonial property, child custody, and child support obligations after divorce.

Despite legal changes, women in all the countries typically are granted or accept child custody after divorce. In several jurisdictions, there has been a slight trend towards joint legal custody, but this has meant joint decision making about the child's welfare rather than shared physical parenting. The advent of joint custody has generated considerable controversy and research in North America about how custody decisions are made and about the impact of various forms of custody on children and custodial mothers. Some men's groups have argued for more joint custody, suggesting that guidelines such as 'the tender years doctrine' and 'the best interests of the child' have really been based on invalid assumptions about women's superior abilities to care for young children. On the other hand, feminists are now arguing that the law should assume that custody will be granted to the parent who was the primary caregiver during marriage, unless that parent chooses otherwise. Joint custody, radical feminists argue, could encourage lower child support for mothers and interference by fathers, while mothers retain the same caregiving responsibilities. In many countries, divorced mothers tend to live in poverty unless the government provides transfer programs to counteract low or sporadic market incomes.

With the advent of no-fault divorce has come the notion of a 'clean break' – the idea that continued dependence on former husbands for financial support should not be encouraged for former wives. A number of researchers, however, have argued that a clean break is not always possible or appropriate when children are involved (Maclean 1990). Mothers who have stayed home with their children for many years are not always able to become self-supporting and are seldom able to make up lost income or earning power. Also, private child support enforcement laws have inadvertently placed the onus of support on mothers because the laws have been ineffective in forcing fathers to pay. Canada and the English-speaking countries are now moving towards limited public enforcement of child support awards. But, these policies seem to be motivated more by the goal of saving welfare money than of improving the living standards of women and their children.

In addition, Canada and several other countries have continued the practice of taxing custodial mothers on child support payments received, while providing separated and divorced fathers with a tax concession on payments made. One argument for this practice has been that a tax concession will encourage fathers to pay. Yet according to all the research, this incentive has not worked. Another argument for the practice has been that men have already paid tax on their income and that most income received is taxed by the government. Nevertheless, mother-led families typically experience high poverty rates, and the government is augmenting this problem by forcing them to pay tax on child support. It is also argued that since married fathers receive no tax concession for supporting their children, neither should divorced fathers. All parents should be expected to support their children and not be provided with a special reward if they do so. In Canada, this issue remains controversial and polarized along gender lines.

Canada and the English-speaking countries continue to focus on debt collection and the enforcement of parental responsibility, viewing unpaid child support as lost revenue. For example, Ontario's Ministry of Community and Social Services estimates that $355 million were lost through defaults on such payments from 1987 to 1993 (Mackie 1994). In the United States, where the trend is to invest public funds in pursuing private resources, fathers were estimated to owe U.S.$4 billion (Can. $5.1 billion) in unpaid child support, and more than half do not pay anything (Maclean 1990).

In contrast, the European governments have focused on assuring that children receive an adequate standard of living (Kahn and Kamerman 1988). Sweden, for example, exempts child support payments received by mothers from income tax and has established a system of social programs in which guaranteed advance payments are combined with other benefits to lone-parent households. In addition, state child support or advance maintenance is not diminished by the mother's earnings (Kindlund 1988). Sweden also maintains a centralized comprehensive system to locate absent parents, establish paternity, collect child support payments, and disburse advance maintenance. The proportion of lone mothers benefiting from some form of government transfer in Sweden is 98 per cent, while in the United States the figure is 57 per cent (Garfinkel and Wong 1990).

In the Scandinavian model, public responsibility for children has minimized the need for private care, there is a commitment to universal programs, and benefit levels are high. All children are treated equally and there is no concept of illegitimacy. By international standards, female participation in the labour force is high regardless of marital status or number of children. Family policies are all founded on the goal of providing full employment for those able to work (Kindlund 1988). Furthermore, human needs are perceived to be a collective rather than a market issue (Lundstrom 1989).

Most countries now require lone parents receiving government benefits to cooperate in the attempt to secure support from the non-custodial parent. Yet establishing paternity and securing awards for unmarried mothers is not as controversial outside the United States (ibid.). The fervour with which Americans focus on making fathers pay partly relates to the number of births outside marriage, which is higher in the United States than in most European countries except Scandinavia. However, it relates more to the American ideology that children are a private responsibility and that public funds should not be 'wasted' on supporting children. It also relates to the residual and punitive nature of American social policies.

The legal obligations on parents to support their children after divorce are quite unequivocal in the countries of this study. In France, for example, non-support of children is a crime, while in Sweden the obligation to support children extends even to step-parents. While there is still a vast gap between legal rhetoric and the social reality of enforcement procedures in most countries, one-parent households are most likely to remain above the poverty line in countries with advance-maintenance systems, universal child benefits, and employment equity policies for women.

9

The effectiveness of
family and social policies

The central question of this book has been why some countries are more generous than others in creating policies which seek to enhance the quality of family life or place a social value on child-rearing. In each chapter, it has been noted that the European countries have developed such policies earlier in the century and with more generosity than Canada and the English-speaking countries. The United States stands out as the only country which has never developed a universal family allowance or statutory maternity/parental benefits.

Chapter 1 looked at explanations of the uneven development of family policies. A combination of political factors influence family policy, including differences in political ideology, the structure of decision making, the strength of various lobby groups and their successful alliances, as well as some demographic and economic changes which serve as an impetus for coalitions and lobbying.

Pampel and Adams (1992) tried to understand why most industrialized countries provide more generous family benefits than the United States by comparing the level of family allowance expenditure in eighteen advanced industrialized countries from 1959 to 1986. They noted that the political context in individual nations shapes the effect population aging has on family allowance transfers. European nations, with older populations and lower fertility rates, tend to spend more on family benefits than does Canada or the United States. For example, as a percentage of gross domestic product in 1986, France spent 3 per cent while Canada spent 0.83 per cent and the United States spent 0 per cent on family allowances. Pampel and Adams concluded that the most decisive factors explaining why some countries have increased spending on family allowances while others have cut back relate to both political and demographic factors. These include a high percentage of the population over the age of sixty-five combined with certain institutional and political conditions, such as corporatism, class-based interest groups, and leftist party rule.

Wennemo (1992, 1994) noted that since the end of the Second World War, most industrialized nations have introduced universal family support, either to raise fertility or to increase the economic well-being of families. There have been two major types of universal support to families: cash benefits and tax reductions. After examining the policies of eighteen OECD countries, she concluded that cash benefit levels are influenced largely by national political trends. Countries with strong left-wing political movements, a history of left political parties in government, and political parties with strong religious affiliations participating in government tend to provide higher levels of cash benefits, but are less likely to support tax reductions. Wennemo found little or no correlation between fertility rates or gross domestic product and cash benefits. Countries delivering benefits through employment-based benefits or a social insurance system (such as France), she noted, provide higher cash benefits than other countries. Once a benefit system is introduced, she argued, it is seldom abolished, even if the political situation changes. As the present study shows, however, Canada, Australia, and Germany are exceptions to her generalization.

Wennemo (1992) also examined the development of tax reductions for families in the eighteen countries. She concluded that the level of gross domestic product per capita (but not economic growth), a high proportion of parents among voters, and the strength of religious parties had a weak positive effect on the development and level of tax allowances for families. Countries with an employment-based system and left-wing governments tend to provide lower levels of tax support for families because they choose to provide higher cash benefits. Wennemo's study also provides strong support for explanations that emphasize the importance of partisan politics in determining the course of family policy development.

Sweden has often been used as an example of a country which has developed strong social supports for families and employment equity for women. The family policy differences between Canada and Sweden can be explained by a combination of factors. In Sweden, the population has always been more homogeneous than in Canada. Women's labour was needed in the Swedish workforce, and married women entered the labour force in larger numbers in earlier decades. Furthermore, rates of divorce, unmarried parenthood, and one-parent families have been higher in Sweden for a longer period of time than in Canada. These social and demographic trends reinforced the demand for changes both in labour policies and in family policies.

Political structures and ideologies sharply differ in Canada and Sweden. Sweden has a central government and a long tradition of social democratic governments which have placed a strong emphasis on citizenship rights and social insurance. In addition, a larger percentage of the population is unionized, many middle-class employees among them, and there has been a long-term alliance between labour unions and the Social Democratic party. Furthermore, corporatism or the formal inclusion of unions, employers, and government in policy formation has provided labour with a stronger voice in policy. All these factors have led to more effective work and family policies initiated at an earlier date in Sweden (Boreham and Compston 1992).

The influences of alliances and political ideology are apparent in recent controversies about family policy in the United States. Despite high rates of female participation in the labour force in the United States, there are no statutory maternity benefits. In the lengthy debate over maternity and parental benefits, small business, the Chamber of Commerce, and conservative politicians formed a strong alliance against attempts to introduce federal statutory benefits, attempts supported by the (declining) union movement and feminists. The business lobby appealed to American values of individualism and non-intervention by government into employment practices. They argued that governments would have to raise taxes if such benefits were legislated and that taxes are already too high. (Although taxes in the United States are lower than in most of the countries in this study, Americans think they are overtaxed.) The alliance argued that if employers had to pay for parental leave, the added payroll costs would have a negative impact on the nation's economic productivity and global competitiveness. These arguments carried a great deal of weight with conservative politicians, who ensured that proposed federal legislation was 'watered down' to a requirement for *un*paid leave to be granted only by medium and large employers. Despite the fact that this legislation passed through Congress, it was vetoed by the U.S. president (which could not happen in Canada). It was not until a Democratic administration under President Clinton came into office that the legislation for unpaid leave was passed.

Because so much family-related legislation is under state jurisdiction in the United States, there is no strong precedent for national
legislation. In addition, the U.S. trade union movement is relatively
weak compared to those in the other countries in this study and has no
tradition of fighting for benefits for working women. Instead, unions
have tried to exclude women and part-time workers. As well, the U.S.
public has never voted a social democratic or left-wing government
into office but has fluctuated between the Republicans (conservative)
and the Democrats (less conservative).

In recent years, an effective alliance has developed between the political right and the 'moral right' or 'pro-family movement.' The U.S.
pro-family movement has supported fundamentalist Christian values
and the male-breadwinner family, but has opposed increased rights for
working women, public child care, sex education, legalized abortion,
family benefits to same-sex couples, and numerous other social policies
affecting family life (Abbott and Wallace 1992).

In terms of demographic factors influencing family policy, the average
age of the U.S. population is relatively low as a result of immigration
trends, and birth rates have remained relatively high. Consequently,
Americans have not been as concerned as Europeans about an aging
population and how to finance future social programs. In addition,
although the participation of women in the labour force is now high
compared to that in the other countries studied, until recently such
participation was largely restricted to working-class women. Consequently, many family benefits, such as child care and income support
programs, are targeted to low-income mothers, especially lone parents.

In many respects, Canada and the United States are similar with
respect to the development of family policies. Yet differences in the
history of social programs, the structure of government, the division of
powers, linguistic and cultural backgrounds, prevalent ideologies, and
the economic status of the two countries have resulted in a number of
differences between the family policies developed in Canada and those
in the United States.

FACTORS INFLUENCING FAMILY POLICY IN CANADA

Demographic influences

Canada has always relied on immigration to settle the land and provide
workers with the required skills. The fact that urbanization and indus-

trialization occurred later in Canada than in Europe delayed women's participation in the labour force and postponed the decline of birth rates. In addition, Canada (along with the United States) experienced a baby boom after the Second World War which kept the North American population relatively young (Beaujot 1990).

Conservative and patriarchal family values accompanied by relatively high birth rates continued until the early 1960s, especially in Quebec, giving Canada a younger population which was less concerned with financing future pension programs than most European nations. Even now, people aged sixty-five and over form a smaller percentage of the population in Canada than in most European countries. These factors have reduced the demand for family policy reform. However, in the past twenty-five years, birth rates have sharply declined, especially in Quebec. This has led to considerable public discussion about how to finance future public pensions, how to reform the health care system to make it more appropriate and affordable for the elderly of the future, and how to reform social services to accommodate an older population. Furthermore, the composition of the Canadian population has changed along with the composition of the typical family.

Economic and labour conditions

Canada's resource-based economy has always depended on foreign capital and markets, and many jobs have been seasonal and in primary industries (such as forestry, mining, and fishing). Before the Second World War, the concept prevailed of a 'family wage' paid to working men which was sufficient to support them and their dependants. As wages declined relative to the cost of living and more women entered the labour force, the concept of a family wage gradually was eroded. Wages are now supposed to be based on individual merit and seniority rather than family status, but real wages have been declining in recent years as a result of high unemployment rates, the growth of non-standard employment, and an increase in the cost of living.

Throughout the 1980s, Canada's unemployment rate has been higher than in all the other countries studied, including the United States. Yet unlike some European countries, neither Liberal nor Conservative Canadian governments have focused on full employment policies. Instead, they have concentrated their efforts on wage subsidies, retraining, temporary job creation, and income security programs (McBride 1987).

Although a globalized economy has necessitated new trade alliances,

Canada's Free Trade Agreement with the United States and the new North American Free Trade Agreement that includes Mexico may contribute to the decline of full-time jobs and the pressure to keep wages and benefits low in Canada. Entering a trade agreement with a much stronger trading partner could gradually pressure Canadian governments to 'harmonize' economic and social programs, especially those related to employment benefits. Although this convergence is not yet very apparent, it has already occurred in family benefits with the recent abolition of the universal family allowance and a reliance on tax credits (Banting 1993). Although European countries are subject to similar international economic trends, the growth of non-standard jobs has not reached the same proportions in some European countries as a result of government regulation and union opposition. Furthermore, the social safeguards for employees and their families built into the European Union provide more protection than Canadians receive.

Political structure and coalitions

In the *British North America Act* of 1867 which established Canada as a nation, jurisdiction was divided between the federal government and provincial governments. Despite several amendments to the Constitution and changes in the political and social climate over the years, family policy has remained a divided jurisdiction. Marriage law, child welfare legislation, the delivery and regulation of child care services, employment legislation affecting maternity and parental leave (but not benefits), the enforcement of support orders after divorce, education, the delivery of health care, and social assistance all reside under provincial jurisdiction. On the other hand, divorce law, most income security programs, income tax concessions (except in Quebec),[1] maternity and parental benefits, and services to Native people living on reserves[2] are under federal jurisdiction.

Because certain aspects of the Constitution have not been clarified and new policy issues have arisen with social and economic change, disputes over jurisdiction have typified Canadian social policy development. Added to this, Canada is a large country, relatively sparsely populated by culturally and racially diverse people from many different backgrounds, with two official languages, and two different systems of civil law.[3] Canada has always had a heterogeneous population and strong regional and cultural concerns, and these differences continue to grow.

Canada's political background as a colonial power and its established political structures influence decision making. The British parliamentary system has always overrepresented the interests of white middle- and upper-class males (Porter 1965), and continues to do so despite the growing multicultural nature of Canadian society and greater demands for the democratization of decision making. Family policies have, until recently, emphasized the nuclear family with a male breadwinner and family head, notwithstanding cultural variations, the growing presence of women in public life, and wide variations in lifestyles. Furthermore, self-reliance, individualism, and family privacy continue to be important values in Canadian law and policies.

Unlike Britain and Australia, Canada has never voted a left-wing government into power in Ottawa, but has essentially alternated between moderate Liberal and Conservative governments. Compared to the rates of unionization in Sweden or Australia, that in Canada has been relatively low (White 1993, 159), although it is much higher than in the United States. Furthermore, alliances between trade unions and left-wing political parties have never been as strong as in Australia or Britain, and they appear to be weakening rather than strengthening in Canada. Unlike Sweden and Australia, Canada has never had a legal avenue through which the voices of labour can be heard in policy decisions, apart from the vote, petitions to members of Parliament, and submissions to parliamentary committees.

While some regions and cultural groups are prosperous, others suffer from serious unemployment and underdevelopment. Cultural and language differences, as well as regional inequalities, are accompanied by varying ideas about which social programs are necessary and how they should be implemented. This diversity makes it difficult for any one point of view to have primacy in influencing government, especially when there are few formal structures through which citizens can express their views. While regions or advocacy groups are divided and argue about policy alternatives, the government may view lack of agreement as an opportunity to pursue its own agenda with minimal consultation.

From the 1920s until the 1970s, the political lobby for women's equality or improved family benefits was weak in Canada. Since the 1970s, however, feminist groups (especially the National Action Committee on the Status of Women [NAC], the Canadian Advisory Council on the Status of Women, and the Women's Legal Education and Action Fund [LEAF]) have developed more widespread support and have become politically sophisticated. At the same time, lesbian and gay rights groups have become an important political force in discussions about how

The effectiveness of family and social policies   339

'family' should be defined and who should be eligible for family benefits. The growing cultural heterogeneity of Canada has also encouraged stronger advocacy for policies which enhance the family life of all Canadians. At the same time, however, a strong lobby from western-based conservative groups, aligned with the fundamentalist Christian churches, continues to promote 'family values,' focusing on a 1950s-style family with a gendered division of labour.

Although these political forces are pressing for reform of family policy, there are structural barriers to change. Canadian policy development has been marked by jurisdictional disputes. Obtaining consensus from ten provinces and two territories, as well as Native peoples, can be time-consuming and difficult. Commitments to specific social programs, such as unemployment insurance, have become entrenched in the practices of employers as well as employees, and the reform of one program impacts on all others. In addition, the idea of change creates uncertainty and caution, especially when mistrust of politicians is as high as it is among Canadians.

The political barriers to changing policy can be illustrated by the 1988 attempt to reform child care funding in Canada, discussed in chapter 6. The federal government proposed to remove child care funding from the Canada Assistance Plan, in which the federal government matches provincial spending, with no spending ceiling set. The proposal was to establish a new funding arrangement under the *Canada Child Care Act*, in which more costs would be shared but a spending ceiling would be placed on federal contributions. The Conservative government which proposed the bill was under growing pressure to reduce government expenditures and balance the budget.

One problem with the proposed legislative change was that child care falls under provincial jurisdiction. The federal government therefore required the support of ten provinces and two territories in order to change the legislation, especially if it wanted to give the new program national objectives. Because child care services had developed unevenly and some provinces had been spending more money than others, a few provincial governments would have gained more money under the new plan while the more prosperous provinces (especially Ontario) would probably have lost if the new funding formula had become law. The federal government was expected to hear the concerns of various advocacy and cultural groups – including unions, child care advocacy groups, feminist groups, 'pro-family' anti-feminist groups, religious groups, and Native peoples' groups – before it changed the legislation. However, it had no legal requirement to amend legislation to incorporate the groups' concerns.

All groups which appeared before the parliamentary committee were opposed to aspects of the bill. For example, the governments of Ontario and Quebec were against the bill because they suspected it would lead to a reduction of federal money to support child care in their provinces, but Quebec also opposed any attempt to create national standards for child care or to 'attach strings' to the transfer. The Child Care Advocacy Association of Canada (formerly the Canadian Day Care Advocacy Association) opposed the transfer of any public money to for-profit day care and argued in favour of national stardards of care. The 'pro-family movement' wanted government support mainly for parents who care for their children at home, while the feminists and the trade unions wanted more subsidized child care spaces, public funding only for not-for-profit care, and better wages for day care workers.

None of these lobby groups was powerful enough to convince the federal Conservative government to amend the legislation. One reason was that the impetus for this bill had largely come from the day care lobby, feminist groups, and unions, but many Conservative members of Parliament were more influenced by the pro-family movement and provincial governments. Second, the bill was introduced just before an election call, indicating that the government may simply have wanted to appear reform-minded without passing the bill. Third, the bill was used in the dispute between the Senate and the House of Commons. While the Conservatives held the majority in the House of Commons, the Liberals held most seats in the Senate. At that time, the Senate was being portrayed by the Conservatives and many citizens as an appointed, unrepresentative, costly, and unnecessary structure of government. When the Senate appeared to be against the child care bill, an election was called, a step which automatically kills any bills not yet passed. Although the Conservative government blamed the Liberal Senate for killing the child care bill, after the Conservatives won the 1988 election, no new child care legislation was introduced.

New trends influencing family policy

Although reforming social policies is difficult in Canada, several trends have altered people's circumstances and motivated political organizing for reform. First, the fact that birth rates are declining and the population is aging has generated considerable discussion about financing future social programs. As in France and Sweden, this trend could lead to pressure from advocacy groups for governments to create policies which encourage child-bearing and/or more social support for child-rearing. The Quebec government has already responded to pressure from nationalists by introducing a wide range of family policies, including additional parental leave, more child care services, housing grants for young families, and cash incentives for each birth.

Second, international comparisons have indicated that child poverty rates are much higher in Canada than in most industrialized countries (except the United States). They have also shown that Canadians remain poor longer than most Europeans because tax and transfer programs are less effective in redistributing income. The risk of negative international publicity combined with encouragement from the United Nations could compel the Canadian government to improve Canada's record. Several parliamentary committees have already noted that if we continue to allow children to live in poverty, they are likely to develop social and psychological problems which will be costly to resolve in the future. A coalition of community and social service groups called Campaign 2000 is pressuring the government to keep its promise of eliminating child poverty by the year 2000. This advocacy group consists of eleven national partners (national groups representing food banks, day cares, seniors, child welfare workers, teachers, mental health associations, and others) and twenty community partners (Hubka 1992b).

The third societal change which could motivate policy reform is the relatively high rate of immigration from developing countries which is making Canadian society increasingly heterogeneous in culture, race, and religion. Cultural diversity has encouraged new ideas about what families should be and do, about the role of government in family life, and about what kinds of social programs are necessary and desirable. For example, increasing cultural diversity has required the immigration department to clarify the definition of 'family' and 'dependant.' In addition, academics, policy analysts, and the gay and lesbian community are placing greater pressure on governments to redefine 'families' to include the caring relationships among same-sex couples.

Fourth, as the cost of social programs rises, more people are questioning whether or not they are getting value for their tax dollars. Despite nation-wide concern about high unemployment in Canada, other concerns about interest charges on the deficit and the 'high' level of taxation are preoccupying politicians from all parties, and ordinary citizens as well. There is still widespread acceptance that government money should be spent on maintaining existing income security programs and services to needy people, and on reducing violence against women and children. But there is also a somewhat contradictory belief among Canadians that social programs should be reformed to move people off 'passive' assistance, such as welfare and unemployment insurance, and into the workforce. Arguments to this effect are gaining strength, even though unemployment rates remain higher in Canada than in other industrialized countries, and new permanent jobs have not yet been created. Without even comparing Canadian social spending or levels of taxation with European countries, Canadians nevertheless *believe* that their social programs are too costly and that taxes should be lower. In comparison to the United States, of course, Canada's income tax rates and social program spending look high, although they are not particularly high by European standards. This perception that Canadians are spending too much on social programs will continue to be a stumbling block for the development of new family policies.

One of the most significant trends for Canadian family policy is the entrance of mothers with preschool children into the paid labour force. This increase in participation rates coincided with growing inflation, the expansion of the number of jobs in the service sector, an increase in part-time work, the widespread use of birth control, the acceptance of more female students into universities, and the development of feminist ideologies. The increase in two-income families and sole-support mothers has generated the need for employment leave for family responsibilities (including maternity/parental leave and benefits), public child care services, and equal pay for work of comparable value. The increasing percentage of sole-support mothers and two-income families also has created the momentum for family law reform, including laws relating to divorce, the division of matrimonial property, child custody, and the calculation and enforcement of child and spousal support. These reforms further encouraged public discussion and debate about values, priorities, and policy options. In addition, family law reform has been the central forum of feminist critiques of social policy, which are beginning to have an impact on policy formulation in many countries.

FEMINIST CRITIQUES OF 'FAMILY VALUES' AND FAMILY POLICY

The difficulty of creating new family policies and reforming existing ones has been due to the diversity of family structures, varying opinions over entitlement, and concerns about the implications of change. Legislators in many countries have attempted to avoid certain controversies by focusing on income security, employment leave for family reasons, child health care, child protection, day care, and the enforcement of child support. In doing so, they have avoided such controversial issues as abortion, benefits for same-sex couples, wages for housewives, and, until recently, violence against women. Behind all family policies, however, lie unavoidable values issues relating to the definition of family, the relative value of domestic and paid work, and the role of government in regulating personal life or resolving work-family conflicts. Consensus on these issues has been difficult, especially in countries such as Canada with a history of cultural diversity, a tradition of individual rather than collective rights, and an ideology of the family as a private realm rather than a field for public concern and government activity.

In the past few years, numerous feminist scholars have critiqued existing family and social policies (including Abbott and Wallace 1992; Abramovitz 1989; Eichler 1988a, 1988b; Heitlinger 1993; Lewis 1993; McDaniel 1990; Pateman 1988, 1989; Sidel 1992; and Spakes 1991, to name only a few). Of course there have been differing opinions among feminist scholars and organizations. 'Liberal feminists' essentially have argued for equal opportunity and focused on obtaining a larger or fairer slice of the pie for women. This has meant the pursuit of equality before the law, equal access to higher education, and equal pay and promotional opportunities in the labour force. On the other hand, more 'radical feminists' and 'socialist feminists' have argued that women's biology and life experiences are different from men's and that we should be emphasizing equality of *outcome* rather than opportunity. Because legal, political, and economic institutions have been designed by men to suit their interests and needs, the argument goes, equal access will not lead to equal outcomes for women. Women need to infiltrate and redesign laws, programs, and practices to focus more on consensus, cooperation, human needs, and environmental protection and less on hierarchy, competition, and profit making.

Despite ideological differences among feminist groups, there is some agreement that 'the family' should *not* be the unit of analysis in social policies. Before social policies are created or amended, the potential impact on individuals needs to be understood, as policy cannot be assumed to be experienced in the same way by all family members (Eichler 1988a). Variations in family structure suggest that a policy will rarely be good or bad for all family structures, yet legislators must create policies which treat all structures equally. Moreover, accurate knowledge about family life is essential before existing policies are amended or new ones created (Eichler 1988b; McDaniel 1990; Spakes 1991).

Both liberal and more radical feminists have argued that in order to become more responsive to the realities of women's lives, social policies should work towards greater gender equality within families, workplaces, and society (McDaniel 1990). Yet radical feminists have perceived this goal as problematic and have further argued that citizenship has historically been defined in the male image. Liberal democracy assumes the active participation of all citizens, and social policy assumes that labour force participation, full-time work, and the ability to achieve a certain wage level are the norm. A system based on such assumptions fails to acknowledge that women's labour force participation is truncated by lack of access to 'good' jobs, lack of child care, and programs which have defined them as men's 'dependants' (Pateman 1989).

The type of family policy a country adopts reflects its ideas about the role of women in families and the labour force (Spakes 1992). For example, the United States uses job-related and income-tested benefits to create a dual system of welfare based on labour force attachment, family status, and social status. Those who are not firmly attached to the labour force or not married are in a disadvantaged economic position, which partly explains the extent of child and family poverty in the United States.

Feminists have also argued that family policies should not assume that families are private and separate from the economy. Rather, policies should acknowledge that raising a family is work, particularly for women. In addition, employees seldom are able to leave behind all of their family concerns when they enter the factory or office. In particular, mothers with young children or employees experiencing family crises such as illness, problems with child care, marital separation, family violence, concerns about members with disabilities, or the death of a family member need some public acknowledgment, both from employers and from the law, of the importance of these responsibilities.

Family policies should have the eradication of family violence as one of their central goals. Although child welfare policies have always dealt with child abuse and child neglect, the law has not always protected women within families. Only in recent decades have laws eliminated a husband's immunity from charges of sexually assaulting his wife. Only in recent decades have police begun to take more seriously verbal threats and sexual and physical violence by men against their intimate partners. The impetus for this change has originated from the feminist movement and more specifically from women who have organized temporary shelters for the 'survivors' of violence against women and children.

Feminists have also argued that policies must acknowledge that family change is ongoing and closely related to other societal trends (McDaniel 1990). Earlier chapters have shown how the entrance into the labour force by married women and mothers has been related to structural changes in the economy, the availability of certain kinds of jobs, the structure of family benefits, the taxation system, laws relating to contraception, employment, divorce, and child support, and altered perceptions about women's personal ambitions and needs. Family policies, therefore, cannot be amended without also considering reform to taxation and labour market policies and without attempting to integrate economic and social policies from different levels of government.

Sweden's family policy is part of a wider labour market policy. Scandinavian policies are often favourably contrasted to American social policies; yet problems remain for women. Although Swedish social policies have enabled women both to reproduce and to participate in the workforce, they have not led to complete equality. Discrimination and segregation remain both within the labour force and in the larger society. For example, in the decision-making processes of corporatist arrangements such as labour unions, women and their interests are not specifically represented. Furthermore, women are even more underrepresented than they were thirty or forty years ago (Bergqvist 1991). Many more mothers than fathers work part time, take leave for family reasons, and receive low wages (Widerberg 1990). As well, controversies continue in Sweden about whether children are being neglected or left too much in the care of non-family members as a result of policies promoting full employment. Encouraging women to accept the 'male model' of employment may result in negative consequences for children.

In many countries (especially Australia, Britain, Canada, and the United States), debates over family values have tended to be politically and socially conservative, influenced by the 'moral right' (Abbott and Wallace 1992). U.S. family policies tend to grant more rights to individuals living within the traditional nuclear family and imply that reproduction is a necessary part of a woman's existence. Feminists have argued that proposals to restore the traditional family of male breadwinner and female homemaker are doomed to failure because recent changes in family life have been influenced by labour market, economic, and ideological trends beyond the control of easy policy manipulation

(Eichler 1988a). Radical feminists have argued that the movement for a national family policy in the United States is not only based on the traditional family model, but has largely been shaped by the judicial system, which follows social tradition and promotes stability rather than change (Spakes 1991). Some feminists are also concerned that an increasing amount of family and social policy in North America is being made through court decisions rather than legislation. However, since both the courts and the legislatures have been designed and numerically dominated by men, it is not clear that governments represent the interests of women more effectively than the courts.

Although recent policies in many countries are written to be 'gender neutral,' some feminists have argued that they are nevertheless biased towards men's interests, occupational patterns, or ways of thinking. For example, Okin (1989) critiqued modern political theories and argued that theories of justice have generally ignored gender issues. Concepts such as tradition, understanding, and fairness in political theory tend to be interpreted from an exclusively male perspective. She argued that the historical exclusion of family from the political domain is inappropriate given that family structures are created by political decisions. In addition, the division of labour within gender-structured families raises barriers for women in other spheres of society. Okin described the 'gender-structured' family as an unequal power situation for women in which, if they work outside the home, they usually receive a lower wage and no value is granted to their work within the home. This places them in a vulnerable situation within marriage and in the event of separation or divorce. Similarly, British feminists have argued that the basic tenets of the welfare state are more relevant to men's values, such as rationality, individuality, and citizenship. Gender-neutral policies ignore that women usually become part of society and of the welfare state not as individuals, but as the mothers, wives, and daughters of men (Pateman 1988).

Okin (1989) argued that a 'just society' must move away from gender-based roles and promote equal sharing by men and women of paid and unpaid work and of productive and reproductive labour. She recommended policies with these goals in mind, such as parental leave that is distinct from pregnancy/childbirth leave and available to both parents, equal splitting of wages between partners, and, in the event of a divorce or separation, fairer custody and support arrangements which produce the same standard of living in the homes of both parents.

Most feminists agree that a woman's position in the market economy influences the division of labour and her bargaining power within her household. Similarly, a woman's position in her household affects earnings and potential earnings in the labour force. Using data from the Luxembourg Income Study from 1979 to 1986, Hobson (1990) demonstrated that countries with a fairly equal distribution of income between the richest and poorest families nevertheless often achieve little equality between partners, whether married or cohabiting. Economic dependency among women still exists in Sweden, for example, although it is considerably less than in other European and North American countries.

Other feminist scholars have illustrated the implicit biases against women within existing policies. For example, Naples (1991) analysed the U.S. *Family Support Act* of 1988, using a socialist feminist analysis. She argued that there are five ways in which the state contributes to women's oppression and impoverishment through this act. First, the legislation uses gender-neutral language which masks the different life experiences of men and women. Second, the legislation stigmatizes certain household structures that do not conform to societal norms, especially lone-parent families. Third, it attempts to control the work of reproduction by forcing unmarried mothers to live with their parents, pushing mothers with young children into the labour force even when they do not have adequate child care, and disallowing tax deductions for child care provided by extended family members. Fourth, women are encouraged to remain in paid and unpaid caregiving roles that are devalued both economically and ideologically. Finally, Naples argued that this legislation and other U.S. social policies fragment social life by undermining families' and women's control over reproduction. At the same time, they do not provide necessary social supports, such as affordable child care services or minimum wages high enough to enable parents to support their families.

Nuccio and Sands (1992) used post-modern feminist deconstruction to uncover male biases in theories of the feminization of poverty. They critiqued themes and statements of leading theorists and U.S. policy makers, while questioning the currently proposed solution to the feminization of poverty: marriage for women and the creation and preservation of well-paid jobs for men. Nuccio and Sands provided an example of a 'phallacy' of poverty by examining the case of the 1991 proposal by Wisconsin Governor Thompson that would cap welfare payments to unwed teenage mothers and pay larger grants to those who marry. Women who marry would receive an extra U.S.$80 (Can. $102) per month, and the couple could earn up to U.S.$14,500 (Can. $18,509) from paid employment without having their welfare payments reduced. The Wisconsin proposal offered an exemplar of policy based on what Abramovitz called the 'family ethic' (Abramovitz 1989), because women can switch their dependence from the welfare state to marriage. In this proposal, marriage was used to rectify social, political, and economic problems, while intruding on women's personal affairs and encouraging an economic motive for marriage.

By using deconstruction, Nuccio and Sands illustrated how theories of poverty blame mother-led families for their poverty. They argued that it is not the erosion of the two-parent family that is impoverishing women and their children, but gender, race, and class discrimination. Women's impoverishment is supported by a patriarchal economic system which allows a gap between the wages of men and women, an inadequate welfare system, and an unreliable system of child support (Nuccio and Sands 1992).

Recent social policy in the United States has been influenced by the fear that two-parent, middle-class families are being eroded by divorce, cohabitation, gay couples, donor insemination, and surrogate parenting (Abramovitz 1992). In addition to the financial concerns related to female-headed households and teenage pregnancies, there are still class and patriarchal biases underlying American family and welfare policies. Recent cuts to welfare spending illustrate the harsh treatment of poor women and their families. Abramovitz criticized the 1988 *Family Support Act* for forcing mothers into a welfare-to-work program called JOBS without adequate child care and without wages enabling them to support their families. She maintained that promoting marriage as a way out of poverty for welfare mothers (as in Wisconsin's 'wedfare') discriminates in favour of the two-parent family. The notion that poor families need to be more self-sufficient, she claimed, ignores government mismanagement of finances and promotes the idea of poverty as an individual responsibility. An example of the precarious position of poor women is the effort to control women's behaviour by advocating the use of Norplant, a long-lasting birth control device. The New Right in the United States is using family policy to further its goals of reduced government intervention in private life and lower taxes (ibid.).

Clearly, social policy is influenced by decision-making structures, social values, and political alliances, and contains both implicit and explicit prescriptions about behaviour. While men and women need equal opportunity to obtain an education, find work, and support their families, their different biology and life experiences require some special policies and programs if women are to enjoy the same autonomy as men (Bacchi 1990, 1991; Meehan 1993). As well, work needs to be redefined to include such unpaid work as child-rearing and domestic labour, and to acknowledge the family responsibilities of paid workers who are also family members.

Through the persistent lobbying efforts of feminists and social welfare reformers, policy makers in Canada and the English-speaking countries are becoming more aware of the links between an individual's family responsibilities and status in the labour force. In addition, they are becoming more concerned about the physical and emotional safety of women and children at home. Although we no longer assume that employees have no family responsibilities or that what takes place at home is of no relevance to governments or employers, there has been little consensus on how best to resolve these difficult policy issues.

GOVERNMENT RESPONSES TO THE RISING COSTS OF SOCIAL PROGRAMS

From 1950 to 1975, many industrialized countries initiated major improvements to social security programs. Since the mid-1970s, however, national economies have declined and increasing concern has been expressed by employers, investors, and the political right about the rising costs of social programs (Mishra 1990). With this economic slow-down has come a questioning of the basic principles underlying the welfare state and, in many countries, a return to more conservative notions about individual and family responsibility.

Although the costs of social programs have increased in all the countries of our study since the Second World War, productivity has also increased. Nevertheless, most governments have felt increasing pressure to rationalize services and to curb social benefits. While some governments have ignored these pressures and maintained programs, others have responded by privatizing the delivery of services, rejecting universality, means-testing benefits, introducing user fees or increased premiums, and emphasizing economics in program evaluations (R. Morris 1988).

Privatization of services has been a prevalent response to rising costs in the United States and Britain. Some programs that were previously subsidized, provided, or funded by governments are now expected to be provided or funded by the private sector, which could include both non-government organizations and families. In some cases, governments have contracted out services such as job training to private educational organizations or home inspections for adoption to private child welfare agencies or professionals. In the United States, child care services were largely privatized under the Reagan administration by providing employer subsidies for workplace child care (Kamerman and Kahn 1989a). Deinstitutionalization of chronic care patients has led to greater emphasis on home care in Britain and North America, which assumes that some family member (usually a woman) is at home to provide daily care. Increasingly, adult women work in the labour force and cannot leave their jobs to care for frail elderly, chronically ill, or disabled family members. Also, women who provide or manage care for their elderly parents may still have children at home and could be caught between the responsibilities of caring for two generations. Conservative governments have emphasized the importance of families as providers of care and economic support without acknowledging these dilemmas, and have shifted to them the burden of delivering services previously offered by government. In this way, family values and family policy have been used to save or rationalize government resources.

In addition, some governments have decided that they cannot afford universal benefits in certain realms. For example, the Canadian government converted the former family allowance from a universal benefit to an income-tested tax benefit in 1993, arguing that universalism was no longer affordable or politically acceptable. Yet universal family allowances provide the message that child-bearing and child-rearing are socially and economically important for governments, not simply something couples or individuals do for themselves. Targeting family benefits, implies that governments have an interest in reproduction only when families are poor.

Another government response to rising costs has been to tighten the eligibility qualifications for family benefits. This could involve transforming universal benefits to income-tested benefits, as in the 1988 change to family allowance in Australia. Or it could involve changing from income-tested benefits to means-tested ones, which are more rigorous. Because means tests involve assets as well as income, recipients may be forced to exhaust all their savings before they may apply for government assistance, with the result that their ability to respond to crises without government assistance is eroded (Sherraden 1991). Another way in which eligibility has been tightened is by increasing the number of weeks worked before an employee is entitled to maternity benefits or unemployment insurance. In Sweden, the wage replacement rate was recently reduced from 90 to 80 per cent for parental benefits, but only after a year of receiving benefits. By Canadian standards,

Swedish parental benefits are still very generous, and the basic philosophy remains intact that governments should support childbirth and infant care from public funds.

The introduction of user fees or increased premiums in some jurisdictions shifts the funding of services from government to individuals or employers. For example, unemployment insurance premiums were raised by the Conservative government in Canada in 1990 (although they were reduced again by the Liberal government in 1994). Hospital user fees were made illegal by the *Canada Health Act* in 1984, yet a decade later they continue to be debated as a solution to the rising costs of health care. In Alberta, user fees were introduced in 1994 for public kindergarten, and in Britain, user fees have been added to some health services (Mishra 1990).

Finally, government reviews of the costs and benefits of social programs have emphasized cost reductions over the benefits for clients. Canada has been reviewing all social programs since 1994. The Unemployment Insurance Program especially has been under scrutiny, partly because it costs about $20 billion per year, but also because it is viewed as a 'passive' program which encourages dependence on government benefits. Although governments always say that evaluations are designed to make programs more efficient, most reviews appear to be motivated by a desire to reduce expenditures which are perceived as too high (C. Walker 1993).

Not all governments have felt the necessity to cut social programs, however, and benefit levels have been maintained in most of the countries studied. Countries such as Sweden have concentrated on high employment and high tax rates in order to afford social programs, and child benefits have increased substantially in Sweden over the past ten years. Parental leave has been extended in all the European countries studied, and child care services have been expanded in most. Although concerns about the rising costs of social programs have led to minor cutbacks in some areas, the welfare state remains relatively intact in the European countries (Mishra 1990; C. Jones 1993). Indeed, some family benefits and services seem to have been expanded as governments are pressured for programs to resolve work-family conflicts or address declining birth rates.

COMPARISON WITH DEVELOPING COUNTRIES

In comparison to programs in developing nations, the social programs in the industrialized countries studied appear very generous. Many developing countries have no social security systems at all, which means no social assistance benefits, no contributory social insurance programs such as unemployment insurance or health insurance, no government pensions, no worker's compensation, no family allowances, and often no income tax system. In these countries, the government's inability to raise sufficient tax money to develop such programs may be due to widespread poverty or the lack of wage labour. In other cases, the government may not be stable enough to enforce income taxes, establish long-term programs, or develop political consensus, or may allocate a disproportionate amount of government revenue to military expenses because of civil war or an external threat. Furthermore, those who lobby for human rights, fair wages, or social programs may be ignored or prosecuted. Where such conditions prevail, protection from poverty remains the concern of individuals, extended families, communities, and religious or other voluntary organizations.

In countries where social welfare benefits are not provided by the government, the rich set aside money for future crises, purchase private insurance, invest their money in other countries in case of political trouble at home, and hire private doctors, nurses, and nannies to whom they pay relatively low wages. In developing countries, the gap between the rich and the poor tends to be wider than in industrialized countries, especially if there is no income tax or only a small one. The poor, who cannot afford to purchase private benefits or hire help, tend to experience more nutrition problems, more illness and disability, higher infant and maternal mortality rates, and lower life expectancies. In developing countries, children from low-income families are expected to leave school early to help support their families, and even if compulsory education laws exist, they are difficult to enforce. Unlike industrialized countries, developing nations are often concerned about high fertility and over-population. Higher levels of industrialization and urbanization, greater numbers of women in the formal workforce, and more fully developed public social services tend to be correlated with lower fertility, longer life expectancy, a higher standard of living, and a smaller gap between the rich and poor.

We can argue that some industrialized countries, such as Sweden, offer better programs for families than do other industrialized countries such as the United States. Yet we cannot forget that the United States may appear generous from the point of view of poor people who come from countries with no social safety net at all. Nevertheless, this should not prevent us from comparing the effectiveness of social programs across industrialized societies or working to improve programs that do not fulfil their own goals.

THE EFFECTIVENESS OF FAMILY POLICY

There are many ways in which this study could measure the effectiveness of family policy. One measure would be the extent to which it reduces child poverty, which has been a concern of the Canadian government for several years. A second measure is how well policies maintain good health and prevent premature death among infants, children, and pregnant women. A third measure is whether or not people readily embrace marriage, child-bearing, and child-rearing, as opposed to non-family lifestyles. A fourth measure is the extent to which policies reduce conflicts between earning a living and raising children. Although another measure of effectiveness might be how well women and children are protected from violence, comparative statistics are not available. Therefore, only the first four measures will be discussed.

Reducing child and family poverty

The first measure of effectiveness is the easiest to discuss because extensive comparative data have already been gathered and analysed using the Luxembourg Income Study data base. Furthermore, Canadian parliamentary studies have focused on this issue, and Parliament made a resolution in 1989 to abolish child poverty by the year 2000. In chapter 3, it was demonstrated that in Canada child poverty rates are high compared to those in the European countries in this study and that poor families with children stay in poverty longer. While European government transfer programs have been instrumental in counteracting the market forces which keep families poor, North American programs have been less effective.

Although poverty among elderly people has been reduced in the past decade through improvements to Canadian pension policies, there is growing government concern about child poverty, especially in lone-parent households (Canada, House of Commons 1991). As the cost of living rises and more families require two earners, lone-parent families become disadvantaged relative to two-parent families. One-parent families headed by women are often cited as those most vulnerable to poverty and most in need of new policy solutions in all the countries of this study (McLanahan, Casper, and Sorenson 1992).

Unlike some of the countries studied (such as Australia and France), Canada provides no special benefit for one-parent families that is not available to all poor families, except the Equivalent to Married Credit (EMC). EMC was fourteen times more valuable than the non-refundable Child Tax Credit before it was abolished. EMC is non-refundable, however, which means that it provides no assistance to the poorest lone-parent families who are below the tax-paying threshold. Lone parents in Canada may also be eligible for subsidized child care, if they are employed, attending school full time, or are enrolled in government-sponsored job training programs. In addition, parents who do not work for pay or who are marginally employed may be eligible for provincial social assistance programs.

The incomes of many families, however, have not kept up with the cost of living because social assistance rates and minimum wages are low, as discussed in chapter 3. Neither is indexed to the rising cost of living (National Council of Welfare 1990b, 25–6). Furthermore, recent changes in the labour force which perpetuate high unemployment and create more non-standard jobs than ongoing full-time positions threaten family security (National Forum on Family Security 1993).

Women, as the heads of about 80 per cent of lone-parent families in Canada (Devereaux 1990, 136), tend to be clustered in low-paying positions which are non-unionized and lack promotional possibilities. For example, only 29 per cent of employed women were unionized compared to 38 per cent of men in 1989 (White 1993, 159). Women often work part time in order to care for their children or because full-time positions are unavailable. For a number of reasons, including movement in and out of the labour force for child-bearing and child-rearing, the percentage of women earning the minimum wage is almost twice that of men (ibid.). From 1975 until 1989, however, minimum wages as a percentage of average earnings declined substantially in all jurisdictions of Canada (National Council of Welfare 1990b). Despite legislation promoting equity, women still earn about two-thirds of men's wages.

The new Child Tax Benefit and existing child care subsidies in Canada are targeted to low-income and middle-income families, eroding the principle that child-bearing and child-rearing have social value and contribute to the nation's future development. In addition, some needy people have had their benefits reduced in recent years. For example, provincial welfare reforms have sometimes reclassified who is 'employable,' and lone mothers who would have been considered better off at home caring for their children a decade ago are now pushed into the labour force. Yet neither permanent jobs nor child care services are always available to assist these women to enter or re-enter the labour force (Lightman 1991b).

Job-training programs have not been effective in assisting people to become self-supporting because they so often train unemployed people for jobs that do not exist, for jobs that are disappearing, or for short-term low-paid work (Pal 1987; Evans 1993). In addition, programs have been based on the assumption that finding a job is a matter of personal choice, requiring only the acquisition of skills or a show of initiative. Employment programs have not always taken account of labour force trends or discriminatory practices against certain categories of workers, such as visible minorities, women, or persons with disabilities.

Policy researchers have reiterated that people who train for new jobs, find work, and move off social assistance need some guarantee that they can live on their incomes and that their jobs will continue. After all, procedures for getting back on welfare or unemployment insurance are time-consuming and bureaucratically complex (Riches 1991; Schragge 1990). In some jurisdictions, social benefits granted to welfare recipients (such as subsidized health insurance, dental care, or child care services) are not available to the working poor. This has made welfare recipients cautious about accepting short-term employment.

Although government income-security programs expanded in the 1960s and 1970s, the real value of some benefits has been eroded during the 1980s and 1990s by changes in eligibility rules, rising living costs, and declining real wages. Changes in the structure of the labour force have reduced the number of full-time unionized jobs, and minimum wages have been allowed to decline relative to average wages (National Council of Welfare 1990b). Governments have not prevented employers from creating part-time temporary positions, nor have they required the same prorated pay and benefits as for full-time positions. Women have been attracted to these part-time positions largely because of child care problems, which governments have done little to resolve.

There have been attempts to bring existing family-related policies more into line with family and labour force trends, but competing advocacy groups have sometimes prevented the introduction of new legislation or reduced its effectiveness. For example, the well-financed and conservative pro-family movement has aligned with employers' groups against feminist organizations and unions. Furthermore, in an attempt to save money, to appease employers and the conservative right, and to acquire immediate and politically acceptable solutions, governments have focused on training lone mothers and making divorced fathers pay for child support rather than improving employment conditions or creating permanent jobs.

Rising divorce rates and family law reform have also increased poverty among divorced women and their children (M.E. Morton 1988). Changes to family law have replaced alimony with temporary spousal support or lump-sum payments, yet women seldom have the same earning capacity as men. In addition, the lack of enforcement of child support has led to considerable public concern about defaulting. Recent legislation, such as Ontario's, should substantially improve the incomes of lone mothers who depend on court-awarded child support payments, but it does nothing to raise social assistance levels or minimum wages. Ontario's pay equity law also appears to be a step in the right direction towards reducing labour force inequality for working women, yet it is unlikely to contribute to rapid or dramatic changes.

Although there are problems with all of our social programs, they are certainly more comprehensive, especially for children and women, than they used to be prior to the Second World War. Definitions of 'family' have been broadened to include one-parent families, cohabiting couples, and, in some cases, lesbian and gay couples. Some real attempts have been made to consider gender equality, such as laws which require equal access to divorce and child custody, equal division of matrimonial property after divorce, the enforcement of court-awarded child support, equal pay for work of comparable value, and the provision of maternity benefits and child care services.

Yet Canadian social policies have not been as effective as those in the European countries of this study in reducing child poverty. Canadian policies have been more effective in diminishing poverty among elderly people with an attachment to the labour force than among young families or those outside the labour force (Battle 1988). Programs for seniors are much more developed than programs for children, and much more federal money is invested in pension programs than in child benefits. There are three types of federal benefits for elderly people in Canada: a universal[4] pension (Old Age Security), two targeted benefits (Spouse's Allowance and Guaranteed Income Supplement), and one work-related pension (Canada/Quebec Pension Plan). Yet, we have maintained only one federal benefit for children which is targeted to middle- and low-income families. However, two work-related benefits may be available in certain circumstances: the child care deduction and maternity/parental benefits. Young families not regularly attached to the labour force must rely on the Child Tax Benefit, their own resources, or provincial social assistance programs.

Canada's policies and programs for families with dependent children are not as generous as those in the European countries studied, although Canada compares favourably to the United States. Neither have Canadian programs been as effective as European ones in keeping children out of poverty, as was shown in chapter 3.

Child and maternal health

Although this study has glossed over policies related to child and maternal health, health can be used as a measure of the effectiveness of family policies. In most industrialized countries, infant mortality and maternal death rates have declined since the 1930s as a result of general improvements in living standards, sanitation, nutrition, and health care. The United Nations gathers international statistics both on maternal death rates (caused by deliveries and complications of pregnancy and childbirth) and on infant mortality. Although many factors could affect these death rates, such as maternal diet, exercise, lifestyle, birthing practices, and personal and professional health care, these death rates provide one rough indication of how Canada compares with other countries in terms of the health and social services available to pregnant women and infants.

As Table 9.1 indicates, Canada's infant, child, and maternal death rates are moderate compared to those in the other countries studied. Yet because there are few variations in the statistics, it is difficult to draw conclusions from these data. However, we can see that Sweden has the lowest and the United States the highest rates of infant mortality, while Sweden also has the lowest rates of child mortality and maternal deaths. Although the statistics themselves offer no reasons for the variations, the research documented throughout this book offers some clues. The high infant mortality rate in the United States could be attributed to lack of public health insurance and preventive services for pregnant women and families, poor nutritional habits, and widespread poverty, especially among blacks and lone-mother families.

Although indicators of child and maternal mortality are moderate in Canada compared to the other countries, we should add that the rates for Native people are extremely high. In 1985, when the infant mortality rate for Canada was 7.9, the rate for Registered Indians was 17.9 and for Inuit, 28.0 per 1,000 live births (Canada, Health and Welfare 1988, 7).

TABLE 9.1
Infant, child, and maternal death rates in eight countries, 1989–1990

Country	Infant mortality rate (under 1 year)*		Deaths of children (1–4 years)**		Maternal death rate (per 100,000 live births)
	Male	Female	Male	Female	
Australia	9.2	7.3	0.5	0.3	4.9
Canada	8.2	5.4	0.4	0.4	4.1
France	8.6	6.4	0.5	0.3	8.5
West Germany	8.9	6.5	0.5	0.4	7.3
Netherlands	8.2	6.2	0.4	0.4	5.3
Sweden	6.7	5.0	0.3	0.3	5.2
United Kingdom	9.1	7.0	0.4	0.3	8.1
United States	11.1	9.0	0.5	0.4	8.4

* Per 1,000 live births
** Per 1,000 children aged 1–4
SOURCE: United Nations 1992, 340–9, 354–7.

These high infant mortality rates for Native people can be attributed to extreme poverty, the high cost of food in the North, lack of health services, substandard accommodation, high rates of substance abuse and poor health, and high rates of suicide and homicide.

Birthing practices differ in the countries of this study and may also shed some light on child and maternal health issues. The experience of childbirth may vary with women's physical and emotional health, the presence or absence of the father, social conditions surrounding the birthing process, and income security and health programs supporting children. In the past few decades, North American health care reformers have argued that childbirth has become unnecessarily medicalized. The assumption is prevalent that births 'delivered' by physicians in hospitals are the only safe ones; but research from Canada, the United States, Britain, and the Netherlands does not support this assumption (Jezioranski 1987, 92).

Prior to the 1920s, most North American births used to take place at home with the assistance of midwives or experienced married women; but now most occur in hospitals. Numerous medical interventions are typically used, including anaesthetics, episiotomies, and Caesarean sections. Some doctors and nurses argue that sterile conditions and medical interventions are necessary for the safety of mother and child; but other people argue that in the United States, where medical interventions are highest, infant mortality rates are also the highest, and that Canadian rates used to be higher than those in some industrialized countries which allow home births and midwives, and where doctors perform fewer Caesareans. However, in recent years Canadian infant mortality rates have declined (M. Baker 1990a).

By the end of the 1950s, childbirth in Canada was generally viewed as an unnatural event or a form of illness requiring hospitalization and medical intervention. Husbands were not allowed in the labour room, and drugs, forceps, and surgery were commonly used in childbirth. With the increasing costs of liability insurance, a desire for regular hours, exclusion from hospital privileges, and technological advances in obstetrics, many family practitioners have stopped delivering babies and allowed specialists to take over. The prevalent use of specialists often means that there is little continuity in maternal health care (Baker 1990a).

Although midwifery is still practised throughout the world in lay form and is the predominant form of birth care, it can now be legally practised in most industrialized countries only if licensed or certified (Jezioranski 1987, 105). Several European countries (most notably the Netherlands, England, Sweden, and Finland) rely extensively on midwives in hospital and home births. In the Netherlands, policy makers concluded early in this century that home births should be encouraged because they were safer than hospitalization. Since then, midwifery has been the predominant form of birth care, and midwives attend deliveries without the supervision of physicians. In the Netherlands, 30 per cent of births take place at home, compared to 1 per cent in Britain, Canada, and the United States, and Dutch general practitioners and midwives both deliver at home. As in other countries, however, the trend in the Netherlands has been towards hospital births assisted by physicians (Torres and Reich 1989, 406).

The Dutch health system, which is based on private insurance, covers the payment for prenatal care, delivery, and postnatal care only if provided by a midwife – not by a physician – as long as a midwife practises in the community and there are no medical indications for specialized care. This policy reduces the cost of childbirth considerably. Health insurance also covers the cost of nursing aides, which makes home birth easier for women (ibid. 407–10).

In the United Kingdom, the centralized planning process of the National Health Service helped facilitate the movement from home to institutional births, and ensured that the lobbying efforts of the medical profession had a major and rapid impact on the location of childbirth (ibid. 409). Although midwives are still the senior persons present at three-quarters of all British births, the scope for their clinical judgment narrowed significantly once birth moved to the hospital setting. Consequently, technological intervention increased considerably during the 1960s and 1970s. At the same time, however, the maternity rights and feminist movements grew in strength and raised objections to much of this intervention (Weitz 1987, 82).

Where midwives are allowed to practise in North America, they generally attend normal low-risk births and refer cases with complications to medical practitioners. The fact that physicians and doctors deal with a greater proportion of high-risk births means that rates of neonatal mortality (up to four weeks after birth) are higher for hospital/physician births. Research which controls for risk factors, however, reveals that mortality rates are comparable for both groups of practitioners or lower for midwife-attended births than for obstetrician care (Jezioranski 1987, 100).

North American physicians have been criticized in recent years for performing Caesarean births which are medically unnecessary. In fact, North American hospitals have the highest rate of Caesarean sections in the world, and the American rate jumped to 25 per cent in 1988 from about 5 per cent in the 1960s. A study by California researchers, published in 1989 in the *New England Journal of Medicine*, found that wealthy women in the United States are nearly twice as likely to undergo a Caesarean section than poor women, regardless of age, race, or complications during pregnancy. Caesareans are particularly likely to be performed in the United States by private physicians rather than physicians working in public hospitals or with patients covered by government health care plans (*Globe and Mail*, 27 July 1989). This implies that some physicians perform Caesareans on women who can afford to pay for this operation, whether or not they really need it (M. Baker 1990a).

In Canada, the rate for Caesarean sections is about seventeen per one hundred births, with a high rate of about twenty in Ontario and Quebec, compared to an average of fifteen in European countries (Hossie 1985). The Netherlands, with an above-average percentage of home births attended by midwives, had a rate of six per hundred live births in 1985 (Torres and Reich 1989). In comparison with vaginal births, Caesareans are associated with higher rates of maternal and foetal mortality, higher rates of infection, and the need for continued medical attention. The extensive use of foetal heart monitors may compound the apparent need for medical intervention during labour because studies suggest that electronic foetal monitors are not accurate predictors of foetal stress. False stress indications increase the likelihood of Caesarean sections, which result in greater mortality and morbidity. These monitors also increase the risk of perforations of the uterus and placenta and lacerations to the foetus (U.S. Dept of HEW 1979).

Midwives tend to rely less on technological monitoring, drugs, and other interventions. There is also evidence that midwives' clients require less postpartum care and recovery time (Fooks and Gardner 1986, 7). But more important for childbirth policy, midwives cost public insurance programs less money than physicians, and for this reason some juris-dictions in Canada, such as Ontario and Quebec, have recently brought them back into the health care system.

This cursory overview of child and reproductive health measures does not lead to many conclusions about the effectiveness of family policy. Using infant and maternal death rates yields few differences among the industrialized countries, although Sweden compares favour-ably and the United States less so. With respect to some birthing prac-tices, it appears as though childbirth is more medicalized in Canada and the United States than in some of the other countries. Furthermore, comparisons of health care costs indicate that Canada's system is rela-tively expensive compared to other public health insurance systems although less expensive than the private system in the United States where millions of people are not covered by any insurance (Fulton 1994). In summary, differences in poverty rates and in child welfare systems show up in death rates, but only between countries at the policy extremes (that is between the United States and Sweden). A closer look at child and maternal health statistics for Native people in Canada, however, makes Canada look more like a developing nation and less like the other industrialized countries.

Fertility and family policy[5]

Several of the countries studied have experienced periods of intense concern about declining fertility. From the 1930s through the 1960s, both France and Sweden developed policies designed to prevent fertil-ity rates from falling farther. Their policies differed considerably, how-ever. Sweden viewed gender equality and universal participation in the labour force as the desired route and developed policies to enable fami-lies better to combine paid work and child-rearing. On the other hand, France focused on pronatalist family policies which encouraged parents to produce more children by providing larger allowances for each child in the family. In addition, by providing a child-rearing allowance, France encouraged mothers with preschool children to stay at home or work part time.

In Canada, Quebec is the only province which has expressed public concern about declining fertility, although similar declines have been experienced by other provinces, such as Ontario. Quebec's definition of the problem has been influenced by the extent and rapidity of the decline in birth rates, as well as by nationalist concerns that the French population, language, culture, and political power could dwindle within Canada as Quebec birth rates fall. In the 1950s, Quebec birth rates were among the highest in the Western world, but they plummeted from the mid-1960s until the late 1980s.

Despite the political attention paid to the low birth rate in Quebec (M. Baker 1994b), the crude birth rate (CBR) is not particularly low in comparison to some European countries. For example, in Belgium, Czechoslovakia, Denmark, East Germany, Finland, Hungary, Italy, the Netherlands, Norway, Spain, Sweden, Switzerland, and the United Kingdom, CBRs are lower than in both Canada overall and Quebec in particular (Statistics Canada 1988, 71). But the CBR is affected by the older average age of European populations. If we use the total fertility rate as a measure (or the average number of births per woman), the Quebec rate is lower than the rate in Canada overall, the United States, and most European countries (Le Bourdais and Marcil-Gratton 1994).

Although most industrialized countries experienced fertility rates below the replacement level of 2.1 children per woman during the 1980s and 1990s, not all governments have responded similarly to this trend. After political pressure from Quebec nationalists (mostly men), the Quebec government developed a comprehensive set of family policies, a government structure to implement and enforce these policies, expanded parental leave and day care spaces, interest-free housing loans for first-time home owners with dependent children, and cash bonuses for parents at childbirth (ibid.). In addition, the Quebec government has attempted to use immigration to delay population decline, although there has been some backlash in response to this policy. For example, the Quebec government announced its intention in 1991 to increase the number of immigrants until the proportion reaches 25 per cent of the Canadian intake. After public opposition from Quebec nationalists, unions, and the unemployed, the proposed immigration target was reduced, allegedly to improve services for existing immigrants (M. Baker 1994b).

From 1987 to 1988, the total fertility rate increased in several Canadian provinces. In Quebec, in 1988, there was a 10 per cent increase in first-order fertility (first-born children in a family) for women of all age groups which did not occur in other provinces (Dumas 1990). Yet the 1988 fertility rate of third-born children was lower in Quebec than in all other provinces, despite the large baby bonus for families with three or more children,[6] and it is falling once again in both Quebec and the rest of Canada (La Novara 1993, 13).

Eastern Europe and the Soviet Union have also experienced an imbalance of the sex ratio and subsequent low marriage and birth rates since the Second World War. Also contributing to low birth rates in these countries, however, were socialist policies derived from a view of the family as an institution contributing to women's oppression and the perpetuation of economic inequality. In the past three decades, concern about declining birth rates and the aging population led Eastern European governments to develop a series of pronatalist policies which were both repressive and supportive of women and families. The repressive policies included restrictions on birth control and abortion, taxes for childless adults, and restrictions on divorce. Romania, Bulgaria, and Hungary severely restricted the use of abortion, and Romania taxed childless adults over twenty-five years of age who held jobs (Lodh 1987). (The ban on birth control, abortion, and divorce in Romania was lifted only with the overthrow of its president, Nicolae Ceausescu, in December 1989.) The supportive policies included generous paid and unpaid maternity and parental leave, state-funded child care services, and special bonuses at the birth of each child.

It is difficult to assess the effectiveness of pronatalist policies in raising the birth rate. Some policies are too recent to have influenced long-term trends, and others are so indirect that it is difficult to say that changes in fertility have been caused by them rather than other factors. In Romania, for example, fertility rates rose in the 1970s but then declined to a point lower than before the pronatalist policies (Romaniuc 1984). In countries with a severe housing shortage, giving priority to parents with children when allocating apartments has served as a relatively successful pronatalist policy (Lodh 1987), but not one likely to be politically acceptable in a democracy such as Canada.

In most countries, inducements to reproduce have been typically insufficient to counter reasons or conditions that favour limiting fertility. Pronatalist policies appear to be more successful in influencing the timing rather than the number of births (Beaujot 1990). Couples or women who have postponed child-bearing may decide to reproduce when financial incentives are in place, but will probably not have more children than they initially planned.

Decisions to reproduce depend on too many other factors, including the economic climate, the availability of jobs, educational plans, opportunities to combine family and work, accommodation costs, the availability of contraception and abortion, and prevailing attitudes about women's role and the desirability of family life. In other words, the decision not to have children is a complex one and cannot be easily altered by policy makers (Eichler 1988a).

According to some Quebec demographers, declining population is politically dangerous because it leads to a reduction in economic productivity, consumption, investment and employment (Mathews 1984; Henripin 1989). This proposition is debatable, however, as other studies indicate that there was no correlation between economic well-being and population growth for OECD countries between the years 1960 to 1985 (Fortin 1989; S.P. Johnson 1987). In addition, Lasserre and colleagues (1988) concluded that increasing the birth rate will not necessarily improve the economic well-being of Canadians (as measured by the gross domestic product). Other changes, however – such as policies that encourage more women to enter the labour force or that require employers to pay women and visible minorities higher wages – would be more effective in improving economic well-being. Falling birth rates and an aging population will probably raise the per capita cost of future programs, especially if reforms are not made to the delivery of medical services and public pensions. Nevertheless, European countries such as Sweden and West Germany have preserved their social programs, economic productivity, and cultural identity despite falling birth rates and an aging population (ibid.).

High fertility rates tend to be associated with developing countries, along with high rates of infant mortality and maternal death, national and family poverty, low levels of female education, low rates of participation in the labour force for women, and increased levels of housework and child care for mothers (S.P. Johnson 1987), Considering these correlations, fertility decline could easily be viewed as a positive demographic trend. In developing countries, a lower rate of population increase is associated with modernization and is often a national goal. Furthermore, having fewer children provides more space and privacy for each family member, possibly more parental attention for each child, a higher per capita income, more money to spend on the children's education, and more time for women to work to raise the household income (Eichler 1988a).

Because children are still perceived to be the responsibility of women, women are less likely than men to view declining birth rates as a 'social problem' and more likely to view declining fertility as an advantage for women (Messier 1985; Le Bourdais and Marcil-Gratton 1994). Furthermore, policies which try to encourage increased fertility might be ineffective, but could also be detrimental to employed women unless they were accompanied by more public support for child-rearing, more subsidized child care spaces, and employment reforms.

If more women reproduce and some have larger families, they will need to take more time off work in the initial stages of their occupational lives. Without courses to up-grade skills or other measures to compensate for lost work time, such absences could reduce any gains that women have made in employment equity. High divorce rates and the fact that mothers usually acquire custody of children make it difficult for lone mothers to support more children, as so many are now living in poverty. Unless women's wages improve, more fathers accept custody of the children, or non-custodial fathers contribute higher child support payments, more women will find themselves on social assistance if they have larger families (M. Baker 1994b).

Increasing birth rates and larger families could also lead to public demand for higher wages to enable parents to support more dependants. Considering that children are so expensive to raise, most people limit reproduction during economic hard times. Although birth rates are likely to decline during a climate of economic restraint, declining fertility has encouraged pronatalist and pro-family sentiments among some conservative sectors of the population. Governments have been known to use pro-family ideologies either to encourage family members to care for each other with minimal government intervention or to withdraw costly government services which were once provided free, most often by women (Glossop 1986).

In Quebec, however, the falling birth rate has been used by nationalists as a rallying point for action to increase Quebec's power within the Canadian federation and to prevent further erosion of the French culture and language – even though increased population does not guarantee the retention of language or culture. Immigration and increasing multiculturalism could substantially alter a society which has been relatively homogeneous in the past, and there is no guarantee that francophones, rather than anglophones or 'allophones,'[7] will be the ones to produce larger families after the introduction of birth incentives. Birth incentives could also expand non-traditional family forms in a way not anticipated by the government – leading to an increase in lone mothers raising children without partners, or more lesbian parents, for example. Incentives to raise the birth rate without providing ongoing financial assistance throughout the children's lives could place more pressure on government-funded social services by encouraging women or couples to have more children than they can afford to raise. In other words, providing financial incentives alone will neither raise the birth rate nor protect French language and culture in Quebec (M. Baker 1994b).

Declining fertility is correlated with a number of factors: rising levels of female education, increased participation in the labour force by women, postponed marriage, improved contraception, postponed pregnancies, an increase in the value placed on individualism, self-development, and occupational success, and higher costs of accommodation and child care. Policies designed to raise the birth rate artificially, without adequately dealing with these other social, ideological, and economic factors, are unlikely to be effective.

In a democracy such as Canada, it is not politically feasible to influence fertility behaviour through coercive measures, even though they have proven slightly more effective than family support programs. The experience of France and Sweden indicates that making the social environment more conducive to child-rearing by providing more generous family allowances, maternity benefits, and child care services will not necessarily *increase* the fertility rate. As we saw in chapter 2, the total fertility rates are similar in Sweden and the United States, despite almost opposite family policies. However, supportive programs for families undoubtedly improve the lives of parents (especially mothers) raising children and might slow the decline of birth rates. Furthermore, supportive programs would improve opportunities for women to combine work and family life more effectively and to make greater gains towards employment equality (Hantrais 1994).

Reducing work-family conflicts

In contrast to the situation a generation ago, most mothers with preschool and school-aged children are now in the Canadian workforce. Juggling paid work and family responsibilities has proven difficult and has become a major source of stress for women (G. Lowe 1989) as well as of lost productivity for employers (Duxbury and Higgins 1994). Part of the problem is the lack of public support for combining work and family life.

Although employed women in Canada can theoretically receive maternity leave and unemployment insurance benefits when they give birth, not all pregnant women in the workforce actually draw benefits for the full period. The eligibility requirements have been relatively strict (dependent upon length of residence in the province and continuous employment with the same employer for a specified period) and exclude those who are self-employed. Some women return to work early because of work-related or financial pressures, while others are ineligible for benefits.

Prior to the amendment to the *Unemployment Insurance Act* in 1990, the lack of parental leave implied that children were the responsibility of women rather than of both parents. Despite the amendment, however, there is still little or no statutory employment leave for family illness. Furthermore, employers' groups such as the Canadian Manufacturers' Association and the Canadian Chamber of Commerce opposed the expansion of parental leave or leave for family responsibilities in the later 1980s (Townson 1988, 13). Female employees often use their vacation or sick leave to care for sick children or disabled family members (MacBride-King 1990; Duxbury and Higgins 1994). In addition, high quality and affordable child care services are often unavailable, especially for children in rural areas, infants, and children of shift workers. Lack of employer and government attention to the family responsibilities of employees implies that reproduction and child-raising are merely personal or family concerns rather than an issue for the entire society to resolve.

The structure of the labour force and the organizations in which most women work were originally designed by men for male workers. Even workplaces with a majority of female workers tend to hire a disproportionate number of men for managerial positions. Consequently, work organizations tend to be more supportive of men's career patterns, values, and needs than of women's. Employers have historically made concessions to the family needs of women workers only when their labour was highly valued, such as in times of labour shortage or when employers have invested considerable money in training employees. Women are still expected to adjust to an employment mentality which implies that work is the only important factor in employees' lives and that another family member is at home dealing with children and household responsibilities.

Women will be unlikely to want to bear and raise more children without substantial changes to government benefits and to the structure of work. Improvements such as increased maternity benefits, longer parental leave, publicly funded child care services, longer vacations, and more extensive leave for family illness or emergencies may create an environment more conducive to child-bearing and family life. Nevertheless, as the case of Sweden indicates, even when statutory benefits are in place, men are less likely than women to take advantage of them. Employees who take the maximum leave are viewed as lacking full commitment to their jobs.

Reinforcing the concept that children are of social value appears to be an essential first step in reducing work-family conflicts. But conflicts between work and family cannot be solved easily through a few changes to increase employment leave for family responsibilities. Policies to assist young families and individuals to be self-supporting need to focus on the following issues:

1. Subsidized child care services should be extended to all preschool children rather than being targeted to children from low-income families.
2. Public kindergarten should be available to four-year-olds in all provinces on a non-compulsory basis.
3. The child care expenses deduction should be converted into a refundable credit to help lower-income earners.
4. Leave provisions should be legislated for family responsibilities, including family emergencies and illness.
5. The replacement level of maternity and parental benefits should be raised to approximate previous earnings more closely (and the level in European countries).
6. The fact that women's average wages are lower than men's needs to be more widely acknowledged, and the income gap needs to be diminished through pro-active legislation which is not based on complaints.
7. We need to ensure that minimum wages and social assistance rates keep pace with the rising cost of living.
8. Legislation is needed to equalize and prorate the wages and benefits associated with full-time and part-time work.

The consequences of ignoring the fact that employees also have families are potentially serious not only for women, but also for labour force productivity, to the future birth rate, and children's well-being.

CONCLUSION

Family policy differs in its intent and focus in the eight industrialized countries of this study. Except in Quebec, family policy in Canada has been largely implicit and inconsistent. In addition, so many jurisdictions are involved that the different levels of government are not always working in concert. For example, while Quebec has been elaborating its family policy in the past few years to make benefits more generous for all parents, the federal government has been targeting benefits to lower-income families.

Typically, discussions of 'family values' in North America have originated from the political right and have had a conservative influence in social policy, promoting family autonomy and lack of government intervention. Those who promote family values tend to support the patriarchal family rather than egalitarian ideals or alternative lifestyles. For example, the pro-family movement uses the concept of family values in expressing disapproval for legalized abortion, contraception, sex education, benefits for same-sex couples, and public child care services. Furthermore, governments have used the concept of 'home care,' with all the accompanying connotations of nurturing by loved ones, as a strategy to reduce public expenditures by asking women to care for family members without remuneration. In general, North American feminists have viewed appeals to 'family values' as emanating from the 'moral right' and as promoting policies that are contrary to their interests.

Feminist researchers have cautioned governments to create not a family policy *per se*, but rather social policies which view the individual rather than 'the family' as the unit of society. They have argued in favour of policies that respect differences in the social and economic experiences of women and men, as well as policies which treat all family configurations equally.

At the same time, feminist researchers have argued that using gender-neutral language in policy may be necessary for the preservation of some individual rights, but must not mask the different social realities of men and women or confuse policy initiatives. For example, using the concept of 'custodial parent' makes it sound as though either mother or father typically cares for children after divorce. In fact, mothers are granted custody by Canadian courts in 73 per cent of cases and fathers in only 13 per cent of cases. Female custodial parents often experience additional problems of wage and promotional discrimination, sexual harassment, poverty, and inappropriate expectations based on the ideology of motherhood which male custodial parents are not subject to.

Another example of how gender-neutral language could blur policy initiatives is the concept of the 'lone-parent family.' There are substantial differences between lone fathers and lone mothers, as well as among lone-parent families created through widowhood, separation and divorce, or birth outside marriage. Focusing on gender differences reveals that women are the heads of 80 per cent of these families and that, as breadwinners, they tend to earn incomes considerably lower than men's when they enter the labour force. Furthermore, lone mothers are less likely than lone fathers to enter the labour force full time because of domestic responsibilities which are viewed as 'women's work.' Consequently, lone fathers are far less likely than lone mothers to work part time, to stay home with their children, to depend on welfare, and to experience poverty.

If we focus on the gendered nature of family poverty, we develop some different solutions than if we regard it as a gender-neutral problem. Potential solutions could include providing subsidized child care services for all preschool children, to enable mothers to enter the labour force. We should also enforce equal pay for work of comparable value, fight labour force segregation based on gender, broaden eligibility for maternity benefits, and legislate prorated wages and benefits for part-time work. Regardless of the gender of parents, solutions to family poverty would also include raising minimum wages, fighting racial discrimination, making workplaces accessible for those with special needs, and, most importantly, creating permanent jobs.

Many researchers have highlighted the fact that those who are the most likely to be poor are women who are unmarried, mothers, and homemakers, as compared to women who are married, childless, and employed (McLanahan, Casper, and Sorenson 1992). The most vulnerable to poverty are those who experience motherhood outside marriage, especially in Canada and the English-speaking countries of this study. If a social security system defines women as men's dependants or bases eligibility on participation in the labour force, as is the case in these countries, then women without men and women without jobs are going to be especially disadvantaged.

This suggests that social programs should not base eligibility on continuing participation in the labour force unless the government also maintains a policy of full employment and is heavily involved in creating jobs and regulating the labour market. This also means that specialized programs are needed to deal with maternity and early child care. Some governments provide an allowance for parents (mothers) caring for preschool children at home, and these programs are sometimes financed through payroll taxes. In other words, employers, employees, and governments are sharing the cost of extended parental leave rather than placing the burden on women and their families.

Neither should programs implicitly encourage poor women to marry or recouple in order to exit from social assistance. Although 'wedfare' programs may temporarily save government money, they can push women into abusive, unhappy, or temporary relationships which could be detrimental for them and their children. Instead of viewing mother-led families as a 'social problem,' we should question *why* women can seldom support themselves and their children outside marriage without government assistance. The answer would lead back to the gendered division of labour in both paid and unpaid work. Solutions include questioning the segregation of paid work, why women's wages tend to be lower than men's, why so many mothers are forced to work part time, and, most important, why work is undervalued when women perform it.

Throughout this book, it has been emphasized that family policy is part of social and economic policy and should not be viewed as a separate entity. The development of family policies and programs, as part of 'the welfare state,' is influenced by political ideologies, the structure of decision making, political advocacy and alliances, the legal system, the taxation system, and labour market trends and strategies. Therefore, any changes to family policy necessarily involve changes to other economic and social policies. For example, child poverty cannot be resolved solely by improving child benefits. Children are poor because their parents are unemployed, underemployed, or already working as unpaid caregivers. Therefore, labour market policies are central, unemployment must be reduced, and 'good jobs' need to be encouraged (National Council of Welfare 1990a). In addition, the taxation system needs to be reformed to assist families with children, instead of overtaxing parents and undertaxing corporate profits and wealthier individuals.

This study has found that nations with a tradition of social democracy, corporatist decision making, long-term concerns about fertility decline, and well-developed social welfare systems tend also to create policies which assist parents to raise their children and help employees manage family responsibilities. Some countries provide support to enable both parents to enter and remain in the labour force (Sweden), while others offer maximum options for children and the family unit (France). The lowest levels of child poverty and the highest levels of gender equality, however, are found in Sweden rather than in France. This suggests that child poverty can be reduced through policies of full employment which especially assist women to gain employment equality with men. At the same time, employers and governments must recognize that women employees in particular need public resources to reduce conflicts between earning a living and caring for dependants.

Because only women gestate and give birth, and because women have historically been the family caregivers and kinkeepers, policies must acknowledge that men and women often experience reality differently. Given equal opportunities to enter higher education and the labour market, women will continue to be presented with and to accept different options and responsibilities throughout their lives. Unless policies are tailored for women's unique experiences, women will become increasingly disadvantaged over time, especially if they marry and raise children. In countries where women have a higher level of representation in policy-making positions (Sweden and the Netherlands), policies are more likely to safeguard women's interests.

In comparing Canada with the seven other countries, I noted that the Canadian government and several provincial governments have emphasized the importance of family as the basic institution in society. Politicians have argued that children should be viewed as a future resource and that we must preserve this resource by eradicating child poverty, child abuse, and child neglect. Governments across the country have reformed family law to ensure equal responsibility by mothers and fathers for child custody and support after divorce. Yet they have not spent much effort or money on improving the child welfare system, eradicating violence against women, or raising the incomes of poor families.

In 1993, Canada abolished the universal family allowance, although it had been allowed to decline in value for years. Yet the countries with the lowest child poverty rates have retained universality and continue to pay higher child allowances than we ever did. Canada's maternity benefits have strict eligibility requirements and replace less than 60 per cent of previous wages, as compared to 80 to 100 per cent in the European countries. Our child care services are subsidized only for low-income parents, but a shortage of subsidized spaces makes it difficult for these parents to benefit from the policy. Furthermore, many parents above the eligibility income also need government assistance with child care.

The federal government allows middle- and higher-income parents to deduct a portion of child care expenses from income tax if they have official receipts, but forces them to locate these services themselves. Yet we know that lack of affordable child care keeps some parents out of the workforce and on welfare, while for others, it reduces their employment productivity and promotional opportunities.

In most Canadian provinces, enforcement procedures for child support have left the onus and cost on custodial mothers, and have offered them little assistance in locating the children's father and securing payment. Yet we know that most lone mothers cannot live independently of social assistance without regular payments from the children's father. In Sweden and several other countries, child support is guaranteed by the government and later retrieved by a central agency from the non-residential parent. Although our governments are talking about introducing a similar system, only a few provinces have implemented such procedures. Because enforcement of child support is under provincial jurisdiction, the federal government cannot create a national system or force the provinces to create their own.

Canada's child welfare systems tend to be reactive to complaints and overburdened with cases of child abuse. Most clients are living in poverty, and many are lone mothers trying to care for their children with minimal support from fathers or governments. Some of these mothers are victims of abuse themselves, but child welfare systems in some provinces are mandated to deal only with children rather than with the entire family. Even when the entire family is the concern of the agency, scarce resources often limit intervention. Many European countries provide community-based preventive services, including regular health and psychological check-ups, an extensive system of visiting homemakers and surrogate parents, state-subsidized child care, generous child allowances, subsidized housing, and holiday homes for the poor. Although we know that these services are effective in reducing family crises and poverty, Canadians have been unwilling to pay for them in higher taxes or by shifting spending priorities.

In comparison with the European countries in this study, Canada appears to provide a rather chilly climate for child-rearing and family life. We have argued that policy differences between Canada and the European countries (especially Sweden and France) have been caused by a combination of political factors which have been influenced by demographic and economic changes. We have never voted a social democratic or left-wing party into office at the federal level, and Canadian governments have been relatively conservative. The trade union movement has been weak and has not created an effective alliance with any political party that has won a federal election. Our political structures, especially federalism and the division of powers between federal and provincial government, have not encouraged rapid policy change. Instead, they have led to disputes, protracted negotiations, and only limited reforms. Our decision-making structures have also excluded the voices of many interest groups, including those of the working classes, cultural minorities, and women.

Canada has been divided by regional, language, and cultural issues, so that finding consensus on social policy issues has been challenging. Historically, women have not been as involved in Canadian political decision making as they have in other countries (such as the Netherlands and Sweden). Only now that women have become more involved in Canadian public life, including the labour force, unions, and government, have policy options for child care, family leave, and child support enforcement been discussed seriously in a public forum. Individualism has been emphasized in our laws, and we have downplayed group rights and social responsibility. Like our neighbours in the United States, we have been unwilling to pay taxes as high as Europeans have been paying in return for better social services (although our income taxes are higher than in the United States).

Demographic trends have also helped to explain the lack of explicit family policy in Canada. After the Second World War, Canada experienced a baby boom that did not occur in Europe, postponing the population decline experienced overseas. In addition, our population has been kept young through continual immigration, while Europe has undergone considerable emigration, especially among young people. This meant that advocacy groups did not form in Canada as they did in Europe to push for policies to encourage child-bearing and family formation.

Changes are apparent in Canada, however, which have led to increased political pressure to reform family policies. Women's participation in the labour force has grown, especially among mothers with young children. Numerous lobby groups have formed to advocate extensions to parental leave and the development of statutory leave for family responsibilities, among them the National Action Committee on the Status of Women, the federal and provincial advisory councils on the status of women, and trade unions. Advocacy groups, especially the coalition of provincial organizations called the Child Care Advocacy

Association of Canada, have also pressured the government for improved child care facilities. These groups have increased government awareness of the need to alleviate some of the conflicts between earning a living and raising children, and have experienced some success in changing policies.

A larger percentage of women now graduate from universities and have entered those professions which influence policy decisions, such as politics, economics, law, policy research, and government administration. This development has provided articulate leadership for the feminist movement, which organized a national coalition called the National Action Committee on the Status of Women (NAC). NAC has undertaken strenuous political lobbying over the past decade on a wide variety of issues, and has been moderately successful in having its views accepted in policy decisions. In addition, the legal advocacy organization called Women's Legal Education and Action Fund (LEAF) has been very active in fighting feminist causes in court and attempting to use the *Canadian Charter of Rights and Freedoms* to further women's interests. At the same time, however, the conservative pro-family movement (especially REAL Women of Canada) and the fathers' rights movement have also been effective in their lobbying efforts against feminist causes.

The birth rate has been declining for years, and at least one provincial government, lobbied by Quebec nationalists, has responded with more government supports for families raising children. In addition, poverty among children and within lone-mother families is now costing provincial governments considerable amounts of money, placing additional political pressure on all levels of government to improve or cut income security programs.

Although advocacy groups are becoming more powerful and politically sophisticated, the pressures are strong from employers' groups and the political right to reduce government spending. We have a long way to go before we reach the level of social spending in Sweden, and a long way to go before we reach the level of family benefits and services in Sweden and France. First, we need to believe that parents make a contribution to the nation by having and raising children. Perhaps this will not happen until our birth rates further decline and children truly become a scarce resource.

Notes

CHAPTER 1 State intervention in family life

1 Terrance Hunsley, from the School of Policy Studies at Queen's University, was my collaborator on this project, which was generously funded by National Welfare Grants.
2 By 'standardized' I mean positions covered by labour standards or legislation. These are usually full-time, full-year positions.
3 A family is defined as 'poor' if family equivalent gross income is less than 50 per cent of median equivalent gross income for the country. Median equivalent gross income is family gross income divided by the OECD equivalence scale which assigns the first adult in the family a value of 1, each additional adult a value of 0.7, and each additional child a value of 0.5.
4 I am grateful to Anna Michetti for helping me with the background research for this section. An earlier version of this section is contained in a portion of chapter 10 in *Canada's Changing Families: Challenges to Public Policy*, edited by Maureen Baker and published by the Vanier Institute of the Family, 1994.
5 In the 1988 election, the New Democratic party won 43 seats in Parliament while the Conservative party won 169. After the 1993 election, the NDP was left with 9 seats while the Conservatives retained only 2.
6 From 1984 to 1990, I worked as a senior researcher on parliamentary committees and experienced first-hand the non-binding nature of submissions from the public.
7 Unless otherwise indicated, the population statistics are taken from: United Nations, *The World's Women, 1970–1990: Trends and Statistics* (New York: United Nations 1991), 22, 67; *The Canadian Global Almanac, 1992* (Toronto:

Global Press 1992); and Doris Anderson, *The Unfinished Revolution* (Toronto: Doubleday Canada 1991).

8 Excluding persons living on Indian reserves
9 Excluding Northern Ireland

CHAPTER 2   Changing family trends

1 Dependency ratios are rough calculations of the 'dependent' portion of the population compared with the 'working' population, based on assumptions about labour force participation. They are usually calculated as the population considered to be economically dependent because of their age (children and retirees) as a ratio of the population considered to be in the labour force because of their age (18–64). These ratios generally do not look at whether or not these people *actually are* in the labour force.

CHAPTER 3   Poverty, labour markets, and social assistance

1 The Luxembourg Income Study (LIS) uses a relative measure of poverty: the percentage of families who live on less than 50 per cent of the country's median income after taxes and adjusted for family size.
2 The two main committees were the Senate Standing Committee on Social Affairs, Science and Technology and the House of Commons Committee on Health and Welfare, Social Affairs, Seniors and the Status of Women, which established a Sub-Committee on Poverty in 1989–90.
3 This report was written for the Senate committee by Dr Joan Vance from the Research Branch, Library of Parliament.
4 The committee was chaired by Toronto MP Barbara Greene.
5 Especially vocal were members of the Fraser Institute, a right-wing think-tank in British Columbia.
6 At the time this manuscript was completed, the 1991 LIS data were not yet available.
7 Social spending includes spending on health care, unemployment insurance, family transfers, disability pensions and services, and old-age pensions. Education is excluded from this figure.
8 Food banks are private organizations which offer food to low-income people who have insufficient funds (even with government assistance) to purchase food.
9 The exceptions are the job search allowance (JSA) and the family allowance (which is income-tested).
10 Health and Human Services

11 The maximum rent assistance was about A.$72 (or Can. $66) for one or two children, and about A.$83 (or Can. $75) for three or more children (Perry 1991).

12 Under the income test applying to maintenance income, entitlement is reduced by one-half of the amount of maintenance in excess of a 'free area' of A.$15 (or about Can. $14) per week plus A.$5 (Can. $4.54) per week for each of the second and subsequent children. Under the test applying to other income, entitlement is reduced by one-half of the amount of such income in excess of the 'free area' of A.$52 (Can. $47) per week plus A.$12 (Can. $11) a week for each of the second and subsequent children.

13 The amount paid in 1992 was A.$53 (Can. $48) or A.$77 (Can. $70) a fortnight per child if under thirteen, A.$77.30 (Can. $70.19) if the child was thirteen to fifteen, and A.$68.00 (Can. $61.74) if the child was sixteen to twenty-four.

14 For lone parents with one child, the income limit is net DM 23,700 (Can. $18,913) per year (for each extra child it is raised DM 4,200 or Can. $3,352) and if a person exceeds the limit, the benefit is reduced by DM 40 (Can. $32) per month for each DM 1,200 (Can. $958) over the limit.

15 If it exceeds an exempt amount of DM 150 (Can. $120) plus DM 70 (Can. $56) per dependent person each week

16 Fl 425 (Can. $303.88) per month up to a maximum payment level of Fl 350 (Can. $250.25) per month

17 Some examples of the personal allowances in 1989–90 are:
   • lone parent over eighteen – £34.90/wk (Can. $68);
   • couple (at least one over eighteen) – £58.40/wk (Can. $115);
   • dependent child (rates vary from £11.75/wk [Can. $23] to £27.40/wk [Can. $54] according to the child's age).

18 Before the introduction of the poll tax in 1989, the Family Expenditure Survey (FES) showed the full level of weekly rent and rates assistance to be £25.93 (Can. $51) in 1988. The average level of housing benefit paid to Income Support recipients was £20.11 (Can. $40) in 1988.

19 The Child Benefit is worth £7.25 (Can. $14) per week for each child, while the One Parent Benefit is worth an additional £5.20 (Can. $10) per week for one child.

20 The limit is usually U.S.$1,500 (or Can. $1,915) with home equity excluded.

21 Or U.S.$3,000 (Can. $3,830) if one member is over sixty

CHAPTER 4   Child allowances and family tax concessions

1 This chapter is a revised version of a paper by Maureen Baker, Terrance

Hunsley, and Anna Michetti prepared for the Sixth Conference on Social Welfare Policy in St John's Newfoundland, 27–30 June 1993.

2 The exchange rate used was based on an average for 1991.

3 The *Report on Social Security for Canada* was prepared by the Advisory Committee on Reconstruction, House of Commons, Special Committee on Social Security, under the direction of Leonard Marsh from McGill University, and was submitted to Parliament in 1943. It contained an outline of existing social security provisions, how they could be improved and extended, and the principles governing the planning of social security in Canada (Guest 1985).

4 Until 1949, immigrant families waited for three years before being eligible for the FA.

5 In 1993, after the Baker (1994) article was written but before it was published, the amount was raised from $7,500 to $8,000 for the third child.

6 Except residents of Quebec, who file on a separate provincial government form

7 Swedish payroll taxes are 33 per cent of payroll but are paid entirely by employers rather than employees.

8 A form of social organization in which key economic, social, and political decisions are made by governments in consultation and negotiation with business corporations, trade unions, professional associations, political pressure groups, and other powerful vested interests

9 For example, a wealth tax or an inheritance tax could be created, and corporations could have their taxation levels increased to the early 1970 levels.

CHAPTER 5 Maternity/parental leave and benefits

1 These include employees who work for banks, in telecommunications and interprovincial or international transportation, and in federal Crown corporations.

2 In 1993, the length of paid parental leave was reduced to sixteen months and the replacement rate to 80 per cent.

3 Two per cent on the first £46 (Can. $90) of earnings, plus 9 per cent on weekly earnings between £46 and a maximum of £350 (Can. $688). This varies to 3.85 per cent for certain married women and widows. Self-employed people contribute £4.55 (Can. $9) per week plus 6.3 per cent of profits between £5,450 (Can. $10,709) and £18,200 (Can. $35,763) a year. Non-employed persons pay £4.45 (Can. $9) a week.

CHAPTER 6   Child care delivery and support

1 I am grateful for the contribution of my research assistant, Erica Penner, who provided the research for this section.
2 I use the term 'not-for-profit' instead of 'non-profit' to distinguish the intent from the outcome. For example, some day care operations which might be considered profit-making ventures do not, in fact, make a profit.
3 Some feminists note that people often say that mothers care for their children but fathers 'babysit.' This implies that fathers are doing something special when they fulfil their legal parental responsibilities.
4 This section is a slight revision of chapter 5, pages 171–4, of *Families in Canadian Society*, 2nd ed., by Maureen Baker (Toronto: McGraw-Hill Ryerson 1993).
5 Personal conversation with Martha Friendly, 6 March 1995

CHAPTER 7   Child protection, family violence, and substitute care

1 Another reason for focusing on children is that some boundaries had to be created for this very broad project. Since there is so much new research on violence against women, and entire books could be written on it, this study touches only briefly on the topic.
2 The term 'in care' means in the care of, or under the jurisdiction of, child welfare authorities or their agents (foster parents, group homes) rather than parents, and is used synonomously with the term 'substitute care.'
3 A version of this section was first published in *Families in Canadian Society*, 2nd ed., by Maureen Baker (Toronto: McGraw-Hill Ryerson 1993), 181–5.
4 This section is a revised version of part of chapter 4 in *Families in Canadian Society*, 2nd ed., by Maureen Baker (Toronto: McGraw-Hill Ryerson 1993).
5 This section is based on research by Carol Cumming Speirs and Maureen Baker, published in 'Eligibility to Adopt: Models of "Suitable Families" in Legislation and Practice,' *Canadian Social Work Review* (Winter 1994). I am grateful to Carol Cumming Speirs for permission to revise and abbreviate this paper.
6 Nova Scotia, Prince Edward Island, and Alberta enacted legislation prior to the First World War; Ontario, Quebec, Manitoba, British Columbia, and Saskatchewan in the 1920s; and Newfoundland, the Northwest Territories, and Yukon in the 1940s.
7 'Custom adoption' refers to the less formalized adoption practices of Native peoples.

CHAPTER 8   Divorce laws, child custody, and child support

1 Statistics Canada 1988, 60
2 To reiterate a point made in chapter 2, this study uses the term 'lone' parent rather than 'single' parent (as does the government of Canada) to eliminate any confusion about the marital status of the parent. 'Single' sometimes implies 'never married' in Canada.
3 Although the legislation is gender neutral, I use the pronoun 'he' for the parent who is expected to pay child support and the pronoun 'she' for the receiver of the payment, because this is the typical situation.
4 Stage two applies only to children who were born or whose parents have separated after 1 October 1989.

CHAPTER 9   The effectiveness of family and social policies

1 Quebec has its own income tax system, which provides different benefits from the federal ones. All other Canadian provinces use the federal income tax form and calculate their tax rates as a percentage of the federal rate, even though they may offer some provincial concessions.
2 There is a continuing dispute about whether or not Native people who have not signed treaties with the federal government should be under federal jurisdiction, or whether they should be treated as any other citizen.
3 While the nine provinces and two territories of 'English' Canada have a legal system derived from English common law, Quebec's *Civil Code* has developed from the French Napoleonic Code.
4 Although this benefit is delivered to people sixty-five and over, it is taxed back from those with higher incomes.
5 This section is an abbreviated version of 'Women and Population Policy in Quebec: Implications for Women,' by Maureen Baker, in *Canadian Journal of Women and the Law*, vol. 7 (1) 1994: 116–32.
6 In 1994, the amount was $8,000 for the birth of third or subsequent children.
7 People who speak languages other than French or English at home

Bibliography

Abbott, Pamela, and Claire Wallace. 1992. *The Family and the New Right*. London: Pluto Press.

Abramovitz, Mimi. 1989. *Regulating the Lives of Women*. Boston: South End Press.

– 1992. 'Poor Women in a Bind: Social Reproduction without Social Supports.' *Affilia* 7 (2): 23–43.

Adams, Carolyn, and Kathryn Winston. 1980. *Mothers at Work: Public Policies in the United States, Sweden and China*. New York: Longman.

Adams, G.C., and C.M. Johnson. 1991. 'Child Care and the Family Support Act: Should States Reimburse Unlicensed Providers?' *Public Welfare* 49(2): 9–12.

Adams, Owen B. 1990. 'Divorce Rates in Canada.' In *Canadian Social Trends*, edited by C. McKie and K. Thompson, 142–5. Toronto: Thompson Educational Press.

Adams, Owen B., and Dhruva Nagnur. 1986. 'Marriage, Divorce and Mortality: A Life Table Analysis for Canada and Regions, 1980–1982.' Paper presented at the conference of the Federation of Canadian Demographers, November.

– 1990. 'Marrying and Divorcing: A Status Report for Canada.' In *Canadian Social Trends*, edited by C. McKie and K. Thompson, 142–5. Toronto: Thompson Educational Press.

Adams, Paul. 1990. 'Children as Contribution in Kind: Social Security and Family Policy.' *Social Work* 35(6): 492–8.

Aguilar, Renato, and Bjorn Gustafsson. 1987. 'Public Sector Transfers and Income Taxes: An International Comparison with Micro Data.' The Luxembourg Income Study, Working Paper no. 10. Göteborg, Sweden.

Aitken, G. 1991. *Reducing Child Poverty: Assessing the Relevance of Australian Initiatives to Canada*. Paper presented to the Fifth Conference of Social Welfare Policy, 25–8 August. Bishop's University.

– 1993. 'Changing Adoption Policy and Practice to Deal with Children in Limbo.' Paper presented to the Sixth National Conference on Social Welfare Policy, 27–30 June. St John's, Newfoundland.

Akyeampong, Ernest. 1992. 'Absences from Work Revisited.' *Perspectives on Labour and Income* 4(1): 44–51.

Albrecht, Stan L., Howard M. Bahr, and Kristen L. Goodman. 1983. *Divorce and Remarriage: Problems, Adaptations and Adjustments*. Westport, Conn.: Greenwood.

Albrecht, Stan L., and P.R. Kunz. 1980. 'The Decision to Divorce: A Social Exchange Perspective.' *Journal of Divorce* 3: 319–37.

Aldous, Joan, and Robert C. Tuttle. 1988. 'Unemployment and the Family.' In *Employment and Economic Problems*, edited by Catherine S. Chilman, Fred M. Cox, and Elam W. Nunnally, 17–41. Newbury Park, Calif.: Sage Publications.

Allen, MaryLee. 1991. 'Crafting a Federal Legislative Framework for Child Welfare Reform.' *American Journal of Orthopsychiatry* 61(4): 610–23.

Ambert, Anne-Marie. 1980. *Divorce in Canada*. Don Mills, Ont.: Academic Press.

– 1983. 'Separated Women and Remarriage Behaviour: A Comparison of Financially Secure Women and Financially Insecure Women.' *Journal of Divorce* 6: 43–54.

– 1984. 'Longitudinal Changes in Children's Behavior toward Custodial Parents.' *Journal of Marriage and the Family* 46: 463–8.

– 1985. 'The Effect of Divorce on Women's Attitude toward Feminism.' *Sociological Focus* 18: 265–72.

– 1988a. 'Relationships between Ex-Spouses: Individual and Dyadic Perspectives.' *Journal of Social and Personal Relationships* 5: 327–46.

– 1988b. 'Relationships with Former In-Laws after Divorce: A Research Note.' *Journal of Marriage and the Family* 50: 679–86.

– 1990a. *Ex-Spouses and New Spouses*. London: JAI Press.

– 1990b. 'Marriage Dissolution: Structural and Ideological Changes.' In *Families: Changing Trends in Canada* (2nd ed.), edited by M. Baker, 192–210. Toronto: McGraw-Hill Ryerson.

– 1990c. 'The Other Perspective: Children's Effect on Parents.' Chapter 7 in *Families: Changing Trends in Canada* (2nd ed.), edited by M. Baker. Toronto: McGraw-Hill Ryerson.

– (1992). *The Effect of Children on Parents*. New York: The Haworth Press.

Ambert, Anne-Marie, and Maureen Baker. 1984. 'Marriage Dissolution: Structural and Ideological Changes.' In *The Family: Changing Trends in Canada*, edited by M. Baker, 85–103. Toronto: McGraw-Hill Ryerson.

Ambert, Anne-Marie, and J.F. Saucier. 1984. 'Adolescents' Academic Success and Aspirations by Parental Marital Status.' *Canadian Review of Sociology and Anthropology* 21: 62–74.

Anderson, Doris. 1991. *The Unfinished Revolution*. Toronto: Doubleday Canada.

Anderson, Elaine A. 1991. 'The Future of Family Policy.' In *The Reconstruction of Family Policy*, edited by E. Anderson and R. Hula. Westport, Conn.: Greenwood Press.

Anderson, Elaine A., and Richard C. Hula. 1991. *The Reconstruction of Family Policy*. Westport, Conn.: Greenwood Press.

Anderson, Karen. 1988. 'Historical Perspectives on the Family.' In *Family Matters*, edited by K. Anderson et al. Scarborough, Ont.: Nelson Canada.

Anderson, Karen L., et al. 1988. *Family Matters. Sociology and Contemporary Canadian Families*. Scarborough, Ont.: Nelson Canada.

Andersson, G. 1986. 'The Adopting and Adopted Swedes and Their Contemporary Society.' In *Adoption in Worldwide Perspective*, edited by R.A.C. Hoksbergen. Berwyn: Swets North America.

– 1992. 'Social Workers and Child Welfare.' *British Journal of Social Work* 22(3): 253–69.

Andrain, Charles. 1985. *Social Policies in Western Industrial Societies*. Berkeley: University of California.

Andrew, Caroline. 1984. 'Women and the Welfare State.' *Canadian Journal of Political Science* 17(4): 667–83.

Angenent, Huub, and Anton DeMan. 1992. *Childrearing. Personality Development and Deviant Behavior*. Toronto: Thompson Educational Publishing.

Archer, Keith. 1990. *Political Choices and Electoral Consequences: A Study of Organized Labour in the New Democratic Party*. Montreal: McGill-Queen's University Press.

Arditti, J.A. 1990. 'Noncustodial Fathers: An Overview of Policy and Resources.' *Family Relations* 39: 460–5.

– 1991. 'Child Support Noncompliance and Divorced Fathers: Rethinking the Role of Paternal Involvement.' *Journal of Divorce and Remarriage* 14(3/4): 107–19.

Armitage, Andrew. 1988. *Social Welfare in Canada. Ideals, Realities, and Future Paths* (2nd ed.). Toronto: McClelland and Stewart.

– 1993. 'The Policy and Legislative Context.' In *Rethinking Child Welfare in Canada*, edited by Brian Wharf, 37–63. Toronto: McClelland and Stewart.

Armstrong, Pat. 1990. 'Economic Conditions and Family Structures.' In *Families: Changing Trends in Canada* (2nd ed.), edited by M. Baker. Toronto: McGraw-Hill Ryerson.

Armstrong, Pat, and Hugh Armstrong. 1984. *The Double Ghetto. Canadian*

Women and Their Segregated Work (2nd ed.). Toronto: McClelland and
Stewart.

– 1988. 'The Conflicting Demands of "Work" and "Home".' In *Family Matters,*
edited by Karen L. Anderson et al., 113–40. Scarborough, Ont.: Nelson
Canada.

– 1990. *Theorizing Women's Work*. Garamond: Toronto.

Aronson, Jane. 1991. 'Dutiful Daughters and Undemanding Mothers: Contrast-
ing Images of Giving and Receiving Care in Middle and Later Life.' In
Women's Caring. Feminist Perspectives on Social Welfare, edited by C. Baines,
P. Evans, and S. Neysmith, 138–68. Toronto: McClelland and Stewart.

Asner, Elizabeth, and David Livingstone. 1990. 'Household Class, Divisions of
Labour and Political Attitudes in Steeltown.' Paper presented at Canadian
Socialist Association Meetings, Victoria, British Columbia.

Atkinson, C., and A. Horner. 1990. 'Private Fostering – Legislation and
Practice.' *Adoption and Fostering* 14(3): 17–22.

Australian Government, Committee on Employment Opportunities. 1993.
Restoring Full Employment. A Discussion Paper. Chaired by Michael Keating.
December. Canberra.

– 1994. *Working Nation. Policies and Programs*. White Paper presented by Prime
Minister P.J. Keating, May. Canberra: Australian Government Publishing
Service.

Ayim, Maryann. 1987. 'Children's Rights in Canada.' Paper presented to the
Canadian Society for Women in Philosophy, November. Montreal.

Bacchi, Carol. 1990. *Same Difference: Feminism and Sexual Difference*. London:
Allen and Unwin.

– 1991. 'Pregnancy, the Law and the Meaning of Equality.' In *Equality Politics
and Gender*, edited by Elizabeth Meehan and Selma Sevenhuijsen. London:
Sage.

Bachrach, Christine A. 1983. 'Children in Families: Characteristics of Biological,
Step- and Adoptive Children.' *Journal of Marriage and the Family* 45 (February): 171–9.

Badgley, Robin (chair). 1984. *Sexual Offences against Children*. Report of the
Committee on Sexual Offences against Children and Youth. Ottawa: Supply
and Services Canada.

Baer, I. 1986. 'The Development of Adoptions in the Federal Republic of
Germany.' In *Adoption in Worldwide Perspective*, edited by R.A.C.
Hoksbergen. Berwyn: Swets North America.

Bagley, Christopher R. 1986. 'The Institution of Adoption: A Canadian Case
Study.' In *Adoption in Worldwide Perspective*, edited by R.A.C. Hoksbergen.
Berwyn: Swets North America.

Bagley, C., B.A. Burrows, and C. Yaworski. 1991. 'Street Kids and Adolescent Prostitution: A Challenge for Legal and Social Services.' In *Canadian Child Welfare Law: Children, Families and the State*, edited by N. Bala, J.P. Hornick, and R. Vogl. Toronto: Thompson Educational Publishing.

Bagley, Christopher R., and Kathleen King. 1990. *Child Sexual Abuse. The Search for Healing*. London: Tavistock/Routledge.

Bagley, Christopher R., and Ray J. Thomlinson, eds. 1991. *Child Sexual Abuse: Critical Perspectives on Prevention, Intervention and Treatment*. Toronto: Wall and Emerson.

Baines, Carol, Patricia Evans, and Sheila Neysmith, eds. 1991. *Women's Caring. Feminist Perspectives on Social Welfare*. Toronto: McClelland and Stewart.

Baker, John. 1986. 'Comparing National Priorities: Family and Population Policy in Britain and France.' *Journal of Social Policy* 15(4): 421–42.

Baker, Maureen. 1982. 'Finding Partners in the Newspaper: Sex Differences in Personal Advertising.' *Atlantis* 7(2): 137–46.

– 1983. 'Divorce: Its Consequences and Meanings.' In *The Canadian Family*, edited by K. Ishwaran, 289–300. Toronto: Gage.

– 1984. 'Women Helping Women: The Transition from Separation to Divorce.' *Conciliation Courts Review* 22: 53–63.

– 1985. '*What Will Tomorrow Bring?*' ... *A Study of the Aspirations of Adolescent Women*. Ottawa: Canadian Advisory Council on the Status of Women.

– 1988. *Aging in Canadian Society: A Survey*. Toronto: McGraw-Hill Ryerson.

– 1990a. 'A New Status for Midwifery: Women and Public Policy.' *Canadian Review of Social Policy* 26: 54–63.

– 1990b. 'The Perpetuation of Misleading Family Models in Social Policy: Implications for Women.' *Canadian Review of Social Work* (Summer): 169–82.

– 1991. 'His and Her Divorce Research: New Theoretical Directions in Canadian and American Research.' In *Continuity and Change in Marriage and Family*, edited by J. Veevers. Toronto: Holt, Rinehart and Winston.

– 1992. 'The Adequacy of Existing Social Programs for Canadian Families: Trends in Emerging Needs.' In *Social Policy in the Global Economy*, edited by Terrance M. Hunsley, 67–79. Kingston: Queen's University.

– 1993a. *Families in Canadian Society* (2nd ed.). Toronto: McGraw-Hill Ryerson.

– 1993b. 'A Sociological Perspective on Child Care Research.' *Proceedings from the Child Care Policy and Research Symposium*. Occasional Paper no. 2. Toronto: University of Toronto, Childcare Resource and Research Unit.

– 1994a. *Canada's Changing Families: Challenges to Public Policy*. Ottawa: Vanier Institute of the Family.

– 1994b. 'Family and Population Policy in Quebec: Implications for Women,' *Canadian Journal of Women and the Law* 7(1): 116–32.

- 1994c. 'Family Poverty and Work/Family Conflicts: Inconsistent Social Policies.' *Canadian Review of Social Policy* 33 (Spring/Summer): 45–61.
Baker, Maureen, ed. 1990. *Families: Changing Trends in Canada* (2nd ed.). Toronto: McGraw-Hill Ryerson.
Baker, Maureen, and Hans J.I. Bakker. 1980. 'The Double Bind of the Middle Class Male: Men's Liberation and the Male Sex Role.' *Journal of Comparative Family Studies* 11(4): 547–61.
Baker, Maureen, Terrance Hunsley, and Anna Michetti. 1993. 'The Use of the Income Tax System to Deliver and Target Family Benefits: A Cross-National Comparison.' Paper presented to the Sixth Conference on Social Welfare Policy, June. St John's, Newfoundland.
Baker, Nancy C. 1978. *Baby Selling: The Scandal of Black Market Adoptions.* New York: Vanguard Press.
Bala, Nicholas. 1991a. 'Child and Family Policies for the 1990s.' In *Children, Families and Public Policy in the 90s*, edited by L.C. Johnson and R. Barnhorst, 105–32. Toronto: Thompson Educational Publishing.
- 1991b. 'An Introduction to Child Protection Problems.' In *Canadian Child Welfare Law: Children, Families and the State*, edited by N. Bala, J.P. Hornick, and R. Vogl. Toronto: Thompson Educational Publishing.
Bala, Nicholas, and Kenneth L. Clarke. 1981. *The Child and the Law.* Toronto: McGraw-Hill Ryerson.
Bala, Nicholas, Joseph P. Hornick, and Robin Vogl. 1991. *Canadian Child Welfare Law: Children, Families and the State.* Toronto: Thompson Educational Publishing.
Bala, Nicholas, and Martha Bailey. 1990–1. 'Canada – Controversy Continues over Spousal Abortion and Support.' *Journal of Family Law* 29(2): 303–15.
Balleyguier, G. 1991. 'French Research on Day Care.' In *Day Care for Young Children: International Perspectives*, edited by E.C. Melhuish and P. Moss, 27–45. London: Tavistock/Routledge.
Bandler, Jean T.D. 1989. 'Family Protection and Women's Issues in Social Security.' *Social Work* (July): 307–11.
Banting, Keith G. 1987a. *The Welfare State and Canadian Federalism.* Kingston and Montreal: McGill-Queen's University Press.
- 1987b. 'The Welfare State and Inequality in the 1980s.' *Canadian Review of Sociology and Anthropology* 24(3): 309–38.
- 1993. 'Globalization, the Labour Market and Social Welfare Spending.' Paper presented to the Sixth Conference on Social Welfare Policy, 27–30 June. St John's, Newfoundland.
Barbier, Jean-Claude. 1990. 'Comparing Family Policies in Europe: Methodological Problems.' *International Social Security Review* 43(3): 326–41.

– 1992. 'Minimum Social Income and Family Policy in France.' In *Social Security and Changing Family Structures*, edited by the International Social Security Association, 201–10. Geneva: ISSA.

Barnes, Gordon E.; Leonard Greenwood, and Reena Sommer. 1991. 'Courtship Violence in a Canadian Sample of Male College Students.' *Family Relations* 40 (January): 37–44.

Barnhorst, Richard, and Laura C. Johnson. 1991a. *Children, Families and Public Policy in the 90s*. Toronto: Thompson Educational Press.

– 1991b. *The State of the Child in Ontario*. Toronto: Oxford University Press.

Barnhorst, R., and B. Walter. 1991. 'Child Protection Legislation in Canada.' In *Canadian Child Welfare Law: Children, Families and the State*, edited by N. Bala, J.P. Hornick, and R. Vogl. Toronto: Thompson Educational Publishing.

Barr, Lynn. 1993. *Basic Facts on Families in Canada, Past and Present*. Catalogue no. 89-516. Ottawa: Statistics Canada.

Bates, F. 1989–90. 'Australia: Forward to the Past – Supporting the Family in 1988.' *Journal of Family Law* 28(3): 397–408.

Bates, Frank. 1990–1. 'Australian Family Law in 1989: How Important Are People Really?' *Journal of Family Law* 29(2): 277–84.

Battle, Ken. 1988. 'Child Benefits in Decline.' *Policy Options* (January): 3–7.

– 1992a. 'Missing a Chance for a Solid Punch at Poverty.' *The Globe and Mail*, 12 March: A15.

– 1992b. 'White Paper Whitewash: The New Child Benefit.' *Perception* 16(2/3): 34–40.

Battle, Ken, and Sherri Torjman. 1993. *Federal Social Programs: Setting the Record Straight*. Ottawa: Caledon Institute of Social Policy.

– 1994. 'Opening the Books on Social Spending: Highlights from a New Study.' *Perception* 17(4): 12–16.

Baxter, Ian F.G. 1987. 'Family Law Reform: A Historical Perspective of the Ontario Experience.' *Canadian Journal of Family Law* 6 (Winter): 247–69.

Bay, R.C., and S.L. Braver. 1990. 'Perceived Control of the Divorce Settlement Process and Interparental Conflict.' *Family Relations* 39: 382–7.

Beaujot, Roderic. 1986. 'Dwindling Families.' *Policy Options* 7 (September): 3–7.

– 1988. 'The Family in Crisis?' *Canadian Journal of Sociology* 13 (Summer): 305–11.

– 1990. 'The Family and Demographic Change in Canada: Economic and Cultural Interpretations and Solutions.' *Journal of Comparative Family Studies* 21(1): 25–38.

– 1991. *Population Change in Canada. The Challenge of Policy Adaptation*. Toronto: McClelland and Stewart.

Bebbington, A., and J. Miles 1989. 'The Background of Children Who Enter Local Authority Care.' *British Journal of Social Work* 19: 349–68.

Bélanger, Lise. 1981. 'The Types of Violence the Elderly Are Victims Of: Results of a Survey Done with Personnel Working with the Elderly.' Paper presented at the Thirty-fourth Annual Scientific Meeting of the Gerontological Association of America, November.

Beller, Andrea H., and S.S. Chung. 1991. 'Child Support and the Feminization of Poverty.' In *The Reconstruction of Family Policy*, edited by E. Anderson and R. Hula. Westport, Conn.: Greenwood Press.

Belliveau, Jo-Anne, Jillian Oderkirk, and Cynthia Silver. 1994. 'Common-Law Unions: The Quebec Difference.' *Canadian Social Trends* 33 (Summer): 8–12.

Bellware, Jo-Ann, and Diane Charest. 1986. *Monoparentalité feminine et aide sociale*. Québec: Services des Politiques et de la Recherche en Securité du Revenu.

Belous, Richard S. 1991. *Demographic Currents: Trends and Issues that Face the United States, the United Kingdom and Canada*. September. Toronto: The British-North America Committee.

Beneteau, Renée. 1990. 'Trends in Suicide.' In *Canadian Social Trends*, edited by C. McKie and K. Thompson, 93–5. Toronto: Thompson Educational Publishing.

Bequele, Assefa, and Jo Boyden, eds. 1988. *Combatting Child Labour*. Geneva: International Labour Organization.

Bergmann, B. 1988. 'A Workable Family Policy.' *Dissent* (Winter): 88–93.

Bergqvist, Christina. 1991. 'Corporatism and Gender Equality – A Comparative Study of Two Swedish Labor Market Organizations.' *European Journal of Political Research* 20 (September): 107–25.

Berkman, B.G. 1986. 'Father Involvement and Regularity of Child Support in Post-Divorce Families.' *Journal of Divorce* 9(3): 67–74.

Bernier, Ivan, and Andrée Lajoie, eds. 1986. *Family Law and Social Welfare Legislation in Canada*. Toronto: University of Toronto Press.

Berrick, Jill D. 1991. 'Welfare and Child Care: The Intricacies of Competing Social Values.' *Social Work* 36: 345–51.

Besharov, Douglas J. 1990a. 'Combating Child Abuse: Guidelines for Cooperation between Law Enforcement and Child Protective Agencies.' *Family Law Quarterly* 24(2): 209–45.

– 1990b. *Recognizing Child Abuse. A Guide for the Concerned*. Toronto: The Free Press.

Bittman, Michael 1994. *Recent Changes in Unpaid Work*. Canberra: Australian Bureau of Statistics.

Blank, H. 1989. 'Child Care and Welfare Reform: New Opportunities for Families.' *Young Children* (May): 28–30.

- 1991. 'Implementing the Child Care and Developmental Block Grant: Initial Reports from the States.' *Young Children* (July): 61–4.
Blau, David M., ed. 1991a. *The Economics of Child Care*. New York: Russell Sage Foundation.
- 1991b. 'Introduction.' In *The Economics of Child Care*, edited by D.M. Blau, 1–9. New York: Russell Sage Foundation.
Blau, D.M., and P.K. Robins. 1988. 'Child-Care Costs and Family Labor Supply.' *The Review of Economics and Statistics* 7: 374–81.
- 1989. 'Fertility, Employment, and Child-Care Costs.' *Demography* 26(2): 287–99.
Blishen, J.A. 1991a. 'The Lawyer's Role: Introduction.' In *Canadian Child Welfare Law: Children, Families and the State*, edited by N. Bala, J.P. Hornick, and R. Vogl. Toronto: Thompson Educational Publishing.
- 1991b. 'Representing the Agency.' In *Canadian Child Welfare Law: Children, Families and the State*, edited by N. Bala, J.P. Hornick, and R. Vogl. Toronto: Thompson Educational Publishing.
Bock, Gisela, and Pat Thane, eds. 1991. *Maternity and Gender Policies. Women and the Rise of the European Welfare States, 1880–1950s*. London: Routledge.
Bolderson, Helen, and Deborah Mabbett. 1991. *Social Policy and Social Security in Australia, Britain and the USA*. Aldershot, England: Avebury.
Bolton, Frank, and Susan Bolton. 1987. *Working with Violent Families: A Guide for Clinical and Legal Practice*. Newbury Park, Calif.: Sage Publications.
Bookman, Ann. 1991. 'Parenting without Poverty: The Case for Funded Parental Leave.' In *Parental Leave and Child Care*, edited by J.S. Hyde and M.J. Essex, 66–89. Philadelphia: Temple University Press.
Boreham, Paul, and Hugh Compston. 1992. 'Labour Movement Organization and Political Intervention – The Politics of Unemployment in the OECD Countries, 1974–1986.' *European Journal of Political Research* 22 (August): 143–70.
Borg, S.G., and F.G. Castles 1981. 'The Influence of the Political Right on Public Income Maintenance Expenditure and Equality.' *Political Studies* 29: 604–21.
Boyd, Monica. 1984. *Canadian Attitudes toward Women: Thirty Years of Change*. Ottawa: Women's Bureau, Labour Canada.
- 1988. 'Changing Canadian Family Forms: Issues for Women.' In *Reconstructing the Canadian Family: Feminist Perspectives*, edited by N. Mandell and A. Duffy, 85–110. Toronto: Butterworths.
Boyd, Monica, and Edward Pryor 1990. 'Young Adults Living in Their Parents' Home.' *Canadian Social Trends*, edited by C. McKie and K. Thompson, 188–91. Toronto: Thompson Educational Publishing.
Boyle, Michael. 1991. 'Child Health in Ontario.' In *The State of the Child in*

Ontario, edited by R. Barnhorst and L.C. Johnson, 92–116. Toronto: Oxford University Press.

Bradshaw, Jonathan. 1993. 'Developments in Social Security Policy.' In *New Perspectives on the Welfare State in Europe*, edited by Catherine Jones, 43–63. London: Routledge.

Bradshaw, Jonathan, and Jane Millar. 1991. *Lone Parent Families in the U.K.* London: Department of Social Security.

Bradshaw, Jonathan, et al. 1992. 'Lone-Parent Families in the United Kingdom: Challenges for Social Security Policy.' In *Social Security and Changing Family Structures*, edited by the International Social Security Association, 185–200. Geneva: ISSA.

Bradshaw, Jonathan, John Ditch, Hilary Holmes, and Peter Whiteford. 1993. *Support for Children: A Comparison of Arrangements in Fifteen Countries.* Research Report 21. London: Department of Social Security.

Brand, Ruth. 1989. 'Single Parents and Family Preservation in the Federal Republic of Germany.' *Child Welfare* 68(2): 189–95.

Bravo, Ellen. 1991. 'Family Leave: The Need for a New Minimum Standard.' In *Parental Leave and Child Care*, edited by J.S. Hyde and M.J. Essex, 165–75. Philadelphia: Temple University Press.

Bridgeford, Jeff. 1991. *The Politics of French Trade Unionism.* London: Leicester University Press.

Brieland, Donald. 1984. 'Selection of Adoptive Parents.' In *Adoption. Current Issues and Trends*, edited by Paul Sachdev, 65–85. Toronto: Butterworths.

Brinkerhoff, Merlin B., and Eugen Lupri. 1983. 'Conjugal Power and Family Relationships: Some Theoretical and Methodological Issues.' In *The Canadian Family*, edited by K. Ishwaran. Toronto: Gage.

– 1988. 'Interspousal Violence.' *The Canadian Journal of Sociology* 13(4): 407–34.

Broberg, A., and C.P. Hwang. 1991. 'Day Care for Young Children in Sweden.' In *Day Care for Young Children: International Perspectives*, edited by E.C. Melhuish and P. Moss, 75–101. London: Tavistock/Routledge.

Brocas, Anne-Marie, et al. 1990. 'Women in Precarious Situations and in Poverty.' In *Women and Social Security*, 97–108. Geneva: International Labour Office.

Bronfenbrenner, Urie. 1992. 'Child Care in the Anglo-Saxon Mode.' In *Child Care in Context: Cross-Cultural Perspectives*, edited by M.E. Lamb et al. Hillsdale, N.J.: Lawrence Erlbaum Associates.

Bronstein, P., and C. Cowan, eds. 1988. *Fatherhood Today: Men's Changing Role in Society.* New York: Wiley and Sons.

Brook, Eve, and Ann Davis, eds. 1985. *Women, the Family, and Social Work.* London: Tavistock.

Brown, Joan. 1988. *Child Benefit – Investing in the Future*. London: Calvert's Press.

– 1992. 'Which Way for Family Policy: Choices for the 1990's.' In *Social Policy Review* no. 4, edited by Nick Manning and Robert Page, 154–74. Social Policy Association. London: Longman Group U.K.

Brown, R.G. 1989. 'Social Security and Welfare.' In *Australian Society*, edited by E. Hancock, 23–43. Cambridge: Cambridge University Press.

Brown, Robert L. 1991. *Economic Security in an Aging Population*. Toronto: Butterworths.

Bryson, L., and M. Mowbray. 1986. 'Who Cares? Social Security, Family Policy and Women.' *International Social Security* 2: 183–200.

Buchanan James M., and Richard E. Wagner. 1977. *Democracy in Deficit: The Political Legacy of Lord Keynes*. New York: Academic Press.

Buhmann, Brigitte, et al. 1987. 'Improving the Luxembourg Income (LIS) Measure: Microdata Estimates of the Size Distribution of Cash and Noncash Income in Eight Countries.' The Luxembourg Income Study, Working Paper no. 13, August.

Bullington, Sandra R. 1993. 'Will Separation or Divorce Increase Your Taxes?' *The Single Parent* 36(1): 12–14, 71.

Bunjes, L.A.C. 1991. 'Born in the Third World: To School in the Netherlands.' In *Adoption: International Perspectives*, edited by E.D. Hibbs. Madison, Conn.: International University Press.

Burch, Thomas K., and Ashok Madan. 1986. *Union Formation and Dissolution: Results from the 1984 Family History Survey*. Statistics Canada, Catalogue no. 99-963E. Ottawa: Supply and Services Canada.

Burke, Mary Anne, Susan Crompton, Alison Jones, and Katherine Nessner. 1991. 'Caring for Children.' *Canadian Social Trends* 22 (Autumn): 12–15.

Burkhauser, Richard V., and Greg J. Duncan. 1988. 'Life Events, Public Policy and the Economic Vulnerability of Children and the Elderly.' In *The Vulnerable*, edited by J. Palmer, T. Smeeding, and B. Torrey, 55–88. Washington, D.C.: Urban Institute Press.

Burrett, Jill F. 1988. *Child Access and Modern Family Law*. Sydney: The Law Book Company Limited.

Burrows, D. 1991. 'Adoption, Wardship and Access – Now and Under the Children Act.' *Adoption and Fostering* 15(1): 50–3.

Buysse, Anne-Marie. 1992. 'Family Models and Social Legislation in EEC Countries: A Comparative Study.' In *Social Security and Changing Family Structures*, edited by the International Social Security Association, 89–103. Geneva: ISSA.

Byrd, A.D. 1988. 'The Case for Confidential Adoption.' *Public Welfare* (Fall): 20–3, 46.

Calciano, E.M. 1992. 'United Nations Convention on the Rights of the Child: Will It Help Children in the United States?' *Hastings International and Comparative Law Review* 15: 515–34.

Caledon Institute of Social Policy. 1992. *Child Benefit Primer: A Response to the Government Proposal*. June. Ottawa.

Callahan, Marilyn. 1993a. 'The Administrative and Practice Context: Perspectives from the Front Line.' In *Rethinking Child Welfare in Canada*, edited by Brian Wharf, 64–97. Toronto: McClelland and Stewart.

– 1993b. 'Feminist Approaches: Women Recreate Child Welfare.' In *Rethinking Child Welfare in Canada*, edited by Brian Wharf, 172–209. Toronto: McClelland and Stewart.

Cameron, David R. 1978. 'The Expansion of the Public Policy.' *The American Political Science Review* 72: 1243–61.

– 1984. 'Social Democracy, Corporatism, Labor Quiescence and the Representation of Economic Interest in Advanced Capitalist Society.' In *Order and Conflict in Contemporary Capitalism*, edited by J.H. Goldthorpe. Oxford: Clarendon Press.

Campaign 2000. 1993. *Child Poverty in Canada, Report Card, 1993*. Ottawa: Centre for International Statistics, Canadian Council on Social Development.

– 1994. *Investing in the Next Generation. Policy Perspectives on Children and Nationhood*. Toronto: Campaign 2000.

Campbell, M. 1991. 'Children at Risk: How Different Are Children on Child Abuse Registers?' *British Journal of Social Work* 21: 259–75.

Canada, Department of Finance. 1994. *Government Revenues in Canada: Basic Facts*. Ottawa: Department of Finance.

Canada, Department of Justice. 1990. *Evaluation of the Divorce Act. Phase II: Monitoring and Evaluation*. Ottawa: Department of Justice.

– 1993. *Custody and Access: Public Discussion Paper*. March. Ottawa: Department of Justice.

Canada, Federal/Provincial/Territorial Family Law Committee. 1991. *Child Support: Public Discussion Paper*. June. Ottawa: Department of Justice.

Canada, Government of. 1993. *Family-Related Leave and Benefits*. Ottawa.

Canada, Health and Welfare. 1974. *Social Security in Canada*. Ottawa: Information Canada.

– 1988. *Health Status of Canadian Indians and Inuit*. Prepared by B. Muir. January. Ottawa: Supply and Services Canada.

– 1991. *Inventory of Income Security Programs in Canada, July 1990*. Ottawa: Health and Welfare Canada.

– 1992. *The Child Benefit. A White Paper on Canada's New Integrated Child Tax Benefit*. Ottawa: Minister of Health and Welfare.

Canada, House of Commons. 1991. *Canada's Children: Investing in Our Future*. Report of the Sub-Committee on Poverty of the Standing Committee on Health and Welfare, Social Affairs, Seniors and the Status of Women. Chaired by Barbara Greene, MP. December. Ottawa.

Canada, New Democratic Party. 1987. *Caring for Canada's Children: A Special Report on the Crisis in Child Care*. Ottawa.

Canada, Senate. Standing Senate Committee on Social Affairs, Science and Technology. 1987. *Child Benefits. Proposal for a Guaranteed Family Supplement Scheme*. June. Ottawa: Senate of Canada.

– 1988. *Proceedings of the Subcommittee on Child Care*. Ottawa.

– 1989. *Child Poverty and Adult Social Problems*. December. Ottawa: Minister of Supply and Services.

– 1991. *Children in Poverty: Toward a Better Future*. Report of the Standing Senate Committee on Social Affairs, Science and Technology. Chaired by Senators Lorna Marsden and Brenda Robertson. January. Ottawa: Minister of Supply and Services.

Canada, Task Force on Child Care. 1986. *Report of the Task Force on Child Care*. Ottawa: Supply and Services Canada.

Canadian Centre for Justice Statistics. 1994. 'Homicide.' In *Canadian Social Trends, Volume 2*, 419–22. Toronto: Thompson Educational Publishing.

Canadian Institute of Child Health. 1989. *The Health of Canada's Children: A CICH Profile*. Ottawa: The Canadian Institute of Child Health.

Carlson, Allan. 1989. 'A Pro-Family Income Tax.' *Public Interest* 94 (Winter): 69–76.

– 1990. *The Swedish Experiment in Family Politics*. London: Transaction Publishers.

Carney, Terry. 1990. 'The Social Security Act: Just Another Act or a Blueprint for Social Justice?' *Australian Journal of Social Issues* 25(2): 103–19.

Casper, Lynne, Sara S. McLanahan, and Irwin Garfinkel. 1994. 'The Gender-Poverty Gap: What We Can Learn from Other Countries.' Luxembourg Income Study, Working Paper no. 112. July. Luxembourg.

Cass, Bettina. 1989. 'Children's Poverty and Labour Market Issues.' In *Child Poverty*, edited by D. Edgar, D. Keane, and P. McDonald, 146–72. Sydney: Allen and Unwin.

– 1992. 'Fightback: The Politics of Work and Welfare in the 1990s.' *Australian Quarterly* 64(2): 140–61.

Castles, Francis G. 1978. *The Social Democratic Image of Society*. London: Routledge and Kegan Paul.

Castles, Ian. 1991. *Yearbook Australia 1991*. Canberra: Australian Bureau of Statistics.

Catala, P. 1991–2. 'Reform of French Family Law: A Peaceful Revolution.'
Tulane Civil Law Forum 6(7): 271–82.

Chambers, D.L. 1988. 'The Federal Government and a Program of "Advance
Maintenance" in the United States.' In *Child Support*, edited by A.J. Kahn and
S.B. Kamerman, 343–9. Newbury Park, Calif.: Sage Publications.

Cheal, David. 1991. *Family and the State of Theory*. Toronto: University of
Toronto Press.

Cherlin, Andrew, and Frank F. Furstenberg. 1988. 'The Changing European
Family – Lessons for the American Reader.' *Journal of Family Issues* 9(3):
291–7.

Child Poverty Action Group. 1994. *Policy Statement on Social Security for Families
with Children*. Toronto: Child Poverty Action Group.

Chilman, Catherine S. 1992. 'Welfare Reform or Revision? The Family Support
Act of 1988.' *Social Service Review* 66 (September): 349–77.

Chilman, Catherine S., Fred M. Cox, and Elam W. Nunnally. 1988. *Employment
and Economic Problems*. Newbury Park, Calif.: Sage Publications.

Christensen, Carole P. 1989. 'Protecting Our Youth: Cultural Issues in the
Application of the Youth Protection Act.' *Intervention* 84 (November): 31–41.

Christensen, D.H., C.D. Dahl, and K.D. Rettig. 1990. 'Noncustodial Mothers
and Child Support: Examining the Larger Context.' *Family Relations* 39:
388–94.

Clark, Susan M. 1993. 'Families in Poverty: Report on a 10-Year Study in Nova
Scotia.' Paper presented at the Sixth Conference on Social Welfare Policy,
29 June. St John's, Newfoundland.

Clement, Wallace, and Rianne Mahon, eds. 1994. *Swedish Social Democracy.
A Model in Transition*. Toronto: Canadian Scholars' Press.

Clerkx, Lily E., and Marinus H. Van Ijzendoorn. 1992. 'Child Care in a Dutch
Context: On the History, Current Status, and Evaluation of Nonmaternal
Child Care in the Netherlands.' In *Child Care in Context*, edited by M. Lamb
et al. Hillsdale, N.J.: Lawrence Erlbaum Associates.

Clifford, R.M., and S.D. Russell. 1989. 'Financing Programs for Preschool-Aged
Children.' *Theory into Practice* 28: 19–27.

Cognetta, C.J., Jr. 1992. 'Foster Care: A Need for New Solutions.' *New York
State Bar Journal* (May/June): 28–30.

Cohen, C.P., and P. Miljeteig-Olssen. 1991. 'Status Report: United Nations
Convention on the Rights of the Child.' *Journal of Human Rights* 8: 367–82.

Cohen, Joyce S., and Anne Westhues. 1990. *Well-Functioning Families for
Adoptive and Foster Children*. Toronto: University of Toronto Press.

Cohen, S., and R.D. Warren. 1990. 'The Intersection of Disability and Child
Abuse in England and the United States.' *Child Welfare* 69(3): 253–62.

Coller, D. 1988. 'Joint Custody: Research, Theory and Policy.' *Family Process* 27(4): 459–69.

Collier, David, and Richard Messick. 1975. 'Prerequisites versus Diffusion: Testing Alternative Explanations of Social Security Adoption.' *American Political Science Review* 69: 1299–1315.

Colton, M.W., W. Hellinckx, R. Bullock, and B. Van Den Bruel. 1991. 'Caring for Troubled Children in Flanders, The Netherlands, and the United Kingdom.' *British Journal of Social Work* 21: 381–92.

Coltrane, Scott, and Neal Hickman. 1992. 'The Rhetoric of Rights and Needs: Moral Discourse in the Reform of Child Custody and Child Support Laws.' *Social Problems* 39(4): 400–20.

Commaille, J. 1990. 'Family Policy in EEC Countries: France.' In *Family Policy in EEC Countries*, edited by W. Dumon. Luxembourg: Commission of the European Communities.

Conway, John F. 1993. *The Canadian Family in Crisis*. Toronto: James Lorimer and Company.

Cook, L.W. 1991–2. 'Open Adoption: Can Visitation with Natural Family Members Be in the Child's Best Interest?' *Journal of Family Law* 30: 471–92.

Corbett, Gail H. 1981. *Barnardo Children in Canada*. Peterborough, Ont.: Woodland Publishing.

Corsini, D.A., S. Wisensale, and G. Caruso. 1988. 'Family Day Care: Systems Issues and Regulatory Models.' *Young Children* 43(6): 17–23.

Coughlin, Richard M. 1980. *Ideology, Public Opinion and Welfare Policy*. Berkeley: University of California.

Council of Europe. 1986. *Implementation of the European Convention on Human Rights in Respect of Young Persons and Children Placed in Care or in Institutions Following a Decision of the Administrative or Judicial Authorities*. Strasbourg: Council of Europe.

Courchene, Thomas J. 1987. *Social Policy in the 1990's: Agenda for Reform*. Scarborough, Ont.: Prentice-Hall.

Craig, John. 1992. 'Recent Fertility Trends in Europe.' *Population Trends* 68 (Summer): 20–3.

Cruickshank, D.A. 1991. 'The Child in Care.' In *Canadian Child Welfare Law: Children, Families and the State*, edited by N. Bala, J.P. Hornick, and R. Vogl, 77–107. Toronto: Thompson Educational Publishing:.

Culkin, M., J.R. Morris, and S.W. Helburn. 1991. 'Quality and the True Cost of Child Care.' *Journal of Social Issues* 47(2): 71–86.

Cuneo, Carl. 1979. 'State, Class and Reserve Labour: The Case of the 1941 Unemployment Insurance Act.' *Canadian Review of Sociology and Anthropology* 16(2): 147–70.

Dahl, Robert, and Edward Tufte. 1973. *Size and Democracy*. Stanford, Calif.: Stanford University Press.

Dalto, Guy C. 1989. 'A Structural Approach to Women's Hometime and Experience-Earnings Profile: Maternity Leave and Public Policy.' *Population Research and Policy Review* 8: 247–66.

Daly, Kerry, and Michael Sobol. 1993. *Adoption in Canada, Final Report*. May. Ottawa: Health and Welfare Canada.

Danzinger, Sheldon. 1990. 'Antipoverty Policies and Child Poverty.' *Social Work Research and Abstracts* 26(4): 17–24.

Danzinger, S.K., and A. Nichols-Casebolt. 1987–8. 'Teen Parents and Child Support: Eligibility, Participation, and Payment.' *Journal of Social Science Research* 11(2/3): 1–20.

– 1990. 'Child Support in Paternity Cases.' *Social Service Review* 64(3): 458–74.

De'Ath, E. 1989. 'The Family Center Approach to Supporting Families.' *Child Welfare* 68(2): 197–207.

Deller Ross, Susan. 1991. 'Legal Aspects of Parental Leave: At the Crossroads.' In *Parental Leave and Child Care*, edited by J.S. Hyde and M.J. Essex, 93–124. Philadelphia: Temple University Press, 1991.

Denny, E., J. Pokela, J.R. Jackson, and M.A. Matava. 1989. 'Influencing Child Welfare Policy: Assessing the Opinion of Legislators.' *Child Welfare* 69(3): 275–87.

Denton, Frank T., Peter C. Pineo, and Byron G. Spencer. 1991. *The Demographics of Employment*. June. Ottawa: Studies in Social Policy.

Devereaux, Mary Sue. 1990. 'Changes in Living Arrangements.' In *Canadian Social Trends*, edited by C. McKie and K. Thompson. Toronto: Thompson Educational Publishing.

Dewar, Marsha. 1988. *The Social Construction of the Family and Child Care Policy*. MSW Research Report, November. Montreal: McGill University.

Diduck, Alison. 1990. 'The Use of Fixed-Term Maintenance to Encourage Financial Independence.' *Manitoba Law Journal* 19: 153–73.

Dierkes, M.W., H.N. Antal, and A.B. Antal, eds. 1987. *Comparative Policy Research*. England: Gower Publishing.

Docksey, Christopher. 1987. *Sharing of Occupational, Family and Social Responsibilities – The Case for Parental Leave*. Paper presented at an Expert Seminar on Independence between Women and Men, 9–13 July. Salzburg.

Dominelli, Lena. 1991. *Women across Continents. Feminist Comparative Social Policy*. London: Harvester Wheatsheaf.

Dopffel, P. 1988. 'Child Support in Europe: A Comparative Overview.' In *Child Support*, edited by A.J. Kahn and S.B. Kamerman, 176–223. Newbury Park, Calif.: Sage Publications.

Dornbusch, Sanford M., and Myra H. Stober. 1988. *Feminism, Children and the New Families*. New York: Guilford Press.

Douthitt, Robin A., and Joanne Fedyk. 1990. *The Cost of Raising Children in Canada*. Toronto: Butterworths.

Downing, J.D., S.J. Wells, and J. Fluke. 1990. 'Gatekeeping in Child Protective Services: A Survey of Screening Policies.' *Child Welfare* 69(4): 357–69.

Downs, Anthony. 1960. 'Why the Government Budget Is Too Small in a Democracy.' *World Politics* 12: 541–63.

Drakich, Janice. 1988. 'In Whose Best Interest? The Politics of Joint Custody.' In *Family Bonds and Gender Divisions*, edited by B. Fox, 477–96. Toronto: Canadian Scholars' Press.

Dranoff, Linda Silver. 1977. *Women in Canadian Life. Law*. Toronto: Fitzhenry and Whiteside.

Drover, Glenn, and Patrick Kerans, eds. 1993. *New Approaches to Welfare Theory*. Brookfield, Vt: Edward Elgar.

DuBray, Robert. 1986. *A Comparison of Compensation in Canada and the United States*. Ottawa: The Conference Board of Canada.

Dudley, J.R. 1991. 'Exploring Ways to Get Divorced Fathers to Comply Willingly with Child Support Agreements.' *Journal of Divorce and Remarriage* 14(3/4): 121–35.

Dulac, Germain. 1994. 'The Changing Faces of Fatherhood.' *Transition* (March): 12–15.

Dumas, Jean. 1990. *Report on the Demographic Situation in Canada 1990*. For Statistics Canada. Catalogue no. 91-209. November. Ottawa: Supply and Services Canada.

– (with Yolande Lavoie). 1992. *Report on the Demographic Situation in Canada 1992*. Catalogue no. 91-209E. November. Ottawa: Statistics Canada.

Dumas, Jean, and Yves Péron. 1992. *Marriage and Conjugal Life in Canada*. Catalogue no. 91-534E. March. Ottawa: Statistics Canada.

Dumon, Wilfrid. 1987. 'La politique familiale en Europe occidentale.' *Année Sociologique* 37: 291–308.

– 1990. *Family Policy in EEC Countries*. Luxembourg: Commission of the European Communities.

Dunbar Amy, and Susan Nordhauser. 1991. 'Is the Child Care Credit Progressive?' *National Tax Journal* 44 (December): 519–28.

Duncan, Greg J., and Willard Rodgers. 1990. 'Lone-Parent Families and Their Economic Problems: Transitory or Persistent.' In *Lone-Parent Families. The Economic Challenge*. Paris: OECD.

Duskin, Elizabeth. 1990. 'Overview.' In *Lone-Parent Families. The Economic Challenge*. Paris: OECD.

– 1992. 'Disadvantaged Lone-Parent Families: Is Family Structure the Problem? Is Social Security the Answer?' In *Social Security and Changing Family Structures*, edited by the International Social Security Association, 115–24. Geneva: ISSA.

Duxbury, Linda, and Christopher Higgins. 1994. 'Families in the Economy.' In *Canada's Changing Families: Challenges to Public Policy*, edited by M. Baker, 29–40. Ottawa: Vanier Institute of the Family.

Duxbury, L., C. Higgins, and C. Lee. 1992. *Balancing Work and Family: A Study of the Canadian Private Sector*. Ottawa: Health and Welfare Canada.

Economic Council of Canada. 1992. *The New Face of Poverty. Income Security Needs of Canadian Families*. Ottawa: Minister of Supply and Services Canada.

Economic Intelligence Units. 1992, 1993. *Country Report* (Australia, Canada, France, Germany, Netherlands, Sweden, United Kingdom, United States). London: Economic Intelligence Units.

Edgar, Don. 1991. 'Tackling Workforce Barriers: Overseas Sole Parents Provisions.' *Paid Work. Is It a Luxury Sole Parents Can't Afford?* Proceedings of a Conference on Workforce Barriers Facing Sole Parents. Melbourne, Australia: Victorian Council of Social Service.

Edgar, Don, D. Keane, and P. McDonald. 1989. *Child Poverty*. Melbourne, Australia: Allen and Unwin (with the Australian Institute of Family Studies).

Eduards, Maud L. 1991. 'Toward a Third Way: Women's Politics and Welfare Policies in Sweden.' *Social Research* 58(3): 677–705.

Eekelaar, J. 1988. 'England and Wales.' In *Child Support*. Edited by A.J. Kahn and S.B. Kamerman, 153–75. Newbury Park, Calif.: Sage Publications.

Eichler, Margrit. 1988a. *Families in Canada Today*. Toronto: Gage Educational Publishing.

– 1988b. *Fifty Questions: Problems and Issues in Developing Policies for Canadian Families*. January. Ottawa: Canadian Centre for Policy Alternatives.

– 1990. 'The Limits of Family Law Reform or the Privatization of Female and Child Poverty.' *Canadian Family Law Quarterly* 7(1).

Ellwood, David T. 1987. *Divide and Conquer: Responsible Security for America's Poor*. New York: Ford Foundations.

– 1988. *Poor Support: Poverty in the American Family*. New York: Basic Books.

– 1990. 'Valuing the United States Income Support System for Lone Mothers.' In *Lone-Parent Families: The Economic Challenge*, 201–22. Paris: OECD.

Ergas, Y. 1990. 'Child-Care Policies in Comparative Perspective: An Introductory Discussion.' In *Lone-Parent Families. The Economic Challenge*, 173–99. Paris: OECD.

Erikson, Robert, and Johan Fritzell. 1988. 'The Effects of the Social Welfare System in Sweden on the Well-Being of Children and the Elderly.' In *The*

Vulnerable, edited by J. Palmer, T. Smeeding, and B. Torrey, 309–30. Washington, D.C.: Urban Institute Press.

Ermisch, John F. 1990. 'Demographic Aspects of the Growing Number of Lone-Parent Families.' In *Lone-Parent Families. The Economic Challenge*, 27–41. Paris: OECD.

– 1991. *Lone Parenthood – An Economic Analysis*. Cambridge: Cambridge University Press.

Ermisch, John F., Stephen Jenkins, and Robert E. Wright. 1990. 'Analysis of the Dynamics of Lone Parenthood: Socio-Economic Influences on Entry and Exit Rates.' In *Lone-Parent Families. The Economic Challenge*, 69–90. Paris: OECD.

Esping-Andersen, G. 1984a. 'Social Policy as Class Politics in Post-War Capitalism: Scandinavia, Austria and Germany.' In *Order and Conflict in Contemporary Capitalism*, edited by J.H. Goldthorpe. Oxford: Clarendon Press.

– 1984b. 'The State as a System of Stratification: Conservatism, Liberalism and Socialism in the Organization of Public Welfare Programs.' Paper presented to the Public Symposium on the Labor Movement and the Welfare State in Western Europe. March. University of Copenhagen.

– 1985. *Politics against Markets – the Social Democratic Road to Power*. Cambridge, Mass.: Harvard University Press.

– 1990. *The Three Worlds of Welfare Capitalism*. Princeton, N.J.: Princeton University Press.

– 1992. 'The Three Political Economies of the Welfare State.' In *The Study of the Welfare State*, edited by J.E. Kolberg. London: M.E. Sharpe.

Evans, Patricia M. 1992. 'Targeting Single Mothers for Employment: Comparisons from the United States, Britain and Canada.' *Social Service Review* 66 (September): 378–98.

– 1993. 'From Workfare to the Social Contract: Implications for Canada of Recent U.S. Welfare Reforms.' *Canadian Public Policy* 19(1): 54–67.

Evans, Patricia M., and Eileen L. McIntyre. 1984. 'Welfare, Work Incentives and the Single Mothers.' In *The Canadian Welfare State*, edited by J.S. Ismael, 101–25. Edmonton: University of Alberta Press.

Fabricant, Michael B., and Steve Burghardt. 1992. *The Welfare State Crisis and the Transformation of Social Service Work*. Armonk, N.Y.: M.E. Sharpe.

Farquhar, K.B. 1990. 'Termination of the In Loco Parentis Obligation of Child Support.' *Canadian Journal of Family Law* 9: 99–129.

Federal/Provincial/Territorial Family Law Committee. *See* Canada.

Felstiner, J.P. 1991. 'Child Welfare Hearings from an Unfamiliar Perspective.' In *Canadian Child Welfare Law: Children, Families and the State*, edited by N. Bala, J.P. Hornick, and R. Vogl. Toronto: Thompson Educational Publishing.

Ferguson, E. 1991. 'The Child-Care Crisis: Realities of Women's Caring.' In *Women's Caring: Feminist Perspectives on Social Welfare*, edited by C. Baines, P. Evans, and S. Neysmith, 73–105. Toronto: McClelland and Stewart.

Ferri, E. 1993. 'An Overview of Research and Policy on the Lone Parent Family in Britain.' In *Single Parent Families*, edited by J. Hudson and B. Galaway. Toronto: Thompson Educational Publishing.

Fillion, K. 1989. 'The Daycare Decision'. *Saturday Night* (January): 23–30.

Finlay, H.A., and R.J. Bailey-Harris. 1989. *Family Law in Australia*. Sydney: Butterworths.

Finnie, Ross 1993. 'Women, Men, and the Economic Consequences of Divorce: Evidence from Canadian Longitudinal Data.' *Canadian Review of Sociology and Anthropology* 30(2): 205–41.

– 1994. *Child Support: Exploring the Guideline Options*. Montreal: Institute for Research on Public Policy.

Flango, Victor. 1990. 'Agency and Private Adoptions by State.' *Child Welfare* 69 (3): 263–75.

Fletcher, C.N. 1989. 'A Comparison of Incomes and Expenditures of Male-Headed Households Paying Child Support and Female-Headed Households Receiving Child Support.' *Family Relations* 38: 412–17.

Flynn, Clifton P. 1991. 'Rethinking Joint Custody Policy: Option or Presumption?' In *The Reconstruction of Family Policy*, edited by E.A. Anderson and R.C. Hula. Westport, Conn.: Greenwood Press.

Flynn, C.P., and H. Rodman. 1991. 'Latchkey Children and After-School Care: A Feminist Dilemma?' In *The Reconstruction of Family Policy*, edited by E.A. Anderson and R.C. Hula, 77–90. Westport, Conn.: Greenwood Press.

Folbre, Nancy. 1991. *Women on Their Own: Global Patterns of Female Headship*. March. Washington: International Centre for Research on Women.

– 1993. *Who Pays for the Kids? Gender and the Structures of Constraint*. New York: Routledge.

Fooks, Cathy, and Bob Gardner. 1986. 'The Implementation of Midwifery in Ontario.' November. Current Issue Paper no. 50. Toronto: Ontario Legislative Library.

Foote, Catherine. 1988. 'Recent State Responses to Separation and Divorce in Canada: Implications for Families and Social Welfare.' In *Canadian Social Work Review* 5.

Foreign and Commonwealth Office. 1991. 'Economic and Scientific Affairs – Taxes and Social Security Contributions.' *Survey of Current Affairs* 21(1): 17–19.

Forestall, Nancy. 1993. 'Workers, Wives and the Welfare State: Workers' Compensation and Ontario Goldminers, 1915–1950.' Paper presented to the Sixth Social Welfare Conference, 27–30 June. St John's, Newfoundland.

Fortin, Pierre. 1989. 'L'impact du choc démographie sur le niveau de vie à long terme.' Allocution du président prononcée le 25 mai 1989 lors du congrès annuel de la Société canadienne de science économique. Mont-Rolland, Québec.

Frank, R., 1987–8. 'Federal Republic of Germany: New Thinking on Maintenance Obligations, Artificial Insemination and Conflict of Laws.' *Journal of Family Law* 26: 101–11.

Frankel, A.J. 1991. 'The Dynamics of Day Care. Families in Society.' *The Journal of Contemporary Human Services* (January): 3–10.

Frankel, H. 1988. 'Family-Centred, Home-Based Services in Child Protection: A Review of the Research.' *Social Service Review* 62 (March): 137–57.

Fraser, Nancy. 1989. *Unruly Practices*. Minneapolis: University of Minnesota Press.

Freed, D.J., and T.B. Walker. 1990. 'Family Law in the Fifty States: An Overview.' *Family Law Quarterly* 24(3): 309–400.

Freeman, M.D.A. 1989–90. 'England: A Year of Abuse.' *Journal of Family Law* 28: 469–90.

– 1990–1. 'England's New Children's Charter'. *Journal of Family Law* 29: 343–57.

Friendly, Martha. 1994. *Child Care Policy in Canada. Putting the Pieces Together*. Don Mills, Ont.: Addison-Wesley.

Fritzell, Johan. 1992. 'Income Inequality Trends in the 1980s: A Five Country Comparison.' April. The Luxembourg Income Study, Working Paper no. 73.

Fulton, Jane. 1994. 'Families, Health and Health Care.' In *Canada's Changing Families: Challenges to Public Policy*, edited by M. Baker. Ottawa: Vanier Institute of the Family.

Furstenberg, Frank, Jr. 1988. 'Marital Disruptions, Child Custody, and Visitation.' In *Child Support: From Debt Collection to Social Policy*, edited by A.J. Kahn and S.B. Kamerman. Newbury Park, Calif.: Sage Publications.

Furstenberg, F., and C. Nord. 1985. 'Parenting Apart: Patterns of Childrearing after Divorce.' *Journal of Marriage and the Family* 47: 893–904.

Galarneau, Diane. 1992. 'Alimony and Child Support.' *Perspectives on Labour and Income* 4(20): 8–21.

Galinsky, Ellen, Diane Hughes, and Judy David. 1990. 'Trends in Corporate Family Supportive Policies.' *Marriage and Family Review* 15(3–4): 75–94.

Garfinkel, Irwin 1985. 'The Role of Child Support Insurance in Antipoverty Policy.' *The Annals of the American Academy of Political and Social Sciences* 479 (May): 119–31.

– 1988. 'Child Support Assurance: A New Tool for Achieving Social Security.' In *Child Support*, edited by A.J. Kahn and S.B. Kamerman, 328–49. Newbury Park, Calif.: Sage Publications.

– 1992. *Assuring Child Support*. New York: Russell Sage Foundation.

Garfinkel, Irwin, and Sara S. McLanahan. 1986. *Single Mothers and Their Children – A New American Dilemma*. Washington: Urban Institute Press.

Garfinkel, I., D. Meyer, and P. Wong. 1990.'The Potential of Tax Credits to Reduce Poverty and Welfare Recipiency.' *Population Research and Policy Review* 9: 45–63.

Garfinkel, I., and M.S. Melli. 1990. 'The Use of Normative Standards in Family Law Decisions: Developing Mathematical Standards for Child Support.' *Family Law Quarterly* 24(2): 157–78.

Garfinkel, Irwin, Donald Oellerich, and Philip K. Robins. 1991. 'Child Support Guidelines – Will They Make a Difference?' *Journal of Family Issues* 12(4): 404–29.

Garfinkel, Irwin, and Patrick Wong. 1990. 'Child Support and Public Policy.' In *Lone-Parent Families. The Economic Challenge*, 101–26. Paris: OECD.

Garrett, P., D. Wenk, and S. Lubeck. 1990. 'Working around Childbirth: Comparative and Empirical Perspectives on Parental Leave Policy.' *Child Welfare* 69(5): 401–13.

Genereux, Anne. 1991. 'The Protection Hearing.' In *Canadian Child Welfare Law: Children, Families and the State*, edited by N. Bala, J.P. Hornick, and R. Vogl, 55–76. Toronto: Thompson Educational Publishing.

Getis, Victoria L., and Maris A. Vinovskis. 1992. 'History of Child Care in the United States before 1950.' In *Child Care in Context: Cross-Cultural Perspectives*, edited by M.E. Lamb et al. Hillsdale, N.J.: Lawrence Erlbaum Associates.

Gibbons, J. 1991. 'Children in Need and Their Families: Outcomes of Referral to Social Services.' *British Journal of Social Work* 21: 217–27.

Gibbs, J.T. 1990. 'Black American Adolescents.' In *Children of Color*, edited by J.T. Gibbs et al., 179–223. San Francisco: Jossey-Bass.

Gilbert, Neil, Harry Specht, and Paul Terrell. 1993. *Dimensions of Social Welfare Policy* (3rd ed.). Englewood Cliffs, N.J.: Prentice-Hall.

Gill, Flora. 1990. 'Social Justice and the Low-Paid Workers.' *Australian Journal of Social Issues* 25(2): 83–101.

Gilliand, Pierre. 1989. 'Evolution of Family Policy in the Light of Demographic Development in Western European Countries.' *International Social Security Review* 42(1): 395–426.

Ginsburg, Norman. 1992. *Divisions of Welfare: A Critical Introduction to Comparative Social Policy*. London: Sage.

Glass, B.L. 1990. 'Child Support Enforcement: An Implementation Analysis.' *Social Service Review* 64(4): 542–58.

Glatzer, Wolfgang, et al. 1992. *Recent Social Trends in West Germany 1960–1990*. Montreal/Kingston: McGill-Queen's University Press.

Glendon, Mary Ann. 1981. *The New Family and the New Property*. Toronto: Butterworths.

– 1987. *Abortion and Divorce in Western Law*. Cambridge, Mass.: Harvard University Press.

Glennerster, H., et al. 1991. 'A New Era for Social Policy: A New Enlightenment or a New Leviathan?' *Journal of Social Policy* 20(3): 389–414.

Glezer, Helen. 1988. *Maternity Leave in Australia. Employee and Employer Experiences. A Survey*. Monograph no. 7. Melbourne: Australian Institute for Family Studies.

Glossop, Robert. 1986. 'Family Time or Prime Time? Jobs, Leisure and Relationships in the 1980s.' A Plenary Address to the Leisure in Motion 1986 Conference of the British Columbia Recreation Association and the National Recreation and Parks Association, Vancouver, 11 May 1986. 'Perspectives Series.' Ottawa: Vanier Institute of the Family.

– 1993. 'Canadian Marriage and Family: Future Directions.' In *Marriage and Family in Canada Today*, edited by G.N. Ramu, 210–25. Scarborough, Ont.: Prentice Hall.

Goelman, Hillel. 1992. 'Day Care in Canada.' In *Child Care in Context: Cross-Cultural Perspectives*, edited by M.E. Lamb et al. Hillsdale, N.J.: Lawrence Erlbaum Associates: 223–63.

Goelman, H., M.K. Rosenthal, and A.R. Pence. 1990. 'Family Day Care in Two Countries: Parents, Caregivers and Children in Canada and Israel.' *Child and Youth Care Quarterly* 19(4): 251–70.

Goldberg, G.S. 1991. 'Women on the Verge: Winners and Losers in German Unification.' *Social Policy* 34: 35–44.

Goldfarb, S.F. 1987. 'Child Support Guidelines: A Model for Fair Allocation of Child Care, Medical and Educational Expenses.' *Family Law Quarterly* 21(3): 325–49.

Gonyo, B., and K.W. Watson. 1988. 'Searching in Adoption.' *Public Welfare* (Winter): 14–22, 43–4.

Gooderham, Mary. 1994. 'Couples Paid up to $30,000 for Babies.' *Globe and Mail* (Toronto), 16 February.

Goodman, Catherine. 1992. 'Income Security and Support for Families in a Changing Social Environment: The Canadian Experience.' In *Social Security and Changing Family Structures*, edited by the International Social Security Association, 53–75. Geneva: ISSA.

Goodnow, J., A. Burns, and G. Russell. 1989. 'Australian Families: Pictures and Interpretations.' In *Australian Society*, edited by E. Hancock, 23–43. Cambridge: Cambridge University Press.

Goodwin, Cynthia. 1984. *Equal Pay Legislation and Implementation: Selected Countries*. Ottawa: Labour Canada.

Gordon, Linda, ed. 1991. *Women, the State and Welfare*. Madison, Wis.: University of Wisconsin Press.

Gordon, Margaret S. 1988. *Social Security Policies in Industrialized Countries: A Comparative Analysis*. New York: Cambridge University Press.

Gordon, Michael. 1971. 'Civil Servants, Politicians and Parties.' *Comparative Politics* 4: 29–58.

Gould, Stephanie G., and John L. Palmer. 1988. 'Outcomes, Interpretations and Policy Implications.' In *The Vulnerable*, edited by J. Palmer, T. Smeeding, and B. Torrey, 413–42. Washington, D.C.: Urban Institute Press.

Grandke, A. 1989–90. 'German Democratic Republic: Social Development, Social Policy and Family Law.' *Journal of Family Law* 28: 495–507.

Granger, J. M. 1989. 'Attitudes toward National Personal Social Services Policy.' *Child Welfare* 68(3): 301–15.

Gray, Grattan. 1990. 'Social Policy by Stealth.' *Policy Options* (9 March): 17–29.

Guest, Dennis. 1985. *The Emergence of Social Security in Canada* (2nd ed.) Vancouver: University of British Columbia Press.

– 1990. 'Dealing with Unemployment.' In *Unemployment and Welfare*, edited by G. Riches and G. Ternowetsky, 30–46. Toronto: Garamond Press.

Gunderson, Morley, and Leon Muszynski. 1990. *Women and Labour Market Poverty*. June. Ottawa: Canadian Advisory Council on the Status of Women.

Gustafsson, Bjorn. 1993a. 'The Income Safety Net: Who Falls into It and Why?' In *Welfare Trends in the Scandinavian Countries*, edited by Erik J. Hansen et al., 267–85. Armonk, N.Y.: M.E. Sharpe.

– 1993b. 'Poverty in Sweden 1975–1985.' In *Welfare Trends in the Scandinavian Countries*, edited by Erik J. Hansen et al., 251–66. Armonk, N.Y.: M.E. Sharpe.

Gustafsson, Bjorn, and Mats Lindblom. 1990. 'Poverty as Inefficiency of the Welfare State. A Cross-country Comparison.' August. The Luxembourg Income Study, Working Paper no. 61. August.

Gustafsson, Siv. 1990. 'Labour Force Participation and Earnings of Lone Parents: A Swedish Case Study Including Comparisons with Germany.' In *Lone-Parent Families. The Economic Challenge*, 151–62. Paris: OECD.

Gustavsson, N., and S. Kopels. 1992. 'Liability in Child Welfare.' *Child and Adolescent Social Work Journal* 9(5): 457–67.

Haas, Linda. 1990. 'Gender Equality and Social Policy – Implications of a Study of Parental Leave in Sweden.' *Journal of Family Issues* 11(4): 401–23.

– 1991. 'Equal Parenthood and Social Policy: Lessons from a Study of Parental Leave in Sweden.' In *Parental Leave and Child Care*, edited by J.S. Hyde and M.J. Essex, 375–405. Philadelphia: Temple University Press.

Hainsworth, T.W. 1992. *The Ontario Family Law Act Manual*. Toronto: Canada Law Book.

Hall, T. 1986. 'The Adoption Revolution in Britain.' In *Adoption in Worldwide Perspective*, edited by R.A.C. Hoksbergen. Berwyn: Swets North America.

Hallett, S. 1991. 'Criminal Prosecutions for Abuse and Neglect.' In *Canadian Child Welfare Law: Children, Families and the State*, edited by N. Bala, J.P. Hornick, and R. Vogl. Toronto: Thompson Educational Publishing.

Hanson, S.H., and M.J. Sporakowski. 1986. 'Single-Parent Families,' *Family Relations* 35: 3–8.

Hantrais, Linda. 1994. 'Comparing Family Policy in Britain, France and Germany.' *Journal of Social Policy* 23 (Part 2): 135–60.

Hardey, Michael, and Graham Crow. 1991. *Lone Parenthood*. Toronto: University of Toronto Press.

Hardey, Michael, and Judith Glover. 1991. 'Income, Employment, Daycare and Lone Parenthood.' In *Lone Parenthood*, edited by M. Hardey and G. Crow, 88–109. Toronto: University of Toronto Press.

Hardiker, P., K. Exton, and M. Barker. 1991. 'The Social Policy Contexts of Prevention in Child Care.' *British Journal of Social Work* 21: 341–59.

Hardin, M. 1988. 'New Legal Options to Prepare Adolescents for Independent Living.' *Child Welfare* 57(6): 529–46.

– 1992. 'Working with the Courts: Some Suggestions for Child Welfare Agency Administrators.' *Children's Legal Rights Journal* 13(4): 12–15.

Harding, Ann, and John Landt. 1992. 'Policy and Poverty: Trends in Disposable Incomes.' *Australian Quarterly* 64(1): 19–48.

Harrell, Andrew. 1985. 'Husbands' Involvement in Housework: The Effects of Relative Earning Power and Masculine Orientation.' Edmonton: Edmonton Area Study Series no. 39.

Harris, D.V. 1988. 'Renewing Our Commitment to Child Welfare.' *Social Work* 33(6): 483–4.

Harris, L. 1980. 'The State and the Economy: Some Theoretical Problems.' In *Socialist Register*, edited by R. Miliband and J. Saville. London: Merlin.

Harrison, Margaret. 1991. 'The Reformed Australian Child Support Scheme: An International Policy Comment.' *Journal of Family Issues* 12(4): 430–49.

Harrison, M., G. Snider, R. Merlo, and V. Lucchesi. 1991. *Paying for the Children*. Monograph no. 10. Melbourne: Australian Institute of Family Studies.

Harvey, W. 1991. 'Preparing Children for Testifying in Court.' In *Canadian Child Welfare Law: Children, Families and the State*, edited by N. Bala, J.P. Hornick, and R. Vogl. Toronto: Thompson Educational Publishing.

Haskey, John. 1993. 'Trends in the Numbers of One Parent Families in Great Britain.' *Population Trends* 71: 26–33.

Haskins, R. 1988a. 'Child Support: A Father's View.' In *Child Support*, edited by A.J. Kahn and S.B. Kamerman, 306–27. Newbury Park, Calif.: Sage Publications.

– 1988b. 'What Day Care Crisis?' *Regulation* 12 (2): 13–21.

– (1992). 'Similar History, Similar Markets, Similar Policies Yield Similar Fixations.' In *Child Care in Context: Cross-Cultural Perspectives*, edited by M.E. Lamb et al. Hillsdale, N.J.: Lawrence Erlbaum Associates.

Hatton, M.J. 1991. 'Representing Parents.' In *Canadian Child Welfare Law: Children, Families and the State*, edited by N. Bala, J.P. Hornick, and R. Vogl. Toronto: Thompson Educational Publishing.

Havemann, Robert, and Barbara Wolfe. 1993. 'Children's Prospects and Children's Policy.' *The Journal of Economic Perspectives* 7(4): 153–74.

Hayes, Cheryl, John L. Palmer, and Martha J. Zaslow, eds. 1990. *Who Cares for America's Children. Child Care Policy for the 1990s*. Washington, D.C.: National Academy Press.

Hayghe, H.V. 1988. 'Employers and Child Care: What Roles Do They Play?' *Monthly Labor Review* (September): 38–44.

Heclo, Hugh. 1974. *Modern Social Politics in Britain and Sweden*. New Haven, Conn.: Yale University Press.

Heidenheimer, Arnold J. et al. 1975. *Comparative Public Policy*. New York: St Martin's.

Heitlinger, Alena. 1987. *Reproduction, Medicine and the Socialist State*. London: Macmillan.

– 1991. 'Pronatalism and Women's Equality Policies.' *European Journal of Population* 7: 343–75.

– 1993. *Women's Equality, Demography, and Public Policy. A Comparative Perspective*. London: Macmillan.

Helgeson, V.S., G.S. Goodman, P.R. Shaver, and J.P. Lipton. 1989. 'Special Report: Attitudes Concerning the Rights of Children and Adults.' *Children's Legal Rights Journal* 10(1): 2–12.

Henderson, D.R. 1989. 'The Supply-Side Tax Revenue Effects of the Child Care Tax Credit.' *Journal of Policy and Management* 8(4): 673–5.

Henripin, Jacques. 1989. *Naître ou ne pas être*. Montréal: Institut québécois de recherche sur la culture.

Hepworth, H. Philip. 1980. *Foster Care and Adoption in Canada*. Ottawa: Canadian Council on Social Development.

Herr, M. 1989. 'Policy Directions for Child Care.' *American Family* 12(3): 3–10.

Hersov, Lionel. 1990. 'Aspects of Adoption.' *Journal of Child Psychology and Psychiatry* 31(4): 493–510.

Hess, Melanie. 1992a. *The Canadian Fact Book on Income Security Programs.* Ottawa: Canadian Council on Social Development.

– 1992b. 'Social Spending in America.' *Perception* 16(2,3): 47–54.

Hessle, S. 1989. 'Families Falling Apart: A Report from Social Services.' *Child Welfare* 68(2): 209–13.

Hibbs, Douglas A., Jr. 1970. 'Political Parties and Macroeconomic Policy.' *American Political Science Review* 70: 1467–87.

– 1978. 'On the Political Economy of Long-Run Trends in Strike Activity.' *British Journal of Political Science* 8: 153–75.

Higgins, C., L. Duxbury, and C. Lee. 1993. *Balancing Work and Family: A Study of the Canadian Private Sector.* London, Ont.: National Centre for Research, Management and Development, University of Western Ontario.

Hill, Malcolm. 1992. 'Free Trade and Social Policy: Are There Lessons from Europe?' *Canadian Review of Social Policy* 29/30 (Summer/Winter): 5–24.

Hill, Michael. 1989. 'Income Maintenance and Local Government.' *Critical Social Policy* 9(1): 18–36.

– 1990. *Social Security Policy in Britain.* Aldershot, Eng.: Edward Elgar.

Hill, M., and J. Triseliotis, 1991. 'Subsidized Adoption across the Atlantic.' *Child Welfare* 70(3): 383–95.

Himel, S.G. 1991. 'Representing Children.' In *Canadian Child Welfare Law: Children, Families and the State,* edited by N. Bala, J.P. Hornick, and R. Vogl. Toronto: Thompson Educational Publishing.

Himmelstrand, U., G. Ahrne, and L. Lundberg. 1981. *Beyond Welfare Capitalism – Issues, Actors and Forces in Societal Change.* London: Heinemann.

Hobart, Charles. 1989. 'Premarital Sexuality.' In *Marriage and the Family in Canada Today,* edited by G.N. Ramu, 53–76. Scarborough, Ont.: Prentice-Hall.

Hobson, Barbara. 1990. 'No Exit, No Voice: Women's Economic Dependency and the Welfare State.' *Acta Sociologica* 33: 235–50.

Hofferth, S.L. 1989. 'What Is the Demand for and Supply of Child Care in the United States?' *Young Children* (July): 28–33.

Hofferth, S.L., and D.A. Phillips. 1987. 'Child Care in the United States, 1970 to 1995.' *Journal of Marriage and the Family* 49 (August): 559–71.

– 1991. 'Child Care Policy Research.' *Journal of Social Issues* 47(2): 1–13.

Hohn, Charlotte. 1987. 'Population Policies in Advanced Societies: Pronatalist and Migration Strategies.' *European Journal of Population* 3: 459–81.

– 1990. 'Federal Republic of Germany.' In *Family Policy in EEC Countries,* edited by W. Dumon, 79–102. Luxembourg: Commission of the European Communities.

Hohn, Charlotte, and Kurt Luscher. 1988). 'The Changing Family in the Federal Republic of Germany.' *Journal of Family Issues* 9(3): 317–35.

Hohnerlein, Eva-Marie. 1992. 'Income Support Benefits for Lone-Parent Families in the FRG and Italy: A Comparative Study.' In *Social Security and Changing Family Structures*, edited by the International Social Security Association, 125–56. Geneva: ISSA.

Hoksbergen, Renée A.C. 1985. 'Adopting a Foreign Child: Principles Governing the Handling of This Complex Phenomenon in the Netherlands.' *International Child Welfare Review* 64/65 (Summer): 34–44.

– 1991. 'Understanding and Preventing "Failed Adoptions."' In *Adoption: International Perspectives*, edited by E.D. Hibbs. Madison, Conn.: International University Press.

Hoksbergen, R.A.C., and L.A.C. Bunjes. 1986. 'Thirty Years of Adoption Practice in the Netherlands.' In *Adoption in Worldwide Perspective*, edited by R.A.C. Hoksbergen. Berwyn: Swets North America.

Hoksbergen, R.A.C., and S.D. Gokhale. 1986. 'Adoption: A World-Wide Phenomenon.' In *Adoption in Worldwide Perspective*, edited by R.A.C. Hoksbergen. Berwyn: Swets North America.

Horne-Roberts, J. 1991. 'The Adoption Law Review.' *New Law Journal* 141: 1657–8.

– 1992. 'Intercountry Adoption.' *New Law Journal* 142: 286–8.

Hossie, Linda, 1985. 'The Midwives Battle for Self-Rule.' *Globe and Mail*, 12 November.

Howe, D. 1987. 'Adopted Children in Care.' *British Journal of Social Work* 17: 493–505.

Howes, C. 1991. 'Caregiving Environments and Their Consequences for Children: The Experience in the United States.' In *Day Care for Young Children: International Perspectives*, edited by E.C. Melhuish and P. Moss, 184–98. London: Tavistock/Routledge.

Howing, P.T., and J.S. Wodarski. 1992. 'Legal Requisites for Social Workers in Child Abuse and Neglect Situations.' *Social Work* 37(4): 330–5.

Huber, Joan, and Glenna Spitze. 1980. 'Considering Divorce: An Expansion of Becker's Theory of Marital Instability.' *American Journal of Sociology* 86(1): 75–89.

Hubka, David S. 1992a. *Countdown 92: Campaign 2000 Child Poverty Indicator Report*. November. Ottawa: The Centre for International Statistics on Economic and Social Welfare for Families and Children, Canadian Council on Social Development.

– 1992b. 'Reporting on Child Poverty: The Efforts of Campaign 2000.' *Perception* 16(4): 17–22.

Hudson, S.S., 1988–9. 'The Broadening Scope of Liability in Child Abuse Cases.' *Journal of Family Law* 27: 697–713.

Hugo, Graeme, 1986. *Australia's Changing Population: Trends and Implications*. Melbourne: Oxford University Press.

Hula, Richard C. 1991. 'Introduction: Thinking about Family Policy.' In *The Reconstruction of Family Policy*, edited by E.A. Anderson and R.C. Hula. Westport, Conn.: Greenwood Press.

Hunsley, Terrance M. 1986. 'A Warming Climate for Reform.' *Policy Options* 7(5): 9–13.

– 1992. 'Fiscal Dimensions of the Canadian Welfare State.' In *Social Policy in the Global Economy*, edited by Terrance Hunsley. Kingston: Queen's University, School of Policy Studies.

– 1994. *An Inventory of Family-Supportive Policies and Programs in Federal, Provincial and Territorial Jurisdictions*. Ottawa: Vanier Institute of the Family.

Hunsley, Terrance M., ed. 1992. *Social Policy in the Global Economy*. Kingston: Queen's University, School of Policy Studies.

Hupe, Peter L. 1993. 'Beyond Pillarization – The (Post-) Welfare State in the Netherlands.' *European Journal of Political Research* 23: 359–86.

Huston, Aletha C. 1991a. 'Antecedents, Consequences and Possible Solutions for Poverty among Children.' In *Children in Poverty*, edited by A. Huston. Cambridge: Cambridge University Press.

– 1991b. 'Children in Poverty: Developmental and Policy Issues.' In *Children in Poverty*, edited by A. Huston. Cambridge: Cambridge University Press.

Huston, Aletha, C., ed. 1991. *Children in Poverty*. Cambridge: Cambridge University Press.

Hwang, C. Philip, and Anders G. Broberg. 1992. 'The Historical and Social Context of Child Care in Sweden. ' In *Child Care in Context: Cross-Cultural Perspectives*, edited by M.E. Lamb et al. Hillsdale, N.J.: Lawrence Erlbaum Associates.

Hwang, C.P., A. Broberg, and M.E. Lamb. 1991. 'Swedish Child Care Research.' In *Day Care for Young Children: International Perspectives*, edited by E.C. Melhuish, and P. Moss, 101–20. London: Tavistock/Routledge.

Hyde, Janet Shibley, and Marilyn J. Essex eds. 1991. *Parental Leave and Child Care. Setting a Research and Policy Agenda*. Philadelphia: Temple University Press.

International Labor Office. 1988a. 'Legal Provisions.' *Conditions of Work Digest* 7(2): 79–142.

– 1988b. 'Maternity/Paternity Leave – Legal Provisions.' *Conditions of Work Digest* (Geneva) 7(2).

International Metal Workers' Federation. 1981. *International Comparison of Average Net Hourly Earnings in 1980 Based on Working Time Required for the Purchase of Various Consumer Items*. Geneva: International Metal Workers' Federation.

International Social Security Association. 1986. 'Developments and Trends in Social Security 1984–1986.' *International Social Security Review* 39: 375–86.
– 1992a. 'Developments and Trends in Social Security 1990–1992.' *International Social Security Review* 45(4): 48–63.
– 1992b. *Social Security and Changing Family Structures*. Studies and Research no. 29. Geneva: ISSA.
– 1992c. 'Worldview – Australia.' *International Social Security Review* 45(3): 83–100.
Ironmonger, Duncan. 1993. 'Why Measure and Value Unpaid Work?' Paper presented to the International Conference on the Measurement and Valuation of Unpaid Work, 28–30 April. Ottawa.
Irving, Howard H., Michael Benjamin, and Nicolas Troeme. 1984. 'Shared Parenting: An Empirical Analysis Utilizing a Large Data Base.' *Family Process* 23 (December): 561–9.
Ismael, Jacqueline, ed. 1987. *The Canadian Welfare State. Evolution and Transition*. Edmonton: University of Alberta Press.
Ismael, Jacqueline, and Yves Vaillancourt. 1988. *Privatization and Provincial Social Services in Canada*. Edmonton: University of Alberta Press.
Jacob, Herbert. 1988. *Silent Revolution – The Transformation of Divorce Law in the United States*. Chicago: University of Chicago Press.
Jencks, Christopher, and Barbara Boyle Torrey. 1988. 'Beyond Income and Poverty: Trends in Social Welfare among Children and the Elderly Since 1960.' In *The Vulnerable*, edited by J. Palmer, T. Smeeding, and B. Torrey, 229–73. Washington, D.C.: Urban Institute Press.
Jenson, Jane. 1994. 'Post-Fordist Restructuring: Consequences for Women's Employment.' Presentation at McGill University, 11 March. Montreal.
Jezioranski, Lisa. 1987. 'Towards a New Status for the Midwifery Profession in Ontario.' *McGill Law Journal* 33(1): 90–136.
Johnson, Andrew F., Stephen McBride, and Patrick J. Smith, eds. 1994. *Continuities and Discontinuities. The Political Economy of Social Welfare and Labour Market Policy in Canada*. Toronto: University of Toronto Press.
Johnson, Holly. 1990. 'Wife Abuse.' In *Canadian Social Trends*, edited by C. McKie and K. Thompson, 173–6. Toronto: Thompson Educational Publishing.
Johnson, Stanley P. 1987. *World Population and the United Nations. Challenge and Response*. Cambridge: Cambridge University Press.
Johnston, Janet R., Marsha Kline, and Jeanne M. Tschann. 1989. 'Ongoing Postdivorce Conflict: Effects on Children of Joint Custody and Frequent Access.' *American Journal of Orthopsychiatry* 59 (October): 576–92.
Johnston, Patrick. 1983. *Native Children and the Child Welfare System*. Toronto: Lorimer.

Jones, Catherine, ed. 1985. *Patterns of Social Policy. An Introduction to Comparative Analysis*. London: Tavistock.

– 1993. *New Perspectives on the Welfare State in Europe*. London: Routledge.

Jones, Ellen, and Fred W. Grupp. 1987. *Modernization, Value Changes and Fertility in the Soviet Union*. Cambridge: Cambridge University Press.

Jones, M.A. 1980. *The Australian Welfare State*. North Sydney: Allen and Unwin.

Jonker, J.M.L. 1990. 'Family Policy and Population Policy in the Netherlands.' *Family Policy in EEC Countries*. Luxembourg: Commission of the European Communities.

Jonsson, J.O. 1993. 'Education, Social Mobility and Social Reproduction in Sweden.' In *Welfare Trends in the Scandinavian Countries*, edited by Erik J. Hansen et al., 91–118. Armonk, N.Y.: M.E. Sharpe.

Joshi, Heather. 1990. 'Obstacles and Opportunities for Lone Parents as Breadwinners in Great Britain.' In *Lone-Parent Families. The Economic Challenge*, 127–150. Paris: OECD.

Judge, Ken, and Ray Robinson. 1988. 'Public Expenditure, Privatization and the Welfare State in Britain.' In *Testing the Limits of Social Welfare*, edited by R. Morris, 39–59. Hanover, N.H.: University Press of New England.

Kadushin, A., and J.A. Martin. 1988. *Child Welfare Services* (4th ed.). New York: Macmillan.

Kagan, S.L. 1988. 'Current Reforms in Early Childhood Education: Are We Addressing the Issues?' *Young Children* (January): 27–32.

– 1990. 'The Changing World of Early Care and Education: Retrofitting Practice and Policy.' *Child and Youth Care Quarterly* 19(1): 7–20.

– 1991. 'Examining Profit and Nonprofit Child Care: An Odyssey of Quality and Auspices.' *Journal of Social Issues* 47(2): 87–104.

Kagan, S.L., and J.W. Newton. 1989. 'For-Profit and Nonprofit Child Care Similarities and Differences.' *Young Children* (November): 4–10.

Kahn, Alfred J., and Sheila B. Kamerman, eds. 1988. *Child Support: From Debt Collection to Social Policy*. Newbury Park, Calif.: Sage.

Kalbach, Warren, and Wayne W. McVey. 1979. *The Demographic Basis of Canadian Society* (2nd ed.). Toronto: McGraw-Hill Ryerson.

Kamerman, Sheila B. 1989. 'Toward a Child Policy Decade.' *Child Welfare* 68(4): 371–90.

Kamerman, Sheila, and Alfred Kahn. 1976. 'Explorations in Family Policy,' *Social Work* 21: 181–7.

– 1980. 'Child Care and Family Benefits: Policies of Six Industrialized Countries.' *Monthly Labour Review* 103 (July-December): 22–8.

– 1982. 'Income Transfers, Work and the Economic Well-Being of Families with Children: A Comparative Study.' *International Social Security Review* 35: 345–82.

- 1983a. 'Income Maintenance, Wages and Family Income.' *Public Welfare* 4(4): 23–30.
- 1983b. *Maternity Policies and Working Women*. New York: Columbia University Press.
- 1987. 'Explaining the Outcomes: Social Policy in the U.S. and Europe.' Paper prepared for the Sloan Foundation Project on 'The Well-being of the Aged and Children in the United States: Intertemporal and International Perspectives.' August.
- 1988a. 'Child Support in the United States: The Problem.' In *Child Support*, edited by A.J. Kahn and S.B. Kamerman, 10–19. Newbury Park, Calif.: Sage Publications.
- 1988b. 'Introductory Note: Child Support in Europe and Israel.' In *Child Support*, edited by A.J. Kahn and S.B. Kamerman, 45–9. Newbury Park, Calif.: Sage Publications.
- 1988c. 'Social Policy and Children in the United States and Europe.' In *The Vulnerable*, edited by J. Palmer, T. Smeeding, and B. Torrey, 350–80. Washington, D.C.: Urban Institute Press.
- 1988d. 'U.S. Issues in International Perspective.' In *Child Support*, edited by A.J. Kahn and S.B. Kamerman, 350–76. Newbury Park, Calif.: Sage Publications.
- 1988e. 'What Europe Does for Single Parent Families.' *Public Interest* 93 (Fall): 70–86.
- 1989a. 'Child Care and Privatization under Reagan.' In *Privatization and the Welfare State*, edited by S. Kamerman and A. Kahn. Princeton, N.J.: Princeton University Press.
- 1989b. 'Family Policy: Has the United States Learned from Europe?' *Policy Studies Review* 8 (3): 581–98.
- 1989c. 'Single-Parent, Female-Headed Families in Western Europe: Social Change and Response.' *International Social Security Review* 42(1): 3–34.
- 1991a. 'Child Care Policies and Programs: An International Overview.' *Journal of Social Issues* 47(2): 179–96.
- 1991b. 'Parental Leave and Infant Care: U.S. and International Trends and Issues, 1978–1988.' In *Parental Leave and Child Care*, edited by J.S. Hyde and M.J. Essex, 11–23. Philadelphia: Temple University Press.
- Forthcoming. 'Family Change and Family Policy: USA.' In *Family Change and Family Policy* (tentative title). Oxford: Oxford University Press.
Kamerman, Sheila, and Alfred Kahn, eds. 1978. *Family Policy: Government and Families in 14 Countries*. New York: Columbia University Press.
Kangas, Olli, and Joakim Palme. 1992–3. 'Statism Eroded? Labor-Market

Benefits and Challenges to the Scandinavian Welfare States.' *International Journal of Sociology* 22(4): 3–24.

Kanter, R. 1977. *Work and Family in the United States*. New York: Russell Sage.

Katarynych, Heather L. 1991. 'Adoption.' In *Canadian Child Welfare Law: Children, Families and the State*, edited by N. Bala, J.P. Hornick, and R. Vogl. Toronto: Thompson Educational Publishing.

Kaul, H. 1991. 'Who Cares? Gender Inequality and Care Leave in the Nordic Countries.' *Acta Sociologica* 34: 115–25.

Kelly, Robert F., and Sarah H. Ramsey. 1991. 'Poverty, Children and Public Policies: The Need for Diversity in Programs and Research.' *Journal of Family Issues* 12(4): 388–403.

Kent, George. 1991. *The Politics of Children's Survival*. New York: Praeger.

Kerans, Patrick. 1990. 'Government Inquiries and the Issue of Unemployment: The Struggle for People's Imagination.' In *Unemployment and Welfare: Social Policy and the Work of Social Work*, edited by G. Riches and G. Ternowetsky, 47–63. Toronto: Garamond Press.

Kesselman, Jonathan R. 1993. 'The Child Tax Benefit: Simple, Fair, Responsive?' *Canadian Public Policy* 19(2): 109–32.

Kessler, D., and A. Masson, 1985. 'What Are the Distributional Consequences of the Socialist Government Policy in France?' *Journal of Social Policy* 14(3): 403–18.

Keyfitz, Nathan, and Wilhelm Flieger, 1990. *World Population Growth and Aging – Demographic Trends in the Late Twentieth Century*. Chicago: University of Chicago Press.

Kiesling, Herbert. 1992. *Taxation and Public Goods*. Ann Arbor: University of Michigan Press.

Kindlund, S. 1988. 'Sweden.' In *Child Support*, edited by A.J. Kahn and S.B. Kamerman, 74–92. Newbury Park, Calif.: Sage Publications.

Kisker, E., and R. Maynard. 1991. 'Quality, Cost, and Parental Choice of Child Care.' In *The Economics of Child Care*, edited by D.M. Blau, 127–43. New York: Russell Sage Foundation.

Kitchen, Brigitte. 1986. 'The Patriarchal Bias of the Income Tax in Canada.' *Atlantis* 11(2): 35–46.

– 1990a. 'Employment Strategies for Women and the Sexual Division of Labour.' In *Unemployment and Welfare*, edited by G. Riches and G. Ternowetsky, 141–60. Toronto: Garamond.

– 1990b. 'Family Policy.' In *Families. Changing Trends in Canada* (2nd ed.), edited by M. Baker, 306–29. Toronto: McGraw-Hill Ryerson.

Kitchen, Brigitte, Andrew Mitchell, Peter Clutterbuck, and Marvyn Novick.

1991. *Unequal Futures: The Legacies of Child Poverty in Canada*. Toronto: Child Poverty Action Group and Social Planning Council of Metropolitan Toronto.

Klein, Rudolf. 1976. 'The Politics of Public Expenditure: American Theory and British Practice.' *British Journal of Political Science* 6: 401–32.

Klerman, Lorraine V. 1991. 'The Association between Adolescent Parenting and Childhood Poverty.' In *Children in Poverty*, edited by A. Huston. Cambridge: Cambridge University Press.

Knoppers, Bartha Maria. 1992. *Canadian Child Health Law. Human Rights and Risks of Children*. Toronto: Thompson Educational Publishing.

Knudsen, Christin, and H. Elizabeth Peters. 1994. 'An International Comparison of Married Women's Labor Supply.' Luxembourg Income Study, Working Paper no. 106, January. Luxembourg.

Kontos, S. 1991. 'Provider Perspectives in Family Day Care: Implications for Regulation and Licensing. Introduction.' *Child and Youth Care Forum* 20(4): 223–4.

Korpi, W. 1978. *The Working Class in Welfare Capitalism – Work, Unions and Politics in Sweden*. London: Routledge and Kegan Paul.

Korpi, W., and M. Shalev. 1980. 'Strikes, Power and Politics in Western Nations.' In *Political Power and Social Theory. Vol.1*, edited by M. Zeitlin. Greenwich, Conn.: JAI Press.

Krane, Julia. 1994. *The Transformation of Women into Mother Protectors: An Examination of Child Protection Practices in Cases of Child Sexual Abuse*. PhD diss., University of Toronto.

Krashinsky, Michael. 1987. 'The Cooke Report on Child Care: A Critique.' *Canadian Public Policy* 13(3): 294–303.

Krasner, Stephen D. 1976. 'State Power and the Structure of International Trade.' *World Politics* 28: 317–47.

Krause, H.D. 1988. 'Reflections on Child Support.' In *Child Support*, edited by A.J. Kahn and S.B. Kamerman, 227–50. Newbury Park, Calif.: Sage Publications.

– 1990. 'Child Support Reassessed: Limits of Private Responsibility and the Public Interest.' *Family Law Quarterly* 24(1): 1–34.

Kuehl, W., and A. Winter-Stettin. 1986. 'Foreign Adoption in the Federal Republic of Germany.' In *Adoption in Worldwide Perspective*, edited by R.A.C. Hoksbergen. Berwyn: Swets North America.

Kumar, Pradeep. 1987. *Recent Wage Deceleration in Canada – Short-Run Response or Situational Change?* Kingston: Industrial Relations Centre, Queen's University.

Kurzman, Paul A. 1988. 'Work and Family: Some Major Dilemmas.' In

Employment and Economic Problems, edited by C.S. Chilman, F.M. Cox, and E.W. Nunnally, 67–83. Newbury Park, Calif.: Sage Publications.

Kyle, I., M. Friendly, and L. Schmidt, eds. 1993. *Proceedings from the Child Care Policy and Research Symposium, Occasional Paper No. 2.* Toronto: The Childcare Resource and Research Unit, Centre for Urban and Community Studies, University of Toronto.

Labour Canada, Women's Bureau. 1990. *Women in the Labour Force 1990–91.* Ottawa: Labour Canada.

Lachapelle, R., and J. Henripin. 1982. *The Demolinguistic Situation in Canada. Past Trends and Future Prospects.* Montreal: The Institute for Research on Public Policy.

Lamb, Michael E., and Kathleen J. Sternberg. 1992). 'Sociocultural Perspectives on Nonparental Child Care.' In *Child Care in Context: Cross-Cultural Perspectives,* edited by M.E. Lamb et al. Hillsdale, N.J.: Lawrence Erlbaum Associates.

Lamb, M.J., K.J. Sternberg, C.P. Hwang, and A.G. Broberg. 1992. *Child Care in Context: Cross-Cultural Perspectives.* Hillsdale, N.J.: Lawrence Erlbaum Associates.

Lamb, M.E., K.J. Sternberg, and R.D. Ketterlinus. 1992. 'Child Care in the United States: The Modern Era.' In *Child Care in Context,* edited by M.E. Lamb et al., 207–21. Hillsdale, N.J.: Lawrence Erlbaum Associates.

Lambert, Suzanne. 1994. 'Sole Parent Income Support: Cause or Cure of Sole Parent Poverty?' *Australian Journal of Social Issues* 29(1): 75–97.

Lane, Christel. 1993. 'Gender and the Labour Market in Europe: Britain, Germany and France Compared.' *The Sociological Review* 41(2): 274–301.

Langan, Mary. 1985. 'The Unitary Approach: A Feminist Critique.' In *Women, The Family and Social Work,* edited by Eve Brook and Ann Davis, 28–47. London: Tavistock.

Langan, Mary, and Ilona Ostner. 1991. 'Gender and Welfare.' In *Towards a European Welfare State?,* edited by Graham Room, 127–50. Bristol: School of Advanced Urban Studies.

La Novara, Pina. 1993. *A Portrait of Families in Canada.* Catalogue 89-523E. Ottawa: Statistics Canada.

Lasch, Christopher. 1977. *Haven in a Heartless World: The Family Besieged.* New York: Basic Books.

Lasserre, Pierre, Evelyne Lapierre-Adamcyk, and Pierre Oulette. 1988. 'Demographie et productivité.' Report prepared for the Review of Demography and Its Implications for Economic and Social Policy. Ottawa: Health and Welfare Canada.

Laxer, James. 1993. *False God. How the Globalization Myth has Impoverished Canada.* Toronto: Lester Publishing.

Leavitt, R.L. 1991. 'Family Day Care Licensing: Issues and Recommendations.' *Child and Youth Care Forum* 20(4): 243–54.

Le Bourdais, Céline, and Nicole Marcil-Gratton (with Danièle Bélanger). 1994. 'Quebec's Pro-Active Approach to Family Policy: "Thinking and Acting Family."' In *Canada's Changing Families: Challenges to Public Policy*, edited by M. Baker, 103–15. Ottawa: Vanier Institute of the Family.

Le Bras, Hervé. 1991. 'Demographic Impact of Post-War Migration in Selected OECD Countries.' In *Migration – the Demographic Aspects*. Paris: OECD.

Lee, G.R. 1977. 'Age at Marriage and Marital Satisfaction: A Multivariate Analysis for Implications for Marital Stability.' *Journal of Marriage and the Family* 39: 493–504.

Legros, Michel, and Bernard Simonin. 1991. 'Minimum Income for Economic and Social Integration and Access to Employment: Some Reflections on the French Experience.' *Labour and Society* 16(2): 193–218.

Lehmbruch, Gerhard. 1977. 'Liberal Corporatism and Party Government.' *Comparative Political Studies* 10: 91–126.

Leibowitz, A., L.J. Waite, and C. Witsberger. 1988. 'Child Care for Preschoolers: Differences by Child's Age.' *Demography* 25(2): 205–20.

Leik, R.K., M.A. Chalkley, and N.J. Peterson. 1991. 'Policy Implications of Involving Parents in Head Start.' In *The Reconstruction of Family Policy*, edited by E.A. Anderson and R.C. Hula, 217–36. Westport, Conn.: Greenwood Press.

LeMay, S.K. 1988–9. 'The Emergence of Wrongful Adoption as a Cause of Action.' *Journal of Family Law* 27: 475–88.

Lenoir, Rémi. 1991. 'Family Policy in France since 1938.' In *The French Welfare State*, edited by J.S. Ambler. New York and London: New York University Press.

Leprince, F. 1991. 'Day Care for Young Children in France.' In *Day Care for Young Children: International Perspectives*, edited by E.C. Melhuish and P. Moss, 10–26. London: Tavistock/Routledge.

Lero, Donna, L. Brockman, A. Pence, H. Goelman, and K. Johnson. 1993. *Workplace Benefits and Flexibility: A Perspective on Parents' Experiences.* Catalogue no. 89-530E, December. Ottawa: Statistics Canada.

Lero, Donna, H. Goelman, A. Pence, L. Brockman, and S. Nutall. 1992. *Canadian National Child Care Study: Parental Work Patterns and Child Care Needs.* Catalogue no. 89-529E. Ottawa: Minister of Supply and Services.

Lero, Donna S., and Karen L. Johnson. 1994. *110 Canadian Statistics on Work and Family.* Ottawa: Canadian Advisory Council on the Status of Women.

Lesemann, Frédéric, and Roger Nicol. 1994. 'Family Policy: International Comparisons.' In *Canada's Changing Families: Challenges to Public Policy*, edited by M. Baker, 117–26. Ottawa: Vanier Institute of the Family.

Leslie, Leigh A., Elaine A. Anderson, and Meredith P. Branson. 1991. 'Responsibility for Children – The Role of Gender and Employment.' *Journal of Family Issues* 12(2): 197–210.

LeSueur, A.P. 1991. 'Public Policies and the Adoption Act.' *Public Law* (Autumn): 326–31.

Levin, Henry M. 1991. 'Cost-Benefit and Cost-Effectiveness Analyses of Interventions for Children in Poverty.' In *Children in Poverty*, edited by A. Huston. Cambridge: Cambridge University Press.

Lewis, Jane. 1989. 'Lone Parent Families: Politics and Economics.' *Journal of Social Policy* 18(4): 595–600.

Lewis, Jane, ed. 1993. *Women and Social Policies in Europe. Work, Family and the State*. Aldershot, Eng.: Edward Elgar.

Lewis, J., and G. Astrom. 1992. 'Equality, Difference and State Welfare: Labor Market and Family Policies in Sweden.' *Feminist Studies* 18(1): 59–87.

Lightman, Ernie S. 1991a. 'Support for Social Welfare in Canada and the United States.' *Canadian Review of Social Policy* 28: 9–27.

– 1991b. 'Work Incentives across Canada.' *Journal of Canadian Studies* 26(1): 120–37.

Lima, L.H., and R.C. Harris. 1988. 'The Child Support Enforcement Program in the United States.' In *Child Support*, edited by A.J. Kahn and S.B. Kamerman, 20–44. Newbury Park, Calif.: Sage Publications.

Lindbeck, Assar. 1974. *Swedish Economic Policy*. Berkeley: University of California Press.

Lindsay, Colin. 1992. *Lone-Parent Families in Canada*. For Statistics Canada, Catalogue no. 89-522E, December. Ottawa: Minister of Industry, Science and Technology.

Lister, Ruth. 1991. 'Social Security in the 1980's.' *Social Policy and Administration* 25(2): 91–107.

– 1994. 'The Child Support Act: Shifting Financial Obligations in the United Kingdom.' *Social Politics* 1(2): 211–22.

Little, Margaret. 1993. 'Single Mothers in Postwar Ontario.' Paper presented to the Canadian Sociology and Anthropology Association Annual Meetings, 4 June. Ottawa: Carleton University.

Lochhead, Clarence. 1993. 'Family Poverty in Canada, 1991.' *Perception* 17(1): 21–4.

Lodh, Françoise. 1987. 'Explaining Fertility Decline in the West (with Special Reference to Canada): A Critique of Research Results from Social Sciences.' Unpublished paper, March. Ottawa: Vanier Institute of the Family.

Lorenz, Walter. 1991. 'The New German Children and Young People Act.' *British Journal of Social Work* 21: 329–39.

Lowe, Graham. 1989. *Women, Paid/Unpaid Work and Stress: New Directions for Research*. March. Ottawa: Canadian Advisory Council on the Status of Women.

Lowe, M.I. 1991. 'The Challenge of Partnership: A National Foster Care Charter in the United Kingdom.' *Child Welfare* 70(2): 151–6.

Lubeck, S., and P. Garrett. 1991. 'Child Care in America: Retrospect and Prospect.' In *The Reconstruction of Family Policy*, edited by E.A. Anderson and R.C. Hula, 191–202. Westport, Conn.: Greenwood Press.

Lundstrom, T. 1989. 'On Swedish Social Policy.' *International Social Work* 32: 261–71.

McAllister, Ian, and Toni Makkai. 1992. 'Resource and Social Learning Theories of Political Participation: Ethnic Patterns in Australia.' *Canadian Journal of Political Science* 25(2): 269–93.

McBride, Stephen. 1987. 'Trends and Priorities in Job Creation Programs: A Comparative Study of Federal and Selected Provincial Policies.' In *The Canadian Welfare State. Evolution and Transition*, edited by Jacqueline Ismael, 151–70. Edmonton: University of Alberta Press.

MacBride-King, Judith. 1990. *Work and Family: Employment Challenge of the 90s*. Report 59-90. November, Ottawa: The Conference Board of Canada.

McBride-Stetson, Dorothy. 1991. 'The Political History of Parental Leave Policy.' In *Parental Leave and Child Care*, edited by J.S. Hyde and M.J. Essex, 406–23. Philadelphia: Temple University Press.

McCarthy, S. 1991. 'The Children Act 1989: Rules and Orders.' *New Law Journal* 11 (October): 1368, 1377–8.

McDaniel, Susan A. 1986. *Canada's Aging Population*. Toronto: Butterworths.

– 1988a. 'Women's Roles and Reproduction: The Changing Picture in Canada in the 1980s.' *Atlantis* 14(1): 1–12.

– 1988b. 'Women's Roles, Reproduction and the New Reproductive Technologies: A New Stork Rising.' In *Reconstructing the Canadian Family*, edited by N. Mandell and A. Duffy, 175–206. Toronto: Butterworths.

– 1990. *Towards Family Policies in Canada with Women in Mind*. Ottawa: Canadian Research Institute for the Advancement of Women.

McDonald, T.P., J.R. Moran, and I. Garfinkel. 1990. 'Absent Father's Ability to Pay More Child Support.' *Journal of Social Service Research* 13(4):1–18.

McEvoy, Maureen. 1991. 'Native Communities Revise and Redesign the Child Welfare System.' *Transition* 21(4): 11–14.

McFadden, E.J. 1991. 'Preface.' *Child Welfare* 70(2): 99–105.

McFate, Katherine. 1991. 'Poverty, Inequality and the Crisis of Social Policy.

Summary of Findings.' Unpublished paper prepared for the Joint Center for Political and Economic Studies, Washington, D.C.

McGillivray, A. 1990. 'Abused Children in the Courts: Adjusting the Scales after Bill C-15.' *Manitoba Law Journal* 19: 549–79.

McGilly, Frank. 1990. *Canada's Public Social Services*. Toronto: McClelland and Stewart.

Mackay, R.D. 1993. 'The Consequences of Killing Very Young Children.' *The Criminal Law Review*: 21–30.

Mackie, Richard. 1994. 'Crackdown on "Deadbeat Dads" Discussed.' *Globe and Mail* (Toronto), 4 August: A1.

MacLachlin, B. 1990. 'Spousal Support: Is It Fair to Apply New-Style Rules to Old-Style Marriages?' *Canadian Journal of Family Law* 9: 131–42.

McLanahan, Sara S., Nan Marie Astone, and Nadine F. Marks. 1991. 'The Role of Mother-Only Families in Reproducing Poverty.' In *Children in Poverty*, edited by A. Huston, 51–78. Cambridge: Cambridge University Press.

McLanahan, Sara S., Lynne M. Casper, and Annemette Sorenson. 1992. 'Women's Roles and Women's Poverty in Eight Industrialized Countries.' The Luxembourg Income Study, Working Paper no. 77. April.

McLanahan, Sara S., A. Sorenson, and D. Watson. 1989. 'Sex Differences in Poverty.' *Signs* 15 (Autumn): 102–22.

McLaren, Angus, and Arlene Tigar McLaren. 1986. *The Bedroom and the State: The Changing Practices and Politics of Contraception and Abortion in Canada, 1880–1980*. Toronto: McClelland and Stewart.

Maclean, Mavis. 1990. 'Lone-Parent Families: Family Law and Income Transfers.' In *Lone-Parent Families. The Economic Challenge*. Paris: OECD.

MacLeod, Linda. 1980. *Wife Battering in Canada: The Vicious Circle*. Ottawa: Canadian Advisory Council on the Status of Women.

– 1987. *Battered but Not Beaten: Preventing Wife Abuse in Canada*. Ottawa: Canadian Advisory Council on the Status of Women.

– 1989. *Wife Battering and the Web of Hope: Progress, Dilemmas and the Visions of Prevention*. Prepared for the Family Violence Prevention Division. May. Ottawa: Health and Welfare Canada.

McLindon, J.B. 1987. 'Separate but Equal: The Economic Disaster of Divorce for Women and Children.' *Family Law Quarterly* 21(3): 351–405.

McQuaig, Linda. 1987. *Behind Closed Doors: How the Rich Won Control of Canada's Tax System*. Toronto: Viking.

– 1993. 'Globalization, Labour Market and Social Welfare Spending: Plenary Session.' Presentation to the Sixth Social Welfare Policy Conference, 29 June. St John's, Newfoundland.

McQuillan, Kevin. 1991. 'Family Change and Family Income in Ontario.' In
  Children, Families and Public Policy in the 90s, edited by L.C. Johnson and
  R. Barnhorst, 153–73. Toronto: Thompson Educational Publishing.
– 1992. 'Falling Behind: The Income of Lone-Mother Families, 1970–1985.'
  Canadian Review of Sociology and Anthropology 29(4): 511–23.
McRoy, R.G. 1991. 'American Experience and Research on Openness.' *Adoption
  and Fostering* 15(4): 99–111.
McVey, Wayne W. and Barrie W. Robinson. 1981. 'Separation in Canada: New
  Insights Concerning Marriage Dissolution.' *The Canadian Journal of Sociology*
  6(3): 353–66.
Magnet, Myron. 1992. 'The American Family, 1992.' *Fortune* 10 (August): 42–7.
Makepeace, J. 1981. 'Courtship Violence among College Students.' *Family
  Relations* 30: 97–102.
Marcil-Gratton, Nicole. 1989. 'Growing Up within a Family: Canadian Children
  and Their Parents' New Lifestyles.' *Transition* 19 (September): 4–7.
Marlow, Christine. 1991. 'Women, Children and Employment: Responses by
  the U.S. and Great Britain.' *International Social Work* 34: 287–97.
Marsh, P. 1990. 'Changing Practice in Child Care – The Children Act 1989.'
  Adoption and Fostering 14(4): 27–30.
Marshall, Katherine. 1993. 'Employed Parents and the Division of Housework.'
  Perspectives on Labour and Income. Statistics Canada, Catalogue no. 75-001E,
  23–30. Autumn. Ottawa: Ministry of Industry, Science and Technology.
Martin, A. 1975. 'Labor Movement Parties and Inflation: Contrasting Re-
  sponses in Britain and Sweden.' *Polity* 7(4): 427–51.
Martin, Ross. 1989. *Trade Unionism*. Oxford: Clarendon Press.
Marx, Karl. 1852, 1963. *The Eighteenth Brumaire of Louis Bonaparte*. New York:
  International.
Mathews, Georges. 1984. *Le choc démographiques: Le déclin du Québec est-il
  inévitable?* Montreal: Boréal Express.
Maurice, Marc, François Sellier, and Jean-Jacques Silvestre. 1982. *The Social
  Foundation of Industrial Power – A Comparison of France and Germany*. Cam-
  bridge, Mass.: MIT Press.
Mayfield, Margie. 1990. *Work-Related Child Care in Canada*. Ottawa: Labour
  Canada.
Maynard, Rona. 1988. 'Were They Better Off Than We Are.' *Report on Business
  Magazine* (May): 39–47.
Meehan, Elizabeth. 1993. 'Women's Rights in the European Community.' In
  Women and Social Policies in Europe. Work, Family and the State, edited by
  J. Lewis, 194–205. Aldershot, Eng.: Edward Elgar.
Meezan, William, Sanford Katz, and Eva Manoff Russo. 1978. *Adoptions without*

Agencies: A Study of Independent Adoptions. New York: Child Welfare League of America.

Melhuish, E.C. 1991. 'Research on Day Care for Young Children in the United Kingdom.' In *Day Care for Young Children: International Perspectives*, edited by E.C. Melhuish and P. Moss, 142–60. London: Tavistock/Routledge.

Melhuish, Edward, and Peter Moss. 1991. 'Current and Future Issues in Policy and Research.' In *Day Care for Young Children: International Perspectives*, edited by E.C. Melhuish and P. Moss, 199–215. London: Tavistock/Routledge.

– 1992. 'Day Care in the United Kingdom in Historical Perspective.' In *Child Care in Context: Cross-Cultural Perspectives*, edited by M.E. Lamb et al. Hillsdale, N.J.: Lawrence Erlbaum Associates.

Mercer, S. 1986. 'Not a Pretty Picture: An Exploratory Study of Violence against Women in High School Dating Relationships.' *Resources for Feminist Research* 17(2): 15–23.

Messere, K., and J. Owens. 1979. 'The Treatment of Dependent Children under Income Tax and Social Welfare Systems.' *International Social Security Review* 32: 50–9.

Messier, Suzanne. 1985. *Refléxion sur les politiques de population. Incidences de la baisse de la fécondité québécoise sur la situation les Québécoises*. April. Quebec: Quebec Advisory Council on the Status of Women.

Messu, Michel. 1992. 'Family Policy and a Social Incomes Policy: The Case of the Single-Parent Allowance in France.' *International Social Security Review* 45(3): 71–81.

Meston, John. 1988. 'Preparing Young People in Canada for Emancipation from Child Welfare Care.' *Child Welfare* 67(6): 625–34.

– 1993. *Child Abuse and Neglect Prevention Programs*. Ottawa: Vanier Institute of the Family.

Meyer, Daniel R., Elizabeth Phillips, and Nancy L. Maritato. 1991. 'The Effects of Replacing Income Tax Deductions for Children with Children's Allowances: A Microsimulation.' *Journal of Family Issues* 12(4): 467–91.

Meyer, Philippe. 1983. *The Child and the State – The Intervention of the State in Family Life*. Cambridge: Cambridge University Press.

Michelson, William. 1985. *From Sun to Sun. Daily Obligations and Community Structure in the Lives of Employed Women and Their Families*. Totowa, N.J.: Rowman and Allanheld.

Miles, J. 1981. 'Sexism in Social Work.' *Social Work Today* 13(1): 14–15.

Millar, Wayne. June 1991. 'Divorces, Canada and the Provinces 1989.' *Health Reports* 3(2): 83–6.

Miller, Kenneth E. 1991. *Denmark: A Troubled Welfare State*. Boulder, Colo.: Westview Press.

Milner, Henry. 1990. *Sweden: Social Democracy in Practice*. New York: Oxford University Press.

Mimoto, H., and P. Cross. 1991. 'The Growth of the Federal Debt.' *Canadian Economic Observer* (June): 3.1–3.18.

Mishra, Ramesh. 1990. *The Welfare State in Capitalist Society*. Toronto: University of Toronto Press.

Mitchell, Andrew. 1987. 'The Cost of Raising a Child in the Toronto Area in 1986.' Prepared for the Social Planning Council of Metropolitan Toronto. *Social Infopac* 6(5): 1–5.

– 1991. 'The Economic Circumstances of Ontario's Families and Children.' In *The State of the Child in Ontario*, edited by R. Barnhorst and L.C. Johnson, 22–47. Toronto: Oxford University Press.

Mitchell, Deborah. 1990. 'Is There a Trade-Off between the Efficiency and Effectiveness Goals of Income Transfer Programs?' The Luxembourg Income Study, Working Paper no. 62. October.

– 1992. 'Welfare States and Welfare Outcomes in the 1980s.' *International Social Security Review* 45(1/2): 73–90.

Moeller, Robert G. 1989. 'Protecting Mother's Work: From Production to Reproduction in Postwar West Germany.' *Journal Of Social History* 22(3): 413–37.

Moors, Hein G. 1990. 'Attitudes towards Demographic Trends and Population Policy: Italy and the Netherlands in a Comparative Perspective.' *Population Research and Policy Review* 9: 179–94.

Moreau, Joanne. 1991. 'Employment Equity.' *Canadian Social Trends* 22 (Autumn): 26–8.

Morfuni, C. 1991. 'Child Abuse and the Family Law Act 1975 (Cth).' *The Australian Law Journal* 65(June): 332–43.

Morris, Lydia. 1993. 'Household Finance Management and the Labour Market: A Case Study in Hartlepool.' *Sociological Review* 41(3): 506–36.

Morris, Robert. 1988. 'Changing Patterns of Public Social Welfare Policy in Nine Countries, 1975–1986: Predicting Future Trends.' In *Testing the Limits of Social Welfare*, edited by R. Morris, 1–38. Hanover, N.H.: University Press of New England.

Morrison, Richard J., and Jillian Oderkirk. 1991. 'Married and Unmarried Couples: The Tax Question.' *Canadian Social Trends* 21 (Summer): 15–20.

Morton, Mary E. 1988. 'Dividing the Wealth, Sharing the Poverty: the (Re)formation of "Family" in Law.' *The Canadian Review of Sociology and Anthropology* 25(2): 254–75.

Morton, Mildred. 1990. 'Controversies within Family Law.' *Families. Changing Trends in Canada* (2nd ed.), edited by M. Baker, 211–40. Toronto: McGraw-Hill Ryerson.

Moss, Peter. 1988. 'The Indirect Costs of Parenthood: A Neglected Issue in Social Policy.' *Critical Social Policy* 8(3): 20–37.

– 1991. 'Day Care for Young Children in the United Kingdom.' In *Day Care for Young Children: International Perspectives*, edited by E.C. Melhuish and P. Moss, 121–41. London: Tavistock/Routledge.

Moss, P., and E.C. Melhuish. 1991. 'Introduction.' In *Day Care for Young Children: International Perspectives*, edited by E.C. Melhuish and P. Moss, 1–9. London: Tavistock/Routledge.

Mossman, Mary Jane, and Morag MacLean. 1986. 'Family Law and Social Welfare: Toward a New Equality.' *Canadian Journal of Family Law* 5 (Summer): 79–110.

Mosteller, R.P. 1992. 'Child Abuse Reporting Laws and Attorney-Client Confidences: The Reality and the Specter of Lawyer as Informant.' *Duke Law Journal* 42(2): 203–78.

Muir, Bernice L. 1988. *Health Status of Canadian Indians and Inuit*. Ottawa: Health and Welfare Canada.

Myles, John. 1989. *Old Age in the Welfare State: Political Economy of Public Pensions* (2nd ed.). Lawrence, Kans.: University Press of Kansas.

NAEYC (National Association for the Education of Young Children). 1987. 'Position Statement on Licensing and Other Forms of Regulation of Early Childhood Programs in Centers and Family Day Care Homes.' *Young Children* 42: 64–8.

Naples, Nancy A. 1991. 'A Socialist Feminist Analysis of the Family Support Act of 1988.' *Affilia* 6(4): 23–38.

Nasmith, A.P. 1991. 'Legal Structure in Child Protection.' In *Canadian Child Welfare Law: Children, Families and the State*, edited by N. Bala, J.P. Hormick, and R. Vogl, 310–16. Toronto: Thompson Educational Publishing.

National Council of Welfare. 1987. *The Tangled Safety Net*. November. Ottawa: National Council of Welfare.

– 1988. *Child Care: A Better Alternative*. December. Ottawa: National Council of Welfare.

– 1989. *The 1989 Budget and Social Policy*. September. Ottawa: National Council of Welfare.

– 1990a. *Fighting Child Poverty*. Ottawa: National Council of Welfare.

– 1990b. *Women and Poverty Revisited*. Summer. Ottawa: National Council of Welfare.

- 1992a. *The 1992 Budget and Child Benefits*. Autumn. Ottawa: Minister of Supply and Services Canada.
- 1992b. *Welfare Incomes 1991*. Summer. Ottawa: National Council of Welfare.
- 1993. *Incentives and Disincentives to Work*. Autumn. Ottawa: National Council of Welfare.
- 1994a. *Poverty Profile 1992*. Ottawa: National Council of Welfare.
- 1994b. *Welfare Incomes 1993*. Ottawa: National Council of Welfare.
National Forum on Family Security. 1993. *Family Security in Insecure Times*. Ottawa: National Forum on Family Security.
Native Women's Association of Canada. 1986. *Presentation to the Special House of Commons Committee on Child Care*. 10 June. Ottawa.
Nelson, M.K. 1990. *Negotiated Care: The Experience of Family Day Care Providers*. Philadelphia: Temple University Press.
- 1991. 'A Study of Family Day Care Providers: Attitudes toward Regulation.' *Child and Youth Care Forum* 20(4) 225–42.
Ng, Edward. 1992. 'Children and Elderly People: Sharing Public Income Resources.' *Canadian Social Trends* 25 (Summer): 12–15.
Nichols-Casebolt, A., and I. Garfinkel. 1987. 'The New Child Assurance Program: The Wisconsin Demonstration.' *Social Work* 32(5): 445–6.
Nichols-Casebolt, A., and M. Klawitter. 1990. 'Child Support Enforcement Reform: Can It Reduce the Welfare Dependency of Families of Never-Married Mothers?' *Journal of Sociology and Social Welfare* 17(3): 23–54.
Nordhaus, William D. 1975. 'The Political Business Cycle.' *Review of Economic Studies* 42: 160–90.
Norton, A.J., and L.F. Miller. 1992. *Marriage, Divorce and Remarriage in the 1990's*. October. Washington, D.C.: U.S. Department of Commerce, Bureau of Census.
Nova Scotia Social Services Council. 1982. *Vulnerable Mothers, Vulnerable Children*. Report to Honourable Edmund L. Morris, Minister of Social Services, June. Halifax.
Novick, Marvin. 1990. 'A New World Agenda: Social Choices for a Healthy Society.' In *Unemployment and Welfare*, edited by G. Riches and G. Ternowetsky, 255–70. Toronto: Garamond.
Nuccio, Kathleen E., and Roberta G. Sands. 1992. 'Using Postmodern Feminist Theory to Deconstruct "Phallacies" of Poverty.' *Affilia* 7(4): 26–48.
Ochiltree, Gay. 1992. 'Child Care in the English-Speaking Countries with Reference to Australia.' In *Child Care in Context: Cross-Cultural Perspectives*, edited by M.E. Lamb et al. Hillsdale, N.J.: Lawrence Erlbaum Associates.
O'Connor, Julia S. 1989. 'Welfare Expenditure and Policy Orientation in Canada in Comparative Perspective.' *Canadian Review of Sociology and Anthropology* 26(1): 127–50.

Oderkirk, Jillian. 1992. 'Food Banks.' *Canadian Social Trends* 24 (Spring): 6–14.

Oderkirk, Jillian, and Clarence Lockhead. 1992. 'Single Parenthood: Gender Differences.' *Perception* 16(2/3): 27–32.

O'Donnell, A.A. 1992. 'Re-Thinking Accountability in Child Welfare.' *Child and Adolescent Social Work Journal* 9(3): 261–70.

O'Donnell, H.B. 1990–1. 'Title I of the Family Support Act of 1988 – The Quest for Effective National Child Support Enforcement Continues.' *Journal of Family Law* 29: 149–70.

OECD (Organization for Economic Co-operation and Development). 1985. *Social Expenditure, 1960–1990: Problems of Growth and Control.* Paris: OECD.

– 1987. *OECD Economic Outlook: Historical Statistics, 1960–1985.* Paris: OECD.

– 1989. *Labour Force Statistics, 1967–1987.* 30–1. Paris: OECD.

– 1990a. *Lone Parent Families – The Economic Challenge.* Based on papers presented at the OECD conference on Social Policy held in December 1987. Paris: OECD.

– 1990b. *The Personal Income Tax Base – A Comparative Survey.* A Report by the Committee on Fiscal Affairs. Paris. OECD.

– 1992a. *Economic Intelligence Unit* (1–4). Paris: OECD, Statistics Directorate.

– 1992b. *The Tax/Benefit Position of Production Workers –1988–1991. Special Feature – Personal Income Tax Thresholds.* Paris: OECD.

– 1993. *Main Economic Indicators.* January. Paris: OECD.

Offe, C. 1984. *Contradictions of the Welfare State.* London: Hutchinson Education.

Offner, P. 1991. 'Child Care and the Family Support Act: Should States Reimburse Unlicensed Providers?' *Public Welfare* 49(2): 6–9.

O'Higgins, M., G. Schmaus, and G. Stephenson. 1989. 'Income Distribution and Redistribution: A Microdata Analysis for Seven Countries.' *Review of Income and Wealth* 35(2): 107–31.

– 1990. 'Income Distribution and Redistribution: A Microdata Analysis for Seven Countries.' In *Poverty, Inequality and Income Distribution in Comparative Perspective. The Luxembourg Income Study,* edited by T.M. Smeeding, M. O'Higgins, and L. Rainwater. Washington, D.C.: Urban Institute Press.

Okin, Susan Moller. 1989. *Justice, Gender, and the Family.* New York: Basic Books.

O'Leary, K.D., et al. 1989. 'Prevalence and Stability of Physical Aggression between Spouses: A Longitudinal Analysis.' *Journal of Consulting and Clinical Psychology* 57: 263–8.

Olsen, Gregg M. 1994. 'Locating the Canadian Welfare State: Family Policy and Health Care in Canada, Sweden, and the United States.' *The Canadian Journal of Sociology* 19(1): 1–20.

Olsson, Ulf. 1991. 'Planning in the Swedish Welfare State.' *Studies in Political Economy* 34: 147–71.

Ontario Fair Tax Commission. 1993. *Fair Taxation in a Changing World. Report of the Ontario Fair Tax Commission.* Toronto: University of Toronto Press.

Ontario Law Reform Commission. 1985. *Report on Human Artificial Reproduction and Related Matters.* Toronto: Ministry of the Attorney General, Ontario.

Ornstein, Michael. 1989. *AIDS in Canada. Knowledge, Behaviour, and Attitudes of Adults.* Toronto: York University Institute for Social Research.

Ostner, Ilona. 1994. 'Back to the Fifties: Gender and Welfare in Unified Germany.' *Social Politics* 1(1): 32–59.

Overall, Christine. 1993. *Human Reproduction: Principles, Practices, Policies.* Toronto: Oxford University Press.

Oxley, Carol. 1987. 'Family Allowance for All? – Provisions of Universal Family Assistance in a Number of Countries.' *Social Security Journal* (Winter): 42–54.

Packman, J., and B. Jordan. 1991. 'The Children Act: Looking Forward, Looking Back.' *British Journal of Social Work* 21: 315–27.

Padilla, M.L., and G.L. Landreth. 1989. 'Latchkey Children: A Review of the Literature.' *Child Welfare* 68(4): 445–54.

Pahl, J. 1989. *Money and Marriage.* London: Macmillan.

Pal, Leslie A. 1987. 'Tools for the Job: Canada's Evolution from Public Works to Mandated Employment.' In *The Canadian Welfare State,* edited by Jacqueline S. Ismael. Edmonton: University of Alberta Press.

Palmer, John L., Timothy Smeeding, and Christopher Jencks. 1988. 'The Uses and Limits of Income Comparisons.' In *The Vulnerable,* edited by J. Palmer, T. Smeeding, and B. Torrey. 9–27. Washington, D.C.: Urban Institute Press.

Palmer, John L., Timothy Smeeding, and Barbara Boyle Torrey. 1988. *The Vulnerable.* Washington, D.C.: Urban Institute Press.

Palmer, Sally E. 1989. 'Mediation in Child Protection Cases: An Alternative to the Adversary System.' *Child Welfare* 68(1): 21–31.

Pampel, Fred C., and Paul Adams. 1992. 'The Effects of Demographic Change and Political Structure on Family Allowance Expenditures.' *Social Service Review* 66(4): 524–46.

Pampel, Fred C., and John B. Williamson. 1988. 'Welfare Spending in Advanced Industrial Democracies, 1950–1980.' *American Journal of Sociology* 93(6); 1424–56.

Paris, Hélène. 1989. *The Corporate Response to Workers with Family Responsibilities.* Report 43-89, August. Ottawa: The Conference Board of Canada.

Pateman, Carole. 1987. 'The Patriarchal Welfare State.' In *Democracy and the Welfare State,* edited by Amy Gutman. Princeton: Princeton University Press.

– 1988. *The Social Contract.* Oxford: Polity Press and Basil Blackwell.

– 1989. *The Disorder of Women.* Oxford: Polity Press and Basil Blackwell.

Payne, Julien D. 1985. 'Family Law Reform and the Law Reform Commission of Canada.' *Canadian Journal of Family Law* 4(4): 355–67.
– 1994. 'Family Law in Canada.' In *Canada's Changing Families: Challenges to Public Policy*, edited by M. Baker. Ottawa: Vanier Institute of the Family.
Pearson, Jessica, and Nancy Thoennes. 1988. 'Supporting Children after Divorce: The Influence of Custody on Support Levels and Payments.' *Family Law Quarterly* 22(3): 319–39.
– 1990. 'Custody after Divorce: Demographic and Attitudinal Patterns.' *American Journal of Orthopsychiatry* 60 (April): 233–49.
Pechman, Joseph A. 1987. *Comparative Tax Systems: Europe, Canada and Japan*. Arlington, Va.: Tax Analysts.
Pechman, Joseph, and G.V. Engelhardt. 1990. 'The Income Tax Treatment of the Family: An International Perspective.' *National Tax Journal* 43(1): 1–22.
– 1991. *The Income Tax Treatment of the Family: An International Perspective*. Washington, D.C.: The Brookings Institute Press.
Peillon, Michel. 1993. 'Welfare and State Centralisation.' *West European Politics* 16(2): 105–21.
Pelton, Leroy H. 1989. *For Reasons of Poverty – A Critical Analysis of the Public Child Welfare System in the United States*. New York: Praeger.
– 1991. 'Beyond Permanency Planning: Restructuring the Public Child Welfare System.' *Social Work* 36(4): 337–43.
Pence, A.R., and H. Goelman. 1991. 'The Relationship of Regulation, Training and Motivation to Quality of Care in Family Day Care.' *Child and Youth Care Forum* 20(2): 83–101.
Perry, David B. 1987. 'Selected Statistics on the Evolution of the Personal Income Tax System since 1970.' *Canadian Tax Journal* 5(1): 207–14.
Perry, Julia. 1991. *Breadwinners or Childrearers: The Dilemma for Lone Mothers*. Australia: OECD Working Party on Social Policy.
Peters, Donald L., and Alan R. Pence, eds. 1993. *Family Day Care. Current Research for Informed Public Policy*. Toronto: Canadian Scholars' Press.
Phillips, A., and P. Moss. 1989. *Who Cares for Europe's Children? The Short Report of the European Childcare Network*. Brussels: ECSC-EEC-EAEC.
Phillips, Deborah A. 1991a. 'Day Care for Young Children in the United States.' In *Day Care for Young Children: International Perspectives*, edited by E.C. Melhuish and P. Moss, 161–84. London: Tavistock/Routledge.
– 1991b. 'With a Little Help: Children in Poverty and Child Care.' In *Children in Poverty*, edited by A. Huston. Cambridge: Cambridge University Press.
Phillips, D., J. Lande, and M. Goldberg. 1990. 'The State of Child Care Regulation: A Comparative Analysis.' *Early Childhood Research Quarterly* 5: 151–79.

Philp, Margaret. 1994. 'Child-Care Reform Package Faces Review.' *Globe and Mail* (Toronto), 12 February.

Phipps, Shelley A. 1993a. 'Canadian Child Benefits: Behavioural Consequences, Income Adequacy and Alternatives.' Working Paper no. 93-03. Halifax: Department of Economics, Dalhousie University.

– 1993b. 'International Perspectives on Income Support for Families with Children.' Paper presented at Canadian Employment Research Forum Workshop on Income Support, 24 September. Ottawa.

– 1994. 'Poverty and Labour Market Change: Canada in Comparative Perspective.' Luxembourg Income Study, Working Paper no. 108. April. Luxembourg.

Phipps, Shelley A., and Peter S. Burton. 1992. 'What's Mine Is Yours?: The Influence of Male and Female Incomes on Patterns of Household Expenditure.' Working Paper no. 92-12. Halifax: Department of Economics, Dalhousie University.

Picton, C. 1986. 'Adoption in Australia.' In *Adoption in Worldwide Perspective*, edited by R.A.C. Hoksbergen. Berwyn: Swets North America.

Pierrehumbert, Blaise. 1992. 'Parental versus Nonparental Child Care in the Early Years, from a French-speaking Swiss Perspective.' In *Child Care in Context*, edited by M. Lamb et al., 135–43. Hillsdale, N.J.: Lawrence Erlbaum Associates.

Pierson, Ruth. 1977. 'Women's Emancipation and the Recruitment of Women into the Labour Force in World War II.' In *The Neglected Majority: Essays in Canadian Women's History*, edited by S.M. Trofimenkoff and A. Prentice. Toronto: McClelland and Stewart.

Pinker, Robert. 1994. 'Golden Ages and Welfare Alchemists: Some Thoughts on Social Change and Social Policy.' Presented as the Maxwell Cummings Lecture, 21 March. Montreal: McGill University.

Pixley, Jocelyn. 1993. *Citizenship and Employment: Investigating Post-Industrial Options*. Melbourne: Cambridge University Press.

– 1994. 'After the White Paper – Where?' Unpublished paper. Sydney: University of New South Wales, Department of Sociology.

Pontusson, J. 1984. 'Behind and Beyond Social Democracy in Sweden.' *New Left Review* 143(Jan/Feb): 69–96.

Porter, John. 1965. *The Vertical Mosaic*. Toronto: University of Toronto Press.

Powell, Lisa M. 1992. *Towards Child Care Policy Development in Canada*. Background paper prepared for the School of Policy Studies Program on Social Policy. Kingston: Queen's University.

Price Waterhouse. 1992. *Individual Taxes – A Worldwide Summary*. New York.

Prince, Michael J. 1987. 'How Ottawa Decides Social Policy.' In *The Canadian*

Welfare State: Evolution and Transition, edited by J. Ismael. Edmonton: University of Alberta Press.

Pritchard, C. 1992. 'Children's Homicide as an Indicator of Effective Child Protection: A Comparative Study of Western European Statistics.' *British Journal of Social Work* 22(6): 663–84.

Prosser, W. 1991. 'Comments on "Child Care Policy and Research": An Economist's Perspective.' In *The Economics of Child Care*, edited by D.M. Blau, 43–9. New York: Russell Sage Foundation.

Proudfoot, P., and K. Jewell. 1990. 'Restricting Application of the Causal Connection Test: Story v. Story.' *Canadian Journal of Family Law* 9: 143–51.

Pulkingham, Jane. 1994. 'Private Troubles, Private Solutions: Poverty among Divorced Women and the Politics of Support Enforcement and Child Custody Determination.' *Canadian Journal of Law and Society* 9(2): 73–97.

Pupo, Norene. 1988. 'Preserving Patriarchy: Women, the Family and the State.' In *Reconstructing the Canadian Family: Feminist Perspectives*, edited by N. Mandell, and A. Duffy, 207–37. Toronto: Butterworths.

Quebec, Minister of State for Social Development. 1985. *Collective Support Demanded for Quebec Families*. Report on the Consultation Held on Family Policy. Quebec: Government of Quebec.

Raban, Colin, and Phil Lee. 1988. *Welfare Theory and Social Policy*. London: Sage Publications.

Rains, R.E. 1991. 'Protecting Children – and Their Families – from Abuse: The Cleveland Crisis and England's Children Act 1989.' *Case Western Reserve Journal of International Law* (Spring): 171–96.

Ram, Bali. 1990a. 'Intermarriage among Ethnic Groups.' *Ethnic Demography. Canadian Immigrant, Racial and Cultural Variations*, edited by S.S. Halli, F. Trovato, and L. Driedger, 213–27. Ottawa: Carleton University Press.

– 1990b. *New Trends in the Family. Demographic Facts and Figures*. Prepared for Statistics Canada, Catalogue no. 91-535E, March. Ottawa: Minister of Supply and Services Canada.

Rappaport, J.S. 1991. 'The Legal System's Response to Child Abuse: A "Shield" for Children or a "Sword" against the Constitutional Rights of Parents?' *Journal of Human Rights* 9: 257–91.

Rashid, Abdul. 1994. 'Changes in Real Wages.' *Canadian Social Trends* 32 (Spring): 16–18.

Ravelet, Michel. 1987. *Le Divorce*. Paris: Editions Fernand Nathan.

Ray, Jean-Claude. 1990. 'Lone Mothers, Social Assistance and Work Incentives: The Evidence in France.' In *Lone-Parent Families. The Economic Challenge*. Paris: OECD.

Raycroft, M.M. 1991. 'Abuse and Neglect Allegations in Child Custody and

Protection Cases.' In *Canadian Child Welfare Law: Children, Families and the State*, edited by N. Bala, J.P. Hornick, and R. Vogl. Toronto: Thompson Educational Publishing.

Rayle, Pierrette. 1988. 'La prestation compensatoire et la Cour d'appel cinq ans plus tard.' *Revue du Barreau* 14: 225–49.

Rehn, Gosta. 1985. 'Swedish Active Labour Market Policy: Retrospect and Prospect.' *Industrial Relations* 24(1): 62–89.

Reitsma-Street, Marge, Richard Carrière, and Adje VandeSande. 1993. 'Three Perspectives on Child Poverty in Canada.' *The Social Worker* 61(1): 6–12.

Richardson, C. James. 1988a. 'Children of Divorce.' In *Family Matters*, edited by K.L. Anderson et al., 163–200. Scarborough, Ont.: Nelson Camada.

– 1988b. *Court-based Divorce Mediation in Four Canadian Cities: An Overview of Research Results*. Ottawa: Minister of Supply and Services.

– 1992. 'Family Law Research in a Decade of Change.' In *Sociology for Canadians* (2nd ed.), edited by A. Himmelfarb and C.J. Richardson, 231–9. Toronto: McGraw-Hill Ryerson.

Riches, Graham. 1986. *Food Banks and the Welfare Crisis*. Ottawa: Canadian Council on Social Development.

– 1990a. 'Child Poverty and Welfare Reform: Robbing the Poor to Pay the Poor.' *Canadian Review of Social Policy* 26: 26–38.

– 1990b. 'Welfare Reform, and Social Work Practice: Political Objectives and Ethical Dilemmas.' In *Unemployment and Welfare: Social Policy and the Work of Social Work*, edited by G. Riches and G. Ternowetsky. Toronto: Garamond.

Riches, Graham, and Gordon Ternowetsky. 1990. *Unemployment and Welfare: Social Policy and the Work of Social Work*. Toronto: Garamond.

Ricketts, Wendell, and Roberta Achtenberg. 1989. 'Adoption and Foster Parenting for Lesbians and Gay Men: Creating New Traditions in Family.' *Marriage and Family Review* 14(3–4): 83–118.

Rimlinger, Gaston V. 1971. *Welfare Policy and Industrialization in Europe, America and Russia*. New York: John Wiley.

Ringen, Stein. 1987. *The Possibility of Politics: A Study in the Political Economy of the Welfare State*. Oxford: Clarendon Press.

Ringen, Stein, et al. 1992. 'Income Distribution and Redistribution in the Nordic Welfare States.' In *The Study of Welfare State Regimes*, edited by John Eivind Kolberg, 69–91. New York: M.E. Sharpe.

Robins, P.K. 1990. 'Federal Financing of Child Care: Alternative Approaches and Economic Implications.' *Population Research and Policy Review* 9: 65–90.

– 1991. 'Child Care Policy and Research: An Economist's Perspective.' In *The Economics of Child Care*, edited by D.M. Blau, 11–49. New York: Russell Sage Foundation.

Rodgers, Harrell R., Jr, ed. 1988. *Beyond Welfare. New Approaches to the Problem of Poverty in America.* Armonk, N.Y.: M.E. Sharpe.

– 1990. *Poor Women, Poor Families. The Economic Plight of America's Female-Headed Households* (rev. ed.) Armonk, N.Y.: M.E. Sharpe.

Roll, Jo. 1990–1. 'One in Ten: Lone Parent Families in the European Community.' *Social Policy Review* no. 4, edited by Nick Manning, 169–86. Social Policy Association. London: Longman.

Romaniuc, A. 1984. *Fertility in Canada: From Baby-Boom to Baby-Bust.* Ottawa: Statistics Canada.

Ronstrom, A. 1989. 'Sweden's Children's Ombudsman: A Spokesperson for Children.' *Child Welfare* 68(2): 123–8.

Rood-de Boer, M. 1986–7. 'The Netherlands: Family Law, More and More Tailor-Made.' *Journal of Family Law* 25: 187–90.

– 1987–8. 'The Netherlands: How to Tackle New Social Problems.' *Journal of Family Law* 26: 141–7.

– 1988–9. 'The Netherlands: Riding the Carousal of Family Law.' *Journal of Family Law* 27: 221–9.

– 1991–2. 'The Netherlands: New Realities in the Nineties.' *Journal of Family Law* 30: 427–30.

Rosenthal, Carolyn J. 1982. 'Family Responsibilities and Concerns: A Perspective on the Lives of Middle-aged Women.' *Resources for Feminist Research* 11(2): 211–2.

– 1985. 'Kinkeeping in the Familial Division of Labour.' *Journal of Marriage and the Family* 47(4): 965–74.

Rosenthal, James A., and Victor Groze. 1990. 'Special-Needs Adoption: A Study of Intact Families.' *Social Service Review* (September): 475–505.

Ross, David. 1988. 'Not a Vintage Decade for Low-Income Canadians.' *Perception* 12(2): 20–2.

Ross, David P., and Richard Shillington. 1989. *The Canadian Fact Book on Poverty 1989.* Ottawa: Canadian Council on Social Development.

Roussel, Louis, and Irene Thery. 1988. 'France: Demographic Change and Family Policy since World War II.' *Journal of Family Issues* 9(3): 336–53.

Rubellin-Devichi, Jacqueline. 1990–1. 'France: The Child First and Foremost and Other Family Law Developments.' *Journal of Family Law* 29(2): 359–69.

Russell, A. 1991. 'Reflections and Expectations.' In *Canadian Child Welfare Law: Children, Families and the State,* edited by N. Bala, J.P. Hornick, and R. Vogl. Toronto: Thompson Educational Publishing.

Russell, Diana E.H. 1990. *Rape in Marriage.* Bloomington, Ind.: Indiana University Press.

Ryburn, M. 1991. 'The Children Act – Power and Empowerment.' *Adoption and Fostering* 15(3): 10–14.

Rycraft, J.R. 1990. 'Redefining Abuse and Neglect: A Narrower Focus Could Affect Children at Risk.' *Public Welfare* 48(1): 14–21.

Ryerse, Catherine. 1990. *Thursday's Child, Child Poverty in Canada: A Review of the Effects of Poverty on Children*. Ottawa: National Youth in Care Network.

Sacco, Vincent, and Holly Johnson. 1994. 'Violent Victimization.' In *Canadian Social Trends, Volume 2*, 415–18. Toronto: Thompson Educational Publishing.

Sachdev, Paul, ed. 1984. *Adoption. Current Issues and Trends*. Toronto: Butterworths.

Sailor, C.B. 1990–1. 'Qualified Immunity for Child Abuse Investigators: Balancing the Concerns of Protecting Our Children from Abuse and the Integrity of the Family.' *Journal of Family Law* 29: 659–77.

Sainsbury, Diane. 1993. 'Dual Welfare and Sex Segregation of Access to Social Benefits: Income Maintenance Policies in the U.K., the U.S., the Netherlands and Sweden', *Journal of Social Policy* 22(1): 69–98.

Saldeen, Ake. 1990–1. 'Sweden: Changes in the Code on Marriage and Plans for Reform in the Areas of Adoption, Child Custody and Fetal Diagnostics.' *Journal of Family Law* 29(2): 431–9.

Samantrai, K. 1992. 'To Prevent Unnecessary Separation of Children and Families: Public Law 96-272 – Policy and Practice.' *Social Work* 37(4): 295–302.

Sanders, Jo. 1988. *Staying Poor: How the Job Training Partnership Act Fails Women*. Netuchen, N.J.: The Scarecrow Press.

Santrock, John, and R.A. Warshak. 1986. 'Developmental Relationships and Legal/Clinical Considerations in Father-Custody Families.' In *The Father's Role: Applied Perspectives*, edited by M.E. Lamb. New York: Wiley.

Saunders, Peter. 1991. 'Selectivity and Targeting in Income Support: The Australian Experience.' *Journal of Social Policy* 20(3): 299–326.

Saunders, Peter, and G. Matheson. 1991. 'Sole Parent Families in Australia.' *International Social Security Review* 34(3): 51–75.

Savoie, Donald J. 1990. *The Politics of Public Spending in Canada*. Toronto: University of Toronto Press.

Scales, P., and B. Brunk. 1990. 'Keeping Children on Top of the States' Policy Agendas.' *Child Welfare* 69(1): 23–32.

Scarth, Sandra. 1993. 'Child Welfare at the Crossroads. Can the System Protect Canada's Most Vulnerable Children?' *Perception* 17(3): 5–8.

Schmitter, P. 1974. 'Still the Century of Corporatism.' *Review of Politics* 36: 85–131.

Schorr, A.L. 1989. 'Sharing without Shaming.' *Child Welfare* 68 (6): 563–71.

Schragge, Eric. 1990. 'Welfare Reform, Quebec Style.' In *Unemployment and Welfare. Social Policy and the Work of Social Work,* edited by G. Riches and G. Ternowetsky. Toronto: Garamond.

Schwartz, Laurie. 1988. *Parental and Maternity Leave Policies in Canada and Sweden.* Kingston: Queen's University Press.

Schwartz, L.J. 1991. 'Religious Matching for Adoption: Unraveling the Interests Behind the "Best Interests" Standard.' *Family Law Quarterly* 25(2): 171–92.

Seaberg, James R. 1990. 'Family Policy Revisited: Are We There Yet?' *Social Work* 35(6): 548–54.

Seccombe, Wally. 1989. '"Helping Her Out": The Participation of Husbands in Domestic Labour When Wives Go out to Work.' Unpublished paper. Toronto: Ontario Institute for Studies in Education.

Seligson, M., E. Fersh, N.L. Marshall, F. Marx, and R.K. Baden. 1990. 'School-Age Child Care: The Challenge Facing Families.' *Families in Society: The Journal of Contemporary Human Services* 71(6): 324–31.

Seltzer, J.A. 1991. 'Relationships between Fathers and Children Who Live Apart: The Father's Role after Separation.' *Journal of Marriage and the Family* 53(1): 79–110.

Sev'er, Aysan. 1992. *Women and Divorce in Canada.* Toronto: Canadian Scholars' Press.

Sexton, Patricia Cayo. 1991. *The War on Labour and the Left – Understanding America's Unique Conservatism.* Boulder, Colo.: Westview Press.

Shalev, M. 1983. 'Class Politics and the Western Welfare State.' In *Evaluating the Welfare State – Social and Political Perspectives,* edited by S.E. Spiro and E. Yuchtman-Yaar. New York: Academic Press.

Sherraden, Michael. 1991. *Assets and the Poor. A New American Welfare Policy.* Armonk, N.Y.: M.E. Sharpe.

Sidel, Ruth. 1992. *Women and Children Last: The Plight of Poor Women in Affluent America.* New York: Penguin Books.

Sigel, Irving E. 1992. 'A Political-Cultural Perspective on Day Care in the Netherlands, Italy and Sweden.' In *Child Care in Context,* edited by M. Lamb et al., 119–33. Hillsdale, N.J.: Lawrence Erlbaum Associates.

Siggner, Andrew J. 1986. 'The Socio-Demographic Conditions of Registered Indians.' In *Arduous Journey,* edited by J.R. Ponting. Toronto: McClelland and Stewart.

Silverman, A.R., and D.E. Weitzman. 1986. 'Nonrelative Adoption in the United States: A Brief Survey.' In *Adoption in Worldwide Perspective,* edited by R.A.C. Hoksbergen. Berwyn: Swets North America.

Simm, Birte. 1993. 'The Gendered Scandinavian Welfare States: The Interplay between Women's Roles as Mothers, Workers and Citizens in Denmark.' In *Women and Social Policies in Europe*, edited by Jane Lewis, 25–48. Aldershot, Eng.: Edward Elgar.

Sinclair, M., D. Phillips, and N. Bala. 1991. 'Aboriginal Child Welfare in Canada.' In *Canadian Child Welfare Law: Children, Families and the State*, edited by N. Bala, J.P. Hornick, and R. Vogl. Toronto: Thompson Educational Publishing.

Singleton, Gwynneth. 1990. *The Accord and the Australian Labour Movement*. Melbourne: Melbourne University Press.

Sloan, Pamela. 1991. 'From School to Work.' In *Children, Families and Public Policy in the 90s*, edited by L.C. Johnson and D. Barnhorst, 175–206. Toronto: Thompson Educational Publishing.

Sloss, Elizabeth, ed. 1985. *Family Law in Canada: New Directions*. Ottawa: Canadian Advisory Council on the Status of Women.

Smardon, Bruce. 1991. 'The Federal Welfare State and the Politics of Retrenchment in Canada.' *Journal of Canadian Studies* 26(2): 122–41.

Smart, Carol, and Selma Sevenhuijsen. 1989. *Child Custody and the Politics of Gender*. London and New York: Routledge.

Smeeding, Timothy. 1987. 'Cross-National Analyses of Social Policy: Value, Resources, and Challenge.' The Luxembourg Income Study, Working Paper no. 14. October.

– 1992. 'Why the U.S. Anti-Poverty System Doesn't Work Very Well.' *Challenge – The Magazine of Economic Affairs* 35 (January/February): 30–5.

Smeeding, Timothy M., Michael O'Higgins, and Lee Rainwater. 1990. *Poverty, Inequality and Income Distribution in Comparative Perspective*. Washington, D.C.: Urban Institute Press.

Smeeding, Timothy, and Lee Rainwater. 1991. 'Cross-National Trends in Income Poverty and Dependency.' Paper prepared for Joint Center for Political and Economic Studies Conference on Poverty, Inequality, and the Crisis of Social Policy, 19–21 September. Washington, D.C.

Smeeding, Timothy M., Lee Rainwater, Martin Rein, Richard Hauser, and Gaston Schaber. 1990. 'Income Poverty in Seven Countries: Initial Estimates from LIS Database.' In *Poverty, Inequality and Income Distribution in Comparative Perspective*, edited by T. Smeeding, M. O'Higgins, and L. Rainwater. Washington, D.C.: Urban Institute Press.

Smeeding, T., B.B. Torrey, and M. Rein. 1988. 'Patterns of Income and Poverty: The Economic Status of Children and the Elderly in Eight Countries.' In *The Vulnerable*, edited by J.L. Palmer, T. Smeeding, and B.T. Boyle. Washington, D.C.: Urban Institute Press.

Smith, B. 1991. 'Australian Women and Foster Care: A Feminist Perspective.' *Child Welfare* 70(2): 175–84.

Smith, Dorothy. 1977. 'Women, the Family and Corporate Capitalism.' In *Women in Canada* (rev. ed.), edited by Marylee Stephenson. Toronto: Women's Educational Press.

– 1987. *The Everyday World as Problematic: A Feminist Sociology.* Toronto: University of Toronto Press.

Smith, S.R. 1989. 'The Changing Politics of Child Welfare Services: New Roles for the Government and Nonprofit Sectors.' *Child Welfare* 68(3): 289–99.

Smith, Vivian. 1994. 'Compared to Europe, Canada Has No Reason to Feel Smug.' *Globe and Mail* (Toronto), 20 January: A6.

Smithburn, J.E. 1989–90. 'Removing Nonconforming Child Support Payments from the Shadow of the Rule against Retroactive Modification: A Proposal for Judicial Discretion.' *Journal of Family Law* 28: 43–69.

Smolowe, Jill. 1992. 'Where Children Come First.' *Time.* 9 November: 40–1.

Södersten, Bo. 1990. 'The Swedish Tax Reform: How Will It Affect the Economy.' *Current Sweden* 370 (October): 1–9.

Sorrentino, Constance. 1990. 'The Changing Family in International Perspective.' *Monthly Labour Review* (March): 41–58.

Southworth, Suzanne, and J.C. Schwarz. 1987. 'Post-Divorce Contact, Relationship with Father, and Heterosexual Trust in Female College Students.' *American Journal of Orthopsychiatry* 57: 371–82.

Spakes, Patricia. 1989. 'A Feminist Case against National Family Policy: View to the Future.' *Policy Studies Review* 8(3): 610–21.

– 1991. 'A Feminist Approach to National Family Policy.' In *The Reconstruction of Family Policy*, edited by E. Anderson & R.C. Hula. Westport, Conn.: Greenwood Press.

– 1992. 'National Family Policy: Sweden versus the United States.' *Affilia* 7(2): 44–60.

Speirs, Carol Cumming, and Maureen Baker. 1994. 'Eligibility to Adopt: Models of "Suitable Families" in Legislation and Practice.' *Canadian Social Work Review* 11(1): 89–102.

Sprague, M.C. 1990. 'Defining the Risks after DeShaney.' *Children's Legal Rights Journal* 11(2): 8–23.

Stanton, David I., and Andrew Herscovitch. 1992. 'Social Security and Sole Parents: Developments in Australia.' In *Social Security and Changing Family Structures*, edited by the International Social Security Association, 157–84. Geneva: ISSA.

Statistics Canada. Annual (a). *Births and Deaths. Vital Statistics Volume 1.*

Catalogue no. 84-204. November. Ottawa: Supply and Services Canada.

– Annual (b). *The Labour Force*. Catalogue no. 71-001. Ottawa: Supply and Services Canada.

– Annual (c). *Marriages and Divorces. Vital Statistics. Volume 2.* Catalogue no. 84-205. Ottawa: Supply and Services Canada. September.

– Annual (d). *Vital Statistics*, Volume 3. Ottawa: Information Canada.

– 1983. *Historical Statistics of Canada* (2nd ed.). Ottawa: Supply and Services Canada.

– 1988. *Health Reports. Marriages and Divorce.* Ottawa: Supply and Services Canada.

– 1989. *The Family in Canada. Selected Highlights.* January. Ottawa: Supply and Services.

– 1990a. *Income Distribution by Size in Canada.* Catalogue no. 13-206. Ottawa: Supply and Services Canada.

– 1990b. *A Portrait of Children in Canada.* Catalogue no. 89-520. Ottawa: Supply and Services Canada.

– 1990c. *Women in Canada. A Statistical Report* (2nd ed.) Catalogue no. 89-503E. January. Ottawa: Supply and Services Canada.

– 1991a. *Education in Canada. A Statistical Review for 1989–90.* Catalogue no. 81-229. August. Ottawa: Supply and Services Canada.

– 1991b. *Health Reports. Marriages 1989.* Catalogue no. 82-003S, Supplement 16, 2(4) 1990. Ottawa: Supply and Services Canada.

– 1992a. *Canada Yearbook 1992.* Ottawa: Minister of Industry, Science and Technology.

– 1992b. *Historical Labour Force Statistics, 1991.* Catalogue no. 71-201. February. Ottawa: Supply and Services Canada.

– 1992c. *Labour Force Annual Averages. 1991.* Catalogue no. 71-220. Ottawa: Ministry of Industry, Science and Technology.

– 1992d. *Quarterly Demographic Statistics. July–September 1991.* Catalogue no. 91-002. 5(3) January.

– 1993a. *Earnings of Men and Women 1992.* Catalogue no. 13-217. Ottawa: Minister of Industry, Science and Technology.

– 1993b. *Families: Social and Economic Characteristics. The Nation.* Catalogue no. 93-320. Ottawa: Ministry of Industry, Science and Technology.

– 1993c. *Fertility. The Nation.* Catalogue no. 93-321. June. Ottawa: Ministry of Industry, Science and Technology.

– 1993d. *Workplace Benefits and Flexibility: A Perspective on Parents' Experiences.* Catalogue no. 89-530E. December. National Child Care Study.

– 1994. *Report on the Demographic Situation in Canada 1993.* Catalogue no. 91-209E. March. Ottawa: Minister of Industry, Science and Technology.

Stebbins, Robert A. 1988. 'Men, Husbands and Fathers: Beyond Patriarchal Relations.' In *Restructuring the Canadian Family: Feminist Perspectives*, edited by N. Mandell and A. Duffy, 27–47. Toronto: Butterworths.

Stets, J., and D. Henderson. 1991. 'Contextual Factors Surrounding Conflict Resolution While Dating: Results from a National Study.' *Family Relations* 40: 29–36.

Stewart, D.G., and L.E. McFadyen. 1992. 'Women and the Economic Consequences of Divorce in Manitoba: An Empirical Study.' *Manitoba Law Journal* 21(1): 80–99.

Stork, Hélène. 1992. 'Comparisons of the Patterns of Child Care in Some European Countries.' In *Child Care in Context: Cross-Cultural Perspectives*, edited by M.E. Lamb et al. Hillsdale, N.J.: Lawrence Erlbaum Associates.

Stout, Cam. 1991. 'Common-Law: A Growing Alternative.' *Canadian Social Trends* 23 (Winter): 18–20.

Strauss, Murray A., and Richard J. Gelles. 1990. *Physical Violence in American Families. Risk Factors and Adaptations to Violence in 8,145 Families*. New Brunswick, N.J.: Transaction Press.

Strike, Carol. 1991. 'AIDS into the 1990s.' *Canadian Social Trends* 21 (Winter): 22–4.

Strong-Boag, Veronica. 1982. 'Intruders in the Nursery: Childcare Professionals Reshape the Years One to Five, 1920–1940.' In *Childhood and Family in Canadian History*, edited by J. Parr. Toronto: McClelland and Stewart.

Sullivan, Terrence. 1992. *Sexual Abuse and the Rights of Children. Reforming Canadian Law*. Toronto: University of Toronto Press.

Sündstrom, M., and F.P. Stafford. 1992. 'Female Labour Force Participation, Fertility and Public Policy in Sweden.' *European Journal of Population* 8: 199–215.

Sutherland, Neil. 1976. *Children in English-Canadian Society: Framing the Twentieth Century Consensus*. Toronto: University of Toronto Press.

Sutherland, Ralph W., and M. Jane Fulton. 1988. *Health Care in Canada*. Ottawa: The Health Group.

Svallfors, Stefan. 1991. 'The Politics of Welfare Policy in Sweden: Structural Determinants and Attitudinal Cleavages.' *British Journal of Sociology* 42(4): 609–34.

Swan, George Steven. 1986. 'The Political Economy of American Family Policy, 1945–85.' *Population and Development Review* 12(4): 739–58.

Swenson, Peter. 1989. *Fair Shares: Unions, Pay and Politics in Sweden and West Germany*. Ithaca, N.Y.: Cornell University Press.

Swift, Karen. 1991. 'Contradictions in Child Welfare: Neglect and Responsibility.' In *Women's Caring*, edited by Carol Baines, Patricia Evans, and Sheila Neysmith, 234–71. Toronto: McClelland and Stewart.

– 1995. *Manufacturing 'Bad Mothers'? A Critical Perspective on Child Neglect*. Toronto: University of Toronto Press.

Syrtash, John. 1992. *Religion and Culture in Family Law*. Toronto: Butterworths.

Tabah, Leon. 1990. *World Demographic Trends and Their Consequences for Europe*. Strasbourg: Council of Europe.

Tarschys, Daniel. 1975. 'The Growth of Public Expenditures: Nine Modes of Explanation.' *Scandinavian Political Studies* 10: 9–31.

Teitelbaum, Michael S., and Jay M. Winter. 1985. *The Fear of Population Decline*. Orlando, Fla.: Academic Press.

Ternowetsky, Gordon W. 1987. 'Controlling the Deficit and a Private Sector Led Recovery.' In *The Canadian Welfare State: Evolution and Transition*, edited by J.S. Ismael. Edmonton: University of Alberta Press.

Ternowetsky, Gordon, and Graham Riches. 1990. 'Economic Polarization and Restructuring of Labour Markets in Canada: The Way of the Future.' In *Unemployment and Welfare*, edited by G. Riches and G. Ternowetsky, 19–31. Toronto: Garamond Press.

– 1993. 'Labour Market Restructuring and the Public Safety Net: Current Trends in the Australian and Canadian Welfare States.' Paper presented at the Sixth Social Welfare Conference, 27–30 June. St John's, Newfoundland.

Terpstra, J. 1989. 'Day Care Standards and Licensing.' *Child Welfare* 68(4): 437–42.

Tester, Frank. 1991. 'The Globalized Economy: What Does It Mean for Canadian Social and Environmental Policy?' *Canadian Review of Social Policy* 27 (May): 3–12.

Textor, M.R. 1991. 'International Adoption in West Germany: A Private Affair.' In *Intercountry Adoption: A Multinational Perspective*, edited by H. Alstein and R.J. Simon. New York: Praeger.

– 1992. 'Adoptions in West Germany: Attitudes of Social Workers.' *British Journal of Social Work* 22: 551–64.

Theilheimer, Ish. 1994. 'Unpaid Work – (How) Can You Measure It? Should You Even Try?' *Transition* 24(2): 4–7.

Therborn, G. 1978. 'Sweden before and after Social Democracy: A First Overview.' *Acta Sociologica* 21: 37–58.

Thoburn, J. 1991. 'Permanent Family Placement and the Children Act 1989: Implications for Foster Carers and Social Workers.' *Adoption and Fostering* 15(3): 15–20.

Thoennes, N., P. Tjaden, and J. Pearson. 1991. 'The Impact of Child Support Guidelines on Award Adequacy, Award Variability, and Case Processing Efficiency.' *Family Law Quarterly* 25(3): 325–45.

Thomlison, Ray J., and Catherine E. Foote, 1987. 'Children and the Law in

Canada: The Shifting Balance of Children's, Parents' and the State's Rights.' *Journal of Comparative Family Studies* 18(2): 231–45.

Thompson, D.A.R. 1991. 'Rules of Evidence and Preparing for Court.' In *Canadian Child Welfare Law: Children, Families and the State*, edited by N. Bala, J.P. Hornick, and R. Vogl. Toronto: Thompson Educational Publishing.

Thompson, G. 1991. 'Preface.' In *Canadian Child Welfare Law: Children, Families and the State*, edited by N. Bala, J.P. Hornick, and R. Vogl. Toronto: Thompson Educational Publishing.

Thompson, P.R., and N. Molyneaux. 1992. 'Enforcing Child Care standards.' *Public Welfare* 50(1): 20–5.

Thorne, Barrie. 1982. 'Feminist Rethinking of the Family: An Overview.' In *Rethinking the Family: Some Feminist Questions*, edited by B. Thorne with M. Yalom. New York: Longmans.

Thorne-Finch, Ron. 1992. *Ending the Silence. The Origins and Treatment of Male Violence against Women*. Toronto: University of Toronto Press.

Torjman, Sherri. 1992. 'A Child Benefit Primer: A Response to the Government Proposal.' *Canadian Review of Social Policy* 29/30: 93–105.

– 1994. 'Crests and Crashes: The Changing Tides of Income Security.' In *Canada's Changing Families: Challenges to Public Policy*, edited by M. Baker. Ottawa: Vanier Institute of the Family.

Torres, Alberto, and Michael R. Reich. 1989. 'The Shift from Home to Institutional Childbirth: A Comparative Study of the United Kingdom and the Netherlands.' *International Journal of Health Services* 19(3): 405–14.

Townson, Monica. 1988. *Leave for Employees with Family Responsibilities*. Ottawa: Labour Canada.

– 1993. *Tax Facts: What Every Woman Should Know*. Ottawa: Canadian Advisory Council on the Status of Women.

Traves, Tom. 1991. 'The Canadian Insurance State: A Comparative Note on Olsson's "Planning in the Swedish Welfare State."' *Studies in Political Economy* 34 (Spring): 173–8.

Trzcinski, Eileen. 1991. 'Employers' Parental Leave Policies: Does the Labor Market Provide Parental Leave?' In *Parental Leave and Child Care*, edited by J.S. Hyde, and M.J. Essex, 209–28. Philadelphia: Temple University Press.

Tunnard, J. 1989. 'Local Self-Help Groups for Families of Children in Public Care.' *Child Welfare* 68(2): 221–7.

Tuominen, Mary. 1992. 'Gender, Class and Motherhood: The Legacy of Federal Child Care Policy.' *Affilia* 7(4): 8–25.

United Kingdom, Central Statistical Office. 1992. 'International Comparisons of Taxes and Social Security Contributions in 20 OECD Countries 1980–1990.' *Economic Trends* 470 (December): 104–16, London: Government of the U.K.

– 1993. 'Households and Families.' *Social Trends* 23. London: Government of the U.K.

United Nations. 1987. *World Population Policies Vol. I.* New York: Department of International Economic and Social Affairs.

– 1989a. *Case Studies in Population Policy: Hungary.* New York: Department of International Economic and Social Affairs.

– 1989b. *World Population Policies Vol. II.* New York: Department of International Economic and Social Affairs.

– 1990a. *Patterns of First Marriage: Timing and Prevalence.* New York: Department of International Economic and Social Affairs.

– 1990b. *World Population Policies Vol. III.* New York: Department of International Economic and Social Affairs.

– 1991a. *Demographic Yearbook 1989.* New York: Department of Economic and Social Affairs.

– 1991b. *World Population Prospects 1990.* New York: Department of International Economic and Social Affairs.

– 1991c. *The World's Women, 1970–1990: Trends and Statistics.* New York: United Nations.

– 1992. *Demographic Yearbook 1991.* New York: Department of Economic and Social Affairs.

United Nations Children's Emergency Fund (UNICEF). 1991. *The State of the World's Children 1991.* New York: Oxford University Press.

Upham, James. 1989. 'Help for Abusing Families: Ten Years Later Placement Not Treatment Still Seems to Be the Answer.' *Intervention* 84 (November): 16–23.

Ursel, Jane. 1992. *Private Lives, Public Policy. 100 Years of State Intervention in the Family.* Toronto: Women's Press.

U.S. Dept of HEW (United States Department of Health, Education and Welfare). 1979. *Cost and Benefits of Electronic Fetal Monitoring: A Review of the Literature.* Publication no. 79-3245. Washington, D.C: U.S. Government.

U.S. Dept. of HHS (United States Department of Health and Human Services). 1991. *Social Security Bulletin, Annual Statistical Supplement.* Washington, D.C.

– 1992. *Social Security Programs throughout the World – 1991.* Washington, D.C.

U.S. (United States) House of Representatives, Committee on Ways and Means. 1991. *Overview of Entitlement Programs – 1991 Green Book.* May 7. Washington, D.C. U.S. Government Printing Office.

U.S. (United States) House of Representatives, Select Committee on Children, Youth and Families. 1990. *Children's Well-Being: An International Comparison.* Washington, D.C.: U.S. Government Printing Office.

Väisänen, Ilkka. 1992. 'Conflict and Consensus in Social Policy Development –

A Comparative Study of Social Insurance in 18 OECD Countries 1930–1985.'
   European Journal of Political Research (22 August): 307–27.
Van Keppel, M. 1991. 'Birth Parents and Negotiated Adoption Agreements.'
   Adoption and Fostering 15(4): 81–90.
Van Pagee, R., W. Van Miltenburg, and E.M. Pasztor. 1991. 'The International
   Transfer of Foster Parent Selection and Preparation Technology: The
   Example of the Netherlands and the United States.' *Child Welfare* 70(2):
   219–27.
Van Stolk, Mary. 1978. *The Battered Child in Canada*. Toronto: McClelland and
   Stewart.
van Wormer, K. 1992. 'No Wonder Social Workers Feel Uncomfortable in
   Court.' *Child and Adolescent Social Work Journal* 9(2): 117–29.
Vander Ven, K. 1991. 'Comment.' *Child and Youth Care Forum* 20(6): 389–91.
Vanier Institute of the Family. 1987. 'Workers With Family Responsibilities in a
   Changing Society: Who Cares?' *Transition* 17(3): 10–11.
– 1988. 'Of Birds, Bees and Petri Dishes.' *Transition* (March): 4–5.
– 1991. *Canadian Families*. Ottawa: Vanier Institute of the Family.
– 1994. *Profiling Canadian Families*. Ottawa: Vanier Institute of the Family.
Verdier, P. 1988. '"Limited Adoption" in France.' *Adoption and Fostering* 12(1):
   41–4.
Vogel, Joachim. 1993. 'Class and Inequality: The Swedish Experience.' In
   Welfare Trends in the Scandinavian Countries, edited by Erik J. Hansen et al,
   119–46. Armonk, N.Y.: M.E. Sharpe.
Vogl, R. 1991. 'Initial Involvement.' In *Canadian Child Welfare Law: Children,
   Families and the State*, edited by N. Bala, J.P. Hornick, and R. Vogl. Toronto:
   Thompson Educational Publishing.
Volgy, Sandra S., ed. 1991. *Women and Divorce, Men and Divorce. Gender
   Differences in Separation, Divorce and Remarriage*. Binghamton, N.Y.: Haworth.
Wachtel, Andy. 1989. *Child Abuse: Discussion Paper*. National Clearinghouse on
   Family Violence. May. Ottawa: Health and Welfare Canada.
Wadhera, Surinder. 1989. 'Trends in Birth and Fertility Rates, Canada, 1921–
   1987.' *Health Reports* 1(2): 211–23.
Wadhera, Surinder, and Wayne J. Millar. 1991. 'Patterns and Change in Canadian
   Fertility 1971–1988: First Births after Age 30.' *Health Reports* 3(2): 149–61.
Wadhera, Surinder, and Jill Strachan. 1991. 'Births and Birth Rates, Canada,
   1989.' *Health Reports* 3(2): 79–82.
– 1992. *Selected Marriage Statistics, 1921–1990*. Catalogue no. 82-552. July.
   Ottawa: Statistics Canada.
Wadlington, Walter. 1990–1. 'The United States: Renewed Focus on Children's
   Issues.' *Journal of Family Law* 29(2): 471–80.

Wald, M.S. 1988. 'Family Preservation: Are We Moving Too Fast?' *Public Welfare* (Summer): 33–8, 46.

Walker, Carol. 1993. *Managing Poverty. The Limits of Social Assistance*. London: Routledge.

Walker, Gillian A. 1990. *Family Violence and the Women's Movement. The Conceptual Politics of Struggle*. Toronto: University of Toronto Press.

Walker, J.R. 1991. 'Public Policy and the Supply of Child Care Services.' In *The Economics of Child Care*, edited by D.M. Blau, 51–77. New York: Russell Sage Foundation.

Walker, Roberta. 1987. 'The Market in Babies.' *Canadian Lawyer* 11(1): 20–3.

Waller, Michael, Stephane Coutois, and Marc Lazar. 1991. *Comrades and Brothers – Communism and Trade Unions in Europe*. London: Frank Cass and Company Limited.

Ward, H., and S. Jackson. 1991. 'Research Note: Developing Outcome Measures in Child Care.' *British Journal of Social Work* 21: 393–9.

Ware, Alan, and R.E. Goodwin. 1990. *Needs and Welfare*. London: Sage.

Warry, Wayne. 1991. 'Ontario's First People: Native Children.' In *Children, Families and Public Policy in the 90s*, edited by L.C. Johnson and R. Barnhorst, 207–30. Toronto: Thompson Educational Publishing.

Watson, K.W. 1988. 'The Case for Open Adoption.' *Public Welfare* (Fall): 24–8, 46.

Weatherly, Richard. 1993. 'Doing the Right Thing: How Social Security Claimants View Compliance.' *The Australian and New Zealand Journal of Sociology* 29(1): 21–39.

Weber, M. 1990. 'CPS Can't Go It Alone.' *Public Welfare* 48(1): 18–19.

Weigl, I., and C. Weber. 1991a. 'Day Care for Young Children in the German Democratic Republic.' In *Day Care for Young Children: International Perspectives*, edited by E.C. Melhuish and P. Moss, 46–55. London: Tavistock/Routledge.

– 1991b. 'Research in Nurseries in the German Democratic Republic.' In *Day Care for Young Children: International Perspectives*, edited by E.C. Melhuish and P. Moss, 56–74. London: Tavistock/Routledge.

Weitz, Rose. 1987. 'English Midwives and the Association of Radical Midwives.' *Women and Health* 12(1): 79–89.

Weitzman, Lenore J. 1985. *The Divorce Revolution: The Unexpected Social and Economic Consequences for Women and Children in America*. New York: Free Press.

– 1988. 'Child Support Myths and Reality.' In *Child Support*, edited by A.J. Kahn and S.B. Kamerman, 251–76. Newbury Park, Calif.: Sage Publications.

Wells, Kathleen, and Paula Reshotko. 1986. 'Cooperative Adoption: An Alternative to Independent Adoption.' *Child Welfare* 65(2) : 177–88.

Wennemo, Irene. 1992. 'The Development of Family Policy.' *Acta Sociologica* 35: 201–17.

– 1994. *Sharing the Cost of Children*. Stockholm: Swedish Institute for Social Research.

Westhues, Anne, and Joyce S. Cohen. 1988. *How to Reduce the Risk: Healthy Functioning Families for Adoptive and Foster Children*. Toronto: University of Toronto Press.

– 1993. 'Intercountry Adoption: A Policy in Need of Reform?' Paper presented at the Sixth Conference on Social Welfare Policy, 27–30 June. St John's, Newfoundland.

Wharf, Brian, ed. 1993. *Rethinking Child Welfare in Canada*. Toronto: McClelland and Stewart.

White, Julie. 1993. *Sisters and Solidarity. Women and Unions in Canada*. Toronto: Thompson Educational Publishing.

Whiteford, Peter. 1987. 'The Costs of Children: The Implications of Recent Research for Income Support Policies.' *Social Security Journal* (Winter): 3–19.

Whiteford, Peter; Bruce Bradbury, and Peter Saunders. 1989. 'Inequality and Deprivation among Families with Children: An Exploratory Study.' In *Child Poverty*, edited by D. Edgar, D. Keane, and P. McDonald, 20–49. Sydney, Aus.: Allen and Unwin.

Widerberg, Karin. 1990. 'Reforms for Women – on Male Terms – The Example of the Swedish Legislation on Parental Leave.' Paper presented to the Twenty-second International Congress of Applied Psychology. July. Kyoto, Japan.

Wiebrens, Casper. 1988. 'The Netherlands.' In *Child Support*, edited by A. Kahn and S.B. Kamerman, 132–52. Newbury Park, Calif.: Sage Publications.

Wilczynski, A., and A. Morris. 1993. 'Parents Who Kill Their Children.' *The Criminal Law Review* (January) 31–6.

Wildavsky, Aaron. 1974. *The Politics of the Budgetary Process* (2nd ed.). Boston: Little, Brown.

Wilensky, Harold. 1975. *The Welfare State and Equality*. Berkeley: University of California.

Willer, B.A. 1990. 'Federal Comprehensive Child Care Legislation: Much Success in 1989 but More Work Ahead in 1990.' *Young Children* (January): 25–7, 49.

Williams, Fiona. 1989. *Social Policy: A Critical Introduction. Issues of Race, Gender and Class*. Cambridge: Polity Press.

Williams, R.J. 1991. 'The Judge's Roles and Responsibilities in Child Protection

Cases.' In *Canadian Child Welfare Law: Children, Families and the State,'* edited by N. Bala, J.P. Hornick, and R. Vogl. Toronto: Thompson Educational Publishing.

Wilson, Elizabeth. 1977. *Women and the Welfare State*. London: Tavistock Publications.

Windschuttle, Keith. 1990. 'Employment Programs and Policies: New Directions for Social Policy.' In *Unemployment and Welfare*, edited by G. Riches and G. Ternowetsky, 223–33. Toronto: Garamond.

Wisensale, Steven K. 1991. 'State Initiatives in Family Policy.' In *The Reconstruction of Family Policy*, edited by E.A. Anderson and R. Hula, 59–75. Westport, Conn. : Greenwood Press.

Wolfe, Alan. 1989. 'The Day Care Dilemma: A Scandinavian Perspective.' *Public Interest* 95 (Spring): 14–23.

Wolfgang, G.; K.O. Hondrich, H.H. Noll, and K.S. Wörndl. 1992. *Recent Social Trends in West Germany 1960–1990*. Frankfurt am Main: McGill-Queen's University Press.

Wong, Yin-Ling Irene, Irwin Garfinkel, and Sara McLanahan. 1992. 'Single-Mother Families in Eight Countries: Economic Status and Social Policy.' The Luxembourg Income Study, Working Paper no. 76. April.

Wright, Robert E. 1991. 'Single Parenthood and Poverty in France.' The Luxembourg Income Study, Working Paper no. 64. March.

Yalnizyan, Armine. 1993. *Defining Social Security, Defining Ourselves*. Toronto: Canadian Centre for Policy Alternatives and Social Planning Council of Metropolitan Toronto.

York, Carolyn. 1991. 'The Labor Movement's Role in Parental Leave and Child Care.' In *Parental Leave and Child Care*, edited by J.S. Hyde and M.J. Essex, 176–86. Philadelphia: Temple University Press.

York, Geoffrey. 1992. 'Michael Wilson's Quiet Revolution.' *Globe and Mail* (Toronto), 24 July.

Young, C.C. 1990–1. 'Abused Children: The Supreme Court Considers the Due Process Right to Protection.' *Journal of Family Law* 29: 679–702.

Young, Iris Marion. 1987. 'Impartiality and the Civic Public: Some Implications of Feminist Critiques of Moral and Political Theory.' In *Feminism as Critique*, edited by Seyla Benhabib and Drucilla Cornell. Minneapolis: University of Minnesota Press.

Ziegert, Klaus A. 1987. 'Children's Rights and the Supportive Function of the Law: The Case of Sweden.' *Journal of Comparative Family Studies* 18(2): 157–74.

Zigler, E.F. 1989. 'Addressing the Nation's Child Care Crisis: The School of the Twenty-First Century.' *American Journal of Orthopsychiatry* 59(4): 484–91.

Zigler, E. 1990. 'Shaping Child Care Policies and Programs in America.' *American Journal of Community Psychology* 18(2): 183–216.

Zimbalist, S.E. 1987. 'A Welfare State against the Economic Current: Sweden and the United States as Contrasting Cases.' *International Social Work* 39: 15–29.

Zimmerman, Shirley L. 1989. 'Myths about Public Welfare: Family Instability, Poverty and Teen Illegitimacy.' *Policy Studies Review* 8(3): 674–88.

– 1991a. 'The Policy Functions of Family Policies in Three States: A Comparative Analysis.' In *The Reconstruction of Family Policy*, edited by E.A. Anderson and R.C. Hula. Westport, Conn.: Greenwood Press.

– 1991b. 'The Welfare State and Family Breakup: The Mythical Connection.' *Family Relations* 38(2): 139–54.

– 1992. *Family Policies and Family Well-Being. The Role of Political Culture.* Newbury Park, Calif.: Sage Publications.

Index